PROPOSALS THAT WORK

FOURTH EDITION

A Guide for Planning Dissertations and Grant Proposals

Lawrence F. Locke
Waneen Wyrick Spirduso
Stephen J. Silverman

Sage Publications, Inc.
International Educational and Professional Publisher
Thousand Oaks ▪ London ▪ New Delhi

For information:

Sage Publications, Inc.
2455 Teller Road
Thousand Oaks, California 91320
E-mail: order@sagepub.com

Sage Publications Ltd.
6 Bonhill Street
London EC2A 4PU
United Kingdom

Sage Publications India Pvt. Ltd.
M-32 Market
Greater Kailash I
New Delhi 110048 India

Printed in the United States of America

Library of Congress Cataloging-in-Publication Data

Locke, Lawrence F.
 Proposals that work: A guide for planning dissertations and
grant proposals / Lawrence F. Locke, Waneen Wyrick Spirduso,
Stephen J. Silverman.—4th ed.
  p. cm.
 Includes bibliographical references (p.) and index.
 ISBN 0-7619-1706-3 (cloth; acid-free paper)
 ISBN 0-7619-1707-1 (paper; acid-free paper)
 1. Proposal writing in research Handboooks, manuals, etc. 2.
Dissertations, Academic Handbooks, manuals, etc. 3. Research grants
Handbooks, manuals, etc. 4. Fund raising Handbooks, manuals, etc.
I. Spirduso, Waneen Wyrick. II. Silverman, Stephen J. III. Title.
 Q180.55.P7 L63 1999
 001.4′4—dc21   99-06594

00 01 02 03 04 05 7 6 5 4 3 2 1

Acquiring Editor:	Peter Labella
Editorial Assistant:	Karen Harlan
Production Editor:	Wendy Westgate
Production Assistant:	Karen Wiley
Typesetter/Designer:	Danielle Dillahunt
Cover Designer:	Ravi Balasuriya

Contents

Preface to the Fourth Edition

This book contains no direct instruction concerning how to do research. Rather, the material herein deals with the problem of how to write a research proposal. Although the two capacities—skill in conducting research and skill in writing about plans for that research—have a close relationship, they are far from coterminous. Individuals who have acquired considerable information about the mysteries of research methods and data analysis do not necessarily know how to undertake the task of planning and effectively proposing their own investigations.

The importance and, therefore, the perceived difficulty of the proposal task will seem greater under some conditions than under others. Even the novice in research is likely to appreciate fully the significance of the research proposal in preparing a grant application. Once the target for inquiry has been selected, it is obvious that the probability for obtaining funding will rest mostly on how clearly and persuasively the proposal displays the author's competence to design and execute the study.

In contrast, few graduate students initially recognize that preparation of the proposal will represent a major hurdle in gaining approval for their thesis or dissertation. In the context of graduate education, however, the research proposal plays a central role—and one that reaches beyond its simple significance as a plan of action. In most instances, the decision to permit the student to embark on a study is made solely on the basis of that first formal document. The quality of the proposal is likely to be used by advisors as a basis for judging the clarity of thought that has preceded the document, the degree of facility with which the study will be implemented if approved, and the adequacy of expository skills the student will bring to reporting the results. In sum, the proposal is the instrument through which the faculty must judge whether there is reasonable hope that the student can conduct research.

Given such an understanding of the importance invested in writing a proposal, our intention in writing this guide is clear and straightforward. Our purpose from start to finish is to assist in achieving one end—a fair and useful hearing for your proposed research. If the proposed study is rejected, it should be because the investigation lacks sufficient merit or feasibility, not because the presentation itself was flawed.

As you read, you will discover that in explanations and illustrations we make frequent use of language and constructs drawn from experimental and quasiexperimental designs for research. Some of that is a simple matter of economy, in that referencing all the variations that exist for any one investigative operation would be endlessly cumbersome. It also is true, however, that the experiment offers a convenient vehicle for introducing a host of constructs and problems that are generic to systematic inquiry. Although those fundamentals assume different forms (and different kinds of significance) in different types of research, there truly is a central set of recurring demands and concerns.

Proposals for historical or philosophical study must reflect canons unique to those areas of inquiry, and plans for qualitative research will begin with some assumptions (described in Chapter 5) that are foreign to the natural science model for investigation. Nevertheless, all must begin with questions, must be grounded in the current status of knowledge, must define data sources, must present plans for analysis, and must convince readers of the author's competence. For our use in this text, then, the value of the experiment rests not in its unique virtues as a tool for research but in how much it shares in common with all modes of inquiry.

SUGGESTIONS FOR USING THE BOOK

This book has been divided into three major parts: Part I, Writing the Proposal, Part II, Money for Research, and Part III, Specimen Proposals. The chapters that constitute Part I represent the core of the book, serving both to present generic information that applies to all research proposals and to discuss some of the problems peculiar to the use of proposals in either graduate education or funding agencies. Chapter headings shown in the table of contents offer a self-explanatory outline of what is covered. We draw your attention to the fact that Chapter 5 deals with the particular demands of proposing studies framed by the assumptions established in the qualitative and critical research paradigms.

In Part II, we offer assistance to those who wish to seek funding for proposed studies. The general topic of locating sources and submitting applications is introduced in Chapter 8. Specific attention is given in Chapter 9 to finding financial support for student research (projects, theses, and dissertations), and Chapter 10 is devoted to the specifics of preparing grant proposals. Collectively, the three chapters in Part II will provide a sound starting place for anyone who wishes to locate and exploit the financial resources available from foundations and agencies (both governmental and private) that have an interest in research. Where required, more detailed information can be found in the books abstracted in Appendix A.

In Part III, four sample proposals are presented. The sections of the first document relate directly to each of the generic proposal tasks presented in Chapter 1. Our short commentaries inserted into the text are used to highlight those key elements. The next three proposals also are accompanied by critical evaluations intended to illuminate their individual strengths and limitations— both as plans for research and as written vehicles for presentation of those plans. Together, the four specimens include documents at both early and late stages of development, both quantitative and qualitative designs, and successful proposals for both graduate student dissertations and research funding.

Readers with different backgrounds will find it useful to employ different methods in using this book. Those who are completely inexperienced in writing proposals should begin with Chapter 1, which deals with the basic functions of the document. Some may find it helpful to couple each task introduced there with the parallel illustration found in the first specimen proposal (Part III). Skimming several of the other proposals to note how various functions are performed will allow the novice researcher to return to the following chapters with some concrete sense of the form actually assumed by proposals.

Readers with some previous experience in research may wish to turn directly to Chapter 3, in which we deal with specific problems in identifying research topics and initiating the proposal process. Those interested in the particular demands and problems presented by the grant proposal should begin with Chapters 8 and 10, subsequently turning to other sections of the guide as needed (including the grant application in Part III). The same pattern of use would be appropriate for those who are considering a qualitative study—in that case starting with Chapter 5 and the corresponding proposal in Part III, using other sections as required.

Finally, in preparing this edition we have again given special attention to the issues of ethics in research and graduate research education. In Chapter 2, we discuss ethical concerns that have become increasingly troublesome for researchers everywhere. Although we believe that all scholars, novice and veteran, should be informed about what constitutes right and wrong behavior in research, it clearly is the unwary novice who is most at risk. Any study can present serious ethical pitfalls, and the proposal is the place to begin thinking about how to avoid them. A close reading of Chapter 2 is not all that you will need to navigate through the full range of ethical problems you might encounter—but it is a reliable guide with which to begin the journey.

Acknowledgments

As in most complex writing endeavors, many persons whose names do not appear on the cover played important parts in its completion. First, we would like to acknowledge the contributions of students in our classes at the University of Massachusetts at Amherst, The University of Texas at Austin, and Teachers College, Columbia University who used earlier versions of this text and provided helpful advice for revision. Drs. Nell Gottlieb, John MacDonald, Shannon Mihalko, and Belinda Minor wrote the excellent specimen proposals used in this edition of the guide. We particularly appreciate their generosity in allowing us to reprint and critique their work.

Our special appreciation goes also to Professors Patt Dodds, Linda Griffin, Pat Griffin, and Judy Placek, whose assistance in preparing the new chapter on proposals for qualitative research was of inestimable value. Thanks also to Dr. Lorraine Goyette, whose careful and repeated attention to the evolving manuscript trapped many of our blunders before they could become public embarrassments; to Margaret Burggren and the staff at the Graduate Student Grant Service of the University of Massachusetts, who were generous with their time and resources in helping us learn about opportunities for funding student research; and to Patricia Moran of Episcopal Social Services of New York, who again shared her insights into the inner workings of foundations and their complex roles in providing financial support. We also are indebted to our editor at Sage, Peter Labella, who got us started again and with gentle prodding kept us on track. Our deepest appreciation, however, must be reserved for Lori, Craig, and Pat, whose patience and understanding once more sustained our effort. As for so much else in our lives, we stand in your debt.

PART

I

WRITING THE PROPOSAL

CHAPTER

1

The Function of the Proposal

A proposal sets forth both the exact nature of the matter to be investigated and a detailed account of the methods to be employed. In addition, the proposal usually contains material supporting the importance of the topic selected and the appropriateness of the research methods to be employed.

FUNCTION

A proposal may function in at least three ways: as a means of communication, as a plan, and as a contract.

Communication

The proposal serves to communicate the investigator's research plans to those who provide consultation, give consent, or disburse funds. The document is the primary resource on which the graduate student's thesis or dissertation committee must base the functions of review, consultation, and, more important, approval for implementation of the research project. It also serves a similar function for persons holding the purse strings of foundations or governmental

3

funding agencies. The quality of assistance, the economy of consultation, and the probability of financial support will all depend directly on the clarity and thoroughness of the proposal.

Plan

The proposal serves as a plan for action. All empirical research consists of careful, systematic, and preplanned observations of some restricted set of phenomena. The acceptability of results is judged exclusively in terms of the adequacy of the methods employed in making, recording, and interpreting the planned observations. Accordingly, the plan for observation, with its supporting arguments and explications, is the basis on which the thesis, dissertation, or research report will be judged.

The research report can be no better than the plan of investigation. Hence, an adequate proposal sets forth the plan in step-by-step detail. The existence of a detailed plan that incorporates the most careful anticipation of problems to be confronted and contingent courses of action is the most powerful insurance against oversight or ill-considered choices during the execution phase of the investigation. With the exception of plans for qualitative research (see Chapter 5), the hallmark of a good proposal is a level of thoroughness and detail sufficient to permit another investigator to replicate the study, that is, to perform the same planned observations with results not substantially different from those the author might obtain.

Contract

A completed proposal, approved for execution and signed by all members of the sponsoring committee, constitutes a bond of agreement between the student and the advisors. An approved grant proposal results in a contract between the investigator (and often the university) and a funding source. The approved proposal describes a study that, if conducted competently and completely, should provide the basis for a report that would meet all standards for acceptability. Accordingly, once the contract has been made, all but minor changes should occur only when arguments can be made for absolute necessity or compelling desirability.

Proposals for theses and dissertations should be in final form prior to the collection of data. Under most circumstances, substantial revisions should be made only with the explicit consent of the full committee. Once the document is approved in final form, neither the student nor the sponsoring faculty members should be free to alter the fundamental terms of the contract by unilateral decision.

REGULATIONS GOVERNING PROPOSALS

All funding agencies have their own guidelines for submissions, and these should be followed exactly. In the university, however, no set of universal rules or guidelines presently exists to govern the form or content of the research proposal. There may be, however, several sources of regulation governing the form and content of the final research report. The proposal sets forth a plan of action that must eventuate in a report conforming to these latter regulations; therefore, it is important to consider them in writing the proposal.

Although it is evident that particular traditions have evolved within individual university departments, any formal limitation on the selection of either topic or method of investigation is rarely imposed. Normally, the planning and execution of student research are circumscribed by existing departmental policy on format for the final report, university regulations concerning theses and dissertation reports, and informal standards exercised by individual advisors or study committees.

Usually, departmental and university regulations regarding graduate student proposals are either so explicit as to be perfectly clear (e.g., "The proposal may not exceed 25 typewritten pages" or "The proposal will conform to the style established in the *Publication Manual of the American Psychological Association*") or so general as to impose no specific or useful standard (e.g., "The research topic must be of suitable proportions" or "The proposal must reflect a thorough knowledge of the problem area"). The student, therefore, should find no serious difficulty in developing a proposal that conforms to departmental and university regulations.

Some universities now allow students to elect alternative dissertation or thesis formats, such as a research paper (or series of papers) with an expanded literature review and supporting materials in the appendix. You might consider such an option because the more compact research paper format can save considerable time in turning the completed dissertation into a publication. Alternative formats for the final report, however, do not alter the need for a complete proposal. A good study requires a sound plan, irrespective of the format used for reporting the results.

Another potential source of regulation, the individual thesis or dissertation committee, constitutes an important variable in the development of the thesis or dissertation proposal. Sponsoring committee members may have strong personal commitments concerning particular working procedures, writing styles, or proposal format. The student must confront these as a unique constellation of demands that will influence the form of the proposal. It always is wise to anticipate conflicting demands and to attempt their resolution before the collection of data and the preparation of a final report.

Committees are unlikely to make style and format demands that differ substantially from commonly accepted modes of research writing. As a general rule, most advisors subscribe to the broad guidelines outlined in this book. Where differences occur, they are likely to be matters of emphasis or largely mechanical items (e.g., inclusion of particular subheadings within the document).

GENERAL CONSIDERATIONS

Most problems in proposal preparation are straightforward and relatively obvious. The common difficulties do not involve the subtle and complex problems of design and data management. They arise instead from the most basic elements of the research process: What is the proper question to ask? Where is the best place to look for the answer? What is the best way to standardize, quantify, and record observations? Properly determining the answers to these questions remains the most common obstacle to the development of adequate proposals.

Simplicity, clarity, and parsimony are the standards of writing that reflect adequate thinking about the research problem. Complicated matters are best communicated when they are the objects of simple, well-edited prose. In the early stage of development, the only way to obtain prompt and helpful assistance is to provide advisors with a document that is easily and correctly understood. At the final stage, approval of the study will hinge not only on how carefully the plan has been designed but also on how well that design has been communicated. In the mass of detail that goes into the planning of a research study, the writer must not forget that the proposal's most immediate function is to inform readers quickly and accurately.

The problem in writing a proposal is essentially the same as in writing the final report. When the task of preparing a proposal is well executed, the task of preparing the final report is more than half done (an important consideration for the graduate student with an eye on university deadlines). Under ideal conditions, such minor changes as altering the tense of verbs will convert the proposal into the opening chapters of the thesis or dissertation, or into initial sections of a research report.

Many proposals evolve through a series of steps. Preliminary discussion with colleagues and faculty members may lead to a series of drafts that evolve toward a final document presented at a formal meeting of the full dissertation or thesis committee, or to a proposal submitted through the university hierarchy to a funding source. This process of progressive revision can be accelerated and made more productive by following these simple rules:

1. Prepare clean, updated copies of the evolving proposal and submit them to advisors or colleagues in advance of scheduled consultations.
2. Prepare an agenda of questions and problems to be discussed and submit them in advance of scheduled consultations.
3. Keep a carefully written and dated record of all discussions and decisions that occur with regard to each item on the consultation agenda.

GENERAL FORMAT

Guidelines for the format of proposals, even when intended only as general suggestions, often have an unfortunate influence on the writing process. Once committed to paper, such guidelines quickly tend to acquire the status of mandatory prescription. In an attempt to conform to what they perceive as an invariant format, students produce proposal documents that are awkward and illogical as plans for action—as well as stilted and tasteless as prose.

Some universities and many funding agencies make very specific demands for the format of proposals. Others provide general guidelines for form and content. Whatever the particular situation confronting the writer, it is vital to remember that *no universally applicable and correct format exists for the research proposal*. Each research plan requires that certain communication tasks be accomplished, some that are common to all proposals and others that are unique to the specific form of inquiry. Taken together, however, the tasks encompassed by all proposals demand that what is written fits the real topic at hand, not some preconceived ideal. It is flexibility, not rigidity, that makes strong proposal documents.

SPECIFIC TASKS

---■---

The following paragraphs specify communication tasks that are present in nearly all proposals for empirical research. Each proposal, however, will demand its own unique arrangement of these functions. Within a given proposal, the tasks may or may not be identified by such traditional section designations as "Background," "Importance of the Study," "Review of Literature," "Methodology," "Definitions," or "Limitations." Individual proposals are sure to demand changes in the order of presentation, or attention to other tasks not specified below. This particularly will be the case with some of the tasks that are specific to grant proposals (see Part II). Finally, it is important to note that some of the adjacent tasks, shown as headings in the following paragraphs, often may be merged into single sections.

As you read each of the tasks below, an illustration can be found by turning to the first proposal in Part III of this guide. In that particular specimen, we have edited the proposal so the sections correspond to the discussion of each task. We have provided a critique preceding each section of the specimen proposal to summarize the suggestions presented in this chapter.

Introducing the Study

Proposals, like other forms of written communication, are best introduced by a short, meticulously devised statement that establishes the overall area of concern, arouses interest, and communicates information essential to the reader's comprehension of what follows. The standard here is a "gentle introduction" that avoids both tedious length and the shock of technical detail or abstruse argument. A careful introduction is the precursor of three other tasks (statement, rationale, and background). In many cases, it may be written simply as the first paragraph(s) of an opening proposal section that includes all three.

For most proposals, the easiest and most effective way to introduce the study is to identify and define the central construct(s) involved. In the sense that constructs are concepts that provide an abstract symbolization of some observable attribute or phenomenon, all studies employ constructs. Constructs such as "intelligence" or "teacher enthusiasm" are utilized in research by defining them in terms of some observable event, that is, "intelligence" as defined by a test score, or "teacher enthusiasm" as defined by a set of classroom behaviors. When the reader asks, "What is this study about?" the best answer is to present the key constructs and explain how they will be represented in the investigation. The trick in these opening paragraphs of introduction is to sketch the study in the bold strokes of major constructs without usurping the function of more detailed sections that will follow.

Relationships among constructs that will be of particular interest or about which explicit hypotheses will be developed should be briefly noted. Constructs with which the reader probably is familiar may be ignored in the introduction, for they are of less interest than the relationships proposed by the author.

The most common error in introducing research is failure to get to the point—usually a consequence of engaging in grand generalizations. For instance, in a proposed study of attributes contributing to balance ability, the opening paragraph might contain a sentence such as "The child's capacity to maintain balance is a factor of fundamental importance in the design of elementary school curriculum." The significance of the construct "balance" in accomplishing motor tasks may make it an attribute of some importance in elementary education, but that point may be far from the heart of a study involving balance. If, for example, the proposed study deals with the relationship of muscle strength to balance, observations about balance as a factor in the design of school curriculum belong, if anywhere, in a later discussion. What belongs up front is a statement that gets to the point: "The task of maintaining static balance requires muscular action to hold the pelvis in a horizontal position. When muscle strength is inadequate to accomplish this, performance is impaired."

Some indication of the importance of the study to theory or practice may be used to help capture the reader's interest, but in the introduction it is not necessary to explain completely all the study's significance. Present the basic facts first and leave the detail of thorough discussion until a more appropriate point. Use of unnecessary technical language is another impediment to the reader's ability to grasp the main idea. Similarly, the use of quotations and extensive references are intrusions into what should be a clear, simple preliminary statement. As a general rule, the first paragraph of the introduction should be free of citations. Documentation of important points can wait until a full discussion of the problem is launched.

Stating the Purpose

Early in the proposal, often in the introductory paragraph(s), it is wise to set forth an explicit statement of your purpose in undertaking the study. We are using the word "purpose" in its general sense as a statement of why you want to do the study and what you intend to accomplish. Such statements can be divided broadly into those related to the desire to *improve* something and those reflecting a desire to *understand* something. In addition to such practical and theoretical purposes, Maxwell (1996) has pointed out that, in some instances, it may be wise to be explicit about more personal purposes as well, including interests related to simple curiosity, a sense of social responsibility, or career demands.

A statement of purpose need not be an exhaustive survey of your intentions, nor need it be written in the formal language of research questions (which are much more specific expressions of what you want to learn). An early and specific announcement of the primary target for the study, and your purpose in aiming at it, will satisfy the reader's most pressing questions—what is this all about, and why is this study being proposed? Succinct answers allow the reader to attend to your subsequent exposition without the nagging sense that he or she still is waiting to discover the main objective. Make your statement of purpose early, be forthright, keep it simple, and be brief.

Providing a Rationale

Once the reader understands the topic of the investigation and has at least a general sense of your purpose, the next task is to address the question "Why bother with that?" in terms that are more detailed and explicit. The development of a rationale that justifies the proposed study usually involves both logical argument and documentation with factual evidence. The intention is to persuade the reader not only that the investigation (with its component questions or hypotheses) is worthy of attention, but also that the problem has been correctly defined.

To that end, it often is helpful to diagram factors and relationships that support your formulation of the problem. Suppose that an assertion proposed for experimental test is that older adults who had oxygen therapy for six months would show superior cognitive function when compared to subjects assigned to a control group. The implication of such an assertion is that there is a relationship between the level of oxygen provided to the brain and cognitive capacity in older adults. The reasons for such a complex supposition can be clarified by diagramming them in a simple form like the one shown in Figure 1.1. Assuming that the constructs have been defined, the rationale can be developed by documenting the information within each box, and then explaining the enormous practical consequences that would attend a positive finding. A sound rationale is one that convinces the reader that you are raising the right question—and that the answer is worth finding.

Figure 1.1. Example of Diagram of Logic for Rationale

In most cases, this early attention to justifying the proposed study should be limited to the basic matters of defining what is to be studied and why it is worth so doing. The detail of rationale for particular choices in methods of data collection and analysis can be deferred until such matters are discussed in subsequent parts of the proposal.

Formulating Questions or Hypotheses

All proposals must arrive at a formal statement of questions or hypotheses. These statements should be written in carefully constructed language that specifies each variable in explicit terms. A statement such as "Studying each day should result in improved learning" is better written as "Sixty minutes of studying each day will result in significantly increased scores on a standardized test of achievement." These statements of questions or hypotheses may be set aside as a separate section or simply included in the course of other discussion. Such statements differ from what was contained in the statement of the purpose in that (a) they are normally stated in formal terms appropriate to the design and analysis of data to be employed, and (b) they display, in logical order, all subsections of the research topic.

The question form is most appropriate when the research is exploratory. The researcher should indicate by the specificity of questions, however, that the problem has been subject to thorough analysis. By careful formulation of questions, the proposed study should be directed toward outcomes that are foreshadowed by the literature or pilot work, rather than toward a scanning of potentially interesting findings.

The hypothesis form is employed when the state of existing knowledge and theory permits formulation of reasonable predictions about the relationship of variables. Hypotheses ordinarily have their origin in theoretical propositions already established in the review of literature. Because the proposal must ensure that the reader grasps how the relationships expressed in theory have been translated into the form of testable hypotheses, it often is useful to provide a succinct restatement of the theoretical framework at a point contiguous to the presentation of formal research hypotheses.

The most common difficulty in formulating a research question is the problem of clarity. Students who have read and studied in the area of their topic for weeks or months often are distressed to discover how difficult it is to reduce all they want to discover to a single, unambiguous question.

The clarity of a research question hinges on adequate specificity and the correct degree of inclusiveness. The major elements of the investigation must be identified in a way that permits no confusion with other elements. At the same time, the statement must maintain simplicity by including nothing beyond what is essential to identify the main variables and any relationships that may be proposed among them. Questions for quantitative studies, for example, must meet three tests of clarity and inclusiveness:

1. Is the question free of ambiguity?
2. Is a relationship among variables expressed?
3. Does the question imply an empirical test?

Applying these standards to the question "Does a relationship exist between self-esteem and reading achievement in children?" apparently identifies the study's main elements apparently in reasonably clear fashion. Self-esteem and reading achievement are variables, and children are the subject population. A relationship is suggested, and correlation of self-esteem and reading scores clearly is implied as an appropriate empirical test of the relationship. The constructs of self-esteem and reading achievement, however, are quite broad and might be taken by some readers to indicate variables different from those intended. These potential sources of ambiguity might be resolved without destroying the simplicity of the question by altering it to ask, "Does a relationship exist between scores on the Children's Test of Self-Esteem and scores on the reading portion of the Tri-State Achievement Test?" Whether it also might be important to provide more specificity for the generic word "children" would depend on whether the intent was to examine self-esteem and reading in a particular type of child. If not, the generic word would be adequate, but if so, the importance of that variable calls for more careful specification in the question.

In the case of qualitative research (discussed at length in Chapter 5), because pre-established hypotheses are seldom used, questions are the tool most commonly employed to provide focus for thesis and dissertation studies. Although there is disagreement among scholars about the use of formal questions in qualitative research, there is no escape from the need to have a question (whether explicit or implicit) that will serve to direct what is observed, or who is interviewed—at least at the outset of the study.

The question(s) frequently are phrased in ways that make them appear very different from those used in the natural science model (and, thereby, discrepant with some aspects of the advice given in this chapter). Some, for example, will sound highly generalized, as in the following examples paraphrased from qualitative proposals.

1. What is going on in this urban school classroom?
2. How do professional wrestlers understand their work?
3. What does residence in a hospice mean to a patient?

Other question statements reflect the intention to use a particular theoretical framework in the study.

1. What perspective do medical students adopt to make sense of their experience in medical school?
2. How do gay and lesbian soldiers manage the presentation of their sexual preference within the social setting of their workplace?
3. How do social roles influence the interaction between teachers and students as they attempt to realize personal goals in the classroom?

In contrast with quantitative research, questions in a qualitative proposal often are treated as more tentative and contingent on the unfolding of the study.

Nevertheless, their careful formulation is no less important. They must give initial direction to planning, bring the power of theoretical constructs to the process of analysis, and reflect the degree of sophisticated thought employed in determining the focus of inquiry.

Experienced qualitative researchers sometimes do, in fact, elect not to package their curiosity, interests, concerns, and foreshadowings into the form of explicit research questions. Graduate students, however, embarking on their first attempt within the qualitative paradigm, often find that their advisors are greatly reassured when the proposal contains a careful accounting of what the data are expected to reveal that is not already known. In other words, it is a good idea for the novice to explicate the questions that motivate their interest, thereby firmly grounding the study in the conventions of scholarly inquiry. How a qualitative investigator's assumptions about the world, and about research, serve to shape those questions will be addressed in Chapter 5.

Research *hypotheses* differ from research *questions* in that hypotheses both indicate the question in testable form and predict the nature of the answer. A clear question is readily transformed into a hypothesis by casting it in the form of a declarative statement that can be tested so as to show it to be either true or false. Getting precisely the hypothesis that is wanted, however, often is more exacting than it appears.

Unlike a question, the hypothesis exerts a direct influence on each subsequent step of the study, from design to preparation of the final report. By specifying a prediction about outcome, the hypothesis creates a bridge between the theoretical considerations that underlie the question and the ensuing research process designed to produce the answer. The investigator is limited to procedures that will test the truth of the proposed relationship, and any implications to be deduced from the results will rest entirely on the particular test selected. Because it exerts such powerful a priori influence, a hypothesis demands considerable attention at the start of a study but makes it easier to preserve objectivity in the later stages of design and execution.

Aside from specific impact on design of the study, the general advantage of the hypothesis over the question is that it permits more powerful and persuasive conclusions. At the end of a study, a research question never permits the investigator to say more than "Here is how the world looked when I observed it." In contrast, hypotheses permit the investigator to say, "Based on my particular explanation of how the world works, this is what I expected to observe, and behold—that is exactly how it looked! For that reason my explanation of how the world works must be given credibility." When a hypothesis is confirmed, the investigator is empowered to make arguments about knowledge that go far beyond what is available when a question has been asked and answered.

We would be remiss here if we did not note the current debate among researchers about the value of hypotheses and statistical significance testing. It has been argued (Schmidt, 1996; Thompson, 1996, 1997) that statistical significance testing (one step in the process of testing hypotheses) has certain technical limitations. For some studies, at least, other types of analyses might provide greater benefits. That debate is beyond the scope of this text. What is certain, however, is that graduate students should discuss the matter with advisors and committee members until a consensus emerges that meets both their expectations and those (if any) of the graduate school. Whether hypotheses are tested or questions are used to guide the research, they should be written with the greatest care for precision and must be exactly appropriate to the purposes of the study.

A hypothesis can be written either as a null statement (conveniently called a null hypothesis), such as "There is no difference between . . .," or as a directional statement indicating the kind of relationship anticipated (called a research or directional hypothesis), such as "When this, also that" (positive) or "When this, not that" (negative). Some clear technical advantages are gained by using the null format, particularly when inferential statistics will be used to analyze the data. Research specialists are not in complete agreement, however, on the wisdom of writing hypotheses in directional form.

Many arguments favor the use of directionality because it permits more persuasive logic and more statistical power. If a pilot study has been completed or the literature review provides strong reasoning for a directional result, then directional hypotheses are clearly appropriate. In some instances, particularly evaluation studies, practical matters may dictate use of a directional hypothesis. For instance, if a therapy program is being evaluated and the only practical consequence would be finding that therapy provides greater gains in stress reduction than the program in current use, a directional hypothesis would permit a direct test of this singular outcome.

Some of the technical debate about the form of hypotheses is beyond the scope of this guide, but a good rule of thumb for the novice is to employ directional hypotheses when pilot data are available that clearly indicate a direction, or when the theory from which the hypotheses were drawn is sufficiently robust to include some persuasive evidence for directionality. If the investigation is a preliminary exploration in an area for which there is no well established theory, and if it has been impossible to gather enough pilot data to provide modest confidence in a directional prediction, the format of the null hypothesis is the better choice. Ultimately, as a researcher pursues a line of questioning through several investigations, directional hypotheses become more obvious and the null format less attractive.

Hypotheses can be evaluated by the same criteria used to examine research questions (lack of ambiguity, expression of relationship, and implication of appropriate test). In addition, the statement must be formulated so that the entire prediction can be dealt with in a single test. If the hypothesis is so complex that one portion could be rejected without also rejecting the remainder, it requires rewriting.

Several small, perfectly testable hypotheses always are preferable to one that is larger and amorphous. For example, in the following hypothesis the word "but" signals trouble. "Males are significantly more anxious than females, but male nurses are not significantly more anxious than female teachers." The F test for the main effect of sex in the implied analysis of variance (ANOVA) will handily deal with males and females, but a separate test as a part of a factorial ANOVA would be required for professional status. Should the tests yield opposite results, the hypothesis would point in two directions at once.

Similarly, the presence of two discrete dependent variables foreshadows difficulty in the following example: "Blood pressures on each of five days will be significantly lower than the preceding day, whereas heart rate will not decrease significantly after Day 3." The implied multivariate analysis of variance (MANOVA) could not rescue the hypothesis by indicating whether we could accept or reject it. The required follow-up test might reject the blood pressure prediction while accepting it for heart rate. In all cases, division into smaller, unitary hypotheses is the obvious cure.

When a number of hypotheses are necessary, as a result of interest in interaction effects or as a consequence of employing more than one dependent variable, the primary hypotheses should be stated first. These primary statements may even be separated from hypotheses that are secondary or confirmatory, as a means of giving prominence to the main intent of the study.

Finally, hypotheses should be formulated with an eye to the qualitative characteristics of available measurement tools. If, for example, the hypothesis specifies the magnitude of relationship between two variables, it is essential that this be supportable by the reliability of the proposed instrumentation. Returning to the earlier example of self-esteem and reading, the fact should be considered that the correlation between scores from two tests cannot exceed the square root of the product for reliability in each test. Accordingly, if reliability of the self-esteem test is .68 and that of the reading test is .76, then a hypothesis of a positive correlation greater than .80 is doomed to failure ($\sqrt{76 \times .68} = .72$).

Delimitations and Limitations

Often, a listing of delimitations and limitations is required to clarify the proposed study. Delimitations describe the populations to which generalizations may be safely made. The generalizability of the study will be a function of the subject sample and the analysis employed. *Delimit* literally means to define the limits inherent in the use of a particular construct or population.

Limitations, as used in the context of a research proposal, refer to limiting conditions or restrictive weaknesses. They occur, for example, when all factors cannot be controlled as a part of study design, or when the optimal number of observations simply cannot be made because of problems involving ethics or feasibility. If the investigator has given careful thought to these problems and has determined that the information to be gained from the compromised aspect of the study is nevertheless valid and useful, then the investigator proceeds but duly notes the limitation.

All studies have inherent delimitations and limitations. Whether these are listed in a separate section or simply discussed as they arise is an individual decision. If they are few in number and perfectly obvious, the latter is desirable. Whatever format is used, however, it is the investigator's responsibility to understand these constraints and to assure the reader that they have been considered during the formulation of the study.

Providing Definitions

All proposals for research use systematic language that may be specific to that field of research or to that proposal. We discuss the use of definitions in greater detail in the section of Chapter 6 titled "Clarity and Precision: Speaking in System Language."

Discussing the Background of the Problem

Any research problem must show its lineage from the background of existing knowledge or previous investigations, or, in the case of applied research, from contemporary practice. The author must answer three questions:

1. What do we already know or do? (The purpose here, in one or two sentences, is to support the legitimacy and importance of the question. Major discussions of the importance and significance of the study will come under the "rationale for the study" section.)

2. How does this particular question relate to what we already know or do? (The purpose here is to explain and support the exact form of questions or hypotheses that serve as the focus for the study.)

3. Why select this particular method of investigation? (The purpose here is to explain and support the selections made from among alternative methods of investigation.)

In reviewing the research literature that often forms the background for the study, the author's task is to indicate the main directions taken by workers in the area and the main issues of methodology and interpretation that have arisen. Particular attention must be given to a critical analysis of previous methodology and the exposition of the advantages and limitations inherent in various alternatives. Close attention must be given to conceptual and theoretical formulations that are explicit or implicit within the selected studies.

By devising, when appropriate, a theoretical basis for the study that emerges from the structure of existing knowledge, by making the questions or hypotheses emerge from the total matrix of answered and unanswered questions, and by making the selection of method contingent upon previous results, the author inserts the proposed study into a line of inquiry and a developing body of knowledge. Such careful attention to background is the first step in entering the continuing conversation that is science.

The author should select only those studies that provide a foundation for the proposed investigation, discuss these studies in sufficient detail to make their relevance entirely clear, note explicitly the ways in which they contribute to the proposed research, and give some indication of how the proposal is designed to move beyond earlier work. The second section of Chapter 4 provides guidelines for preparing the literature review.

It is important for students and novice proposal writers to resist the impulse to display both the extent of their personal labors in achieving what they know and the volume of interesting, but presently irrelevant, information accumulated in the process. The rule in selecting studies for review is exactly the same as that used throughout the proposal—limit discussion to what is essential to the main topic. A complete list of all references used in developing the proposal (properly called a bibliography as distinct from the list of references) may be placed in an appendix, thereby providing both a service to the interested reader and some psychological relief to the writer.

Whenever possible, the author should be conceptually or theoretically clear by creating organizing frameworks that encompass both the reviewed studies and the proposed research. This may take the form of something as obvious and practical as grouping studies according to certain methodological features (often for the purpose of examining divergent results), or something as esoteric as identifying and grouping the implicit assumptions made by various researchers in formulating their statement of the problem (often for the purpose of clarifying the problem selected in the present proposal).

In many proposals, creating an organized conceptual framework represents the most important single opportunity for the application of original thought. In one sense, the organizing task is an extension of the need to achieve clarity in communication. A category system that allows division of diverse ideas or recondite events into easily perceived and remembered subsets is an organizational convenience for the author, as well as for the reader. Beyond convenience, however, organizing frameworks identify distinctive threads of thought. The task is to isolate the parallel ways by which researchers, working at different times and in varying degrees of intellectual isolation, have conceived of reality. In creating a schema that deals meaningfully with similarities and dissimilarities in the work of others, the author not only contributes to the body of knowledge but also deals with the immediate needs of communicating this research to others.

Even relatively simple organizing or integrating systems demand the development of underlying conceptual plans and, often, new ways of interpreting old results and presumed relationships. The sequence of variables in the study may provide a simple and generally adequate place to begin arranging the review. Such questions as "What is the relationship between social class and school achievement when ability is held constant?" consist of concepts placed within a convenient sequential diagram. In turn, such conceptual schemata often contain useful assumptions about causal relationships and thus can serve as effective precursors to explanatory theory. The most elegant kind of research proposals achieve exactly that sort of linkage, using the framework for organizing the review of literature as a bridge connecting existing knowledge, a proposed theory, and the specific, theory-based hypotheses to be empirically tested.

Explaining Procedures

All proposals for empirical research must embody a plan for the careful and systematic observation of events. The methods selected for such observations determine the quality of data obtained. For this reason, the portion of the proposal dealing with procedures the researcher intends to employ will be subject to the closest critical scrutiny. Correspondingly, the presentation of methodology requires great attention to detail. The discussion of method must include sources of data, the collection of data, and the analysis of data. In addition, the discussion must show that the specific techniques selected will not fall short of the claims established in previous sections of the proposal.

The section(s) dealing with methodology must be freely adapted to the purpose of the study. Whatever the format, however, the proposal must provide a step-by-step set of instructions for conducting the investigation. For example, most studies demand explication of the following items:

1. Identification and description of the target population and sampling methods to be used
2. Presentation of instruments and techniques for measurement
3. Presentation of a design for the collection of data
4. Presentation of procedures for collecting and recording data
5. Explanation of data analysis procedures to be used
6. Development of plans for contingencies such as subject mortality

Many justifications for particular method selections will emerge in the development of background for the problem. The rationale for some choices, however, will most conveniently be presented when the method is introduced as part of the investigation plan.

In describing such elements, proposals can include pages of description that fatigue and frustrate the reader without yielding a clear picture of the overall pattern. In many cases, this problem can be avoided by the use of diagrams. Although Figure 1.2 displays a counterbalanced treatment design of moderate complexity, it would require no more than a brief paragraph of accompanying text to provide a clear account of the procedure.

When data are to be gathered from multiple subject groups, the proposal can consume pages of explanatory text without providing the reader with an adequate sense of how subject variables are related. Figure 1.3, however, shows a complex design in which a subject population is divided into 16 subgroups using the four variables of gender, role, subject matter, and affective state, with immediate transparent clarity. Diagrams also are helpful when presenting statistical models that will be tested later, once the data are collected. Note how clearly the interrelations of a hypothetical statistical model appear in Figure 1.4. In the figure, the ovals represent clusters of variables, the boxes show the variables in each cluster, and the various arrows represent interrelationships. Imagine how many words it would take to describe these relationships! Given a brief exposure to these figures, however, most readers would find further explanation unnecessary.

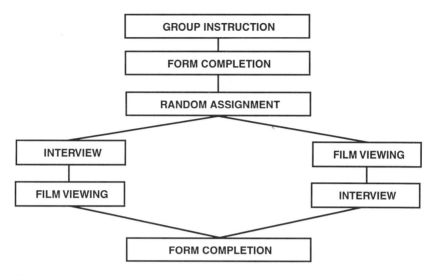

Figure 1.2. Example of Method Flow Chart

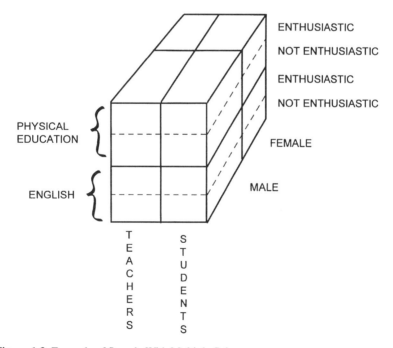

Figure 1.3. Example of Sample With Multiple Subgroups

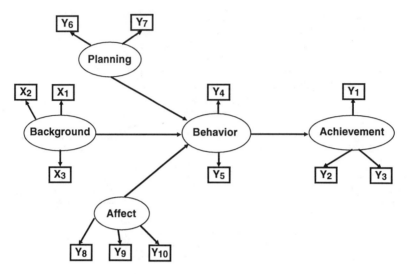

Figure 1.4. Example of Statistical Model

Providing Supplementary Material

For the purpose of clarity and economical presentation, many items may be placed in appendices keyed to appropriate references in the main text. So placed, such materials become options available to the reader as needed, rather than distractions or impediments to understanding the main themes of the proposal. Included in the appendices may be such items as the following:

1. Specifications for equipment
2. Instructions to subjects
3. Letters and other relevant documents
4. Subject consent forms
5. Raw data or tabular material from pilot studies
6. Tabular materials from related research
7. Copies of paper and pencil instruments
8. Questions for structured interviews
9. Credentials of experts, judges, or other special personnel to be employed in the study

10. Diagrammatic models of the research design
11. Diagrammatic models of the statistical analysis
12. Schematics for constructed equipment
13. Chapter outline for the final report
14. Proposed time schedule for executing the study
15. Supplementary bibliographies

2

—◻︎—

Doing the Right Thing

"The Habit of Truth"

The foundation of scholarship as a collective human enterprise is neither intellect nor technical skill. It is simple honesty. If scholars did not have what Jacob Brownowski (1965) called "the habit of truth," there could be no accumulation of reliable knowledge, and thus no science. The rules for this habit of conscience are absolute: no compromises, no evasions, no shortcuts, no excuses, and no saving face. Planning, conducting, and reporting research make sense only so long as the social contract among scholars is honored—*everyone tells the truth as well as he or she can know it.*

Certainly, there is no reason to believe that researchers are paragons of virtue. Nor should we expect that by some magic of nature or nurture they have been exempted from the human frailties of temptation. Pride, selfishness, greed, sloth, and vindictiveness are possibilities for them as much as for anyone else, and the opportunities to succumb are fully as plentiful in the course of inquiry as they are in any other human undertaking.

Why the habit of truth is sustained in any individual scholar is a complex, personal matter. Intellectual integrity, like love, may defy complete analysis. Of this much we can be certain. Researchers understand that there is no way to cheat "just a little." Any dishonesty, large or small, corrodes and contaminates both the process and the products of inquiry—doing harm to guilty and innocent alike by denying truth to all. To this we add another fact that should be noted by anyone proposing to do research: To be discovered, to be caught at cheating in scholarship, brings swift and awful consequences. In this game, the spoilsport is never forgiven.

There may once have been a time when science, as the avocation of people with the leisure to pursue their curiosity, did not invite unethical conduct, but our world has changed, and so has research as a social process. In business, the defense industry, medicine, and the university, research often is a deadly serious contest, played for big stakes and fraught with the tension of competition.

In commercial laboratories with astonishing budgets, large staffs of investigators race around the clock to beat other research teams to lucrative patents and new contracts. In university departments, professors struggle to attract external funding, keep the favor of the institution's managers, and court the possibility of academic honors. Meanwhile, young assistant professors grind out publications in a sometimes desperate pursuit of tenure and promotion. Everywhere, graduate students hurry to complete dissertations so they can win a faculty appointment and rise at last above the enforced penury of teaching assistantships. Anyone who does not see fertile ground for unethical conduct in all of that simply does not understand human nature.

As with any social statistic, it is difficult to know whether the incidence of scientific cheating has undergone an increase that is truly out of proportion to the growth of the research industry itself. What is certain, however, is that we now hear and read regularly about senior investigators, assistants, and graduate students who have been caught doctoring the data, plagiarizing information, or otherwise violating the canons of good scholarship by failing to tell the truth about their work (Adler, 1991; Bell, 1992; Safrit, 1993; Swazey, Anderson, & Lewis, 1993; Taubes, 1995). In their haste to complete the project and reap the rewards, they have broken the fragile habit of truth.

In some cases, of course, that habit never was adequately established. In the preparation of researchers, many universities fail to socialize students into the ethical norms of honest scholarship with the same thoroughness and rigor employed to induct them into the mysteries of sound data analysis. Courses in the philosophy of science and seminars on ethical issues in scholarship have been crowded out of the curriculum. Professors, busy in the frantic pace of their own studies, fail to give time to mentoring students in the complexities of what is acceptable and unacceptable behavior among scholars. We believe that the academic community will be living with the consequences of that neglect for many years to come.

This chapter is no substitute for thorough, on-the-job indoctrination into the ethical standards of inquiry in your field. What we can accomplish here is only to flag with warnings those areas in which the proposal writer is likely to encounter problems related to the ethics of scholarship. One set of those issues attends the process itself (acquiring the cooperation of subjects, gaining access to research sites, gathering data, writing reports, and publishing results). A second category contains ethical problems encountered in relationships, personal and professional, with mentors (notably in the case of professors and graduate students) and colleagues.

Throughout the chapter, we will note sources for learning more about the topic of ethics in research. We urge, however, that you use every opportunity to initiate informal discussions about ethics with active researchers, that you seek out courses and seminars dealing with the moral dimensions of scholarship, and that you attend symposia and workshops on ethical issues whenever they are offered at research conferences in your own field. You also may wish to do some self-study; the cases presented by Penslar (1995) and Macrina (1995) are good places to start. In scholarship, as elsewhere, proper behavior is shaped less by good intentions and far more by healthy doses of forewarning and forearming.

ETHICS AND THE RESEARCH PROCESS

———————■———————

What constitutes ethical behavior in research, as elsewhere in life, is the product of social definition. As a social construct, it is relative to a particular place, time, and set of people. In the instance of research-based scholarship (what is commonly called "science"), however, there is an important difference. Because science must be cumulative and self-correcting over time, and uniform across cultures (and national boundaries), standards for ethical behavior have evolved that constitute a widely agreed-to social contract among the participants.

In North America, for example, members of the National Academy of Sciences (NAS) have defined what constitutes scientific misconduct (breaches of ethical behavior) in explicit detail (Panel on Scientific Responsibility and the Conduct of Research, 1992). These have been divided into three broad categories (not all the individual items deal directly with research activity): (a) scientific misconduct (e.g., falsifying data, plagiarism), (b) questionable research procedures (e.g., keeping inadequate records, careless data collection), and (c) other misconduct (e.g., violation of government regulations, sexual harassment in the workplace).

Our own experience as well as the results from recent studies (Adler, 1991; Swazey et al., 1993) confirm that all the NAS categories of ethical concern deal with problems that have a very real presence in the places where research is done. In the particular context of planning and proposing a study, however, we have found that inadequate provision for the protection of human subjects is among the most common sources of research procedures that fail the test of ethical behavior. In part, this arises from the fact that the risks to participants are not always obvious. It also is true that devising safe, equitable, and respectful treatment for the people who make themselves available for study can sometimes be difficult. Nevertheless, observance of the social contract for ethical research begins with the proposal. That ethical failures as often involve acts of omission as acts of commission within that document makes them no less dangerous—to both people and the enterprise of scholarship.

The Protection of Human Subjects

All universities that receive funding from a federal agency must have in place a system of mandatory review of all research proposals that involve the use of human subjects. The purpose of the review is to ensure protection of the participants' health and welfare. The process may operate at one or several levels, in some cases functioning through a department or college committee and in others by means of a university board (in some institutions, both are employed). Whatever the structure of review procedures, most institutions have published guidelines that lay out the process for obtaining approval and specify the ethical issues to be addressed in the proposal. We strongly recommend that you obtain that document and digest its contents *before* beginning to prepare your proposal. The humane treatment of human beings is far easier to build in than it is to add on!

In addition to the institutional review of protection given human participants, some research journals now have ethical guidelines that must be met if a manuscript is to be considered for review. Professional and scholarly organizations have published standards that should govern research conducted by members. In all of these, attention is given to how the researcher must think and act concerning the people who make themselves available for scrutiny. We believe this body of writing reflects a vital dialogue to which every novice researcher should be a witness—and in which, over the course of their careers, they may become participants.

The proposal for a thesis or a dissertation is not intended just to prepare graduate students to undertake and finish a study. For all, it is basic instruction about what science must be if it is to serve us well and wisely, and for some it is the first rite of initiation into a career of scholarship. Accordingly, all students should invest time in learning and thinking about human rights and the ways in which they become entangled with research. If you have no convenient vehicle for that exercise, a valuable first step can be achieved by reading *Ethical Standards of the American Educational Research Association* (American Educational Research Association, 1992), *Ethical Principles of Psychologists* (American Psychological Association, 1990), *Ethical Principles in the Conduct of Research With Human Participants*, published by the American Psychological Association (1982), and *On Being A Scientist* (1995), prepared by the Committee on Science, Engineering, and Public Policy, National Academy of Science, National Academy of Engineering, and Institute of Medicine for students about to begin their first research study. Also available are a number of books on the topic of ethics in research (for example, Burgess, 1989; Kimmel, 1988; Reece & Siegel, 1986; and Sieber, 1992). Finally, for vivid examples of the complex tensions between our desire to protect participants against unethical use in research investigations and our need to preserve the integrity of research designs, we suggest a review of the problem by Kroll (1993).

It is easy for the novice to feel overwhelmed by all the responsibilities that seem to come with the direct study of other human beings. It is true that in recent years the domain of concerns about the health and welfare of participants has expanded. In large part, this reflects the fact that a greater volume and diversity of research activity has necessitated a wider definition of what constitutes ethical behavior for the investigator and reasonable protection for the subjects of investigation. Indeed, even at a great distance from the physical intrusions required to study human physiology, there is much to consider in writing that required proposal section on "Protection of Human Subjects."

An Ethical Benchmark

In the thickets of ethical complexity faced by the novice researcher, it sometimes is difficult to keep one's moral bearings. Our suggestion is to keep sight of something basic in your value system and use it as a benchmark to test each decision. For us, the starting place is simpler and far more encompassing than any of the now traditional concerns about the physical and psychological safety of participants. We believe that the right to protection begins with the right of free and informed choice.

Every human has the right not to be used by other people. That means the investigator's need for a human source of data is always subordinate to the other person's right to decide whether to provide it or not. The right not to be used applies with equal force to fifth graders, college sophomores, trash collectors, professional athletes, and residents in retirement communities. People who are asked to participate in a study have a right to know what they are getting into and the right to give or withhold their cooperation on the basis of that information.

The Self-Interest of Respect

The fact that an investigator uses volunteers responding to a newspaper advertisement, or paid subjects from a prison population, does not alter the participant's right not to be used as chattel. Research workers have both a responsibility and a special interest in protecting that right. That the rule of informed consent has so often been ignored or compromised in the past accounts in large measure for the difficulties, both obvious and subtle, in obtaining cooperation from prospective participants. Subjects do not always miss (or choose to ignore) the fact that they have suffered the disrespect of having been used by a researcher. They may remember such violation of their person for a long time and on the next occasion may protect themselves by not cooperating. Worse still, they may take a measure of revenge by finding a way to make mischief in the study.

The Danger of Seeming Innocent

What constitutes an unethical use of people is not always clearly established. Social scientists, for example, disagree on the degree to which the use of psychometric instruments, questionnaires, and survey interviews should be circumscribed by procedures to protect respondents' right to informed consent. At the least, this is an issue to be discussed with advisors during development of a proposal that involves such methods.

Our own position on such questions is unequivocal. Concern for the rights of participants should accompany the use of research tools such as questionnaires and interviews, just as it does any other form of data collection. The procedures used to protect the participant's rights may be much less elaborate than those used in an experiment involving physical discomfort or some degree of risk, but they should nonetheless be designed with care and applied with scrupulous uniformity.

It is the ubiquity of questionnaires, the conversational friendliness of interviews, the seeming innocuousness of a Likert-like scale, and the innocence of jotting field notes in social settings that present the greatest danger. Where hazards may be obvious, as for example in medical studies, careful attention to subject protection is the norm. Where risks are less obvious, and where they attach to intangibles such as "the right to full disclosure," the need for protection may be brushed aside as a mere formality, and abuse itself then becomes the insidious norm.

Each time people are treated as though they have no right to the privacy of their bodies, their thoughts, or their actions, the implication is that such treatment is right and acceptable. It is not. In contrast, when an investigator treats entry into the private world of a participant as a special privilege, granted by a fellow being as an act of informed cooperation, the opposite instruction is given—and it will be learned. From that lesson, we all profit.

A Protocol for Informed Consent

At minimum, you should consider the following standards for any proposed study that involves the use of human subjects.

1. Participants should be informed of the general nature of the investigation and, within reasonable limits, of their role in terms of time and effort. A script may be used when such information is transmitted orally. (However this is accomplished, a complete, word-for-word account of the information provided should be placed in the appendix of the proposal.)

2. Participants should be informed of procedures used to protect their anonymity. It should be made clear that anonymity cannot be guaranteed. All that should be promised is the use of rigorous procedures for protection.

3. Participants should, after reasonable consideration (including the right to ask questions), sign a document affirming that they have been informed of the nature of the investigation and have consented to give their cooperation. (A copy of this should be included in the proposal.) Specimens of such documents and a checklist for preparing informed consent forms are included here in Appendix B.

4. In experimental studies, participants should receive an explanation of all treatment procedures to be used and any discomforts or risks involved. If risks, physical or

psychological, are more than minimal, procedures that will be taken to protect the well-being of the subject should be fully explained.

5. Participants should be told what benefits they will receive by participating in the study and what alternative benefits are being made available to other subjects in the study.

6. Participants should be explicitly instructed that they are free to withdraw their consent and to discontinue participation in the study at any time. In some circumstances it is essential that they also be assured that no reprisal will attend such a decision. (Complicated issues, such as setting a time limit on this right or establishing the right to withdraw data already provided if cooperation is withdrawn, require careful attention in the proposal.)

7. Participants should be provided with the name of the person responsible for the study, to whom they can direct questions related to their role or any consequence of their participation. In the case of research conducted by graduate students, this should include the name, address, and telephone number of both the student and the supervising professor.

8. Participants should be offered the opportunity to receive feedback about the results of the study. This should be in a form that is appropriate to the needs and interests of the participant.

The Reactive Effects of Honesty

Arguments to the effect that procedures for informed consent introduce unknown bias effects are, for the most part, spurious. All contacts between investigators and participants hold the potential for generating unknown effects. The procedures for ensuring the rights of subjects do no more to produce response biases than any other interaction. On the other hand, respectful observance of these protections, quite aside from their ethical import, can exercise a measure of steadying influence over the most fundamental (and sometimes the most capricious) of all subject-related variables—the participant's cooperation.

Omission of Information

If it seems essential to withhold some specific item of information from participants, then the omission may be considered. This can be done, however, only after a careful search for any harm or substantial disadvantage that might occur. The use of placebo treatments and control groups sometimes involves exactly this form of limitation on full disclosure. The fact that such procedures are commonplace, however, does not make them less ethically problematic.

The seriousness of any decision to limit what the participant knows is underscored by the fact that deception in the form of giving false information about the nature of the study or the risks of participation (actual deception) is absolutely prohibited in every field of inquiry. As everyone knows, the boundary between sins of omission and commission is dangerously thin!

When participants are not given complete disclosure, they should know, in virtually every instance, that this is the case before making a decision about joining the study. When any information is withheld from the participants, the proposal must present explicit detail about how and when they will be debriefed and how any disadvantage created by the omission will be rectified.

Cooperation by Coercion

There is a spirit as well as a letter to be observed in rules about informed consent. When individuals are under the supervision or control of another individual, it may be difficult for them to refuse an invitation to participate in a study. In a sense, it may truly be impossible for them to freely give their cooperation. Thus, a graduate student may be loath to refuse an advisor's request to serve as a subject, or an undergraduate may feel reluctant to decline a teaching assistant's suggestion that he or she become a participant in a dissertation study. Secretaries and classified staff may be too intimidated to refuse a chairperson's invitation. Any of these individuals may sign the consent form and participate but inwardly feel resentful. People's rights are violated just as much by coercion that is unintended as by that which is so designed.

Many researchers feel that it is good ethical practice not to use students who are in their classes or under their supervision. Some institutions now have regulations that forbid such practice. It may be wise to use the media to solicit volunteers or, in the case of students, to invite only those from other departments or from places outside the purview of your authority.

Reciprocity

If participants give cooperation, time, effort, and access to what is by right theirs to control (not least of all their privacy), what does the researcher give in return? Once that question is allowed legitimacy, satisfying answers may prove more scarce than the novice might expect. It is difficult to establish what is proper compensation for serving as a study participant. In any case, few researchers could afford the purchase price for what their subjects contribute. In some measure, serving as a participant in a research study always has to take the form of a gift, which makes the demand that the gift be freely given and fully acknowledged all the more important.

Among the means of reciprocity are small symbols that show appreciation: a handwritten note, a free lecture or question and answer session on a topic of interest to the participants, or even just a sincere "thank you!" Pride also is its own reward when participants feel that they have contributed to the search for knowledge (or to finding solutions for practical problems), though that wears thin when the required investment of time or effort is large. Qualitative researchers often find that giving a respectful, nonjudgmental ear to participants' accounts of their experiences can have important value as a return for cooperation. An opportunity to satisfy curiosity, or for participants to learn something about themselves (or even about research), also may have some place in an honest exchange. In the end, however, the researcher always is left to answer two hard questions: For whose benefit is this work being done, and where are the interests of my subject in the calculus by which I find the answer?

THE ETHICS OF WRITING

Plagiarism

Ideas, and the words that express those ideas, are the valuables of scholarship. The people who create them have a right to receive credit for them. When one person appropriates the ideas or text of another person and presents them as his or her own, it is theft. The technical term is plagiarism, but it is theft, and the ethics of scholarship make no provision for petty crime—it is all grand theft.

Yes, gray areas exist where ideas, phrases, and even entire ways of thinking about things pass into the public domain where acknowledging their origin no longer is obligatory. And yes, the distinction between a paraphrase in your words and one that derives too much from the original author is a judgment call. For problems of that kind, we leave you to other resources—and your conscience.

What we are talking about here is thievery, and that includes failure to use quotation marks where they belong, omitting citations that credit material found in someone else's work, shoddy carelessness in preparing the list of references, and failure to obtain permission for the use of figures, tables, or even illustrations from another document—whether published or not. In each of those, doing the right thing does not involve knowing the niceties of custom or the precise reading of an obscure rule. You know exactly what is ethical without any coaching. All you need to remember is what your mother said: *"Don't cheat!"* If you need more motivation than that, you might consider the proposition that it is prudent to treat the property of others as you hope they will treat yours.

Providing All the Facts

The purpose of a proposal, you will remember, is to help other people understand what you plan to do. To accomplish that, they need all the relevant facts, not just those favorable to your inclinations. Deliberate omission of information hostile to some part of your proposal is dishonest. Accidental omission of important information (that includes simply not having learned it) is incompetence. Either way, an incomplete account defeats one of the main purposes in writing the proposal—to provide the basis for obtaining good advice.

Manufacturing the Facts

Once the study is under way, frequent opportunities will occur to fabricate data (creating it rather than collecting it) and falsify data (tampering with it to make it appear to be what it is not). Although obviously a violation of ethical practice, it is surprising how reasonable such fraud can seem. If you are collecting data on a subject over five days, and she happens to miss the third day, and your final record sheet shows scores of 10, 20, (?), 40, and 50, what is so unreasonable about inserting the 30 *except that it is a lie?*

Temptations like that are not rare in research. In fact, such situations are more the rule than the exception. In the rush to finish before a deadline, how reasonable will a small lie seem to you? In your response will reside the answer to another question: What kind of scholar do you want to become? (In case you wondered, in many forms of data analysis there are appropriate ways to deal with missing data. All you need to do is use the correct procedure and then be honest— describing in your report exactly how data were handled.)

Inappropriate use of data is no different from making it up. Using raw scores when you know they should be transformed before analysis is just another kind of falsification. Data dredging—repeatedly changing your analysis when results do not come out as anticipated—is another way to fudge. Use the data you have, use it correctly, and tell the reader exactly what you did. With those simple rules, it is hard to go wrong.

Other falsehoods do not directly involve the data. For example, it may be tempting to describe testing procedures as having more rigor than you actually were able to maintain or to report taking the precautions against contamination that you had proposed, when, in fact, it proved impossible to do so. It may be easy to allow the reader to infer that a standard protocol was used unchanged, when, in fact, it had to be modified, or to give the impression that your selection of observation sites was random, when, in fact, you had to pick the ones closest to your office. All are breaches of ethics, all undercut the value of your research, and all serve to create an insidious pollution in the atmosphere of science.

Discussion of your findings provides one last temptation to tilt the facts in a way that favors your personal interests but falls short of an honest accounting. The researcher has a perfect right to emphasize the results that seem most important. That power is abused, however, when disconfirming data are left out of the discussion, or are included without a clear notation of their implications.

Graduate students can be particularly vulnerable to the natural attraction of selective reporting. There often is subtle pressure to present the results that advisors expect. If having to find a way to deal with equivocal or counterintuitive findings is likely to delay graduation, the temptation to simply "not have them" grows ever more attractive. The choice to do the right thing can be inconvenient, expensive, and even painful. No experienced investigator would claim that research is a rose garden.

ETHICS IN PUBLICATION

Sending off the manuscript to a journal, mailing your abstract to the review committee for a national conference, finding your name in the table of contents— those are golden moments, and any researcher who no longer finds them so should consider a long vacation. The route to those wonderful moments, however, is strewn with ethical pitfalls for the unwary novice. There is a lot to know about the rules that govern ethics in publication, and much of that is beyond the purview of this handbook.

As an example, in the case of research studies to which a number of people contribute, there are rules (both written and unwritten) about whose names appear on the report, in what order they appear, and who should be acknowledged but not given status as an author. Unfortunately, these rules come in versions established by universities, journals, scholarly organizations, government agencies, laboratories, and even individual professors. The best we can do is to advise that you make it a point to find out the regulations (or local conventions) that apply in your circumstance. In such matters as whose name will appear on publications and who (or what entity) will have ownership of research products, it is prudent that you locate this information *early* in the proposal development process—and for this purpose, formal documents are always more appropriate than informal conversations.

We will note here only three of the many ethical concerns related to publication, one of them because it is among the first and most obvious, and two because they are well-disguised pitfalls that may not be recognized for the dangers they present. First, can you submit your manuscript to more than one journal at the same time? The short answer is: No, don't ever do it. If you have a fertile mind, you will recognize at once that there are dozens of questions that surround that simple rule. For example, can you submit a manuscript to a journal after the abstract for the same study was published in a conference proceedings? (The answer is yes.) For each of these subsidiary problems, you will have to find what is considered ethical in the particular situation. Just do not forget the basic rule—duplicate submissions are absolutely prohibited, and the event of duplicate publication brings swift and draconian consequences.

A second temptation will come early in your study, and it is that timing that gives it both great attraction and serious danger. Almost every researcher we know has been tempted to submit an abstract to a prestigious conference (to be held well after the proposed conclusion of the study), when the analysis has not been finished, or even when all the data are not yet in hand. The motive is understandable. Researchers are excited about their work and always eager to join the great conversation that represents scholarship in their field. Writing up an abstract that is incomplete or that projects anticipated results seems a minor transgression, but one thing can lead to another. What if the final analysis contradicts your confident projection? What if the work slows down and still is incomplete when the conference date arrives? Among embarrassing alternatives are withdrawing the paper or making a public confession. Worse, however, there will be temptation into serious violation of ethics, such as covering your tracks by faking results or downplaying findings that do not harmonize with the earlier abstract. Cooking up an abstract so you can reserve a place on the program is risky business. Our advice is to do what you know is the right thing—just wait until next year.

A third pitfall lies waiting beyond presentations and journal articles, in a seemingly risk-free document—your résumé. Most beginners in academe do a bit of padding by including fairly minor accomplishments that later will be omitted as publication lists begin to lengthen, but this practice has limitations and points at which it becomes dishonesty rather than innocent enthusiasm. Employers and promotion committees have become increasingly restive about the kind of unethical padding that has proliferated in academic résumés. Among the truly dishonest inclusions are abstracts from presentations that are given a title different from an ensuing published report—so that the two appear to be different studies, when they are not. Another is listing research articles or grant proposals in a way that allows the reader to assume you were a coinvestigator, when in fact you contributed only a minor part to the submission. Contributions to the "Brief Research Notes" sections of journals are found displayed as though they were major achievements.

All such forms of padding are not innocent enthusiasm; they are dishonesty. Happily, a simple procedure can be adopted that will keep you safe from any complaint about your résumé—and still allow you to take credit for everything. Put your accomplishments in categories headed by labels that clearly describe what each contains, and cross-reference where citations represent the same piece of work.

PERSONAL AND
PROFESSIONAL RELATIONSHIPS
————————————■————————————

A very fine distinction separates violations of research ethics (that include most of what has been discussed to this point) and ethical misconduct. For a helpful discussion that defines those and other categories in the domain of ethics, see volume 1 of *Responsible Science*, a publication prepared by the Panel on Scientific Responsibility and the Conduct of Research (1992). It is that latter category of misconduct, which includes the ethics of how scholars treat one another in their personal and professional relationships, to which we will now attend.

Relationships With Faculty Mentors

As has been described in a number of recent publications (Guston, 1993; National Academy of Science, National Academy of Engineering, and Institute of Medicine, 1997; Roberts, 1993), in the ideal situation, the relationship between graduate student and advisor gradually matures until at the completion of the degree the student and professor have become colleagues. Unfortunately, what is ideal is not always real. Some dysfunctions in professor/student relationships are no more than the collision of personality styles, the abrasion of conflicting intellectual interests, or the tensions of differing personal politics. Those are painful, and even harmful if not addressed, but they do not necessarily involve unethical behavior by anyone. Certain types of interpersonal behavior, however, are not acceptable because they are dangerous, or violations of what is equitable, or both.

First among these are instances in which pressure is put on a student to go beyond the expected academic or professional relationship. In our judgment, any attempt by a faculty member to coerce a student into an expanded relationship is inappropriate.

Perhaps not obvious as a form of ethical misconduct is pressure from faculty that urges students to perform tasks that are not part of the academic program—and that they do not wish to do. These subtle abuses include requesting errand service, assigning attendance at social functions, and even the expectation of jogging together. In most collegial relationships, such activities are normal. People who work closely together often exchange favors and socialize. The problem is that the relationship between professors and students is not truly collegial. There is an enormous imbalance of power. In the most innocent and well-intended invitations, students often find the hidden force of coercion.

The point at which inappropriate pressures shade into reasonable requirements is a gray area. An important part of any graduate program is gaining research experience by hands-on engagement. Working with faculty members on their projects can be a valuable source of such training. There are limits to be observed, however, and care needs to be taken so that apprenticeship does not become servitude in disguise.

When the task performed is so narrow as to yield no new skill or knowledge, when the student's own work has to be unreasonably delayed, and when the topic of inquiry is not remotely related to the student's specialization, the line between education and abuse has been crossed. By then, it may be too late to extricate yourself comfortably. For that reason, we suggest prior discussion of all such research opportunities with other faculty advisors, the prospective research mentor, and other graduate students.

Much more serious examples of abusing the faculty-student imbalance of power are all the forms of sexual harassment. The form taken may range from subtle comments to direct demands for sex. Although it is obvious that what one person considers as offensive another person may regard as repartee or humor, that understanding does not make remarks with sexual connotations any more acceptable or any less serious as breaches of ethical conduct. Students have an absolute right to be free of such discomforts. Subtle or glaring, intended or inadvertent, sexual harassment is wrong and not to be tolerated.

If you encounter such problems, we suggest confronting them immediately, rather than allowing them to fester. Some faculty members may not understand that you find something troubling, and a private discussion may set everything straight. Repeated incidents or any invitation or pressure for a sexual relationship should be brought to the attention of someone you can trust—another faculty member, the department chair, the dean, or perhaps the best choice of all, the university ombudsperson.

It is to everyone's advantage that student/professor relationships stay at the formal level of teacher and pupil. If you want a mentor/mentee relationship to turn into something more, we urge that you acquire a new mentor before allowing that to happen. Human relationships are complex, but those that attempt to bridge stations of unequal power are doubly so.

Where goodwill reigns and a modicum of sensitivity is the norm, the relationship between professor and student is not a mine field of hidden risks; it is the place for a rare and invaluable kind of human exchange. Given even reasonable nurture and protection, it will flourish and grow—into collegiality.

Discovery and Obligation

What if it really happens? What if you discover or have strong reason to suspect unethical behavior on the part of a colleague or faculty member? Our first advice is to think carefully, very carefully, about how to protect yourself from involvement or reprisal. Also consider the terrible consequences of an accusation that proves false. Whether or not you take action will be a matter of conscience, and your conscience should tell you that cheating in research can never be condoned or tolerated. What course of action you choose, however, will be a function of circumstance, prudence, and courage.

Talking with the person(s) involved is one course of action. If you judge that to be unreasonable, then you must find other options. In most universities, appropriate authorities are available, and again the ombudsperson will know who they are. Any institution that receives federal research funds will have procedures for investigating violations of research ethics. In some instances, there are provisions to protect the "whistle-blower" (Miceli & Near, 1992), though that is not always possible.

In the end, anyone accused of a violation has a proper claim to due process, and even well-intentioned reports of ethical violations that cannot be sustained when investigated will rebound to the discomfort (and often disadvantage) of the accuser. Again, take the time to review the pages of *Responsible Science* (Panel on Scientific Responsibility and the Conduct of Research, 1992) before you act. Doing the right thing may not be easy, but at least it can be done the right way.

None of us can decline to take responsibility. Every study is part of a shared enterprise—the work of scholarship. When anyone does not do what is right, everyone is harmed.

CHAPTER

3

=□=

Developing the Thesis
or Dissertation Proposal

Some Common Problems

The general purposes and broad format of the proposal document have now been presented. There remain, however, a number of particular points that cause a disproportionate amount of difficulty in preparing proposals for student-conducted research. In some cases, the problems arise because of real difficulty in the subtle and complex nature of the writing task. In other cases, however, the problems are a consequence of confusion, conflicting opinions, and ambiguous standards among research workers themselves and, more particularly, among university research advisors.

As with many tasks involving an element of art, it is possible to establish a few general rules to which most practitioners subscribe. Success in terms of real mastery, however, lies not in knowing, or even following, the rules but in what the student learns to do within the rules.

Each student will discover his or her own set of special problems. Some will be solved only through practice and the accumulation of experience. While wrestling with the frustrations of preparing a proposal, the student should try to remember that the real fascination of research lies in its problematic nature, in the search for serviceable hypotheses, in selecting sensitive means of analyzing data, and in the creative tasks of study design.

Some of the problems graduate students face cannot be solved simply by reading about them. What follows, however, is an effort to alert you to the most common pitfalls, to provide some general suggestions for resolution of the problems, and to sound one encouraging note: Consultation with colleagues and advisors, patience with the often slow process of "figuring out," and scrupulous care in writing will overcome or circumvent most of the problems encountered in preparing a research proposal. In the midst of difficulty, it is useful to remember that problems are better encountered when developing the proposal than when facing a deadline for a final copy of the report.

The problems have been grouped into two broad sections: "Before the Proposal: First Things First" and "The Sequence of Proposing: From Selecting a Topic to Forming a Committee." Each section contains a number of specific issues that may confront the student researcher and provides some rules of thumb for use in avoiding or resolving the attendant difficulties. Readers should skim through the two sections selectively, because not all the discussions will be relevant to their needs. Chapter 4 ("Content of the Proposal: Important Consid-erations"), Chapter 6 ("Style and Form in Writing the Proposal"), and Chapter 7 ("The Oral Presentation") deal with specific technical problems and should be consulted after completing a review of what follows here.

BEFORE THE PROPOSAL:
FIRST THINGS FIRST

─────────────■─────────────

Making Your Decision: Do You Really Want to Do It?

The following idealized sequence of events leads to a thesis or dissertation proposal.

1. In the process of completing undergraduate or master's level preparation, the student identifies an area of particular interest in which he or she proposes to concentrate advanced study.

2. The student selects a graduate institution that has a strong reputation for research and teaching in the area of interest.

3. The student identifies an advisor who has published extensively and regularly chairs graduate student research in the area of interest.

4. Based on further study and interaction with the advisor, the student selects and formulates a question or hypothesis as the basis for a thesis or dissertation.

Because we do not live in the best of all possible worlds, few students are able to pursue the steps of this happy and logical sequence. For a variety of reasons, most students have to take at least one of the steps in reverse. Some even find themselves at the end of several semesters of study just beginning to identify a primary area of interest, in an institution that may be less than perfectly appropriate to their needs, and assigned to an advisor who has little or no experience in that particular domain. For this unfortunate state of affairs, we offer no easy solution. We do believe that one significant decision is, or should be, available to the student—the decision to do, or not to do, a research study. Faced with conditions such as those described above, if the option is available, the more rational and educationally profitable course may be to elect not to undertake a research study. You can determine whether this option is available before the school is selected, or at least before the program of study is selected.

There are sound reasons to believe that experience in the conduct of research contributes to graduate education. There also are good and substantial reasons to believe that other kinds of experiences are immeasurably more appropriate and profitable for some students. The question is, "Which experience is right for you?"

If you are, or think you might be, headed for a career in scholarship and higher education, then the decision is clear. The sooner you begin accumulating experience in research activities, the better. If you are genuinely curious about the workings of the research process, interested in combining inquiry with a career of professional service, or fascinated by the problems associated with a particular application of knowledge to practice, again the decision is clear. An experience in research presents at least a viable alternative in your educational plans.

Lacking one of these motives, the decision should swing the other way, toward an option more suited to your needs. Inadequately motivated research tends not to be completed or, worse, is finished in a pedestrian fashion far below the student's real capacity. Even a well-executed thesis or dissertation may exert a powerful negative influence on the graduate experience when it has not been accepted by the student as a reasonable and desirable task.

One problem touches everyone in graduate education, faculty and students alike—the hard constraints of time. Students want to finish their degree programs in a reasonable period of time. The disposition or circumstances of some, however, may define reasonable time as "the shortest possible time." Others find the thought of any extension beyond the standard number of semesters a serious threat to their sense of adequacy. For students such as these, a thesis or dissertation is a risky venture.

Relatively few research studies finish on schedule, and time requirements invariably are underestimated. Frequent setbacks are almost inevitable. This is one aspect of the research process that is learned during the research experience: Haste in research is lethal to both quality of the product and worth of the experience. If you cannot spend the time, deciding to initiate a research project endangers the area of inquiry, your advisor, your institution, your education, your reputation, and any satisfaction you might take in completing the task. In short, if you can't afford the time, then don't do it at all.

Choosing Your Turf:
Advisors and Areas

Once a firm decision has been made to write a thesis or dissertation, the choice of an advisor presents a less difficult problem. Here, area of interest dictates selection because it is essential to have an advisor who is knowledgeable. Further, it always is preferable to have one who is actively publishing in the domain of interest.

Competent advisement is so important that a degree of student flexibility may be required. It is far better for students to adjust their long-range goals than to attempt research on a topic with which their advisor is completely unfamiliar. It may be necessary for the thesis or dissertation to be part of the advisor's own research program. As long as the topic remains within the broad areas of student interest, however, it is possible to gain vital experience in formulating questions, designing studies, and applying the technology and methods of inquiry that are generic to the domain.

It is desirable for student and advisor to interact throughout the development of the proposal, beginning with the initial selection and formulation of the question. On occasion, however, the student may bring an early stage proposal to a prospective advisor as a test of his or her interest or to encourage acceptance of formal appointment as advisor. Experience suggests that this strategy is most likely to produce immediate results if the proposal is in the primary interest area of the advisor. If the proposal involves replication of some aspect of the advisor's previous research, the student may be amazed at the intensity of attention this attracts.

Finding Your Question:
What Don't We Know That Matters?

Before launching into the process of identifying a suitable topic for inquiry, we suggest a short course of semantic and conceptual hygiene. The purpose of this small therapy is to establish a simple and reliable set of terms for thinking through what can sometimes be a difficult and lengthy problem—what do I study?

All research emerges from a perceived problem, some unsatisfactory situation in the world that we want to confront. Sometimes the difficulty rests simply in the fact that we don't understand how things work and have the human itch to know. At other times, we are confronted by decisions or the need for action when the alternatives or consequences are unclear. Such perceived problems are experienced as a disequilibrium, a dissonance in our cognition. Notice, however, they do not exist out in the world, but in our minds.

That may sound at first like one of those "nice points" of which academics are sometimes fond, but for the purposes of a novice researcher, locating the problem in the right place and setting up your understanding of exactly what is unsatisfactory may represent much more than an arbitrary exercise. Thinking clearly about problems, questions, hypotheses, and research purposes can prevent mental logjams that sometimes block or delay clear identification of what is to be investigated.

The novice will encounter research reports, proposals, and even some well-regarded textbooks that freely interchange the words "problem" and "question" in ways that create all sorts of logical confusion (as in "The question in this study is to investigate the problem of . . ." or "The problem in this study is to investigate the question of . . ."). The problem is located alternately in the world or in the study, the distinction between problems and questions is unclear, and what is unsatisfactory in the situation is not set up as a clear target for inquiry.

We suggest that you be more careful as you think through the question of what to study. Define your terms from the start and stick with them, at least until they prove not to be helpful. The definitions we prefer are arbitrary, but it has been our experience that making such distinctions is a useful habit of mind. Accordingly, we suggest that you use the following lexicon as you think and begin to write about your problem.

> *Problem*—the experience we have when an unsatisfactory situation is encountered. Once carefully defined, it is that situation, with all the attendant questions it may raise, that can become the target for a proposed study. Your proposal, then,

will not lay out a plan to study the problem but will address one or several of the questions that explicate what you have found "problematic" about the situation. Note that in this context neither situation nor problem is limited to a pragmatic definition. The observation that two theories contradict each other can be experienced as a problem, and a research question may be posed to address the conflict.

Question—a statement of what you wish to know about some unsatisfactory situation, as in the following: What is the relation between . . .? Which is the quickest way to . . .? What would happen if . . .? What is the location of . . .? "What is the perspective of . . .? As explained below, when cast in a precise, answerable form, one or several of these questions will become the mainspring for your study—the formal research question.

Purpose—the explicit intention of the investigator to accumulate data in such a way as to answer the research question posed as the focus for the study. The word "objective" is a reasonable synonym here. Although only people can have intentions, it is common to invest our research design with purpose (as in "The purpose of this study is to determine the mechanism through which . . .").

Hypothesis—an affirmation about the nature of some situation in the world. A tentative proposition set up as a convenient target for an investigation, a statement to be confirmed or denied in terms of the evidence.

Given this lexicon, the search for a topic becomes the quest for a situation that is sufficiently unsatisfactory to be experienced as a *problem*. The proposal has as its *purpose* the setting up of a research *question* and the establishment of exactly how (and why) the investigator intends to find the answer, thereby eliminating or reducing the experience of finding something problematic about the world. Problems lead to questions, which in turn lead to the purpose of the study and, in some instances, to hypotheses. Table 3.1 shows the question, purpose, and hypotheses for a study. Note that the hypotheses meet the criteria established in Chapter 1 and are the most specific.

The research process, and thus the proposal, begins with a question. Committed to performing a study within a given area of inquiry and allied with an appropriate advisor, students must identify a question that matches their interests as well as the resources and constraints of their situation. Given a theoretically infinite set of possible problems that might be researched, it is no small wonder that many students at first are overwhelmed and frozen into indecision. The "I can't find a problem" syndrome is a common malady among graduate students, but fortunately one that can be cured by time and knowledge.

Research questions emerge from three broad sources: logic, practicality, and accident. In some cases, the investigator's curiosity is directed to a gap in the logical structure of what already is known in the area. In other cases, the

TABLE 3.1 Problem, Questions, Purpose, and Hypotheses

Problem—Extensive teacher planning of lessons requires large investments of time and energy, and often must compete with other important responsibilities—both professional and personal.

Question—Is the amount or kind of lesson planning done by teachers positively related to student in-class learning behaviors such as time-on-task?

Purpose—The purpose of this study is to examine the relationships between several categories (types) of teacher lesson planning and student time-on-task in a high school automobile mechanics class.

Hypotheses (Note that directional hypotheses are used for Hypotheses 1-3 and that even Hypothesis 4, stated in the null form, could be based on data from a pilot study.)

1. The number of teacher lesson planning decisions that relate to design and use of active learning strategies will be positively related to student time-on-task when those lessons are implemented.

2. The number of class management planning decisions related to particular lesson components will be positively related to student time-on-task when those components are implemented.

3. Teacher lesson planning decisions that require students to wait for the availability of tools or work sites will be negatively related to student time-on-task when those lessons are implemented.

4. The total number of teacher planning decisions (irrespective of category) will not be related to student time-on-task when those lessons are implemented.

---

investigator responds to the demand for information about the application of knowledge to some practical service. In yet other cases, serendipity operates and the investigator is stimulated by an unexpected observation, often in the context of another study. It is common for several of these factors to operate simultaneously to direct attention to a particular question. Personal circumstance and individual style also tend to dictate the most common source of questions for each researcher. Finally, all the sources depend on a more fundamental and prior factor—thorough knowledge of the area.

It is this latter factor that accounts for the "graduate student syndrome." Only as one grasps the general framework and the specific details of a particular area can unknowns be revealed, fortuitous observations raise questions, and possible applications of knowledge become apparent. Traditional library study is the first step toward the maturity that permits confident selection of a research question. Such study, however, is necessary but not sufficient. In any active area of inquiry, the current knowledge base is not in the library—it is in the invisible college of informal associations among research workers.

The working knowledge base of an area takes the form of unpublished papers, conference speeches, seminar transcripts, memoranda, dissertations in progress, grant applications, personal correspondence, telephone calls, and electronic mail communications, as well as conversations in the corridors of conference centers, restaurants, hotel rooms, and bars. To obtain access to this ephemeral resource, the student must be where the action is.

The best introduction to the current status of a research area is close association with advisors who know the territory and are busy formulating and pursuing their own questions. Conversing with peers, listening to professorial discussions, assisting in research projects, attending lectures and conferences, exchanging papers, and corresponding with faculty or students at other institutions are all ways of capturing the elusive state of the art. In all of these, however, the benefits derived often depend on knowing enough about the area to join the dialogue by asking questions, offering a tangible point for discussion, or raising a point of criticism. In research, as elsewhere, the more you know, the more you can learn.

Although establishing a network of exchange may seem impossible to young students who view themselves as novices and outsiders, it is a happy fact that new recruits generally find a warm welcome within any well-defined area of intensive study. Everyone depends on informal relationships among research colleagues, and this rapport is one source of sustaining excitement and pleasure in the research enterprise. As soon as you can articulate well-formulated ideas about possible problems, your colleagues will be eager to provide comment, critical questions, suggestions, and encouragement.

In the final process of selecting the thesis or dissertation problem, there is one exercise that can serve to clarify the relative significance of competing questions. Most questions can be placed within a general model that displays a sequence of related questions—often in an order determined by logic or practical considerations. Smaller questions are seen to lead to larger and more general questions, methodological questions are seen necessarily to precede substantive questions, and theoretical questions may be found interspersed among purely empirical questions. The following is a much simplified but entirely realistic example of such a sequential model. It begins with an everyday observation and leads through a series of specific and interrelated problems to a high-order question of great significance.

> OBSERVATION: Older adults generally take longer than young adults to complete cognitive tasks, but those who are physically active seem to be quicker mentally, especially in tasks that demand behavioral speed.
> 1. What types of cognitive function might be related to exercise?
> 2. How can these cognitive functions be measured?

3. What are the effects of habitual exercise on one of these types of cognitive function—reaction time?
4. Are active older adults faster on a simple reaction time task than sedentary older adults?
5. Are active older adults faster on a more complex reaction time task, such as choice reaction time, than older sedentary adults?

QUESTION: What effect does habitual exercise have on choice reaction time in older adults?

By making the twists and turns of speculation visible in the concrete process of sequential listing, previously unnoticed possibilities may be revealed or tentative impressions confirmed. In the simple example given above, the reader may immediately see other questions that could have been inserted or alternative chains of inquiry that branch off from the main track of logic. Other diagrammatic lists of questions about exercise and cognitive function might be constructed from different but related starting points. One might begin, for example, with the well-established observation that circulation is superior in older individuals who exercise regularly. This might lead through a series of proximal experiments toward the ultimate question, "What is the *mechanism* by which exercise maintains cognitive function?"

Building such diagrams will be useful for the student in several other ways. It is a way of controlling the instinct to grab the first researchable question that becomes apparent in an area. Often such questions are inferior to what might be selected after more careful contemplation of the alternatives. A logical sequence can be followed for most questions, beginning with "What has to be asked first?" Once these serial relationships become clear, it is easier to assign priorities.

In addition to identifying the correct ordering and relative importance of questions, such conceptual models also encourage students to think in terms of a series of studies that build cumulatively toward more significant conclusions than can be achieved in a one-shot thesis or dissertation. The faculty member who has clear dedication to a personal research program can be a key factor in attracting students into the long-term commitments that give life to an area of inquiry.

Researchable questions occur daily to the active researcher. The problem is not finding them but maintaining some sense of whether, and where, they might fit into an overall plan. Although this condition may seem remote to the novice struggling to define a first research topic, formulating even a modest research agenda can be a helpful process. The guidance of a sequential display of questions can allow the student to settle confidently on the target for a proposal.

THE SEQUENCE OF PROPOSING:
FROM SELECTING A TOPIC TO FORMING A COMMITTEE

———————————■———————————

A Plan of Action: What Follows What?

Figure 3.1 can be useful for the novice if one central point is understood. A tidy, linear sequence of steps is not an accurate picture of what happens in the development of most research proposals. The peculiar qualities of human thought processes and the serendipity of retrieving knowledge serve to guarantee that development of a proposal will be anything but tidy. Dizzying leaps, periods of no progress, and agonizing backtracking are more typical than is a continuous, unidirectional flow of events. The diagram may be used to obtain an overview of the task, to establish a rough time schedule, or to check retrospectively for possible omissions, but it is not to be taken as a literal representation of what should or will happen.

To say that development of a proposal is not a perfectly predictable sequence is not to say, however, that it is entirely devoid of order. Starting at the beginning and following a logical sequence of thought and work has some clear advantages. When the proposal has been completed, a backward glance often indicates that a more orderly progression through the development steps would have saved time and effort.

For instance, although the mind may skip ahead and visualize a specific type of measure to be used, Step 11 ("Consider alternative methods of data collection") should not be undertaken until Step 6 ("Survey relevant literature") is completed. Many methods of measurement may be revealed and noted while perusing the literature. Sometimes suggestions for instrumentation materialize in unlikely places or in studies that have been initially categorized as unlikely to yield information concerning measurement. Additionally, reported evidence of the reliability and validity of the scores from alternative procedures will be needed before any final selection can be made. Thus, a large commitment of effort to consideration of alternative methods can be a waste of time if it precedes a careful survey of the literature.

For simplicity, many important elements have been omitted from Figure 3.1. No reference is made to such pivotal processes as developing a theoretical framework, categorizing literature, or stating hypotheses. Further, the detailed demands that are intrinsic to the writing process itself, such as establishing a systematic language, receive no mention. What are presented are the obvious steps of logic and procedure—the operations and questions that mark development toward a plan for action. Finally, the reader who begins to make actual use of the diagram will find that the sequence of steps at several junctures leads into what appear to be circular paths. For example, if at Question F a single form of inquiry does not present itself as most appropriate, the exit line designated "NO" leads back to the previous procedural step of considering alternative forms of inquiry. The intention in this arrangement is not to indicate a trap in which beginning researchers are doomed forever to chase their tails. In each case, the closed loop suggests only that when questions cannot be answered, additional input is required (more study, thought, or advice), or that the question itself is inappropriate to the case and must be altered.

For the most part, Figure 3.1 is self-explanatory. We have assumed that students will be working with, and obtaining advice from, their advisor as they navigate the various steps. In the pages that follow, however, we have selected a few of the steps and questions for comment, either because they represent critical junctures in the proposal process or because they have proven particularly troublesome for our own advisees. It will be helpful to locate in the diagram sequence each of the items selected for discussion so that the previous and succeeding steps and questions provide a frame for our comments.

Step 3: Narrow down. "What do I want to know?" Moving from general to specific is always more difficult for the beginner than is anticipated. It is here that the student first encounters two of the hard facts of scientific life: logistic practicality and the perverse inscrutability of seemingly simple events. Inevitably, the novice must learn to take one small step, one manageable question, at a time. In other words, the proposal must conform in scope to the realistic limitations of the research process itself. At their best, research tools can encompass only limited bits of reality; stretched too far, they produce illusion rather than understanding.

It may be important to think big at first, to puzzle without considering practicality, and to allow speculation to soar beyond the confines of the sure knowledge base. From such creative conceptual exercises, however, the researcher must return to the question, "Where, given my resources and the nature of the problem, can I begin?" Delimiting questions such as "In which people?" "Under what conditions?" "At what time?" "In what location?" "By observing which events?" and "By manipulating which variables?" serve the necessary pruning function.

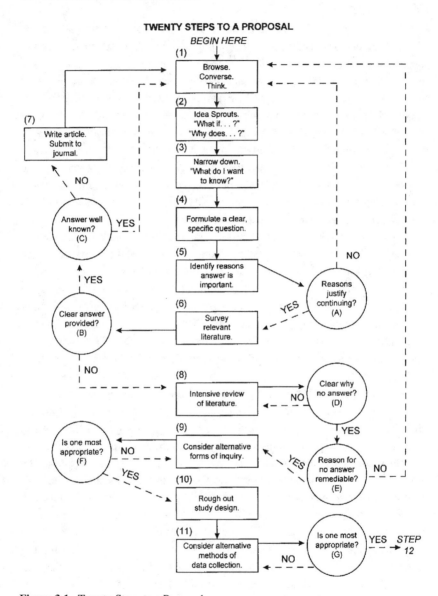

Figure 3.1. Twenty Steps to a Proposal

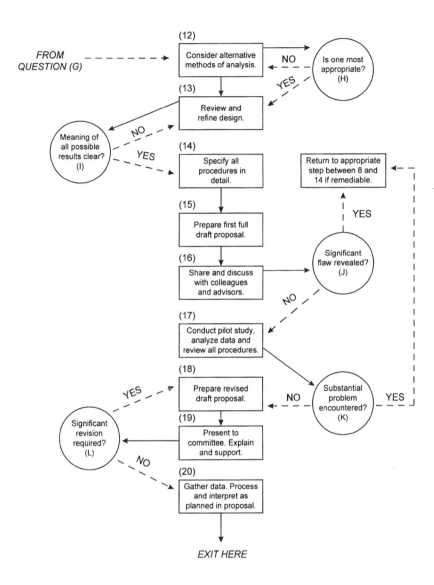

Figure 3.1. *Continued*

NOTE: Boxes represent major procedural steps, and unbroken lines trace the main sequence of those steps. Circles represent the major questions to be confronted, and broken lines lead to the procedural consequences of the alternative YES or NO answers.

Step 5: Identify reasons answer is important. This step places the proposed research in scientific-societal perspective. The study should contribute to the generation or validation of a theoretical structure or subcomponent or relate to one of the several processes by which knowledge is used to enhance professional practice. The trick here is to justify the question in terms appropriate to its nature. Inquiry that is directed toward filling a gap in the structure of knowledge need not be supported by appeals to practical application (even though later events may yield just such a return). Inquiry that arises directly from problems in the world of practice need not be supported by appeals to improve understanding of basic phenomena (even though later events may lead to this). Each kind of question has its own correct measure of importance. The task of distinguishing the trivial from the substantive is not always easy; do not make it even more difficult by attempting to apply the wrong standard.

Question A: Reasons justify continuing? In examining a list of reasons that support the importance of a question, the issue of worth may be viewed from several dimensions: worth to the individual contemplating the answer and worth to the profession, to the academic community, and ultimately to society. Question A, "Reasons justify continuing?" is the question that the researcher must answer in terms of personal interests and needs. The world is full of clearly formulated and specific questions that may not, once seen in their formal dress, seem worth the effort of answering. Because researchers are human, perfectly legitimate questions may seem dull, interesting veins of inquiry may peter out into triviality, and well-defined issues may fail to suit for no better reason than a clash with personal style. On the other hand, some questions are supported by the researcher's immediate need to enhance teaching in a vital subject area or to quench curiosity about a long-held hunch.

The basic rule is to be honest before proceeding. If you really don't care about answering the question, it may be better to start again while the investment still is relatively small.

Step 6: Survey relevant literature. A preliminary scanning of the most obvious, pertinent resources, particularly reviews of the literature, is a way of husbanding time. It is far better to abandon a line of thought after several weeks of selective skimming than to work one's way via slow, thorough digestion of each document to the same conclusion after several months of effort.

Conscientious students sometimes feel vaguely guilty about such quick surveys. Keeping in mind the real purpose, which is to identify questions that already have satisfactory answers, is one way of easing such discomfort.

Question E: Reason for no answer remediable? In some cases, the literature contains an empty area because the state of technology, the available knowledge framework, ethical considerations in completing the study, or the logistic demands peculiar to the question have made it impossible or unreasonable to conduct appropriate forms of inquiry. So long as the gap in knowledge seems to exist because no one has yet defined the question or become interested in pursuing the answer, it is reasonable to proceed. There are other reasons for empty or ambiguous areas in the literature, however, and they signal caution before proceeding.

Question I: Meaning of all possible results clear? The tighter the logic, the more elegant the theoretical framework, the more closely the design is tailored to produce clarity along one dimension—in short, the better the quality of the proposal—the greater the risk that the proposer will be lured into an unfortunate presumption: that the result of the study is known before the data are in hand. That student researchers sometimes are confronted by the stunning news that their treatment produced a reverse effect is in itself neither surprising nor harmful. Being unable to make an intelligent interpretation of such a situation, however, is unfortunate and in most cases avoidable.

Unanticipated results raise a fundamental question that the investigator must confront. Does the finding truly reflect what is resident in the data, or is it only an artifact of the analysis? If there is any doubt about the appropriateness of the analysis, particularly if the procedures were not perfectly aligned with the research question, the latter possibility must be considered. If reexamination of the analysis provides no accounting for findings that are sharply incongruent with expectations, another explanation must be sought. All of this is made more difficult if the possibility of discrepant findings has never been contemplated. A strong proposal, constructed in an orderly, step-by-step sequence, will enhance the likelihood that the student can manage the unexpected with at least a degree of dignity.

Through serious consideration of alternative outcomes at the time of constructing the proposal, it may be possible to include elements in the study that will eliminate ambiguity in some of the most likely results. One method of anticipating the unexpected is to follow through the consequences of rejecting or failing to reject each hypothesis of the study. If the hypothesis was rejected, what is the explanation? How is the explanation justified by the rationale for the study? What findings would support the explanation? Conversely, if the findings of the study fail to provide a basis for rejection, what explanations are to be proposed? At the least, some careful preliminary thought about alternative explanations for each possible result will serve as a shield against the panic that produces such awkward post hoc interpretations as "no significant differences were observed because the instruments employed were inadequate."

Step 16: Share and discuss with colleagues and advisors. There is a well-known syndrome displayed by some who attempt research, characterized by the inclination to prolong the period of writing the final report—indefinitely. Some people simply cannot face what they perceive to be the personal threat implied in opening their work to challenge in the public arena. These individuals are terribly handicapped and only rarely can become mature, productive scholars. An early sign of this is seen in students who cannot bring themselves to solicit advice and criticism for their proposals.

Sometimes students experience severe criticism because they present their ideas before they have been sufficiently developed into a conceptual framework that represents careful preparation. Many professors avoid speculative conversations about "half-baked" ideas that have just arrived in a blinding flash of revelation to the student. Few professors, however, refuse a request for advice concerning a proposal that has been drafted as the culmination of several weeks of hard thought, research, and development. Even at that, having one's best effort devastated by pointed criticism can be an agonizing experience. Nevertheless, the only alternative is to persist in error or ignorance, and that is untenable in research.

If the student is fortunate enough to be in a department that contains a vigorous community of inquiring minds, with the constant give and take of intellectual disputation, the rough and tumble soon will be regarded as a functional part of producing good research. The novice will solicit, if not always enjoy, the best criticism that can be found.

The notion that it is vaguely immoral to seek assistance in preparing a proposal is at best a parody of real science and at worst, as in the form of an institutional rule, it is a serious perversion arising from ignorance. Research may have some game-like qualities, but a system of handicaps is not one of them. The object of every inquiry is to get the best possible answer under the circumstances, and that presumes obtaining the best advice available. It is hoped that the student will not be held to any lesser standard.

It should be obvious that students, after digesting and weighing all the criticism received, must still make their own choices. Not all advice is good, and not all criticism is valid. There is only one way to find out, however, and that is to share the proposal with colleagues whose judgments one can respect, if not always accept.

Step 19: Present to committee. Explain and support. Presentation of your proposal may take place before a thesis or dissertation committee on an occasion formally sanctioned by the graduate school, or at an informal gathering in the advisor's office. In either instance, the purpose served and the importance assumed will depend on both local traditions and the relationships that have evolved to that point among the chairperson, committee members, and student.

If, for example, the chairperson has closely monitored the developing proposal and is satisfied that it is ready for final review and approval, the nature of the meeting is shaped accordingly. In addition, if other committee members have consulted on the proposal at various stages of writing, the meeting may serve primarily as an occasion for final review and a demonstration of presentation skills, rather than evaluation, extensive feedback, and judgment. When these conditions do not apply, the meeting assumes far greater significance, in itself, and the length and nature of the presentation will be affected.

Whatever the circumstances, both a prudent respect for the important function the committee members must perform and a proper desire to demonstrate the extent to which the efforts of your advisors have been effective make careful preparation and a good presentation absolutely necessary. Much of our advice about that is contained in Chapter 7. For the present purpose, we want to underscore the following points.

1. The more you can work with committee members before an official meeting, the more that meeting can focus on improving (and appreciating) your proposal—rather than just on understanding it.

2. As committee members talk with you and with each other at the meeting, it is natural that new insights and concerns will surface. So long as those are accurately recorded, and so long as there is clear provision for how the committee will manage subsequent revisions in the proposal, that process is all to your advantage. The object is not simply to get the proposal (as it stands) accepted; it is to create the best possible plan for your dissertation or thesis.

3. Where you have had to make difficult choices, accept compromises in method for pragmatic reasons, or leave some final decision(s) for a later point in time, it is best to bring such matters directly to the attention of your committee. Don't wait to be questioned. Take the initiative and lay out the problematic aspects for your advisors as you go through the presentation. You need not make the proposed study appear to be mired in difficulty. Propose solutions and give your rationale, but never ignore or gloss over what you know requires more attention—and the help of your committee.

4. If the proposal is approved with the understanding that certain revisions or additions will be made, the best procedure is to obtain signatures on documents

while at the meeting. The signed forms can then be held by your chairperson until he or she has approved the final draft.

Step 20: Gather data. Process and interpret as planned in proposal. This is the payoff. A good proposal is more than a guide to action, it is a framework for intelligent interpretation of results and the heart of a sound final report. The proposal cannot guarantee meaningful results, but it will provide some assurance that, whatever the result, the student can wind up the project with reasonable dispatch and at least a minimum of intellectual grace. If that sounds too small a recompense for all the effort, consider the alternative of having to write a report about an inconsequential question, pursued through inadequate methods of inquiry, and resulting in a heap of unanalyzable data.

Originality and Replication:
What Is a Contribution to Knowledge?

Some attention already has been given to considerations that precede the proposal, the critical and difficult steps of identifying and delimiting a research topic. One other preliminary problem, the question of originality, has important ramifications for the proposal.

Some advisors regard student-conducted research primarily as an arena for training, like woodchopping that is expected to produce muscles in the person who holds the axe, but not much real fuel for the fire. Whatever may be the logic of such an assumption, students generally do not take the same attitude. Their expectations are more likely to resemble the classic dictum for scholarly research, to make an original contribution to the body of knowledge.

An all-too-common problem in selecting topics for research proposals occurs when either the student or an advisor gives literal interpretation to the word "original," defining it as "initial, first, never having existed or occurred before." This is a serious misinterpretation of the word as it is used in science. In research, the word "original" clearly includes all studies deliberately employed to test the accuracy of results or the applicability of conclusions developed in previous studies. What is not included under that rubric are studies that proceed mindlessly to repeat an existing work either in ignorance of its existence or without appropriate attention to its defects or limitations.

One consequence of the confusion surrounding the phrase "original contribution" is that misguided students and advisors are led to ignore one of the most important areas of research activity and one of the most useful forms of training for the novice researcher—replication. That replication sometimes is regarded simply as rote imitation, lacking sufficient opportunity for students to apply and develop their own skills, is an indication of how badly some students misunderstand both the operation of a research enterprise and the concept of a body of knowledge.

The essential role of replication in research has been cogently argued (Gall, Borg, & Gall, 1996). What has not been made sufficiently clear, however, is that replication can involve challenging problems that demand creative resolution. Further, some advisors do not appreciate the degree to which writing proposals for replicative studies can constitute an ideal learning opportunity for research trainees.

In direct replication, students must not only correctly identify all the critical variables in the original study but also create equivalent conditions for the conduct of their own study. Anyone who thinks that the critical variables will immediately be apparent from a reading of the original report has not read very widely in the research literature. Similarly, an individual who thinks that truly equivalent conditions can be created simply by "doing it the same way" just has not tried to perform a replicative study. Thorough understanding of the problem and, frequently, a great deal of technical ingenuity are demanded in developing an adequate proposal for direct replication.

As an alternative to direct replication, the student may repeat an interesting study considered to have been defective in sample, method, analysis, or interpretation. Here the student introduces deliberate changes to improve the power of a previous investigation. It would be difficult to imagine a more challenging or useful activity for anyone interested in both learning about research and contributing to the accumulation of reliable knowledge.

In writing a proposal for either kind of replicative study, direct or revised, the student should introduce the original with appropriate citation, make the comments that are needed, and proceed without equivocation or apology to the proposed study. Replicative research is not, as unfortunate tradition has it in some departments, slightly improper or something less than genuine research.

The cross-validation study is another type of investigation that sometimes is characterized as unoriginal, and even may be confused with replication. An excellent example of a cross-validation study has been provided by Willoughby and Bixby (1991). Cross-validation studies most frequently appear in conjunction with or following prediction studies, in which the investigator attempts to determine an equation by which to predict a variable or variables. The equations that are derived for the sample used, however, may have been affected by chance correlations and errors of measurement to the extent that the investigator cannot be sure how predictive the selected set of variables would be for other samples.

Two techniques of cross-validation are used. In one technique, the investigator computes a predicted score for each subject—on the basis of the equation derived from the original study—and then correlates predicted scores with the scores that actually were measured in the second sample. In some situations, the total sample is split into two groups to provide equal samples for the crossvalidation. If a very high correlation is obtained between those predicted scores and the measured scores in an entirely different sample, the original set of independent variables with their given weights has been validated as being generally predictive of the dependent variable. A second technique is to use the second sample to derive a new equation and set of regression weights and a new multiple R statistic for the originally selected independent variables.

Another situation in which cross-validation is used involves studies in which an investigator selects from a large pool of test items those that significantly discriminate between two or more groups. Again, chance plays a role in the differentiation of the groups—perhaps creating spuriously large differences or an inflated correlation between the criterion and the sample on which the selection of items was based. In studies of this type, cross-validation on additional groups is required.

Irrespective of the situation in which cross-validation is used, or the technique used to accomplish it, it should be readily apparent that cross-validation does not require a completely original effort. Nevertheless, it is a technique sorely needed in the behavioral sciences, where the body of knowledge would be expanded and refined much more rapidly if many of the hundreds of theses undertaken each year were careful cross-validations or replications rather than inexperienced and misguided attempts at originality.

Given the limitations of research reports, it often is useful to discuss the source study for the replication or cross-validation with the original author. Most research workers are happy to provide greater detail and in some instances raw data for inspection or reanalysis. In a healthy science, replication is the most sincere form of flattery. A proposal appendix containing correspondence with the author of the original report, or data not provided in that report, often can serve to interest and reassure a hesitant advisor.

Getting Started:
Producing the First Draft

The student who has never written a research proposal commonly sits in front of a desk and stares at a blank piece of paper or an empty video monitor for hours. The mind is brimming with knowledge gleaned from the literature, but how does one actually get started? The concept of "a research proposal" conjures up ideas of accuracy, precision, meticulous form, and use of a language system that is new and unpracticed by the neophyte researcher. The demands can suddenly seem overwhelming. The student should realize that this feeling of panic is experienced by nearly everyone, not only those who are new to the writing endeavor but those who are skilled as well. Fanger (1985) expressed it beautifully: "I have come to regard panic as the inevitable concomitant of any kind of serious academic writing" (p. 28). For anyone temporarily incapacitated by a blank page or empty monitor, the following suggestions may be helpful.

Make an outline that is compatible with the format selected to present the communication tasks listed in Chapter 1. An initial approval of the outline by the advisor may save revision time later. Gather the resource materials, notes, and references, and organize them into groups that correspond to the outline topics. For instance, notes supporting the rationale for the study would be in one group, and notes supporting the reliability of an instrument to be used would be in another group.

Once the outline is made and the materials gathered, tackle one of the topics in the outline (not necessarily the first) and start writing. If the section to be written is labeled "The Purpose," try imagining that someone has asked, "What is the purpose of this study?" Your task is to answer that question. Start writing. Do not worry about grammar, syntax, or writing within the language system. Just write. In this way you can avoid one of the greatest inhibitions to creativity— self-criticism so severe that each idea is rejected before it becomes reality. Remember, it is easier to correct than to create. If all the essential parts of a topic are displayed in some fashion, they can later be rearranged, edited, and couched within the language system. With experience, the novice will begin thinking in the language system and forms of the proposal. Until that time, the essential problem is to begin. Awkward or elegant, laborious or swift, there is no substitute for writing the first draft.

One way to approach writing is to use the outline feature on your word processor, which allows you to develop your outline and then go back and progressively fill in the detail under each heading. Learn to use this feature. The effort needed to learn its use will be repaid many times over. Word processing programs provide the opportunity for writers to edit, rearrange text easily, and store manuscript copy for future revisions. There is a significant psychological advantage in the ease with which revised drafts can be produced. This encourages the author to make revisions that might otherwise be set aside under the press of limited time, and has greatly enhanced the ability of proposal writers to revise and polish their work.

Selecting Your Thesis
or Dissertation Committee

Master's thesis committees vary in number from one professor to a committee of five or six faculty members. A doctoral dissertation committee typically consists of four to six members. In some instances, all committee members are from within the department of the student's major. In other instances, the committee is multidisciplinary, with faculty representing other departments on campus.

At most universities, students have some opportunity to request specific faculty members for their committee. If the student does have some freedom to exercise choice, committee membership should be designed to maximize the support and assistance available. A student interested in the study of behavioral treatment of drug abuse in young upwardly mobile women could tap the value of different faculty perspectives and skills by blending members from several departments. For this purpose, individuals with multiple interests are particularly useful. For example, a faculty member in the psychology department might be selected for both statistical competence and interest in behavior modification, someone in the school of social work might bring epidemiological expertise regarding drug usage, and a faculty member in the school of public health might be a part of the committee because of expertise in both experimental design and therapeutic compliance techniques.

Because students know from the beginning of the graduate program that faculty eventually will have to be selected for such a committee, it behooves them to be thinking about these matters during the selection of elective courses throughout the program. If a choice has to be made between two professors for an elective course, and one of them is more interested in the student's probable area of research, that may carry the day in determining which course to take. Although it is not essential that students have taken their committee members' classes, it is easier to ask a known faculty member to serve on your committee. That person is likely to take a greater interest in your work, and you have a good idea of his or her standards and methods of scholarship.

4

—◻︎—

Content of the Proposal

Important Considerations

The topics covered in this chapter are designed to assist the true beginner. Most experienced proposal writers may want to go directly to Chapter 7 or simply skim this chapter for review.

REVIEWING THE LITERATURE:
FINDING IT FIRST

—■—

Areas of inquiry within the disciplines exist as ongoing conversations among those who do the work of scholarship. The published literature of an area constitutes the archival record of those conversations: research reports, research reviews, theoretical speculation, and scholarly discourse of all kinds. You join the long conversation of science as you join any other, by first listening to what is being said, and only then formulating a comment designed to advance the dialogue.

The metaphor of scholarship as an extended conversation works well at a variety of levels—because at heart it is an accurate representation. The process of locating the voices of individual conversants, for example, is called *retrieval*. That involves searching through the accumulated archive of literature to find out what has been said (when, by whom, and on the basis of what evidence). The process of listening carefully to the ongoing discourse about a topic of inquiry is called *review*. That involves studying items previously retrieved until both the history and the current state of the conversation are understood. It does not stretch the metaphor too far to observe that writing the proposal is a step in preparing yourself to have your own voice be heard—to do research and enter what you learn into the long conversation.

Retrieval, review, proposing and conducting research, and even report writing are tasks that have their own sets of requisite technical skills. Each also has a place for art and instinct as well as intelligence and accumulated knowledge. This chapter deals with what goes into the proposal (content) once the topic and terms of discourse have been defined. It follows, then, that it must begin with what you have learned by listening in on the conversation—a review of the literature. In your review, you will establish what has been said to this point as the basis for proposing your own contribution. Retrieval, however, comes first in the order of things. You can't review what you haven't found. That brings us to the technical skill and fine art of searching the literature.

We will not burden you with the specifics of a particular search procedure. The demands made by proposals differ widely, as do the background and skills of each proposal writer. Further, the facilities for retrieval vary enormously at different institutions and, of course, each discipline and subspecialty has its own peculiar mechanisms for searching the literature. What we can do here is set forth the small number of general rules that, if observed from the outset, have the power to make any retrieval effort more efficient.

Knowing what you need to know is the obvious first step in formulating a retrieval strategy. Knowing how much you really need to know, however, is a vital second step—and one not always properly appreciated by the novice in research. Discussion with your advisor, consultation with colleagues who have written proposals, inspection of proposals previously accepted by the graduate school, and the preliminary reading already done during the process of identifying the topic of your proposed study will all serve to identify what you need to know—and thereby the literature you will seek. Normally that includes research reports and reviews related to your questions or hypotheses. This literature provides information about research methodology in the area and items dealing with both theory and application as they are related to your study.

Deciding how much you need to know is a more complex decision—in part because you often cannot answer that question until after some retrieval and review already has been accomplished. This is a matter of defining the purpose to be served by what you retrieve. Acquiring a broad overview of previous work in an area leads to one kind of retrieval strategy. If your purpose is to know what a small set of senior scholars have reported in the last two years, the strategy will be different, as will be the case if your purpose is to do an exhaustive search in which every scrap of fugitive literature is doggedly pursued until acquired.

What we suggest is that you talk with your advisor about the question of "how much?" and that you stay in touch with him or her on that topic as you proceed. The notion that every search of the literature needs to be exhaustive is one of the more destructive mythologies that persists in graduate student culture. When you have enough sense of the conversation to argue persuasively that the target for your proposed study is sound, and that the methods of inquiry are correct, you know enough for the purpose of the proposal.

Over a longer period of time, you may have plenty of motivation to read more widely and deeply than anything demanded by your proposal, but that is a different matter. For the present, it is wise to acquire some sense of how much you need to know so that you can shape the size of your review task accordingly—and thereby know what and how much to retrieve. Until you have done some retrieval and review, it is likely that neither you nor your advisor will be able to set that target with precision, but some careful preliminary thought will serve you well.

Retrieval Rule 1. Do not begin by going to the library or your computer and starting to search for literature. Talk first to your advisor (or entire thesis or dissertation committee) and research colleagues who have some familiarity with the area of your proposal. Make a list of what they think you should read. Locate the items, skim them, and record full citations for all that appear to be appropriate. These form the core of your retrieved literature base. Go over the reference lists in the items that appear to be most directly relevant to your needs and make those citations the priority for retrieval when you return to the library.

Retrieval Rule 2. When you go to the library, do not begin by starting to search for literature. Talk first to the reference specialists who can identify the retrieval systems that are most likely to be productive for your topic. Then, we urge you to take advantage of seminars and classes on using specific retrieval systems that are offered at many academic libraries. Retrieval is one part sweat and two parts knowing where to look.

For every scholar, the marvels of computerized retrieval are available at your university library, through the university computer network, or on the Internet. The databases that any given system can access, however, differ in important and subtle ways. Attending introductory seminars and asking for expert help can save hours. Swift, accurate, flexible, and powerful beyond anything we could have dreamed when the first edition of this book appeared, computer retrieval systems are, nevertheless, only as good as their search structures, and those are just as full of limitations and idiosyncratic quirks as any of the printed indexes that scholars used in the past.

That observation leads to two items of advice. First, plan to devote a considerable amount of retrieval time to learning how each system works. Second, by all means use computerized systems, but do not automatically assume that manual search is without value. In other words, all but a very small number of highly technical topics can profit by a visit to whatever is the equivalent to the *Reader's Guide to Periodical Literature*—on CD-ROM or in the printed version—in your particular subject area.

Retrieval Rule 3. From the outset, think of your retrieval effort as consisting of a series of stages. It is unlikely that you will (or should) march through them in perfect sequence; it is more a matter of moving back and forth among the stages in ways that will make best use of your time.

Stage 1: Identification—Find and record citations that seem potentially relevant. This is work done with indexes, bibliographies, reference lists, and, most often, the computer.

Stage 2: Confirmation—Determine that the items identified can be obtained for use. This is work done with the library holdings of serials and books, reprint services, interlibrary loan personnel, microfiche files, and the telephone.

Stage 3: Skimming and Screening—Assess each item to confirm that it actually contains content to be reviewed (to be read and studied with care). This is work that demands enough mastery of the system language and the constructs related to your topic to recognize what is and is not of potential use. Much of this (though not all) can be accomplished without taking the resource item into your physical possession. This means time in the stacks and time at the microfiche reader. The most important retrieval skill here is the ability to resist the temptation to stop the work of skimming and screening and immerse yourself in the conversation.

Stage 4: Retrieval—Acquire the literature. This is work done by checking out books, copying articles from journals, ordering microfiche and reprints, and initiating requests for interlibrary loans. Not everything must be (or should be) retrieved. There is a strong argument for not having every article immediately at hand when you are drafting the review of literature, and one way to ensure that is to take notes from references that then stay in the stacks.

Stage 5: Review—Read and study the literature that records the conversation about your topic. Subsequent sections of this chapter will deal with how to use what you learn to build your proposal.

Retrieval Rule 4. From the first moment of your search, keep a log of all the words used to name what you have to learn about. These will become the keywords used by indexing systems (often they are specifically designated as keywords by the authors) for accessing their holdings. Building a keyword list is like acquiring a set of master keys to a large building. They can open doors in a variety of locations, and without them you can wander for hours without gaining entry to anywhere you want to be. Although most databases now provide the option of searching titles, authors, abstracts, and keywords—or all of them—knowing what phrases produce the greatest yield will help now and in the future. In almost every case, the novice will be astonished at the variety of words and phrases employed to categorize items that appear to be identical.

Retrieval Rule 5. Always take maximum advantage of other people's work. For that reason, research reviews in your area always should have the highest priority in your search plan, as should annotated bibliographies and the reference list at the back of every article and book you retrieve. For the same reason, your first stop in the library should be the bound or computerized version of *Dissertation Abstracts International* (and *Masters Abstracts*). What could be a better search strategy than reading the reviews of literature crafted by students who have worked on similar problems? Dissertations are the *Yellow Pages* of research retrieval. From the start, let your fingers do a lot of the walking.

Retrieval Rule 6. Record a complete citation for every item you identify. Whether with index cards or a computer program that alphabetizes and sorts by keywords, keep a complete running record of what you find—whether immediately reviewed or not. No frustration can match that of having to backtrack to the library for a missing volume or page number.

Retrieval Rule 7. Whatever notes you may take during the stages of Skimming and Screening or Review, never write anything down in which there could be the slightest confusion at a later date as to whether the words are your own—or those of another author. If you take down a quotation, take it verbatim and attach the proper page citation. If you write anything other than a direct quotation, make absolutely sure it is a paraphrase in your own words. There is no place for anything in between those two species of notes.

Retrieval Rule 8. Be cautious about computerized systems that seem too good to be true. There are reference retrieval systems, for example, with which writers can simply highlight a phrase and the computer then automatically imports the phrase to a designated point in your own document, complete with citations in the text and a reference at the back. Writers using such a system don't have to read the full article or do the intellectual work required to truly understand how it fits into the wider conversation among investigators in the area. What seems quick and efficient may serve to undercut the ability to make informed decisions about source material and, ultimately, to write a sound proposal.

If you follow these eight rules, if you build a reasonable sense of how much you really need to know, and if you persist, you may have one of the most wonderful epiphanies a scholar can experience. As you look down a page of references, you will recognize all the names, and the voices of their conversation will fill your ears. At that moment, you are current and you are ready to take part. Given the pace of work in many areas of science, that moment will be brief, but savor it! That is the sweet fruit of retrieval.

REVIEWING THE LITERATURE: WRITING THE RIGHT STUFF

By much deserved reputation, the reviews of literature in student research proposals are regarded as consisting of clumsy and turgid prose, written as *pro forma* response to a purely ceremonial obligation in the planning format. Even when carefully crafted with regard to basic mechanics, they make dull reading, and when not so prepared they are excruciating torture for most readers. Much of this problem arises from a misunderstanding of the task served by reviewing the literature, and none of it need be true.

To begin, the common designation used in proposals, "review of the literature," is a misleading if not completely inappropriate title. A research proposal is not the place to review the body of literature that bears on a problematic area, or even the place to examine all the research that relates to the specific question raised in the proposal. A variety of methods for "reviewing the literature" do exist, such as best evidence synthesis, critical reviews, and even meta-analysis, but they are rarely appropriate for proposals. Analyses of that kind may be useful documents publishable in their own right. Indeed, some journals such as the *Review of Educational Research* are exclusively devoted to such critical retrospectives on scholarship. The task to be performed in the proposal, however, is different. It is not inferior to the true review, it simply is different.

In writing a research proposal, the author is obligated to place the question or hypothesis in the context of previous work in such a way as to explain and justify the decisions made. That alone is required. Nothing more is appropriate, and nothing more should be attempted.

Although the author may wish to persuade the reader on many different kinds of points, ranging from the significance of the question to the appropriateness of a particular form of data analysis, sound proposals devote most of the literature review to explaining (a) exactly how and why the research question or hypothesis was formulated in the proposed form and (b) exactly why the proposed research strategy was selected. What is required to accomplish these tasks is a step-by-step explanation of decisions, punctuated by reference to studies that support the ongoing argument. In this, the writer uses previous work, often some critique of previous work, and sometimes some exposition of the broad pattern of knowledge as it exists in the area to appeal for the reader's acceptance of the logic represented in the proposed study.

Whatever particular arguments must be sustained in the review of the literature, there is no place for the "Smith says this . . ." and "Jones says that . . ." paragraph-by-paragraph recital that makes novice proposals instruments for dulling the senses. This is the place to answer the reader's most immediate questions: What is it the author wants to know, and why has this plan been devised to find the answer? In a good review, the literature is made to serve the reader's query by supporting, explicating, and illuminating the logic now implicit in the proposed investigation.

It follows, then, that where there is little relevant literature, or where decisions are clear-cut and without substantial issues, the review should be brief. In some cases, the examination of supporting literature may best be appended or woven into another section of the proposal. To write a review of literature for the sake of having a review in the document is to make it a parody and not a proposal.

Remember, the writer's task is to employ the research literature artfully to support and explain the choices made *for this study*, not to educate the reader concerning the state of science in the problem area. Neither is the purpose of the section to display the energy and thoroughness with which the author has pursued a comprehensive understanding of the literature. If the author can explain and support the question, design, and procedures with a minimum demand on the reader's time and intellect, then that reader will be more than sufficiently impressed with the applicant's capabilities and serious purpose.

None of this is intended to undervalue the task that every researcher must face, that of locating and thoroughly assimilating what is already known. To do this, the student must experience what Fanger (1985) described as "immersion in the subject" by reading extensively in the areas that are either directly or indirectly related to the topic of study. This may lead at first to a sense of frustration and confusion, but perseverance usually leads out of the wilderness to the point at which what is known about the topic can be seen in the light of what is not known. The goals of the proposed study can be projected against that backdrop.

The proposal is the place to display the refined end products of that long and difficult process. It is not uncommon, for example, for the study's best support to emerge from a sophisticated understanding of gaps in the body of knowledge, limitations in previous formulations of the question, inadequate methods of data collection, or inappropriate interpretation of results. The review of the literature section then becomes a vehicle for illustrating why and how it all can be done better. What readers need, however, is not a full tour retracing each step the author took in arriving at the better mousetrap, but a concise summary of the main arguments properly juxtaposed to the new and better plan for action.

Most students will agonize over the many studies discovered that, although fascinating and perhaps even inspiring during the immersion process, in the final stages of writing turn out to fail the test of critical relevance and therefore merit exclusion from the proposal. It is tempting to see discarded studies and unused note cards as wasted time, but that misses the long view of learning. The knowledge gained through synthesis and evaluation of research results builds a knowledge base for the future. The process of immersion in the literature provides not only the information that will support the proposal but also the intellectual framework for future expertise. What may appear in the crush of deadlines and overload stress to have been pursuit down blind alleys, ultimately may provide insights that will support new lines of thought and future proposals.

Writing the section on related literature often is no more complex than first describing the major concepts that led you to your research question or hypothesis and then describing the supporting research findings already in the literature. It may be as simple as hypothesizing that A is greater than C. Why do you hypothesize that A is greater than C? Because evidence suggests that A is greater than B, and B is greater than C; therefore, it is reasonable to hypothesize that A must be greater than C.

In the review of the related literature, you would present those conceptual relationships in an organized fashion and then document each with previously reported studies. For example, the first section would include the most important studies indicating that A is greater than B, and the second section would present similar evidence supporting the proposition that B is greater than C. The literature section would then conclude with the argument that given such information, it is reasonable to hypothesize that A is greater than C. In addition, either interwoven throughout, or in separate sections, material from the literature would be presented in support of decisions about design and measurement in the proposed study.

Look at the example in Table 4.1, which also is represented diagrammatically in Figure 4.1. In this table, the general research question is posed, followed by the specific hypothesis through which the question will be answered. They are shown here merely to establish the frame of reference for the outline. In this example of the development of the related literature, three major concepts are necessary to support the legitimacy of this hypothesis. In Table 4.1, the question suggests that the way physical fitness and cognitive function are related is

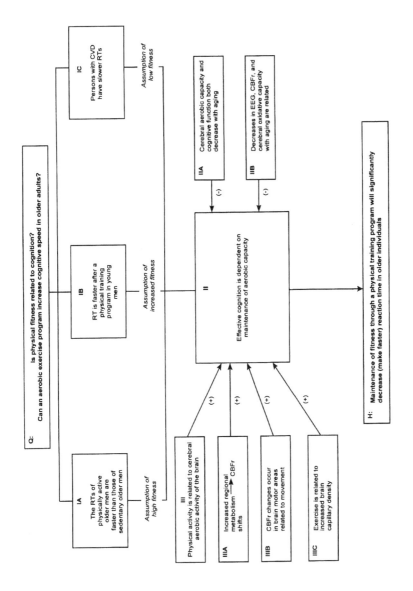

Figure 4.1. Example of a Diagrammatic Overview of the Related Literature

TABLE 4.1 Preparing the Related Literature Section

QUESTION: Is physical fitness related to cognition in older adults? More specifically, can an aerobic exercise program increase cognitive processing speed in older adults?

HYPOTHESIS: Maintenance of physical fitness through a physical training program will significantly decrease (make faster) reaction time in older individuals.

First Stage Outline: Develop the Concepts That Provide the Rationale for the Study

   I. Reaction time is related to physical fitness level.

   II. Maintenance of cognitive function is dependent on maintenance of aerobic capacity of the brain.

   III. The aerobic capacity of brain tissue is affected by physical activity-related regional cerebrovascular changes.

Second Stage Outline: Development of Subtopics for Each Major Concept

   I. Reaction time is related to physical fitness level.

     A. Comparisons of the reaction time of physically active and inactive subjects.

     B. Training effects on reaction time.

     C. Reaction time of those in poor physical condition (cardiovascular disease, hypertension).

   II. Maintenance of cognitive function is dependent on maintenance of aerobic capacity of the brain.

     A. Relationship of cognitive function and brain aerobic capacity in aging individuals.

     B. Relationship of neurological measure of brain function, electroencephalography (EEG), to cerebral blood flow and cerebral oxygen uptake in older subjects.

   III. The aerobic capacity of brain tissue is affected by physical activity-related regional cerebrovascular changes.

     A. Increased metabolism in specific regions leads to cerebral blood flow shifts to those regions.

     B. Regional blood flow shifts in motor areas of the brain are related to physical movement.

     C. Exercise is related to changes in brain capillarization.

Third Stage Outline: Add the Most Important References That Support Each Subtopic

   I. Reaction time is related to physical fitness level.

     A. Physically active individuals have faster reaction times than do sedentary individuals (Clark & Addison, 1987; Cohen, 1993, 1995; Jones, 1998, 1999; Jones & Johnson, 1991; Lloyd, 1994).

     B. Reaction time is faster after a physical training program (Black, 1992, 1997; Dougherty, 1987; Morgan & Ramirez, 1991; Ramirez, 1994; Richards, 1995, 1997; Richards & Cohen, 1989; Roe & Williams, 1995; Walters, 1991).

     C. Cardiovascular-diseased patients have slower reaction time than normal individuals (Brown, 1991; Brown, Mathews, & Smith, 1998; Miller, 1991, 1992; Miller & Roe, 1990; Smith, Brown, & Rodgers, 1999; Smith & Rodgers, 1998).

TABLE 4.1 *Continued*

   II. Maintenance of cognitive function is dependent on maintenance of aerobic capacity of the brain.

      A. Both cognitive function and aerobic capacity decrease with age (Gray, 1988; Petty, 1985).

      B. EEG, cerebral blood flow, and cerebral oxidative capacity decrease with age and are related (Doe & Smith, 1999; Doe, Smith, & Snyder, 1997; Goldberg, 1998; Smith & Doe, 1991; Waters, 1989, 1993; Waters & Crosby, 1992).

   III. The aerobic capacity of brain tissue is affected by physical activity-related regional cerebrovascular changes.

      A. Increased regional metabolism leads to blood flow shifts (Green & Neil, 1966; Lewis, 1979; Thomas, 1976).

      B. Regional blood flow shifts to motor areas of the brain are related to physical movements being controlled (Caplan, Myerson, & Morris, 1991; Goldsmith, 1993, 1994; Johnson, Goldsmith, & Rodriguez, 1990).

      C. Exercise is related to changes in brain capillarization (Meyers & Templeton, 1991; Patrick, 1993; Patrick & Stone, 1995; Robinson & Spencer, 1990).

---

through a change in brain aerobic capacity as a result of training. If this is a reasonable question to ask, one would have to show that there have been some prior studies in which physical fitness level has been related to some measure of cognitive function (Concept I). Second, some evidence that cognitive function might be altered by aerobic functional capacity of the brain should be shown (Concept II). Finally, some evidence should exist that physical movement can alter blood flow shifts in the brain, and that blood flow shifts are related to aerobic capacity (Concept III).

Generally, the major concepts are supported by two or three subtopics, all of which lead to the formalization of the main concept. For example, the concept that reaction time and physical fitness level are related (I) can be supported in three different ways, by showing (a) that reaction time is faster in physically fit persons than in sedentary persons, (b) that physical training enhances reaction time, and (c) that reaction time in those on the lowest end of the physical fitness continuum is the slowest of all. Each of these subtopics is supported by the findings from several studies, as shown in the third stage outline section of the table.

Writing the related literature section is much easier if an outline is developed in stages of increasingly greater detail, as shown in Table 4.1, prior to the actual writing. Once the outline is developed, this section of the proposal can be written in a straightforward manner, with little backtracking necessary. If meticulous care is taken in selecting each reference, an enormous amount of time will be saved in the long run.

Another easy way to conceptualize the organization of the related literature is to diagram it, as shown in Figure 4.1. In this figure, the question (Q) is shown in the first box, and then the major components of the rationale are shown as they relate to one another. Component I refers to the behavioral observations that have been reported in the research literature. Component II refers to the literature in which the effects of aging on cerebral aerobic capacity and cognitive function are described. Because these relationships have negative outcomes, they are shown with a negative sign. Component III refers to all literature that provides support for a relationship between physical activity and cerebral aerobic activity. In this case, these are all positive relationships, which are shown with plus signs. Finally, the last box depicts how all these relationships lead to the hypothesis (H) of the study.

Both the outline and diagram format can be very helpful in conceptualizing the related literature. The entire process can be summarized in the 15 steps in Table 4.2. Table 4.3 contains guidelines for evaluating the related literature section.

SPADEWORK:
THE PROPER USE OF PILOT STUDIES

The pilot study is an especially useful form of anticipation, and one too often neglected in student proposals. When it comes to convincing the scholarly skeptic (sometimes your own advisor), no argument can be so effective as to write, "I tried it and here is how it worked."

It is difficult to imagine any proposal that could not be improved by the reporting of actual preliminary work. Whether it is to demonstrate the reliability of scores produced by the proposed instrumentation, the practicality of procedures, the availability of volunteers, the variability of observed events as a basis for power tests, subjects' capabilities, or the investigator's skills, the modest pilot study is the best possible basis for making wise decisions in designing research.

The pilot study, for example, is an excellent means by which to determine the sample size necessary to discover significant differences among experimental treatments.[1] Sample size estimation or "power analysis" recently has become commonplace in quantitative research. Although it always has been an important component of good research, it has become more frequently used because of the availability of easy-to-use books and computer programs. A particularly useful introduction to power analysis, replete with examples and tables, is *How Many Subjects?* (Kraemer & Thiemann, 1987). In addition, a number of computer programs are available—some of which only require the user to answer a few questions before calculating sample size. Because software is being updated quickly, we suggest inquiring at your institution's statistical consulting office or computer center to find out what is available.

Pilot data and a few decisions (primarily related to the error rates you want for the study) allow researchers to estimate the sample size needed to find significance, if in fact it exists in the data. It is possible that the estimated sample size required will be so large as to be prohibitive, in which case method and measurement tools should be reexamined. In the ideal case, a power analysis will inform the researcher of an appropriate sample size based on permissible error and the data—not just from arbitrary guessing. It is better to find the appropriate sample size in advance, rather than after the fact. Both a sample size that precludes a significant finding and the use of more subjects than needed are wastes of time and effort.

The use of even a few subjects in an informal trial can reveal a fatal flaw before it can destroy months of work. The same trial may even provide a fortunate opportunity to improve the precision of the investigation or to stream-line cumbersome methods. For all these reasons, students and advisors should not insist on holding stringent, formal standards for exploratory studies. A pilot study is a pilot study; its target is the practicality of proposed operations, not the creation of empirical truth.

Examples of purposes that pilot studies might serve include the following:

1. To determine the reliability of measurement in your own laboratory.
2. To ensure that differences that you expect to exist, do in fact exist—that is, if you are studying the different effects of gender on motivation, make sure the gender difference exists.
3. To "save" a sample that is difficult to obtain until the real research project is undertaken—that is, it is prudent to test available subjects until procedural bugs are worked out before testing world-class athletes.
4. To determine the best type of skills to use as an independent variable; for example, effects of different ankle braces on knee mobility—test jumping vertically, horizontally, and while running, then select one.

The presentation of pilot study results sometimes does create a troublesome problem. Readers may be led inadvertently to expect more of pilot work than it

TABLE 4.2 Steps in Writing the Related Literature Section

---

1. Determine the major concepts (generally no more than two or three) that are pertinent to the proposed research question. That is, what are the concepts that must be true for your question to be appropriate or hypotheses tenable?

2. List concepts either in descending order of importance or in terms of logical presentation. That is, does one concept have to be understood before another can be introduced?

3. Prepare an outline with these major concepts as the major headings (such as the one in Table 4.1, concepts I, II, and III).

4. Under each major heading, list the articles that are most directly related (authors and dates only).

5. If the articles under a major heading cluster themselves and suggest a subheading, then arrange the clusters under the major topics in logical order. For example, you might note that of the nine studies pertaining to the notion of a relationship between reaction time and physical fitness, in five of these reaction times of animals were reported, whereas in the other four studies, the reaction times were from humans. The interpretation of these studies, when clustered in terms of type of subject, might be different and have substantial bearing on the potential outcome of the proposed research.

6. Without referring to the details in the articles, summarize in one paragraph the combined findings of each cluster of studies. For example, in concept I.A of Table 4.1, the summary might be that reaction time of physically active men and women is faster than that of sedentary individuals, as long as the subjects are over 60 years old. The summary of concept I.B might be that aerobic training improves reaction time, but strength training in older individuals does not improve reaction time. At some point, you will have to discuss the interpretation to be made from different results of physical fitness on reaction time, depending on the way physical fitness as an independent variable is measured.

7. Write an introductory paragraph explaining what the two or three major areas are and in what order they will be discussed. Explain why the order used was selected, if that is important. Explain why some literature may be omitted if it might seem logical to the reader that it would be included.

8. Write a statement at the end of each section summarizing the findings within each cluster of studies. Show how this summary of findings relates to those in the cluster of studies described in the following paragraphs.

9. Write a paragraph at the end of each major topic (I, II, and III in Table 4.1), with a subheading if appropriate, that summarizes the major points, supports the cohesiveness of the subtopics, and establishes the relevance of these concepts to the proposed research question.

10. Write a paragraph or short section (with the appropriate heading) at the conclusion that draws together all the major summarizing paragraphs.

11. Read the paragraphs and subject them to Steps 1-7 in the "Guidelines for Evaluating the Related Literature Section" (Table 4.3).

12. After all these concepts and subtopics have been carefully introduced, described, and summarized, return to the beginning and insert the documentation for each of the concepts in the proper location. That is, document the statements made in each of the paragraphs by describing the studies leading to them or verifying them.

TABLE 4.2 *Continued*

13. Each time a reference is inserted, place the complete citation in a special file for eventual compilation of a reference list.

14. After a week has passed, reread the related literature section and use the complete "Guidelines for Evaluating the Related Literature Section" that are provided in Table 4.3. Make whatever revisions seem necessary and wait one more week.

15. Read the entire related literature section for coherence, continuity, and smoothness of transition from one concept to another. Check carefully for accuracy of all citations and, again, edit for mechanics.

TABLE 4.3 Guidelines for Evaluating the Related Literature Section

After you have written the first draft of the related literature section (Steps 1-11 in Table 4.2) and then again as you prepare the penultimate draft (Step 14 in Table 4.2), answer the appropriate questions below. Mark the manuscript where the answers to each of these questions are located.

1. Is there a paragraph outlining the organization of the related literature section?

2. Does the order of the headings and subheadings represent the relative importance of the topics and subtopics? Is the order of headings logical?

3. Are there summary paragraphs for each of the two or three major sections and an overall summary at the end?

4. Is the relation of the proposed study to past and current research clearly shown in the summary paragraphs?

5. What new answers (extension of the body of knowledge) will the proposed research provide?

6. What is distinctive or different about the proposed research compared with previous research? Is this clearly stated? Is this introduced in just a few paragraphs?

7. Have the results from your own pilot studies, when appropriate, been interwoven into the synthesis of the related literature?

8. What are the most relevant articles (no more than five) that bear on this research? Underline these references. Are they listed under the first topical heading?

9. Are these articles presented in a way that denotes their importance? Are some cited so many times they lose their power through repetition?

10. Has the evaluation of these key articles, as well as all other articles, been presented succinctly in terms of both procedures and interpretation of results?

can reasonably deliver. Their concerns with the limitations may distract from its limited use in the main line of the argument being advanced by the author. Accordingly, the best course is to make no more of the pilot study than it honestly is worth—most are no more than a report of limited experience under less than perfectly controlled conditions—and do so only when the report will best illuminate the choices made in the proposal.

Brief reference to pilot work may be made in supporting the broad research strategies selected consequent to the review of research. Some pilot studies may, in fact, be treated as one of the works worthy of review. More commonly, however, the results of exploratory studies are used in supporting specific procedures proposed in the section dealing with methodology.

When the pilot study represents a formal and relatively complete research effort, it is proper to cite the work in some detail, including actual data. When the preliminary work has been informal or limited, it may be introduced as a footnote to the main text. In the latter case, it may be desirable to provide a more detailed account of the work in a section of the appendix, leaving the reader the choice of pursuing the matter further if desired.

MURPHY'S LAW: ANTICIPATING THE UNEXPECTED

Murphy's Law dictates that, in the conduct of research, if anything can go wrong, it probably will. This is accepted by experienced researchers and research advisors but rarely is considered by the novice.

Within reasonable limits, the proposal is the place to provide for confrontation with the inexorable operation of Murphy's Law. Subject attrition cannot be prevented, but its effects can be circumscribed by careful planning. The potentially biasing effects created by nonreturns in questionnaire studies can be examined and, to some degree, mitigated by plans laid carefully in the proposal. The handling of subjects in the event of equipment failure is far better considered at leisure, in writing the proposal, than in the face of an unanticipated emergency. Field research in the public schools can provide a range of surprises, including indisposed teachers, fire drills, and inclement weather, all better managed by anticipation than by snap decisions forged in the heat of sudden necessity.

Equipment failure may interrupt carefully timed data collection sequences, or temporary computer breakdowns may delay data processing and analysis. At best, such accidents will do no more than alter the time schedule for the study. At worst, they may require substitutions or substantive changes in the procedures. Each step of the research process should be studied with regard to potential difficulty, and plans in the event of a problem should be stated in the appropriate place within the proposal. For instance, if unequal subject attrition occurs across groups, the type of analysis to be used with unequal Ns should be stated in the analysis section of the proposal.

It is impossible to anticipate everything that can happen. A good proposal, however, provides contingency plans for the most important problems that may arise in the course of conducting the study.

ANTICIPATING THE ANALYSIS: DO IT NOW

The proposal is the proper place to reveal the exact nature of the analysis, as well as anticipated plans in the event of emergency. For many students, especially master's candidates, the analysis, if statistical, may represent new knowledge recently acquired and not fully digested. In addition, the customary time limitation of 12 to 16 months, by which the master's candidate is bound, adds to the difficulty. The candidate may even be in the middle of a first formal course in techniques of data reduction and analysis during the same period of time used for constructing the proposal. Consequently, students find themselves in the awkward position of having to write lucidly about their analytic tools without yet knowing the entire armamentarium available. As untenable as this position is, and as much sympathy as may be generated by the student's advisor or friends, the omission of a full explanation of the analysis in the proposal may prove to be disastrous. Countless unfortunates have found themselves with files full of unanalyzable data, all because the analysis was supposed to take care of itself. A step-by-step anticipation of the analysis to be used is also a double check on the experimental design.

Descriptive, survey, and normative studies require extensive data reduction to produce meaningful quantitative descriptions and summaries of the phenomena of interest. Techniques for determining sample characteristics may be different from those anticipated on the basis of pilot results, or the study sample may be skewed, resulting in the need to discuss techniques for normalizing the data.

Statistical techniques are founded on assumptions relating to sample characteristics and the relationship between that sample and its respective population. The methods one intends to use to determine whether the sample meets the assumptions implicit in the anticipated analysis should be clearly stated. For example, many statistical techniques must be used only when one or more of the following assumptions are met: (a) normal distribution of the sample, (b) random and independent selection of subjects, (c) linear relationships of variables, (d) homogeneity of variance among groups (in regression analysis, this is called homoscedasticity), (e) independence of sample means and variances, and (f) units of measure of the dependent variable on an interval or ratio scale.

Accordingly, the process of selecting a statistic brings with it a number of subsequent questions. What methods will be employed to determine that assumptions have been met? What analyses will be used in the event the assumptions are not met? Will the planned analyses be appropriate in the event subjects are lost so that there are unequal numbers of subjects or trials in the different conditions?

The analysis section of the proposal should be outlined to correspond with the objectives of the study so that each analysis will yield evidence relating to a corresponding hypothesis. In addition, the reader should be able to determine how all data collected are to be analyzed. An efficient way of accomplishing this is by using a graphic model similar to the one shown in Figure 4.2.

If data are to be presented in tabular or graphic form in the completed report, an example of one such table, including predicted figures, often will be helpful to the reader. The purpose of a table or figure in a research report is to summarize material and to supplement the text in making it clearly understandable. Tables and graphic presentation may serve the same purpose in a proposal.

Because of their display quality, the inclusion of tables in the proposal may expose errors of analysis or research design. For instance, some committee readers may not detect the use of an incorrect error term from a reading of the text, but one glance at the degrees of freedom column in an analysis of variance table will reveal the error. In analysis of variance comparisons, inclusion of several tables may expose the presence of nonindependent variables. Although most completed theses and dissertations no longer include analysis of variance tables, at the proposal stage they may be valuable for stimulating feedback from your committee.

If the analysis activity of the project is studied carefully in advance, many headaches as well as heartaches may be avoided. It may seem to take an inordinate amount of time to plan the analysis, but it is time that will not have to be spent again. As the analyses are completed, the results can immediately be inserted in the results section, and the researcher can complete the project with a feeling of fulfillment rather than a frantic scramble to make sense out of a puzzle for which some of the pieces may prove to be missing.

Hypothesis	Variable	Analysis
1. The self-concept of 7-year-olds is higher than that of 5-year-olds.	Sum of self-concept subscales	MANOVA with follow-up if age factor is significant
2. The self-concept of 9-year-olds is higher than that of 7-year-olds.	Sum of self-concept subscales	MANOVA with follow-up if age factor is significant
3. There is no difference between rural or suburban children's self-concept for 5- and 7-year-olds.	Sum of self-concept subscales	MANOVA with follow-up if location factor is significant
4. Nine-year-old suburban children will have higher self-concept than 9-year-old rural children.	Sum of self-concept subscales	MANOVA with follow-up if location factor is significant
5. The peer sociability of 7-year-olds is higher than that of 5-year-olds.	Peer Sociability Index	MANOVA with follow-up if age factor is significant
6. The peer sociability of 9-year-olds is higher than that of 7-year-olds.	Peer Sociability Index	MANOVA with follow-up if age factor is significant
7. Suburban children will have higher peer sociability than urban children.	Peer Sociability Index	MANOVA with follow-up if location factor is significant

Figure 4.2. Example of a Table Showing How Each Hypothesis Will Be Tested

NOTE: This is presented for illustrative purposes. An actual study may have additional hypotheses.

THE STATISTICAL WELL: DRINKING THE GREATEST DRAUGHT

Students usually can expect help from their advisors with the design of statistical analysis. At minimum, an experienced advisor will have some suggestions about the type of analysis that would be most appropriate for the proposed investigation. Many departments include specialists who have statistical consultation with graduate students as a primary part of their professorial responsibility. Other departments work closely with outside statistical and computer consulants who may be in departments of educational psychology, psychology, computer science, or business administration.

The student should not, however, operate under the faulty impression that when the data are collected they can be turned over to a handy statistical expert who, having an intimate relationship with a computer, will magically transform raw data into a finished form of findings and conclusions. Just as the student cannot expect the analysis of data to take care of itself, neither can the student expect a statistical consultant to take care of it.

The assistance of a statistician or computer consultant, invaluable though it may be, ordinarily is limited to the technology of design and data analysis and help with using a packaged statistical program on a computer. The conceptual demands of the study and the particular form and characteristics of the data generated are the investigator's province—to be explained to the consultant, not vice versa. Likewise, the interpretation of results is a *logical*, not a technical, operation and thus is a responsibility for which only the investigator is properly prepared.

On Finding a Friendly Computer

A variety of interrelated decisions must be addressed as the student contemplates the analysis phase of the study. First, what statistical tools are needed to analyze the data correctly? Then, after the statistical methods are selected, what is the most efficient way to do the analysis? (Note that it is not a good idea to reverse the order of these two questions.) At one time, students had few choices with regard to methods of analysis. Either they calculated the statistics themselves on hand or table calculators, or they used the university mainframe computer to complete the analysis. Today, a variety of statistical packages are available for desktop computers. These packages are extremely versatile and, after a user learns the basics, are relatively easy to use. Part of research planning involves making choices among a growing number of attractive options for analysis.

The first step in selecting a computer and program to analyze your data is to find out what computers and packages are available. The student's advisor, other graduate students, and the university computer center can be helpful. Many universities will have both mainframe and microcomputer consultants to help students and faculty and may have agreements with software companies that greatly reduce the cost of the software. In addition, if a needed program is not available on a computer in your department, most universities have them available in a centralized site.

The first step in deciding on how to analyze your data is to eliminate all packages (and computers) that will not allow you to do the desired analysis. This may involve more than assuring yourself that the proposed statistical operation is available. For instance, you should be interested in the number of subjects and variables the program or computer can handle, whether data can be converted to other forms if you need to conduct additional analyses at a later date, and, should data assume an unexpected form, whether other tests that might be needed are available with the same computer and package.

Fortunately, the most common and powerful statistical packages (Statistical Analysis System [SAS] and Statistical Package for the Social Sciences [SPSS]) now are available for both mainframe and personal computers. The packages can accommodate relatively large data sets for analysis and storage (the limits, of course, will depend on the configuration of the personal computer if one is being used for the analysis), can perform virtually any statistical test researchers require, and are available on most university campuses. Although some may find these packages slightly more difficult to master than most spreadsheets that have statistical options and those programs designed to perform a specific task on one type of computer, several benefits accrue from learning to use one or more of the large statistical packages. Among these advantages are that

1. You will be able to obtain help with your data analysis because many faculty members, graduate students, and consultants are experienced with the larger, well-known statistical packages.
2. If the data must be reanalyzed, it is very likely that the package can complete the analysis without the time-consuming problem of reformatting or retyping data.
3. Familiarity with a commonly used program will serve a student well when moving on to an academic appointment—the packages are available on most campuses and little start-up time will be wasted on learning a new program to analyze data.

No matter what type of computer or package you choose, it is absolutely essential to back up your files. This can be accomplished by simply saving computer files on both the hard disk and a diskette or on multiple diskettes or, if you are employing a mainframe computer, by using a tape cartridge or downloading the files to your personal computer. No matter how diligent you are about saving and backing up your files, you also should save a hard copy (a printout of your data) in more than one place. This applies equally to word processing text for the proposal document. As a matter of practice, have both a printout and an electronic copy of the data in at least two places. An extra word of caution—*save frequently*. You can do this manually or by using the autosave feature of your word processor, or, just to be safe, both. Remember, data are like eggs—they are most secure when stored in more than one basket.

Selecting the wrong statistical package rarely is fatal in the research process. The selection of a computer or package that does not meet all your needs may require additional time for entering data or may delay completion of the analysis. A little careful planning, however, may eliminate waste and reduce aggravation at a later date.

The Care and Nurture of Consultants

To obtain technical help from an advisor or consultant, the student should be prepared to provide basic concepts about the content domain of the investigation, including a concise review of what is to be studied, a clear picture of the form data will take, and a preliminary estimate of alternative designs that might be appropriate to the demands of the proposed research. In addition, whether advice concerning design, statistics, or computer programming is sought from the student's project advisor, from a departmental specialist, or from an expert source external to the department, basic rules exist that must be considered if the student is to glean the most information and help for the smallest cost in valuable consultation time.

Rule 1: Understand the consultant's frame of reference. As with any other situation involving extended communication, it is useful to know enough about the language, predilections, and knowledge base of the consultant to avoid serious misunderstandings and ease the process of initiating the transaction. Research consultants are professionals whose primary interest is in the process of research design, statistical analysis, and the application of computers in research. They use a system language unique to statistics and data management and appreciate those who understand at least the rudiments of this vocabulary. Correspondingly, your consultant will not necessarily understand the system language to be used in the proposal, nor the peculiar characteristics of the data. For example, it cannot be assumed that the consultant knows that some of your data consist of repeated measures. Similarly, it would be unlikely for a statistician to know whether these data are normally distributed across trials.

The consultant cannot be expected to make decisions that relate to the purpose of the study, such as those regarding the balance between internal and external validity. Some designs may maximize the validity of the differences that may be found, but correspondingly trade off external validity, and thus the generalizability of the findings. Decisions concerning the acceptability of such research designs must be made by the proposer of the study. The grounds for such a determination rest in the purpose of the study and thus in conceptual work completed long before the consultation interview.

Consultants can be expected to evaluate a proposed experimental design, assist in selection from a group of alternative designs, suggest more efficient designs that have not been considered, and propose methods for efficiently completing the analysis. Often they can be most helpful, however, if preliminary models for design and statistical analysis have been proposed. This provides a starting place for discussion and may serve as a vehicle for considering characteristics of the data that will impose special demands. Consultants can provide information about computer programs, the appropriateness of a particular program for the proposed design, and the entry techniques into these programs. Again, some preliminary preparation by the student can make the consultant's advisory task easier and work to guarantee an optimal selection of procedures for processing raw data. This preparation might include talking with other students presently engaged in computer use, reviewing material on computer language and packaged statistical programs, and visiting the computer center for an update on available services.

Normally, the statistics and computer specialists in a university setting are besieged by frantic graduate students and busy faculty colleagues, all in addition to the demands of their own students. Further, they may be responsible for the management of one or more functions in their own administrative unit or in the computer center. Finally, as active scholars they will be conducting their own research. Both the picture and the lesson should be equally clear to the student seeking assistance: Statisticians and consultants are busy people. They can provide effective assistance only when investigators come with accurate expectations for the kind of help a consultant can properly provide and come fully prepared to exercise their own responsibilities in the process.

Rule 2: Learn the language. The system languages of measurement, computer science, experimental design, and both inferential and descriptive statistics are used in varying degrees in the process of technical consultation for many research proposals. No one, least of all an experienced consultant, expects fluent mastery in the novice. The student must, however, have a working knowledge of fundamental concepts. These ordinarily include measures of central tendency and variability, distribution models, and the concept of statistical significance. Basic research designs, such as those described in introductory research method books, should be familiar to any novice.

It is, of course, preferable to complete at least one statistics course before attempting any study that will demand the analysis of quantitative data. If, as sometimes is the case, the student is learning basic statistics concurrently with the preparation of the proposal, special effort will have to be concentrated on preparing for consultations concerning design and analysis. The situation will be awkward at best, although many consultants will remain sympathetic and patient if students are honest about their limitations and willing to exert heroic effort once it becomes clear which tools and concepts must be mastered.

Beyond the problem of mastering enough of the language to participate in useful discussion is the more subtle problem of understanding the particular analysis and techniques selected for the study. The student must not drift into the position of using a statistical tool or a measurement technique that really is not understood—even one endorsed and urged by the most competent of advisors. Ultimately, the student will have to make sense out of the results obtained through any analysis. At that point, shallow or incorrect interpretations will quickly betray a failure to understand the nature of the analysis. The student also will have to answer questions about the findings long after the advisor is not around. Expert technical advice can be an invaluable asset in devising a strong proposal, but in the final analysis, such advice cannot substitute for the competence of the investigator.

Rule 3: Understand the proposed study. If the novice researcher does not understand the study sufficiently to identify and ask important and explicit questions, that lack is a major obstacle to a successful consultation. Only when the consultant understands the questions of central interest in the study is it possible to translate them into the steps of statistical analysis and selection of the appropriate computer program. Even if you employ a consultant only to help you with data preparation and analysis, if you cannot communicate exactly what you want, you may get back a printout from an analysis that is irrelevant to your needs. Further, a host of specific constraints associated with the nature of the study will condition the consultant's decision about which analysis to recommend.

The student should be ready to provide answers to each of the following questions:

1. What are the independent variables of the study?
2. What are the dependent variables of the study?
3. What are the potential confounding variables of the study?
4. What is the measurement scale of each variable (nominal, ordinal, interval, or ratio)?

5. Which, if any, of the variables are repeated measures?

6. What, for each variable, are the reliability and validity of the scores produced by the instruments?

7. What are the population distribution characteristics for each of the variables?

8. What difference between dependent variables would be of *practical* significance?

9. What are the monetary, safety, ethical, or educational risks involved if a Type I error is made?

10. What is the nature of the loss if a Type II error is made?

In summary, before consulting with a technical specialist, the student must be able to express exactly what the study is to be designed to accomplish, identify the help needed in producing such a design, and provide all the explicit details the consultant will need in formulating advice.

THE SCIENTIFIC STATE OF MIND:
PROOF, TRUTH, AND RATIONALIZED CHOICES

Scientific inquiry is not so much a matter of elaborate technology or even rigorous method as it is a particular state of mind. The processes of science rest, in the end, on how scientists regard the world and their work. Although some aspects of scientific thinking are subtle and elusive, others are not. These latter, the basic attitudinal prerequisites for the conduct of scientific inquiry, are reflected in the way a novice speaks and writes about proposed research. More directly, the proposal will reflect the degree to which the author has internalized critical attitudes toward such matters as proof, truth, and publicly rationalized choices.

What matters is not the observance of particular conventions concerning phrasing, but fundamental ways of thinking that are reflected in the selection of words. When, for example, students write, "The purpose of this study is to prove (or to demonstrate) that . . .," there always is the dangerous possibility that the intent is to do just that—to prove what they have decided must be true.

Such phrasing cannot be dismissed simply as awkward or naive. Students capable of writing such a sentence without hearing at once its dangerous implications are students with a fundamental defect in preparation. They should be allowed to go no further until they apprehend both the nature of proof and the purpose of research in the scientific enterprise, for clearly neither is understood.

Proof, if it exists at all in any useful sense, is a probabilistic judgment based on an accumulation of observations. Ordinarily, only a series of careful replications can lead to the level of confidence implied by the word "proved." Research is not an attempt to prove or demonstrate, it is an attempt to ask a careful question and to allow the nature of things to dictate the answer. The difference between "attempting to prove" and "seeking proof" is subtle but critical, and a scientist must never confuse the two.

If scholars have no illusions about proof, it is wrong, nevertheless, to believe that they never care about the direction of results obtained from their research. As humans, they often are painfully aware of the distinction between results that will be fortunate or unfortunate for their developing line of thought. As scientists, however, they recognize the irrelevance (and even the danger) of allowing personal convenience or advantage to intrude in the business of seeking knowledge. In the end, researchers must sit down before their facts as children and allow themselves to be instructed. The task lies in arranging the context for instruction so that the answers to questions will be clear, but the content of the lesson must remain in the facts as revealed by the data.

A second critical sign of the student's ability to adopt the scientific viewpoint is the general way the matter of truth is treated in the proposal. When students write, "The purpose of this study is to discover the actual cause of . . .," there is danger that they think it is possible to do just that—to discern the ultimate face of reality at a single glance. The most fundamental remediation will be required if such students ever are to understand, much less conduct, scientific inquiry.

Experienced researchers seek and revere veridical knowledge; they may even choose to think of research as the search for truth, but they also understand the elusive, fragile, and probabilistic nature of scientific truth. Knowledge is regarded as a tentative decision about the world, always held contingent on the content of the future.

The business of the researcher is striving to understand. Correspondingly, a high value is placed on hard-won knowledge. Truth is held gently, however, and the experienced investigator speaks and writes accordingly. It is not necessary to lard a proposal with reservations, provisos, and disclaimers such as "it seems." It is necessary to write with respect for the complexity of things and with modesty for what can be accomplished. The researcher's highest expectation for any study is a small but perceptible shift in the scale of evidence. Most scientific inquiry deals not in the heady stuff of truth, "establishing actual causes," but in hard-won increments of probability.

A third sign by which to estimate the student's scientific maturity is the ability (and willingness) to examine alternative interpretations of evidence, plausible rival hypotheses, facts that bid to disconfirm the theoretical framework, and considerations that reveal the limitations of the methodology. It is important not only to lay out the alternatives for the reader but also to explain the grounds for choice among them. The student who neither acknowledges alternatives nor rationalizes choices simply does not understand research well enough to bother with a proposal.

The mature researcher feels no compulsion to provide perfect interpretations or to make unassailably correct choices. One does the best one can within the limits of existing knowledge and the present situation. The author of a proposal is compelled, however, to make clearly rationalized choices from among carefully defined alternatives; this is one reason readers outside the scientific community find research reports tedious in their attention to detail and explanation. It is the public quality of the researcher's reasoning that makes a community of scientific enterprise possible, not the construction of a facade of uniform certainty and perfection.

Student-conducted research often contains choices that must be rationalized less by the shape of existing knowledge and the dictates of logic and more by the homely facts of logistics: time, costs, skills achieved, and available facilities. The habit of public clarity in describing and rationalizing choices must begin there, with the way things are. An honest accounting of hard and often imperfect choices is a firm step for the student toward achieving the habits of a good researcher—the scientific state of mind.

NOTE

1. Statistical significance, of course, is not synonymous with scientific significance in terms of the evolution of knowledge, or practical significance in terms of solving professional problems. Statistical significance largely depends on sample size and selection of an *alpha* level (the level of confidence necessary to reject the null hypothesis). It can be demonstrated between almost any two groups using almost any variable selected, if the sample size is large enough and the power of the test sufficiently high. Such differences between groups may be statistically significant but scientifically trivial and professionally worthless. The pilot study is an excellent device by which the probability of a Type I error may be estimated and an appropriate sample size selected. In this way, the investigator can increase the probability that a statistically significant result also will reflect a difference of scientific and practical significance.

5

=◻=

Preparation of Proposals for Qualitative Research

Different Assumptions

THE ONLY CONSTANT IS CHANGE

When this book first reached print (1976), the probability that any of our readers would elect a qualitative study for their dissertation or grant proposal was small. Only students in sociology or anthropology would have been likely to know that such an option existed. In that year, most graduate students and young scholars would have begun their apprenticeship in research with studies cast in the familiar quantitative mode of natural science.

Those studies would have presumed views of the world and the process of inquiry that were then so pervasive in the disciplines of natural and social science (and applied professional fields such as education, nursing, and social work) as to be called simply "the scientific method." It was an orderly, understandable, and innocent time. There was only one way to do good research; one learned it, and then did it. Because science is not a static set of prescriptions, however, the natural evolution of the enterprise was to produce some dramatic alterations in that familiar landscape.

What changed was not the viability of the then dominant natural science tradition. Experimental and quasi-experimental designs (with all their assumptions about the nature of truth and reality) remain the choice for many scientific purposes. What changed was our growing understanding that quantitative measurement, manipulative experiments, and the search for objective truth are not the only way to do research—and certainly not the only means of systematic investigation that deserve to be called scholarship.

A reconsideration of assumptions about such fundamental things as the nature of reality, what constitutes knowledge, and the role of human values in the process of research led scholars to challenge the adequacy of some of the established norms for inquiry. Such challenges led, in turn, to the development of new strategies for formal inquiry in the social sciences. Those alternatives created both the necessity of an expanded curriculum in research training programs and new options for research proposals.

As a convenient simplification, the alternative way of thinking about research questions (and the new forms of inquiry that it produced) is referred to in this text as "qualitative research." As an alternative paradigm, some forms of qualitative research have had long histories of use in particular areas of social science (for example, cultural anthropology) but until recently were not a significant part of mainstream scholarship or research training in other disciplines or applied professional fields.[1] In the last two decades, however, contributions from qualitative research have burgeoned in the literature of virtually every area of social science.

The same has been true of publications about qualitative research. At the end of the 1960s, only a handful of relatively obscure books and journal articles dealing with qualitative research existed. Suddenly, a mountain of print appeared containing discussions of theory, alternative designs for inquiry, and debates about technical applications and qualitative standards. Inevitably, then, qualitative research has been a "work in progress." Full of zesty academic disputation and exploratory studies pushing the envelope of acceptable science, qualitative research is slowly being defined by the uses of its practitioners.

That evolution has been reflected in successive editions of *Proposals That Work*. Certainly, our own vision of what constitutes a sound proposal for qualitative study has changed. For example, readers with access to earlier versions of this chapter would detect that we have altered our advice concerning the use of mixed (qualitative and quantitative) methods, the necessity for including a comprehensive review of the literature in the proposal document, the appropriate way to address threats to validity, and the distinction to be made between the researcher's purposes and his or her research questions. We make no apology for those (and other) changes in opinion and shifts in emphasis. To the contrary, we believe that the experiences of our own scholarship, as well as what we continue to learn from our students and colleagues, have given us a better understanding of the particular demands and problems involved in writing proposals for qualitative research.

DISAGREEMENTS AND DIVERSITY

———————————■———————————

We recognize that some of you will come to this chapter unfamiliar with (or unclear about) qualitative research. For your use (as well as for the purpose of establishing a common point of reference for all readers), we will provide a brief introduction to the qualitative paradigm. First, however, we must establish several important caveats.

Because this type of inquiry is relatively new in some areas of scholarship and because it is everywhere undergoing a singular spurt of development and diversification, the field is anything but tidy. In consequence, we anticipate that some of the definitions employed in this chapter will be unsatisfactory (if not outright heresy) to some of our academic colleagues. This book, however, was not written for established researchers who already appreciate the subtle distinctions in the field—and who already know how to prepare proposals.

Further, there is no agreement on a universal label for this kind of research. In the literature of social science and applied professional fields, such terms as *interpretive, naturalistic, constructivist, ethnographic,* and *fieldwork* are variously employed to designate the broad collection of approaches that we call simply qualitative research. Some of those terms reflect important distinctions in the minds of the people who employ them. In contrast, we have selected the generic label "qualitative" as an arbitrary convenience.[2] It is intended to be a working term for writing about research proposals and should not be assigned any particular theoretical or ideological connotation.

Also, despite the deceptive simplicity of the single term *qualitative,* you will be confronted at the outset by the need to choose from among a number of possible formats for inquiry. Every research proposal must reflect the author's selection from among alternative approaches to doing research. If, for example, traditional quantitative inquiry seems most appropriate to a research question, there still remains the problem of determining which design offers the best fit. Will you employ an experiment, quasi-experiment, descriptive survey, case study, or mixed methodology?

Qualitative researchers must face a similar question. If the broad assumptions of the qualitative worldview seem appropriate (for reasons that typically mix the demands of the question with the investigator's practical intentions, the availability of resources, prior training, and personal dispositions), there still remains the problem of deciding which of the various qualitative traditions will best serve the needs of the study.[3] Do you think it appropriate to utilize the assumptions and methods that characterize ethnography, grounded theory, phenomenology, critical theory, or mixed methodology—or would a more generic qualitative format best serve your purposes?

Although true beginners may have the freedom to make such decisions more in theory than in practice (in graduate schools, for example, the availability of advisors often constrains the actual range of possibilities), they nevertheless should be aware of the alternatives. The choice is important, the different research traditions present very real advantages and limitations, and the decisions made in selecting from among them have profound consequences for the proposed study.

To survey some of the traditions under the generic umbrella of qualitative research, we suggest one or several of the following resources. They provide not only the economy of an overview (often with emphasis on contrasts across several perspectives and their characteristic strategies) but also a sense of the tensions that attend the process by which scholars begin to stake out territorial claims in a new enterprise.

In his textbook *Research Design: Quantitative and Qualitative Approaches* (1994), Creswell focuses on the relative advantages (and demands) of qualitative and quantitative designs for study. In a more recent textbook (1998), however, he describes the consequences of selecting a particular qualitative approach. To illustrate, he examines the respective traditions of biography, phenomenology, grounded theory, ethnography, and case study. The 1998 text is briefly annotated in Appendix A.

In addition, edited collections such as the *Handbook of Qualitative Research* (Denzin & Lincoln, 1994), *The Handbook of Qualitative Research in Education* (LeCompte, Milroy, & Preissle, 1992), and *Qualitative Inquiry in Education: The Continuing Debate* (Eisner & Peshkin, 1990) contain chapters that illuminate distinctions among various qualitative approaches. Several authors also have explored the major qualitative traditions for the purpose of developing useful taxonomies that clarify both differences and similarities. Among those are Jacob (1987, 1988, 1989), Lancy (1993), Tesch (1990), and Thornton (1987).[4]

Finally, two particularly distinctive alternatives are available for grounding your proposed design—so distinctive that some scholars consider them to constitute separate paradigms rather than subspecies of the broad qualitative perspective. Mixed methodology, sometimes referred to as the "pragmatic paradigm," can be examined by a reading of Tashakkori and Teddlie (1998; a text abstracted in Appendix A). Critical theory research, which involves a complex, variegated, and sometimes controversial approach, is described in accessible terms by Carspecken (1996), Thomas (1992), and Gitlin (1994). We will return to the topics of both critical theory and mixed methods at several later points in this chapter.

Even readers with only a rudimentary background in social science will find that most of the sources noted above are not overly difficult as introductions. Obtaining such an overview of the diversity within qualitative research will have the salutary effect of reminding you to hold your commitments lightly—until you have a complete map of the territory.

Given such rich possibilities for inquiry, you might reasonably ask why we have opted for a generic model in the introduction that follows. Aside from the need to avoid overwhelming readers who are just starting to learn about research, and the obvious need to keep this text to a reasonable size, the answer lies in our purpose.

All the forms of qualitative research with which we have experience have at least some characteristics in common. For example, a concern for maintaining flexibility in the execution of the research design is virtually universal among the different traditions. We also have found it true that all qualitative approaches make some demands that are different from those encountered in quantitative designs. A clear illustration is seen in the fact that the relatively straightforward recipes used to confront investigator bias in quantitative studies (such as the double-blind experiment and analyses that identify investigator effect) are not possible in qualitative research. In consequence, no matter which of the qualitative research traditions is involved, the problem must be approached in a manner very different from, for example, what might be used in an experiment.

Observations like those have led us to conclude that for the purpose of helping novices make decisions about proposals, it is exactly the basic similarities and distinctions that really matter. Our simple, dichotomous division of paradigms into quantitative and qualitative, and our use of a rudimentary generic model to exemplify the latter, are practical if inelegant teaching strategies. We leave to others the task of discerning and illustrating all the fine distinctions that lie both between and within the broad paradigms for inquiry in the social and behavioral sciences.

A BRIEF DESCRIPTION
OF QUALITATIVE RESEARCH
————————————■————————————

What is qualitative research, and how is it done? On first hearing, the answer seems disarmingly simple. It is a systematic, empirical strategy for answering questions about people in a particular social context.[5] Given any person, group, or locus for interaction, it is a means for describing and attempting to understand the observed regularities in what people do, or in what they report as their experience.

For example, one of the most common purposes of qualitative research is served when investigators pose the basic question, "What's going on here?" Venues for their question might include a religious community, a hospital's administrative staff, a halfway house for paroled felons, a classroom, or a school district in which textbook selection has created controversy. Alternatively, the experience of being a first-year social worker, an older adult returning to a community college, a Little League coach, or a nurse in a hospital's intensive care unit might be the focus for study. In each instance, it is the total context that creates what it means to be present, to be a participant, to be a member, and to have a role to play. It is the participant's experience in that context that the researcher seeks to capture and understand in this kind of qualitative investigation.

The matter of definition is complicated, however, by the fact that the paradigm actually is a collection of research traditions, each with its own priorities, political agenda, preferred means of data collection and analysis, and—unhappily for the beginner—technical jargon. "What's going on here?" is just one of the many kinds of questions that can be raised about people. Further, such questions can be answered in very different ways when investigators start with different assumptions about what matters, and where and how to search. That is exactly the case for the different approaches to inquiry that are commonly grouped under the rubric of qualitative research.

The sometimes uneasy and frequently fractious scientific bedfellows collected under the qualitative umbrella are bound together (albeit loosely) by several key assumptions about the social world, the nature of social realities, and the consequent nature of inquiry. It is not always easy, however, for the beginner to discern exactly what those shared assumptions may be. Part of the problem arises from the distinction between theoretical models and real life.

Because the development of a qualitative paradigm was stimulated by a rejection of the assumptions identified with quantitative science (the form of inquiry shaped by its roots in the philosophy of logical positivism), it has been common to describe qualitative research by noting how it differs from that older paradigm. Lists of assertions that purport to distinguish the belief systems of investigators are used to define quantitative and qualitative ways of understanding the world—and doing research.

We have some grave doubts, however, about the veracity of such dichotomous portrayals when applied to real people. Those reservations may prove to be useful as you negotiate your proposal through networks that may include advisors, reviewers, or co-investigators—all of whom will bring their own assumptions to your document.

Our careers have allowed us to become acquainted with a considerable number of active research workers from a variety of disciplines and applied fields. We can testify with confidence that it is difficult to find any investigator who will profess to all the beliefs that purportedly are required of an adherent to either qualitative or quantitative research. Put another way, when it comes to worldviews and personal philosophy, researchers are like most other people: They are capable of remarkable and often highly creative inconsistencies in their thinking. Accordingly, our advice is to take those lists of various assumptions about the world as pedagogical tools that can help you understand the qualitative paradigm, but not as portraits that accurately describe the beliefs of everyone you actually encounter on that (or any other) side of the paradigmatic street! With that caveat in mind, we offer you the following brief description of assumptions commonly attributed to (if not perfectly shared by) all who employ the qualitative paradigm.

> Qualitative researchers assume that there are aspects of reality that cannot be quantified. More particularly, they believe it is both possible and important to discover and understand how people make sense of what happens in their lives. That includes asking research questions about the meanings people assign to particular experiences, as well as discovering the processes through which they achieve their intentions in particular contexts. It also is assumed that all persons construct their individual accounts of each event in which they are participants. Those subjective constructions are accepted as the realities of the social world. Thus, what is real is regarded as invariably multiple and immutably relative to person and context.
>
> Given those assumptions, it is presumed appropriate and effective to inquire about specific social processes or particular persons' perspectives through direct contact with those involved—observing, interacting, and asking questions—in natural contexts where people function. In doing so, it is accepted that the

investigator must be the primary instrument for data collection, and thus part of rather than separate from whatever is investigated. In turn, that requires the assumption that the researcher's own perspectives and values inevitably will become part of the research process and, ultimately, the findings and conclusions.

Over time, the assumptions laid out above have led qualitative researchers to generate a plethora of different designs for study, methods of data collection and analysis, and conventions for discourse about work within each tradition. Although the result sometimes resembles an academic Tower of Babel, those designs, methods, and conventions do reflect (with varying degrees of explicitness) the broad philosophic perspective assumed by the overarching paradigm.

To illustrate the conceptual difficulties that confront newcomers to the world of qualitative research, we can point to the incorrect (though commonplace) assumption that there are such entities as "qualitative research methods." We say "incorrect" because, absent the underlying assumptions, there is nothing in the long list of research procedures commonly employed by qualitative researchers that could not be employed in a quantitative study. Use of a method of data collection commonly employed in qualitative research, however, does not make a quantitative study one whit less quantitative in its scientific nature—unless that method is used (and the accumulated data subsequently interpreted) in accord with the assumptions of the qualitative paradigm. Of course, the reverse also is true. The possibility of actually mixing research models (paradigms) within the same study is a topic we will address later in this chapter.

Having argued that no research methods are exclusively "qualitative" in nature, however, we have to admit that some research tools and conventions are closely identified with qualitative inquiry. In that sense, it is fair to say that some strategies for inquiry are characteristic of much, if not all, qualitative research. Those characteristics include many of the following (though in any one study it would be rare for all to be represented).

1. Qualitative researchers usually work inductively, trying to generate theories that help them understand their data. This is in contrast, for example, to the experimental tradition in quantitative research for which hypotheses usually are set a priori and then deductively tested with the collected data.

2. In most qualitative studies, the central problems are to identify how people interact with their world (what they do), and then to determine how they experience and understand that world: how they feel, what they believe, and how they explain structure and relationships within some segment of their existence.

3. Interviews and various forms of observation are the most common means of data collection, though they are sometimes supplemented by the collection of documents.

4. Data most commonly take the form of words (field notes, interview transcripts, diaries, etc.), although quantities, frequencies, and graphic representations also can be used.

5. It is common for reports of qualitative research to contain detailed descriptions of participants, as well as both the physical and social structures of the context within which the study takes place.

6. In many forms of qualitative research (though certainly not all), the investigator collects data in the field—the place where the behaviors of interest naturally occur.

7. Qualitative research designs frequently involve collection of data from different sources (sometimes by means of different methods) within a setting for the explicit purpose of cross-checking information, called "triangulation." Inspection of such data sets and subsequent follow-up where discrepancies appear make this a primary means for establishing the truthfulness of sources.

8. It is rare for a qualitative researcher to introduce a deliberate intervention in the field of study. For the most part, investigators try to be nonintrusive, reducing the causes of participant reactivity to the smallest possible number. The exceptions here are participatory action research studies in which the investigator plays an active (though circumscribed) role.

9. It is common for qualitative researchers to have a primary interest in identifying and understanding the social processes by which particular end results are created, rather than simply describing the results themselves.

10. Although a researcher may make use of interview guides, systematic formats for recording observation data, and even material from responses to questionnaires, in the final analysis the researcher is the primary instrument for inquiry in qualitative research. With rare exceptions, he or she must interact directly with study participants, determining from moment to moment how to behave, what to notice and record, and how a particular line of inquiry does or does not offer promise for answering the research question at hand.

11. Qualitative researchers try to be conscious of the perspective they bring to a study. For that reason, they often explain their own background and particular interest in the research question as part of the research report. Researcher bias, however, in the sense of a vested personal interest in producing a particular finding, is regarded as a different matter. Bias must be controlled if the results of a study are to seem truthful. Accordingly, tactics for countering the inclination to see and hear what is desired often are central elements in qualitative research designs.

12. Irrespective of the paradigm, participant reactivity to the investigator or to the conditions of the study is a threat to the integrity of research. For a variety of

reasons, however, this is a particularly sensitive problem in qualitative research. Accordingly, many studies include tactics intended to limit that source of data distortion.

13. Only rarely are samples of participants created by random procedures. Selection is more likely to be purposeful, with the intention of maximizing the utility of data for the research goals intended.

14. Designs for qualitative studies usually are carefully thought out during a period of planning and preparation. In some instances, the plan may be specified in considerable detail in the form of an extensive written proposal. Nevertheless, absolute fidelity in execution of a particular design does not offer the same benefit it yields in quantitative studies. Instead, it is common in qualitative research for plans to be regarded as tentative and contingent on the realities presented by data collection and analysis. At least in the case of experienced investigators, in-course adjustments are regarded as part of doing good research rather than fatal breaches of protocol.

15. Qualitative research reports often are written in the first person and may employ expressive language intended to make findings both accessible and powerfully persuasive.

Those are characteristics typical of studies that would belong under the qualitative umbrella. A particular scholar might add or delete one or several, or might modify some of our explanations, but we believe that when taken together, the 15 items collectively come close to a consensus model of what it means to do qualitative research. There are, however, several options for inquiry that cannot be classified cleanly into either the quantitative or qualitative camps.

A paradigm that shares much with the qualitative perspective is called "critical theory." It is well established in both the social sciences and some areas of professional study (notably education). Except for the brief comment that follows, we will not attempt here to address the implications of critical theory for the production of a research proposal. As noted at an earlier point in this chapter, Thomas (1992) provides an introduction to the paradigm that is notable for its accessibility. A more formal accounting is offered by both Carr and Kemmis (1986) and Carspecken (1996), while the collection edited by Gitlin (1994) captures the power of the ideological arguments involved. Chapters dealing with critical theory also may be found in the two handbooks for qualitative research: Denzin and Lincoln (1994) and Lecompte et al. (1992).

As with its paradigmatic neighbors, critical theory shelters a number of traditions that are only loosely (and not always comfortably) related. Participatory, empowering, action, materialist, and feminist research perspectives are among those. At the most fundamental level, what they share is an interest in and a concern for the ways that power is distributed and maintained in social settings—and how those arrangements can be challenged.

On the surface, that kind of interest appears not to require a new set of assumptions about inquiry. As the fundamental concerns of critical theory begin to shape the relationship between the researcher and the researched, however, they begin to have important implications for both method and what some scholars regard as appropriate purposes for research. In some forms of critical theory, research becomes a vehicle for urging or facilitating the redistribution of power and improving the life circumstances of the participants. At that point, where the imagined line between politics and scholarship begins to blur, you can be sure that we have moved into new and controversial territory—and a place where not all qualitative researchers are equally comfortable.

Some investigators who do what is called "feminist" research have made claims to a separate paradigmatic status for their perspective—a tradition that they regard as distinct from both critical theory and the larger collectivity of qualitative research. We suggest that if you are interested in the way gender enters into research, you take a short excursion into the often lively literature on that topic. Good places to begin would be Lather (1991); the chapters dealing with the feminist approach in the collections edited by Eisner and Peshkin (1990), Gitlin (1994), LeCompte et al. (1992), and Denzin and Lincoln (1994); or Maguire's (1987) monograph on feminist participatory research. The more recent book edited by Ribbens and Edwards (1997) emphasizes the considerable difficulties that have attended efforts to pursue a consistently feminist viewpoint in qualitative research.

PREPARING A PROPOSAL
FOR QUALITATIVE RESEARCH

With regard to advice concerning proposals for qualitative research, we wish to make one point clear from the outset: Virtually all of what has been said about function, development, writing style, organization, and format for quantitative proposals will apply here. The qualitative proposal is not substantively a different kind of document. Our experience, however, has convinced us that it does present a particular set of problems that will demand your attention—either because they constitute common sources of difficulty for reviewers, or because they are matters better confronted in the proposal than at the later point of preparing a report.

In drawing up the following list of 13 key points, we have made three assumptions about your situation. First, we have presumed that your proposal will not be subject to review by someone who does not accept qualitative research as genuine scholarship. When that is the case, the proposal must undertake to defend the legitimacy of a paradigm—a task we think is better reserved for seasoned scholars. On the other hand, reviewers who simply are unfamiliar with qualitative research usually can be dealt with by patient explanation and by providing a judiciously short selection of introductory readings.

Second, we have assumed that at least one of the reviewers (for graduate students, most commonly the committee chair) will be familiar with the design and methods you propose, as well as the literature that explicates those choices. Without the support of such expertise, the burden of explaining, certifying, and persuading may be greater than can be born by a document of modest length.

Third, and finally, we have assumed that reviewers for your proposal will be looking for answers to a familiar set of questions. For example, do you appear to know the conceptual and methodological turf? Does your plan reflect careful thought? Do the parts of the proposal fit together? Is there evidence that you are fully aware of the problems to be overcome? Is the nature and scope of the study reasonably well matched to your skills and resources? If the three assumptions noted above are met, the following items can be used as a checklist and, when coupled with the generic advice about proposals offered in the other chapters of this book, should help you deal successfully with the problems that are particular to qualitative research.

1. *Why qualitative?* Make absolutely clear that a qualitative design is appropriate to both the study's general purpose (why you are doing the study) and the more specific research goals (such as formally stated research questions). Your training and personal values are not irrelevant to this argument. In the end, however, it is the match between the paradigm and the problem that must carry the day.

2. *Plan flexibility.* Present a plan describing what you will do from the outset to the finish of your study. If you are a novice, adhering closely to the general specifications of that plan is prudent policy. Qualitative research frequently involves some circumstances, however, for which a degree of anticipated flexibility also is wise. Some procedures must be responsive to what actually happens during data collection, as well as to the nature of the data that begin to accumulate. If there are such points within your proposed plan, showing that you have anticipated the necessity of selecting (or devising) alternative courses of action

always is reassuring to reviewers. There is a delicate balance to be maintained in this aspect of a proposal for qualitative research. Present a careful plan and stick to it unless there are compelling reasons not to do so (dependence on "emergent design" is for experienced investigators). Give clear indication, however, that you have given careful thought to alternatives—should they be required.

3. *Build a framework.* Present a conceptual framework that helps to explain and clarify your proposed design. Define the main constructs and show their relationship to one another, to the research questions, to the methodology, and to the related literature. Absent a contrary regulation, this should not take the form of an extended general review of the literature. Previous scholarship is best limited to assistance in defining the precise conceptual territory of the proposed study. The literature can provide construct definitions, theoretical frameworks, examples of successful research strategies used in parallel circumstances, and a display of where your study would fit into the ongoing conversation among scholars. The primary emphasis, however, should be on the concepts and relationships assembled for your own study. A graphic format often is useful for achieving clarity here (see the excellent examples provided by Maxwell, 1996).

4. *Articulate the parts.* Take special care at each step to write brief but explicit explanations of how the parts fit together—purpose with question, question with framework, framework with methods, and collected data with means of analysis. In the absence of the structure provided by standardized designs, it is easy for authors of qualitative proposals to lose the sense of cohesive unity among the several parts.

5. *Plan for validity.* Deal directly with the issue of validity.[6] If you complete the proposed study, everyone who reads the report will have a perfect right to ask "Why should I believe you?" If you want to be prepared with a persuasive answer, the proposal is the place to search out the threats to validity inherent in your plans. Maxwell (1996) suggests that qualitative proposals should have a separate section devoted to answering the question, "How could I be wrong?" That is a tough question, but a healthy one.

   At the least, you must deal with the three threats to validity that most commonly attend the procedures used in qualitative research. (a) How will you ensure that descriptions of participants and context are accurate and complete? (b) Are your personal biases a threat? If not, why not, or if so, what do you plan to do about them? (c) In what ways and to what degree will participant reactions to you (and to the procedures used in the study) impede acquisition of valid data, and what are your plans for dealing with that problem? Again, experiences (and data) cited from pilot work are powerful ways of showing that you are prepared to deal realistically with threats to validity.

6. *Illustrate analyses.* Be sure to discuss your plans for analysis, giving practical examples whenever possible. Qualitative research seems to invite accounts of

proposed analysis that are superficial—often in the form of brief sections devoted to wholly theoretical discussion that is not convincing as a demonstration of competence. If you are going to use "triangulation of the data," show readers that you know how to perform the appropriate steps of logic with reasonable facility.

7. *Plan for records.* Explain exactly how you will maintain a paper trail. For example, if you propose to use some form of category system for analysis of transcripts, how and when will you record the exact source of each category? Where will you document revisions as they become necessary? Likewise, how will you record your speculations about the data, the participants, the study, or yourself when such thoughts cannot be handled as bracketed insertions into field notes or interview transcripts? We can confirm that such records will be essential when writing the report—many weeks or months later. The length and complexity of most qualitative studies virtually guarantee that you will lose important information if there is no planned regimen for recording it promptly and in adequate detail. We also urge that all records be maintained in duplicate—at separate locations.

8. *Demonstrate procedures.* Avoid the sin of nominalism. Because qualitative research traditions usually are rich with specialized nomenclature, it is easy to slip into the habit of using the names of complex operations as though they were magic incantations. To say that you will produce "grounded theory," or employ "analysis through constant comparison," "triangulation of data sources," or a "peer debriefer," tells the reader little more than that you know how to spell the words. Explaining why you will employ the operation, showing exactly how you will use it in the context of your design, and giving citations for the literature sources you have consulted constitute a far more persuasive presentation.

9. *Don't anticipate findings.* Be careful about using language that might appear to build your personal expectations about findings into the study procedures. For example, a research question such as, "How do student interns deal with feelings of hostility toward supervisory staff?" presumes that such affective states will be experienced by the participants. Whether that assumption is correct or incorrect, the question too easily translates into interview questions that can cue participants as to how they "ought" to feel. Of course, you will have anticipated at least some aspects of what is going on for your participants. In most studies, the conceptual framework itself reflects, directly or indirectly, what the investigator suspects is going on—or at least what he or she believes is worthy of attention. Such expectations, however, become bias (threats to validity) when they go unrecognized, unmonitored, and unchecked. The proposal should be written in a manner that is sensitive to such dangers.

10. *Quantify correctly.* If you decide to use quantitative information (frequencies, measures of association, descriptors for central tendency, etc.) in describing your data or some aspect of the research context, it is your responsibility to demon-

strate that you know how to do so appropriately. Adopting a qualitative perspective does not prohibit you from employing quantitative descriptors, but neither does it exempt you from the conventions for correct application.

11. *Plan entry and exit.* Think through procedures for entry to and exit from your research context (both the site and the human relationships) and make those plans explicit in the proposal. Negotiating conditions for your presence and departure can be delicate matters that have both ethical and practical consequences. This aspect of your study is likely to contain problems that would not be encountered in a typical quantitative study—not least of which are close personal relationships with some or all of the participants.

12. *Transfer cautiously.* Be careful to write about the potential generalizability (application to populations outside your study) of your conclusions in ways that match the proposed procedures for selecting participants. Absent random sampling, claims to acquisition of valid knowledge about other groups (either within the study context or external to it) almost always are inappropriate. Careful and thorough description of the context and participants can make it possible to challenge readers of your report with the later question, "Why would these conclusions not apply in another context?" That, however, is not the same as attempting to generalize your findings to another setting.

13. *Name your perspectives.* Either in the main body or in an appendix to the proposal, include a brief statement highlighting those aspects of your personal biography (work experiences, education, mentors, salient events) that have shaped your perspective on the proposed study—its questions, participants, venue, and general purpose. Reviewers at this stage, as well as readers who will later consult your report, have important reason to know what baggage you bring to the proposed study in the form of relevant beliefs, values, concerns, commitments, and intentions. You will be the primary research instrument, and publicly naming the ways you relate to your study is a vital part of preparing for qualitative research.

To close this section on a note of encouragement and optimism, it is fair to observe that decisions about each of the planning points noted above probably are more "forgiving" than they tend to be in quantitative research. After reading an impressive report from a field investigation, for example, it is easy for novice researchers to believe that wonderfully insightful and cooperative participants were the critical element. The selection of participants (or a study site), however, usually is not as critical as the uninitiated might think. Experienced research workers are more inclined to credit friendly and respectful treatment of participants, perceptive analysis of data—and luck. Few of the decisions made for the proposal are likely to make or break a first effort, even though they are decisions that must be made. Our advice is to plan as carefully as possible but to keep a healthy respect for the surprises to be encountered.

RESOURCES FOR QUALITATIVE RESEARCH

Our recommendations for resources that will assist in preparing a qualitative proposal have been divided into 12 topical areas. We caution you not to treat these as an exhaustive set designed to include all the resources that are relevant to qualitative research. Our purpose here is more limited. We have selected books and journals that attend directly to topics that novice investigators (principally our own students) typically have found relevant to the two steps of creating a study design and writing the proposal. The order of topics begins with the needs of a novice at the earliest stage, and then adds in serial order those investments in reading that would accompany preparation of a qualitative proposal.

1. *User-Friendly Introductions*—The first step in considering use of a qualitative approach is to gain some sense of what it can and cannot accomplish as a research strategy, and what sort of skills are required to design studies, collect and analyze data, and write reports. Our personal favorites for this purpose are Bogdan and Biklen (1992) and Merriam (1998), both of which have the virtue of careful revision after long periods of extensive use. Glesne and Peshkin (1992), Delamont (1992), and Rossman and Rallis (1998) are equally competent as introductions, however, and may better fit your taste in textbooks. For proposals involving smaller scale qualitative studies, Denscombe's *The Good Research Guide for Small Scale Research Projects* (1998) is aptly named and thoroughly practical. Stake (1995) offers an eminently readable survey of qualitative case study research in all of its many permutations. Finally, even at the introductory level you will encounter a good deal of unfamiliar vocabulary, much of which will not be found in a standard dictionary. Fortunately, a dictionary devoted exclusively to the language conventions (a kindly label for jargon) of qualitative inquiry is available (Schwandt, 1997). With suggested readings and cross-references given in most entries, this is an instance for which cover to cover reading of a dictionary might represent an eminently practical strategy.

2. *Specimens*—Almost any modern research journal in the social sciences or applied professional fields will contain qualitative studies (the exceptions, of course, are those explicitly devoted to quantitative scholarship). It will be wise to locate journals that publish such reports in your own area of interest, and we

urge you to do so early in the process of exploring the qualitative option. Only concrete examples can make theoretical discussions come alive. If you need a convenient starting place, *Qualitative Sociology* offers many reports that are relatively brief, intrinsically interesting for most readers, and quite undemanding of technical background. Many areas of study also have collections of qualitative research reports in book format. An excellent example is Riessman's *Qualitative Studies in Social Work Research* (1994).

3. *Theory*—Books dealing with the theoretical foundations of qualitative research are notoriously difficult—and for the uninitiated, ponderously dull. Sooner or later, however, you will have to make a start. Many beginners find it best temporarily to bypass texts that deal with the epistemological roots of the paradigm, and start instead by reading material that deals with how to do research that is faithful to those philosophical origins. The standard in the field for that purpose is Lincoln and Guba (1985), a book that is consulted, cited, quoted, and, in most cases, owned by virtually all who are active in qualitative research. A treatment of foundational theory that will be even more accessible for many readers is offered by Patton (1990) in a textbook notable for the author's light touch. Another gentle way to ease yourself into this literature is to consult the book by Creswell (1998), in which the author illustrates how each of five different qualitative research traditions shapes the nature of study design. If you become serious about doing a qualitative study, there will be many more challenging theoretical mountains to climb. For the present, however, this is enough.

4. *About Qualitative Proposals*—If you have gone this far, you probably are going to write a proposal for qualitative research. There presently are two textbooks devoted to that topic, and in this case our suggestion is that you purchase and use both of them. Marshall and Rossman (1999) and Maxwell (1996) are both ideal for the novice in qualitative research. With contrasting styles and emphases, they form a perfect complementary pair. Brief descriptions of other textbooks dealing with the preparation of proposals may be reviewed in Appendix A. Finally, available on its Website (http://www.ssrc.org), the Social Science Research Council provides a copy of its guide for authors, *The Art of Writing Proposals* (Przeworski & Salomon, 1995). Prepared by veteran reviewers, the advice offered is eminently practical and applicable to proposals for either qualitative or quantitative research.

5. *Ethics in Qualitative Research*—We placed ethics here in the topical order, before the categories dealing with methodology, because we think this is where it belongs. Thinking through the design for a study should be framed in terms of the ethical consequences that might attend each decision. To do so requires acquainting yourself with such problems early in the proposal process. As we noted in Chapter 2, the topic too often receives short shrift in research training

at all levels and, sad to say, that continues to be true of qualitative research. Aside from a passing encounter with a human subjects review protocol, most beginners give scant thought to the question of how they wish to treat their participants—until they walk headlong into one of the nasty dilemmas that abound in qualitative research (see the examples in Chapter 2). You can begin with our discussion of ethics but should add readings that are more directly focused on qualitative inquiry. Either Sieber (1992) or Kimmel (1988) will provide an introduction, as will the chapters devoted to ethical questions in Eisner and Peshkin (1990), Denzin and Lincoln (1994), or LeCompte et al. (1992). Finally, Bailey (1996) offers a guide to field research that gives consideration to ethical problems in each of its chapters.

6. *Methods*—Taken in the generic sense, methods are the tools for doing research. They include the procedures and instruments used by the investigator to generate data, as well as the techniques used to analyze data. Although we ordinarily think of interviewing (listening and conversing), observing (watching people), and document analysis (reading) as the primary means for collecting data in qualitative studies, a quick survey of published reports will reveal that there are many others. Questionnaires, surveys, systematic observation instruments, unobtrusive measures, videotapes, and photographs also serve as data sources. Likewise, there are dozens of methods for organizing data for the purpose of analysis. No single source can cover all methods, so it is necessary to narrow any search to what can be found in more specialized texts. We have provided suggestions below for such sources in the broad topic areas of interviewing, field notes, computer management of data, and analysis.

A useful first step in retrieving sources that explain particular research methods is to use a dictionary or glossary of qualitative terminology to look up the synonyms, definitions, and standard references associated with the method about which you want information. Again we suggest Schwandt (1997) as particularly helpful for that purpose. A second step would be to consult the index to Denzin and Lincoln's *Handbook of Qualitative Research* (1994), tracking down citations for method-related articles and books. Finally, you might scan recent listings from publishers that offer books and monographs dealing with social research in various disciplines and applied fields (for example, Corwin Press, Falmer Press, Jossey-Bass, Longman, Pine Forge Press, Sage Publications, and Teachers College Press).

As a final note about the topic of methods, we have observed that many of our graduate students considered proposing designs involving "mixed methods" (the use of tools for data collection or analysis that ordinarily are associated with studies in a paradigm other than the one adopted to frame the proposal). Further, a smaller number of students even have contemplated the possibility of combining several different paradigms across all the stages of a design. Such studies thus would involve what Tashakkori and Teddlie (1998) have called "mixed models." That raises the question of the compatibility of paradigm models, a topic that has been examined by Howe (1988) and Delamont and Atkinson (1995).

We think concern about the difficulty of such mixing is legitimate, and it is reflected in Item 10 (above) on our list of key problems in preparing a qualitative proposal. As Datta (1994) has succinctly pointed out, "mixed-up" methods and models (those that are used incorrectly, inconsistently, or without reference to any kind of consistent philosophical orientation) are not to be confused with mixed methodology!

Aside from the problem of correct applications, however, it has become clear to us that mixing methods now is a commonplace strategy in qualitative studies (and one that students should learn to execute correctly). In contrast, the mixing of paradigmatic models is much less common and, although clearly feasible, we still think it a less than prudent option for the average graduate student. From the outset, the investigator must have mastered both the instruments and the world-view of two very different systems of thought. Then, in the course of the study, he or she must have sufficient flexibility of mind to move back and forth between two vantage points when contemplating the data. That is asking a great deal of anyone who is less than perfectly confident of his or her technical powers.

Whether you are a veteran investigator or a novice still in training, however, if you are going to consider mixing either methods or models, we think it will be helpful to consult *Mixed Methodology* by Tashakkori and Teddlie (1998). On one hand, we believe that this small paperbound monograph might encourage the initial inspiration to enrich your study design with methods from several research traditions. On the other hand, we suspect the book will leave you with a much more realistic (and sober) appraisal of what will be involved in designing and executing that more ambitious investigation.

7. *Interviewing*—Because this is a particularly common form of data collection, interviewing is accorded a chapter in nearly every qualitative research textbook. In that regard, we think that Patton (1990) and Merriam (1998) constitute good places to begin. Seidman (1998) and Rubin and Rubin (1995) are more special-ized, yet quite accessible. To those we can add two sources that deal with focus groups as an interview format for generating data: Greenbaum (1997) and Morgan and Krueger (1997). Finally, Kvale (1994) has catalogued the most common objec-tions to the use of interview data—and some appropriate responses.

8. *Field Notes*—Again, virtually every basic textbook covering qualitative research offers a chapter on the art of recording observations in the field—the ubiquitous "field notes." Lofland and Lofland (1995) provide a thoughtful treatment that has guided several generations of students in the social sciences. More extended instruction in the techniques of writing ethnographic field notes is available in Emerson, Fretz, and Shaw (1995).

9. *Computer Management of Data*—Computers make it possible to perform the complex tasks of data management, coding, retrieval, and manipulation with a speed, economy, and accuracy never before available to qualitative researchers. They also make it possible to waste time and resources, make egregious errors, and create the illusion of substance where there is none—more swiftly than ever before. Read, consult, reflect, and plan before you decide whether (or how) a computer might serve your proposed study.

Although many of the older textbooks can provide an adequate introduction to the potential uses and abuses of computer software for manipulating qualitative data, the frequent appearance of new software quickly serves to date most of their commentary on particular systems. At the time of this writing, the texts with the most recent publication dates are Weitzman and Miles (1995), a survey with ratings of 24 commercially available programs; Fielding and Lee (1998), a broad examination of the uses and impact of computer-assisted qualitative data analysis; and Gahan and Hannibal (1998), a guide to using the leading software package for developing, supporting, and managing qualitative data analysis.

10. *Data Analysis*—Whether you use a sophisticated computer program or something as simple as a large accounting ledger, analysis requires a plan, and the place to sketch out the initial shape of that element of your methodology is in the proposal. The strategy you employ for making sense out of your data will be determined in the first instance by the particular qualitative tradition you have adopted for the study. Some traditions offer little flexibility, whereas others make no prescription about the particular form of analysis to be employed. The purpose of your study, the nature of the data set, and even how much time you have available will influence the decision, and thus the resource texts that will be relevant.

By far the most comprehensive collection of analytic strategies can be found in the second edition of Miles and Huberman's sourcebook *Qualitative Data Analysis* (1994). On a scale that more closely resembles standard textbooks, however, several other sources offer excellent overviews of what is available. Creswell (1998) compares techniques of analysis and data representation across five qualitative traditions, and Coffey and Atkinson (1996) use a single data set to demonstrate how different techniques of analysis can be employed in a complementary fashion.

You will find that one of the most carefully defined and fully explicated forms of analysis is employed in the social science tradition of "grounded theory." Although the term sometimes is used in nonspecific ways to refer to any approach for developing theoretical ideas that somehow begins with data, when employed to indicate a specific qualitative research tradition something very different is denoted. Grounded theory involves a specific set of highly developed, rigorous, and intellectually demanding analytic techniques for generating substantive theories of social phenomena.

Among various steps and techniques, the grounded theory model of analysis employs the operation called "constant comparison." That term, unfortunately, has been considerably misused by graduate students to give an air of scientific respectability to proposals for analysis by means of unsystematic data-snooping. If you wish to avoid the stigma of such amateur usage, we urge you to read *Basics of Qualitative Research* by Strauss and Corbin (1998). Although demanding, with reasonable diligence it is an accessible source, particularly when coupled with the extensive collection of reports and readings found in *Grounded Theory in Practice* (Strauss & Corbin, 1997).

11. *Writing and Publication*—There now is no scarcity of resources intended to help you write the report of your study. Although that task might be considered beyond the purview of the proposal, that is not at all the case. There are aspects of the report that are not encountered in the task of writing the proposal, but the work of crafting clear and precise prose about a study, whether proposed or completed, is the same. Just a few hours expended on a survey of what will be demanded in a sound report can have a powerful influence not only on how you write, but also on what you propose to do during the study.

    We suggest that you begin with Becker's *Writing for Social Scientists* (1986), an elegant and highly personal exposition by a master of the craft, and continue with Golden-Biddle and Locke (1997), a lively introduction to the qualitative report as a form of "storytelling." Van Maanen (1988) has long been a standard reference for preparing ethnographic reports, and Wolcott's (1990) small mono-graph on "writing up" qualitative research (volume 20 in Sage Publications' Qualitative Research Methods series) is, itself, a model of good writing.

    Finally, if you can allow yourself to dream beyond the labors of writing, there are the more attractive venues of presenting papers, designing poster sessions, locating an appropriate outlet for publication, and using your work to influence practical decisions made by others (as well as the less salubrious task of dealing with your first rejection notice). To sample some of those delights, we suggest the unusual collection edited by Morse (1997), prepared by 24 active researchers in the field of health care. The focus of *Completing a Qualitative Project* is on what remains to be done after your data analysis is finished—moving through the final stages of a long journey for which your proposal constitutes the first step.

12. *Standards for Qualitative Research*—If there were clear, explicit, and reasonably parsimonious standards for quality at the other end of the research pipeline (criteria for evaluating the adequacy of completed qualitative studies), those could be used for critiquing and strengthening the designs presented in proposals. We are sure you will not be surprised to learn that this is not possible, at least not in any simple and straightforward way. One obvious impediment rests in the diversity of qualitative research traditions, many of them still evolving, and all of them infused with distinctive intentions and commitments that would have to shape judgments about the adequacy of each study. Less apparent to the beginner,

however, will be the fact that there has been a distinct reluctance on the part of members of the research community to engage with the question of qualitative criteria for qualitative studies. The most common explanation for this aversion has been a desire not to impose rigid guidelines for process within a paradigm that puts the creative and individual journey toward understanding at the center of inquiry. Whether that explanation is entirely true or not, there recently has been some tentative movement toward elucidation of standards to be held when reviewing a report of qualitative research.

If you wish to make use of that literature as part of your preparation for writing a proposal, we suggest beginning with the brief and unpretentious discussion of standards offered by Rossman and Rallis (1998). If that seems helpful, more extensive discussions of the art and science of critiquing qualitative research may be found in Lincoln (1995) or in the triad of chapters authored, respectively, by Sally Thorne, Phyllis Stern, and Judith Hupcey in the collection edited by Morse (1997).

Some of the best writing about reasonable expectations for quality have appeared in discussions about the nature of validity in qualitative research. A useful introduction to that topic can be found in Johnson (1997). If that brief overview seems fruitful for thinking about your proposed study, however, you will wish to consult much more thorough discussions such as those offered by Maxwell (1992), Eisenhart and Howe (1992), or Altheide and Johnson (1994).

In closing this section dealing with resources, we draw your attention to several more that, while overlapping many of the 12 topical categories above, constitute by themselves an important repository for information about qualitative research. Whatever you are unable to find in the places we have suggested, you surely can locate in one of the following.

In 1986, Sage Publications initiated a series in Qualitative Research Methods. Rapidly approaching the 50th volume at the time of this writing, the collection is one of the most comprehensive efforts ever undertaken to provide support for qualitative research. Packaged in the form of paperbound monographs of 50-100 pages in length, the series provides beginners and veteran researchers with a resource that is both inexpensive and carefully targeted at the most troublesome aspects in the planning and execution of qualitative studies. Though not limited to qualitative designs, the parallel Applied Social Research Methods series from Sage Publications contains a number of monographs that may be equally useful in preparing a proposal. Those dealing with case study research (Yin, 1993, 1994), ethnography (Fetterman, 1998), participant observation (Jorgensen, 1989), and qualitative research design (Maxwell, 1996) represent excellent introductory sources.

The handbook format has become a standard means for periodically collecting and reviewing research in various disciplines, as well as presenting discussions of technical matters and broad issues attending the research enterprise itself. The *Handbook of Qualitative Research* (Denzin & Lincoln, 1994) provides a generic overview of the paradigm, including its many component traditions, strategies for inquiry, methods of data collection and analysis, practical applications, and future development. Although less ambitious in scale and more specific to the field of education, *The Handbook of Qualitative Research in Education* (LeCompte et al., 1992) offers coverage of many broad topics that relate to qualitative research in any applied field of professional service.

A number of journals in the social sciences and applied fields have long included qualitative research reports in their coverage, but four have been devoted exclusively to that form of inquiry. The *International Journal of Qualitative Studies in Education* began publication in 1988 and now represents an invaluable resource for locating original reports, research reviews, theoretical and technical articles, and book reviews. Now in its third decade of issue, *Qualitative Sociology* deals with the qualitative interpretation of social life. Including both research reports and articles on theoretical and technical topics, the journal is made particularly useful by its frequent thematic issues and the inclusion of book reviews in an extended review-essay format. In the broad field of health care, the journal *Qualitative Health Research* offers an interdisciplinary forum for studies that employ qualitative methods. It has been particularly effective as a resource for encouraging alternative approaches to inquiry in the applied fields of medicine. Finally, a relative newcomer to this specialized group, *Qualitative Inquiry*, focuses primarily on interdisciplinary and cross-paradigm research methods. Accordingly, research reports appear only when they present points of special methodological or theoretical interest.

THE DECISION TO GO QUALITATIVE

The decision to undertake a qualitative study brings two types of problems: those that are external and mostly antecedent to the proposal, and those that are internal and associated with devising an appropriate design for the study (and then writing the proposal document). To this point, this chapter has been concerned with the latter—the design and its written presentation. Here, however, we want to turn briefly to the background precursors and surrounding circumstances that will exert their influence on that process.

The problems that precede the preparation of a qualitative proposal begin with the author as a person. Everyone who is tempted to employ a qualitative design should confront and honestly answer one question: "Why do I want to do a qualitative study?" Some novice researchers, traumatized by a fourth-grade encounter with fractions, see qualitative research as a way of avoiding numbers in general and statistics in particular. So long as question and paradigm truly are well matched, however, a choice made on such personal grounds, taken by itself, is neither improper nor inevitably dysfunctional.

As professors who have long labored in graduate-level research training programs, we emphatically endorse the proposition that no student should graduate from such a curriculum without having studied both qualitative and quantitative research—at least through the introductory level. Reasonable academic literacy, if not basic competence, demands at least that much in the way of liberal background. We see no conflict whatever between that standard and the proposition that personal biography is a wise consideration in locating questions and research methods about which one can be enthusiastic.

It also is true, however, that finding certain kinds of questions appealing is not the same as having the personal capacities and intellectual interests demanded in the conduct of a qualitative study. If avoiding statistics is not so much a bad reason for electing to go qualitative as it is an *irrelevant* reason, then personal values that are compatible with a qualitative worldview are not so much an irrelevant rationale as they are *insufficient*. Determining a mode of inquiry that matches both your research goals and your research capabilities requires a more elaborate calculus.

We are not suggesting here that qualitative research must presume unusual capabilities or exceptional intellect. To the contrary, our experience has been that a large proportion of properly trained individuals can do perfectly competent qualitative research—if they are strongly motivated to do so. The demands, however, are very real, and your capacity to meet them should be considered with honest care. At the least, factors such as interactive social skills (people skills), a sensitive ear for nuanced language, and analytic capability (pattern recognition) are far more relevant to success than either an interest in social dynamics or a bad case of math anxiety!

In the same vein, a graduate student who elects qualitative research because it appears either to be relatively "quick" in terms of time commitment or "easy" in terms of intellectual demands has, in the first instance, simply never talked with anyone who has completed such a study and, in the second instance, not read published reports of field research with much care. Qualitative studies are never quick and rarely are completed within the projected time lines. The analysis of qualitative data demands a sustained level of creative thought rarely required of the investigator once data are collected in a quantitative study. Qualitative research may be enormously valuable for many purposes, as well as immensely satisfying to the investigator, but quick and easy it is not.

The vital codicil to this discussion of personal factors in selection of a research paradigm is that whatever one's abilities or interests, it still is necessary to match the procedures of inquiry with the purposes of inquiry. Put another way, a close and comfortable match between your abilities and predilections on one hand, and the nature of qualitative research on the other hand, as genuinely desirable as that may be, still will not make it possible to fit round methods into square questions. If you start out committed to doing qualitative research, then you have limited yourself to questions that best yield to that scientific paradigm. Selection of the means for inquiry prior to identification of the question always bears that restriction.

A second preproposal problem centers on the investigator's ability to move out of the quantitative mode of thought. For many graduate students, the process of adopting assumptions that are consistent with the qualitative perspective means breaking well-worn habits of thought. For most of us, the assumptions of quantitative research have been presented and learned as "science" through many years of school and university education. The unspoken premise of the perspective used in the physical and natural sciences is that if something truly exists, it must exist in some quantity, and exist "out there" in some finite form. Although that certainly represents the most extreme formulation of positivist thought, in functional terms it marks the distinction between what is "real" and "not real" in much of our everyday life. To adopt a different and unfamiliar perspective is sometimes more difficult than one might expect.

To think and write in a consistent fashion with the assumption that people construct reality, allowing truth to reside as much in our heads as "out there," requires a sharp alteration in the habits of intellect. Even imperfectly accomplished, this is difficult for most, and, as experience warns us, impossible for some. It is important to confront this problem during the early apprenticeship stage of research training, when patient and sympathetic mentors can assist with the difficult transition between familiar ways of perceiving and conceptualizing, and a different vantage point—the qualitative worldview.

Before making the final decision to go qualitative, there also are logistic questions to consider. Preparation for qualitative research is most effective when it takes the form of apprenticeship, with intensive field experiences and closely supervised opportunities to practice the analysis of actual data. Where those opportunities are not available, some hard questions must be addressed. Will it be cost-effective to acquire training and experience through some alternative source? Is there sufficient time to invest in both a reasonable level of preparation and a lengthy study? Will the best solution be transfer to another department or institution? These are hard questions, but better raised early than too late.

Finally, it is a simple and well-documented fact that in some departments (or whole institutions), qualitative research is not yet an acceptable form of inquiry (Miller, Nelson, & Moore, 1998). Individual professors may undertake to enlighten or reeducate their colleagues, or to work for revision of graduate school policies (written or unwritten), but individual graduate students are likely to find themselves overmatched in any such effort. A realistic appraisal of the political territory, including the existence of precedents and the fate of similar efforts, should come before final commitment to prepare a full-scale proposal. Have qualitative studies actually been accepted by the graduate school? Have potential committee members or needed consultants seen a prospectus or mini-proposal and indicated their willingness to support a clearly qualitative design? How has the human subjects review committee responded to qualitative proposals in the past? Those questions may sound uncomfortably political, but they are eminently practical to raise before you decide to go qualitative.

Having fulfilled our obligation to sound reasonable cautions, however, the last thing we would wish is to leave the impression that the opportunity to do qualitative research is anything less than an exciting, thoroughly fascinating, and deeply fulfilling option. Here is a form of research that invites questions that deal with how real people think and feel. Here is a way to produce findings that are thoroughly grounded in the stuff of a recognizable reality—the world as it is experienced. Finally, here is an opportunity to join with other scholars in an enterprise characterized by fresh ideas, energetic expansion, and as-yet-unexplored possibilities. If all of that sounds appealing to you, then "yes," you should consider going qualitative.

NOTES

———————————————■———————————————

1. The word "paradigm," as used here, denotes a conceptual framework that provides a particular way of thinking about meaning in the context of formal inquiry. Thus, taken collectively,

the beliefs, values, perspectives, commitments, and consequent methods of inquiry shared by a group of investigators constitute a scientific paradigm. Just as each person has a cognitive schema for making sense out of his or her daily experience in the world, scholars who share the assumptions of a paradigm have a particular way of making sense out of their scientific world. Social scientists who perform experiments, for example, share a general perspective on their work that is distinctly different from that shared by investigators who do studies in the feminist tradition of qualitative research. Accordingly, it would be asserted, for example, that experimental (quantitative) and feminist (qualitative) research have their roots in different scientific paradigms. Any modern textbook on qualitative methodology will provide a starting place for defining the qualitative paradigm, but nearly all of them will lead you back to Guba and Lincoln (1994) and Lincoln and Guba (1985), and from there to the modern origins of the term "paradigm" in Kuhn (1970).

2. Our use of the term *quantitative* also is arbitrary. The simple presence of numbers in a study, per se, does not serve to distinguish one paradigm from another. Both quantitative and qualitative research can employ quantification. It is the underlying assumptions about those numbers that provide the distinctive differences.

3. The term *tradition* in this context represents a convention for collectively designating the various distinctive forms of qualitative research. It does not carry the general, common-use sense of something passed down, generation to generation, over a long period of time. Instead, it is employed in the narrower sense of designating a coherent body of precedents intended to govern some set of actions—in this case, a mode of thought and a related set of research procedures. Hence, phenomenological research is a tradition within the qualitative paradigm, as are ethnography, life history, symbolic interactionism, grounded theory, and case studies.

4. Taxonomies for qualitative approaches to research may be extended beyond what has been touched on in the present chapter by including artistic as well as scientific modes of inquiry. For an introduction to that topic, see Eisner (1981) and Thornton (1987).

5. Our use of the term *empirical* here is not employed as it sometimes is in the discipline of philosophy, to designate the family of theories called "empiricism." We use it only in the common-use sense of designating inquiry based on the data of experience, things that the investigator saw or heard that can then be employed as the warrant for a claim. In that sense, all qualitative research is empirical.

6. Readers should be aware that the word "validity" is not commonly used in the rhetoric of qualitative research. In fact, there is considerable discomfort with and even some rejection of the construct. Our decision, nevertheless, to employ it throughout this chapter is based on two simple facts. First, most of our readers will be familiar with the general use of the term to denote a datum that accurately represents the phenomenon to which it refers (it is true), or a research finding for which persuasive evidence has been presented (it is certain). Second, the formal language that has been invented by qualitative researchers to replace the construct of validity is extensive, complex, and far from sufficiently universal to constitute a reliable system language. If you decide to write a proposal for qualitative research, it will be necessary to assimilate this new language (we suggest that you begin with Lincoln and Guba, 1985; Guba and Lincoln; 1989; and Kvale, 1995), but for our present purpose the single term "validity" will suffice.

6

Style and Form in
Writing the Proposal

The writing style of the thesis or grant proposal may be the most important factor in conveying your ideas to graduate advisors or funding agencies. Even experienced researchers must critically evaluate their writing to ensure that the best laid plans are presented in a clear, straightforward fashion. The sections that follow represent primary concerns for proposal writers.

PRAISING, EXHORTING,
AND POLEMICIZING: DON'T

For a variety of motives arising principally from the reward system governing other writing tasks, many students use their proposal as an opportunity to praise the importance of their discipline or professional field. Some use exhortative language to urge such particular points of view as the supposed importance of empirical research in designing professional practice. Others use the proposed research as the basis for espousing the virtues of particular social or political positions.

There is no need or proper place in a research proposal for such subjective side excursions. The purpose of a proposal is to set forth for a reader the exact nature of the matter to be investigated and a detailed account of the methods to be employed. Anything else distracts and serves as an impediment to clear communication.

As a general rule, it is best to stick to the topic and resist the temptation to sound "properly positive and enthusiastic." Do not attempt to manipulate the opinions of the reader in areas other than those essential to the investigation. The simple test is to ask yourself this question: "Does the reader really need to consider this point in order to judge the adequacy of my thinking?" If the answer is "no," then the decision to delete is clear, if not always easy, for the author.

QUOTATIONS: HOW TO PICK FRUIT
FROM THE KNOWLEDGE TREE

Too often, inexperienced writers are inclined to equate the number of citations in a paper with the weight of the argument being presented. This is an error. The proper purposes served by the system of scholarly citation are limited to a few specific tasks. When a document has all the citations needed to meet the demands of those few tasks, it has enough. When it contains more citations, it has too many and is defective in that regard. Reviewers deem the use of nonselective references as an indication of poor scholarship, an inability to discriminate the central from the peripheral and the important from the trivial in research.

The proper uses of direct quotation are even more stringently limited than the use of general citations for paraphrased material. The practice of liberally sprinkling the proposal with quoted material—particularly lengthy quotations— is more than pointless; it is self-defeating. The first truth is that no one will read them. The second truth is that most readers find the presence of unessential quotations irritating and a distraction from the line of thought being presented for examination. When quotations are introduced at points for which even general citations are unnecessary, the writer has displayed clear disregard for the reader.

There are two legitimate motives for direct use of another scholar's words: (a) the weight of authoritative judgment, in which "who said it" is of critical importance, and (b) the nature of expression, in which "how it was said" is the important element. In the former instance, when unexpected, unusual, or genu- inely pivotal points are to be presented, it is reasonable to show the reader that another competent craftsperson has reached exactly the desired conclusion, or observed exactly the event at issue. In the latter instance, when another writer has hit on the precise, perfect phrasing to express a difficult point, it is proper to employ that talent on behalf of your own argument. The rule to follow is simple. If the substance of a quotation can be conveyed by a careful paraphrase, followed, of course, by the appropriate credit of a citation, with all the clarity and persuasive impact of the original, *then don't quote*. In almost all instances, it is best for the proposer to speak directly to the reader. The intervention of words from a third party should be reserved, like heavy cannon in battle, for those rare instances when the targets are specific and truly critical to the outcome of the contest.

A beneficial technique for students who recognize their own propensity toward excessive quotation is to use the critical summary form of note-taking. In this format, after carefully recording a full citation, each article is critically examined and then paraphrased on reference cards in the student's own words. During note-taking, a decision is made on whether the aesthetics of phrasing or the author's importance in terms of authority justify the use of direct quotation. Except in rare instances, quoted material is not transferred to the note cards. Thus, direct quoting becomes less tempting during the subsequent writing phase when the student has recourse to notes. This technique also prevents unintentional plagiarism.

If using a computer for note storage and retrieval, similar precautions should be taken. When retrieving information from the computer, you should make certain that each item can clearly be identified either as your paraphrase or as a direct quotation. It is possible to lose this information as you switch back and forth between notes, computer, and proposal document. One way to ensure identification, which can be used both on the computer and on handwritten note cards, is to use quotation marks for all direct quotations, listing the page number on which the text was found in parentheses immediately after the closing quotation mark. As you work between notes, computer, and writing of the proposal, transfer all of this to your draft.

CLARITY AND PRECISION: SPEAKING IN SYSTEM LANGUAGE

The language we use in the commerce of our everyday lives is common language. We acquired our common language vocabulary and grammar by a process that was gradual, unsystematic, and mostly unconscious. Our everyday language serves us well, at least as long as the inevitable differences in word meanings assigned by different people do not produce serious failures of communication.

The language of science, specifically the language of research, is uncommon. The ongoing conversation of science, for which a research proposal is a plan of entry, is carried on in system languages in which each word must mean one thing to both writer and reader. Where small differences may matter a great deal, as in research, there must be a minimum of slippage between the referent object, the word used to stand for the object, and the images called forth by the word in the minds of listeners and readers.

The rules of invariant word usage give system languages a high order of precision. Minute or subtle distinctions can be made with relative ease. Evaluative language can be eliminated or clearly segregated from empirical descriptive language. More important, however, the language of research affords the reliability of communication that permits scientists to create a powerful interdependent research enterprise rather than limited independent investigations. When a chemist uses the system language of chemistry to communicate with another chemist, the word "element" has one and only one referent, is assigned to that referent on all occasions, is used for no other purpose within the language system, and consistently evokes the same image in the minds of everyone, everywhere, who has mastered the language.

Various domains of knowledge and various research enterprises are characterized by differing levels of language development. Some disciplines, such as anatomy or entomology, have highly developed and completely regularized language systems, whereas others, particularly the behavioral sciences, employ languages still in the process of development. Irrespective of the area of investigation, however, the language of any research proposal must, as a minimum requirement, be systematic within itself. The words used in the proposal must have referents that are clear to the reader, and each must consistently designate only one referent. When the investigation lies within a subject area with an existing language system, then, of course, the author is bound to the conventions of that system.

Obviously, the researcher should be familiar with the system languages that function in the area of proposed investigation. Reading and writing both the specific language of the subject matter area and the more general languages common to the proposed methodology (statistics, experimental design, psychometrics, computer languages, etc.) are clear requirements for any study. Less obvious, however, is the fact that research proposals, by their exploratory nature, often demand the extension of existing language into new territory. Operations, observations, concepts, and relationships not previously specified within a language system must be assigned invariant word symbols by the investigator. More important, the reader must carefully be drawn into the agreement to make these same assignments.

Advisors and reviewers misunderstand student proposals far more often then they disagree with what is proposed. The failure of communication often occurs precisely at the point where the proposal moves beyond the use of the existing system language. This problem involves a failure of careful invention rather than a failure of mastering technique or subject matter. The following rules may be of some help as the student attempts to translate a personal vision of the unknown into the form of a carefully specified public record.

1. Never invent new words when the existing system language is adequate. If the referent in established use has a label that excludes what you do not want and includes all that you do want, then it needs no new name.

2. If there is reasonable doubt as to whether the word is in the system or the common domain, provide early in the proposal the definition that will be used throughout. Readers may give unnecessary time and attention to deciphering the intended meaning unless you put their minds at ease.

3. Words that have been assigned system meaning should not be used in their common language form. For example, the word "significant" should not be used to denote its common language meaning of "important" in a proposal involving the use of statistical analysis. The system language of inferential statistics assigns invariant meaning to the word "significant"; any other use invites confusion.

4. Where a system language word is to be used in either a more limited or a more expanded sense, make this clear when the word first is introduced in the proposal. If the norms for local style requirements permit, this is one of the legitimate uses of footnotes to the text.

5. Where it is necessary to assign invariant meaning to a common language word to communicate about something not already accommodated within the system language, the author should choose with great care. Words with strong evaluative overtones, words with a long history of ambiguity, and words that have wellen-trenched usage in common language make poor candidates for elevation to system status. No matter how carefully the author operationalizes the new definition, it is always difficult for the reader to make new responses to familiar stimuli.

6. A specific definition is the best way to assign invariant meaning to a word. When only one or two words require such treatment, this can be accomplished in the text. A larger number of words may be set aside in a section of the proposal devoted to definitions. The best definition is one that describes the operations that are required

to produce or observe the event or object. For example, note how the following words are assigned special meaning for the purpose of a proposal.

    a. A common language word is assigned invariant use:
       Exclusion will be deemed to have occurred when both of the following happen: The student no longer is eligible to participate in extracurricular activities under any provision of school district policy, and the student's name is stricken from the list of students eligible for extracurricular activities.

    b. A system language word is employed with limitations not ordinarily assigned:
       The curriculum will be limited to those after-school activities that the current *School District Manual* lists as approved for secondary school students.

    c. A system language word is operationalized by describing a criterion:
       Increased motivation will be presumed when, subsequent to any treatment condition, the time spent in any extracurricular activity rises more than 10% of the previous weekly total.

    d. A common language word is operationalized by describing a criterion:
       Dropouts are defined as all participants who fail to attend three consecutive activity meetings.

    e. A system language word is operationalized by describing procedure:
       Reinforcement will refer to the procedure of listing all club members in the school newspaper, providing special hall passes for members, and listing club memberships on school transcripts.

    f. A common language word is operationalized by describing procedure:
       Instruction will consist of five 10-minute sessions in which the club sponsor may employ any method of teaching so long as it includes no fewer than five attempts for each student to complete the activity.

EDITING: THE CARE AND
NURTURE OF A DOCUMENT

A proposal is a working document. As a primary vehicle for communication with advisors and funding agencies, as a plan for action, and as a contract, the proposal performs functions that are immediate and practical, not symbolic or aesthetic. Precisely because of these important functions, the proposal, in all its public appearances at least, should be free from distracting mechanical errors and the irritating confusion of shoddy format.

At the privacy of your own desk, it is entirely appropriate to cross out passages, add new ones, and rearrange the order of paragraphs. The series of rough drafts is part of the process through which a proposal evolves toward final form. When, however, the proposal is given to an advisor, sent to a funding agency, or presented to a seminar, the occasion is public and calls for an edited, formally prepared document. The document should be easy to read—for which a good printer and high-quality duplication are the first essentials.

Every sentence must be examined and reexamined in terms of its clarity, grammar, and relationship with surrounding sentences. A mark of the neophyte writer is the tendency to resist changing a sentence once it is written, and even more so when it has been typed. A sentence may be grammatically correct and still be awkward within its surroundings. The tough test is the best test here. If, in reading any sentence, a colleague or reviewer hesitates, stumbles, or has to reread the sentence to understand the content, then the sentence must be examined for possible revision—no matter how elegant, obvious, and precise it seems to the author.

Aside from meticulous care in writing and rewriting, the most helpful procedure in editorial revision is to obtain the assistance of colleagues to read the proposal for mechanical errors, lack of clarity, and inadequacies of content. An author can read the same error over and over without recognizing it, and the probability of discovery declines with each review. The same error may leap at once to the attention of even the most casual reader who is reading the proposal for the first time. One useful trick that may improve the author's ability to spot mechanical errors is to read the sentences in reverse order, thus destroying the strong perceptual set created by the normal sequence of ideas.

Although format will be a matter of individual taste or departmental or agency regulation, several general rules may be used in designing the layout of the document:

1. Use double spacing, substantial margins, and ample separation for major subsections. Crowding makes reading both difficult and unpleasant. *Always* number pages so that readers can quickly refer to a specific location.

2. Make ample use of graphic illustration. A chart or simple diagram can improve clarity and ease the difficult task of critical appraisal and advisement.

3. Make careful and systematic use of headings. The system of headings recommended in the *Publication Manual of the American Psychological Association* (1994) is particularly useful for the design of proposals.

4. Place in an appendix everything that is not immediately essential to the main tasks of the proposal. Allowing readers to decide whether they will read supplementary material is both a courtesy and good strategy.

IN SEARCH OF A TITLE:
FIRST IMPRESSIONS AND THE ROUTE TO RETRIEVAL
————————————■————————————

The title of the proposal is the first contact a reader has with the proposed research. First impressions, be they about people, music, food, or potential research topics, generate powerful anticipations about what is to follow. Shocking the reader by implying one content domain in the title and following with a different one in the body of the proposal is certain to evoke a strong negative response. The first rule in composing a title is to achieve reasonable parity between the images evoked by the title and the opening pages of the proposal.

For the graduate student, the proposal title may well become the thesis or dissertation title and therefore calls for careful consideration of all the functions it must serve and the standards by which it will be judged. The first function of the title is to identify content for the purpose of retrieval. Theses and dissertations are much more retrievable than was once the case. In fact, they have become a part of the public domain of the scholar. The increasing use of microfiche and microfilm has made the circulation of unpublished documents many times faster and far broader in geographic scope. Titling research has become, thereby, an important factor in sharing research.

In less sophisticated times, titles could be carelessly constructed and the documents would still be discovered by diligent researchers who could take the time to investigate items that appeared only remotely related to their interests. Today, scholars stagger under the burden of sifting through enormous and constantly increasing quantities of material apparently pertinent to their domain. There is no recourse other than to be increasingly selective in choosing which documents to actually retrieve and inspect. Hence, each title the researcher scans must present at least a moderate probability of being pertinent, on the basis of the title alone, or it will not be included on the reading list for review. In short, the degree to which the title communicates a concise, thorough, and unambiguous picture of the content is the first factor governing whether a given report will enter the ongoing dialogue of the academic community.

Word selection should be governed more by universality of usage than by personal aesthetic judgment or peculiarly local considerations. Computer retrieval systems, on which more and more scholars are depending for leads to related studies in their research field, classify titles according to a limited set of keywords. As we discussed in Chapter 4, researchers construct search plans that will identify all studies categorized by keywords known to be associated with their area of interest. Thus, both readers and writers of research reports must describe the research in similar terms or, in too many instances, they will not reach each other.

The title should describe as accurately as possible the exact nature of the main elements in the study. Although such accuracy demands the use of specific language, the title should be free of obscure technical terms or jargon that will be recognized only by small groups of researchers who happen to pursue similar questions within a narrow band of the knowledge domain.

Components Appropriate
for Inclusion in the Title

The elements most commonly considered for inclusion in the title are the dependent and independent variables, the performance component represented by the criterion task or tasks, the treatment or treatments to be administered, the model underlying the study, the purpose of the study (predicting, establishing relationships, or determining differences), and any unusual contribution of the study.

Dependent and independent variables ordinarily should be included, although they may be presented under a more general rubric. For instance, the independent variables of a study might be simple reaction time, discriminatory reaction time, movement time, and reflex time. In the title, the four measures might appear as "neuromuscular responses." Similarly, the performance components of the study also may be summarized into a single categorical term.

A clever author can, by careful selection of words, provide information in the title that a theory is being tested by using a word that often is associated with the theory. For instance, the title "Generalizability of Contingency Management and Reinforcement in Second-Grade Special Education Classes" implies that the investigator is testing the applicability of behavioral theory to a specific population. Much has been communicated by including the single word "generalizability" in the title.

The ultimate purpose of the study in terms of predicting, establishing relationships, or determining differences can be expressed without providing an explicit statement. For example, when variables are expressed in a series, such as "Anthropometrics, Swimming Speed, and Shoulder-Girdle Strength," a relationship generally is implied. If the same study were titled "Anthropometrics and Shoulder-Girdle Strength of Fast and Slow Swimmers," the reader would anticipate a study in which differences were determined.

Any aspect of the study that is particularly unusual in terms of methodology, or that represents a unique contribution to the literature, should be included in the title. A treatment that is unusually long or of great magnitude (e.g., "Longitudinal Analysis of Human Short-Term Memory From Age 20 to Age 80"), a method of observation that is creative or unusually accurate (e.g., "Hand Preference in Telephone Use as a Measure of Limb Dominance and Laterality"), a sampling technique that is unique (e.g., "Intelligence of Children Whose Parents Own Personal Computers"), and a particular site for measurement that sets the study apart from others (e.g., "Perceptual Judgment in a Weightless Environment: Report From the Space Shuttle") are examples of such aspects.

Components Inappropriate for Inclusion in the Title

Such factors as population, research design, and instrumentation should not be included in the title unless they represent a substantial departure from similar studies. The population, for instance, should not be noted unless it is a population never sampled before, or is in some way an unusual target group. In the title "Imbedded Figures Acuity in World-Class Chess Masters," the population of the subjects is critical to the rationale for the study. The population in "Running Speed, Leg Strength, and Long Jump Performance of High School Boys" is not important enough to occupy space in the title.

Similarly, research design and instrumentation are not appropriate for inclusion in the title unless they represent an unusual approach to measurement or analysis. The type of research method expressed in "Physiological Analysis of Precompetitive Stress" is common in studies dealing with stress, and surely some other aspect of the study would make a more informative contribution to the title. The approach in "Phenomenological Analysis of Precompetitive Stress," however, represents a unique approach and signals the reader that the report contains information of an unusual kind.

Mechanics of Titling

Mechanically, the title should be concise and should provide comfortable reading, free from elaborate or jarring constructions. Excessive length should be avoided because it dilutes the impact of the key elements presented; two lines generally should be adequate. Some retrieval systems place a word limitation on titles, thus enforcing brevity. Redundancies such as "Aspects of," "Comments on," "Study of," "Investigation of," "Inquiry Into," and "An Analysis of" are expendable. It is obvious that a careful investigation of a topic will include "aspects of" the topic, whereas the research report has as its entire purpose the communication of "comments on" the findings of a study. It is pointless to state the obvious in a title.

Attempts to include all subtopics of a study in the title sometimes result in elephantine rubrics. The decision to include or exclude mention of a subtopic should be made less in terms of an abstraction, such as complete coverage, and more in terms of whether inclusion actually will facilitate appropriate retrieval. One useful way to construct a title is to list all the elements that seem appropriate for inclusion, and then to weave them into various permutations until a title appears that satisfies both technical and aesthetic standards.

7

—=▢=—

The Oral Presentation

The processes for consideration of your proposal may not require an oral presentation, and the written document may be the only opportunity to explain (and sell) the study. In many universities, however, formal presentation of your ideas for a thesis or dissertation (particularly at the point of an initial prospectus) is a standard expectation, often performed in the context of a graduate seminar. It is less common to have an opportunity to make an oral presentation of a grant proposal, but interviews with site visitors and even command performances before review panels do occur.

Our advice is that if an opportunity occurs to stand up before an audience and talk about what you propose to do—you should take it. Even if your oral presentation is only to your peers in a study or support group, do it! The feedback and exchange of ideas may prove to be invaluable as you shape the final form of the written document. Further, such exercises are excellent preparation for a later thesis or dissertation defense—the final hurdle before graduation at many institutions.

Of equal importance, however, is the valuable training in research presentation skills that will be used when you have later opportunities to share your completed work. Whether with teachers at a local school, with students and faculty at a nearby college, with professional colleagues at a state conference, or in the rarified atmosphere of an international research symposium, talking about your study and findings is an important extension of the research process. Learning to do it with clarity, economy, and confidence will serve both you and your audiences well—and explaining your proposal is the perfect way to develop and refine those skills.

We do not propose to give a tutorial here on public speaking. What we will do, however, is note those points at which the task of explaining research to a live audience creates demands that require thoughtful preparation. Careful planning is as much needed for presenting a proposed study as for reporting its results.

A slick presentation will not finesse a weak design, but a clear explanation of dilemmas encountered and hard choices yet to be made will improve the quality of assistance you receive. Further, a brisk and economical presentation recruits support because it shows that you understand exactly what is salient for a reviewer's consideration. Best of all, at the other end of the research process, a graceful and lucid discussion of your findings will allow others to share the fruits of your labor—and may even produce invitations to present your work to fellow investigators in exciting and distant venues.

Before launching into a consideration of oral presentations, it will be helpful to review briefly how talking about research is different from writing about it. Each of these differences bears consequences for how the task of speaking is planned and executed.

1. *Time*—The temporal limits for explaining your study to a live audience invariably are more restrictive than the time requirements for accomplishing a written presentation of the same study. Put another way, 20 minutes of a listener's time allow you to cover far less than 20 minutes of a reader's time. The reasons for this are complex and not all of them are obvious, but the end result is a demand for selectivity in content and economy in delivery. Finally, because the listener is not free to go back and hear a presentation over again, as a reader is free to restudy a text, the speaker must achieve absolute clarity on the first attempt.

2. *Interaction*—Oral presentations of research almost always include interchange with the audience. Indeed, in the case of presenting a proposal for a committee or seminar, that exchange is the purpose of the occasion, some or all of the audience having already read your prospectus or full proposal. Questions, comments, advice, and discussion often follow the talk and sometimes are interspersed within the flow of presentation. This fact not only calls for the use of interactive skills (at the least, the need to think on your feet) but has consequences for planning and delivery as well.

3. *Adjustment*—The speaker can monitor the ongoing reactions of a live audience, responding to the array of nonverbal signals by adjusting pace and content.

Boredom, puzzlement, surprise, distraction, and close interest are not visible on the reader's face while you are writing. While you speak, however, all of them can be observed from moment to moment, and such reactions can be useful information. Responding in appropriate ways not only increases the effectiveness of communication but also ties speaker and audience together in a mutual enterprise that is impossible to achieve through the written page.

4. *Anxiety*—If the range of skills demanded for speaking is not wider than the collective span of those needed for writing, at the least, many of them are different. For most students, the skills for making formal oral presentations are much less used, and thereby are less well honed. The need to display unpracticed skills in a public setting, when added to the normal concern about winning approval or obtaining needed assistance, produces an occasion for anxiety. For some, the spontaneous variables at play in a live setting add zest and a sense of rich possibility. For others, a live listening audience simply adds a discomfort for which there is no parallel in the work of writing. For those people, the consequence is a need to prepare in such a way that anxiety (or outright terror) is held within bounds and becomes facilitating arousal rather than debilitating inhibition.

Those are some of the most distinctive differences between writing and speaking. Their existence means that preparing and delivering an oral presentation involves all the problems of using a new medium to communicate familiar content. Accordingly, we have some advice that may provide users of this book with a helpful set of guidelines for getting started. Our suggestions cluster into seven areas that occur in natural sequence: (a) preparing content, (b) preparing materials, (c) practice and revision, (d) preparing the environment, (e) oral presentation, (f) managing interaction, and (g) the aftermath. What we have to say about each of these topics will seem different, in some respects, from what you may have seen in books or heard in public speaking courses. There are several reasons for that, and knowing them may help you digest what is to follow.

First, our advice is tailored to the task of talking about research to other researchers, or, at the least, to people who have working familiarity with scholarship. Customs of language, format, and demeanor allow (or demand) a form of communication that is different from what would be appropriate with another kind of audience. Although much may be shared among all kinds of public speaking, we are not dealing in this text with a generic form of public discourse. Second, the source here is our own experience as people who have frequent occasion to do oral presentations dealing with research. Although that background certainly is helpful in sorting out ideas about what distinguishes effective from ineffective public speaking, it does not provide much occasion to move from specific rules to higher order generalizations. We are not communication specialists, nor are we competent to offer a tutorial on effective use of language. This chapter is about "how to do it," not "how to understand it."

PREPARING CONTENT

In determining what to cover, the particulars of circumstance will dictate most of the decisions. How long do you have? Who will be present, and what will they expect you to do? What will the audience already know? What will your listeners need to learn from you to play their part in the occasion? For your purpose, what is absolutely essential to explain, and what is not? What content requires emphasis, and what may be given only a passing note? To what extent must you contend with uneven prior knowledge on the part of members of the audience? Is the presentation a follow-up of a previously distributed document (a review leading into discussion), or is it the only access the audience will have to your work? If you can specify the answers to those questions, you will have a rough map of what to include in your presentation. In the process of using that map, the following guidelines will assist in shaping the final product.

1. Don't confuse what you already know with what the members of the audience already know. If there was not something they needed to learn from you, why would you be doing the presentation? The right question to start with is *not* "What do I want to talk about?" or "What is in my proposal?" or "What were my results?" The right questions are "What don't they know that they need or want to know?" and "In what order do they need to learn things to make sense of what I have to say?" You are going to lead the listeners through a sequence of logic, or the events of a study, step by step. In that sense, a research presentation is teaching, not ritual display. You begin with, stay with, and end with a concern for what you want your audience to learn. That requires a highly selected version of what you know.

2. In deciding what to cover in the time you have available, less often is more. People will understand more, remember more, and make better use (in subsequent discussion) of what you explain if you explain less. Locate the essentials and make them the center of your presentation. It often will serve you well to note for the audience particular sections of detail you are leaving out (or simply designating by name) and, perhaps, why you are doing so. You even may make clear that you have the material and would be pleased to provide it at another time. That strategy prevents people from being distracted by thoughts about what you are not saying. Having less to talk about allows an easier pace; more opportunity for emphasis, illustration, and review; and less tension in the whole process.

If it is genuinely impossible to communicate what is essential to the purpose of the presentation in the time provided, don't complain about it in your speech. Negotiate an extension of your time, ask for a change in the goals to be accomplished by the presentation, or, as a last resort, make brief public note of what it has been necessary to exclude. Trying to crowd everything in is a lose-lose proposition. It won't work, it will irritate your audience, and it will leave you feeling inadequate.

3. Try to anticipate the needs and reactions of your audience, and build this in as part of your presentation. As with the point made above about noting omissions, there are a number of predictable concerns or needs among audience members that can be dealt with as you proceed. If there is a point about which you are unsure, acknowledge it and invite comment or advice in the following discussion. If there is a point on which you know some of the audience will disagree with what you say, make a polite note of the fact—and perhaps invite subsequent discussion of alternatives. If some people already know something that must be explained for others, recognize the situation and ask those who don't need your tutorial to bear with you. If there has been discussion about a point on a previous occasion, or if there have been revisions in or additions to your work, note them, even if you elect not to discuss them.

All of this serves to assure the audience that you are thinking specifically about them and that you are aware of their unique relationships with the content of your presentation. In addition to helping to maintain their close attention, this strategy allows you to maintain a degree of control (or, at least, influence) over what will be given attention in any discussion that ensues.

PREPARING MATERIALS

Unless you are blessed with the happy facility of perfect memory, the primary task here is to prepare something to guide your presentation. The most obvious purpose of the guide (or script) is to ensure that you say the right things, about the right topics, in the right order. Less obvious are the reasons for trying so hard to get it right—the fact that you have just one chance to achieve transparent clarity, and the fact that making things easy for the audience is the best way to get them to be helpful (and friendly).

It does not matter what form your guide takes, so long as it serves the purpose of getting it right and is constructed to allow effective delivery of your message. The first rule of delivery is *never read!* The second rule is *if you have to read, never appear to be doing so!* By disconnecting speaker and listeners, reading defeats the purpose of doing an oral presentation. It is impossible for the audience to feel other than insulted. Accordingly, your guide has to take a form that allows you to spend most of your time looking at and reacting to your audience, and only brief instants being reminded of what comes next.

The possibilities for accomplishing this are endless. They range from small note cards with key words listed in bold type, through pages of text in traditional outline format, to verbatim scripts with key words or phrases highlighted in fluorescent colors. In designing your own guide, however, remember that there are other needs to be serviced beyond having a memory aid. For example, whatever you use should be visible in a way that requires only a quick glance to find your location and pick up a cue to trigger recall of the next sequence. If you want to move about while speaking, then your guide should be comfortably portable. Pages should be boldly numbered in sequence to avoid the unfortunate accident of missing or jumbled notes, and reminders for the use of each visual aid should be inserted exactly where it is to be introduced.

As an example, this is what one of the present authors does for each presentation. A rough script is typed with double spacing. Some sentences are laid out in complete form, whereas others are indicated just by the opening phrase. All, however, begin at the left margin (essentially, the format is a sequential list of individual sentences). Only the top one third of each sheet is used, the lower two thirds being left entirely blank. Then the typed pages are darkened and enlarged by 10% on a copy machine. (On a computer, all of this could be accomplished by using a larger font and the top half of the page.) Finally, a key word or phrase in each sentence is marked with a highlighter pen.

Placed on a lectern, the script, which occupies only the top portion of the page, now rests at a level directly on the speaker's line of sight to the audience. All the highlighted words are read from peripheral vision, and eye contact with the audience is never broken by having to look down to read the lower portion of the page. Sheets are transferred silently from right to left as used and never become visible distractions for the listeners. The effect given is that of articulate, completely extemporaneous speech, delivered with close attention to the audience.

Some of what the audience sees and hears is illusion, made possible by the idiosyncratic speaking guide described above—a guide that, in truth, serves to disguise a poor memory and poor eyesight. In a like fashion, you must devise a guide that will best serve your unique strengths and limitations as a speaker. The purpose is not to enhance your reputation for oral presentation beyond what you deserve. The purpose is to serve each audience—by making it easy for its members to understand what you have to say.

Another strategy that many speakers use is to place key words and phrases on slides or overhead transparencies. This can be very effective for several reasons. It allows you full freedom to move around, and the display of key words helps the audience remember your main points. This strategy, however, has two potential drawbacks. One is irksome and the other is disastrous. Having the words on the screen tempts the speaker to look at the screen instead of the audience. The second potential problem is that the slide or overhead projector can break down, leaving you with no guide at all. A paper copy of your slides or transparencies, with a few extra notes, allows you the freedom to use either slides or notes and should prevent any serious disaster.

In addition to some form of speaking guide, you may wish to prepare aids that will support your oral presentation. There are several reasons for electing to do so. Not the least of these is the fact that any audience of more than a few individuals will contain some people who learn best (or only) when they can inspect a concrete example. The more complex the object or relationship, the more they are disadvantaged by purely verbal imagery. Photographs, models, tables, figures, graphs, outlines, data specimens, diagrams, and demonstrations are just a few of the supporting illustrations that can give your words concrete representation.

There are other important reasons to consider the use of graphic aids. Economy of communication is one. Although not all pictures can replace a thousand words, some certainly can. Other graphics, such as diagrams or key word outlines, help the audience keep track of sequence and relationship in otherwise convoluted explanations. A good example is a flowchart that helps you take your audience through your methodology. Finally, some illustrations provide focus and heighten impact, as in an audiotape segment or transcript excerpt from an interview.

In deciding whether to make use of such aids, subject each possibility to this basic question: "Will the prop really help people (or at least some people) to understand what I am saying?" If you can't honestly conclude that introducing the supplement to your presentation will cause better or quicker learning, don't use it. Each use of an aid consumes valuable time. Each requires the transfer of audience attention from one object to another, with consequent risk of leaving someone behind. Each, therefore, involves a trade-off to be weighed with great care. Be sure your audience gets back more than it has to give.

One simple aid is almost always appropriate. An outline of what you plan to talk about (and do), laid out in sequence, is appreciated by most listeners. Keep it to a single sheet, include no details, and indicate beginning and ending times. Knowing what is to come (and being able to tick off major segments as they are completed) is a reassuring convenience. It also is the first sign of careful planning and concern for the listeners.

Visual aids such as slides, transparencies, newsprint diagrams, and chalkboard illustrations should be *used*—not simply displayed. Present them, explain their significance, allow the audience a brief moment to digest or ask questions, and then remove the aid from sight, firmly directing attention to the next element of the presentation. Leaving aids visible invites continued inspection or simple distraction (as with the case of projectors running without a slide or transparency in place).

There is a hard rule about quality for visual aids, one never to be violated. *If you use it, everyone should be able to see it!* Large print, high magnification, sharp contrast, and reduction of content to bare essentials are basic qualifications for any illustration. Further, every aid has to be judged relative to the limitations of the environment in which you will be speaking. If it can't be seen by everyone, in every part of the room, don't use it. Under most circumstances, this disqualifies newsprint, chalkboards, and even overhead projectors for any but small group presentations. In such cases, slide projectors or handout sheets are the better choice.

We would be remiss if we did not acknowledge the availability of technologies for the production and display of graphic material that now have relegated chalkboards, overhead projectors, and, perhaps, even the 35 mm carousel slide projector to the status of horse and buggy artifacts. Among those are computer-driven video panels and projectors that permit computer images to be projected directly on the screen, Internet-linked projection, and integrated slide and videotape presentations.

Perhaps even more directly relevant to preparation for a typical student oral presentation are equipment and software that allow the creation of both an original graphic and the necessary slide or videotape with a desktop computer. Some software programs allow you to print out miniaturized copies of your slides. Lined spaces adjacent to each slide allow members of the audience to conveniently take notes or write questions as they listen. To all that magic we say, "Use it, if you have it!" But do profit from the experience of many students (and professors) who have entered the new wonderland of graphic technology before you. You might wish to copy these simple rules and pin them over your computer.

1. No matter what it says on the box, you can bet that effective use of software will take more time and more skill than you expect. Learn how to use any new method for production of graphics well in advance of need—and practice several times.

2. Remember that with the best equipment and software in the world, if there is any step in the process that depends on someone else (e.g., film developing, slide duplicating, tape editing, scanning), they may not be able to meet your demand for last-minute service. Give everyone involved, including yourself, plenty of time.

3. If a computer is involved in any step in the process, save early, save often, and save again!

4. Some of the same familiar rules that applied to now antique equipment still apply to high-tech displays. For example, don't clutter anything you show the audience—"white space" is a virtue when it serves to frame and enhance what you really want people to see. That applies as much to a video panel as it did to magic lantern projectors or filmstrips.

5. When you want people to listen to you, as in transitions between slides or tape segments, don't distract them with too much action of any kind. Even changes in color background or framing in a display can engage attention at the wrong location.

6. Until you become a practiced expert, pay attention to the suggestions for color schemes that accompany production software. What looks really cool (to you) on your monitor may turn into a disastrous chromatic soup when projected onto a large screen. Even worse, some colors dim or even disappear when printed on certain types of slide film. If you do not leave enough time to preview *and correct* such defects, you will be in the unenviable position of asking your audience to "imagine" a line running from point a to point b.

7. Technologies, particularly those involving computer projectors, become doubly prone to catastrophic failure when you try to employ them as a visitor in an unfamiliar venue. Connecting cables, port specifications, type of projector resolution, and other compatibility problems must be resolved in advance—a difficult accomplishment over the telephone, and often an impossible one at short notice. Under those conditions, our advice is to be old fashioned and at least bring a backup. A carousel tray full of slides makes for a good sleep the night before.

8. Make certain you know how to use all the equipment required for your presentation—including what to do should any item malfunction. The time you take to learn and practice will be repaid by a smooth and satisfying performance. Using part of your presentation time to figure out what just went wrong—and what to do next—not only will distract your audience but also is likely to leave you flustered and prone to make other blunders. Electronic aids can be a wonderful enhancement for virtually any presentation. They also are a prime target for Murphy's Law—if anything can come unplugged, it probably will!

Some presentation formats appropriately utilize a continuous stream of graphic aids, as in large-scale lectures. Those special instances aside, the rule again is that less usually will be more. Even with high-quality graphics, there is the risk that overuse of aids will dilute the focus of what you are saying and begin to intrude between you and the audience. Select only the aids that will advance your cause, use them deliberately for that purpose, then never let them remain as distractors. As a general rule, with you to point out what is salient, a well-constructed aid should yield its main message in a few seconds and should do so for everyone in the room. This means that for your audience, illustrations should feel like a natural continuation of the presentation rather than an interruption.

PRACTICE AND REVISION

Explaining any research study, or its results, is a difficult task. To the extent that you genuinely care about communicating with an audience, it will be natural and proper to do the job well. If the quality of presentation enhances or restricts the possibility of achieving your goal, practice makes sense. To do so also signals respect for a significant form of craft knowledge in the world of scholarship, a craft that will serve your work—even if you are just explaining a proposal to the members of a small committee.

There are three main varieties of practice: silent reading, solitary speaking, and trial runs before a live audience. Silent reading gives familiarity to the guide and gradually allows memory to free attention from the bondage of literal reading. It does not, however, give a correct estimate of time required (silent reading always is faster than reading aloud) or give any clue as to how what you say will sound in the ears of an audience.

In contrast, solitary speaking gives both a better estimate of timing and an opportunity to listen to the sounds and sequences of your presentation. You will discover that the syntaxes and rhythms of written text are not those of normal speech, and adjustments will be required if you are to avoid the stilted and unnatural sound of reading aloud. The most common adjustments are simplification of content (often by painful excisions), longer pauses, and more frequent use of words that provide transition between topics.

The use of a mirror, a lectern, and a tape recorder can markedly increase the value of solitary practice, particularly if you now include actual use of graphic aids. This kind of practice accelerates both the fine tuning needed to give confidence and acquisition of automaticity in performing mechanical tasks—such as managing your note cards. The latter is vital because it allows you to spend more and more time looking into the mirror that is standing in for a live audience.

Finally, practice before a real audience allows you to move toward personalization, the ability to speak with the relaxed informality of serious conversations in everyday social interaction. We say "move toward" because there are some conventions that govern formal presentations that are absent in ordinary conversation. Just the matter of how long one person speaks, who controls the topic, and who is free to interrupt mark the rules of formal presentation as different. The intent to instruct (and influence) also is different, not in kind, but in the degree of conscious purpose. Those distinctions (and others) notwithstanding, the audience always is made more comfortable and attentive by a speaker who adopts the tone and cadence of "talking with" rather than "talking at." To achieve that kind of grace, nothing equals live practice.

Friends, relatives, peers, and professors can be drafted for the purpose of live practice. The only absolute qualification is a desire to help you prepare. Of course, the presence of anyone with sufficient background to raise questions about content can elevate the trial to a new level. Questions and comments allow you to revise defective explanations or, at the least, to anticipate reactions and to determine whether the questions raised reveal problems in the proposed study that you must address or whether the questions reflect only an inadequate explanation. Further, now you can practice using aids in ways that truly support rather than interrupt, and now you will discover how much longer everything is going to take than you had first imagined.

Even though not everyone in the audience may be able to help you with the details of the study, all are competent to give feedback about your delivery. Once they understand that critique of practice is helpful (albeit sometimes disconcerting) and not destructive, anyone can notice and report distractors such as the ubiquitous "OK?" or "aaah" that so often intrude without the speaker's awareness. Gestures or postures that erode audience attention such as rubbing the nose, gripping the lectern with white knuckles, staring fixedly above the heads of listeners, swaying from side to side, making eye contact only with individuals on the left, and fiddling with a pointer are so common as to be almost predictable in novice speakers. Good friends will tell you all about them.

When live practice and feedback yield substantial revisions, second and third trials may be needed. A good practice sequence to follow is solitary speaking followed by three presentations to (a) two or three good friends, (b) your advisor, and finally (c) a small group of people who have some competence in research—all prior to the official presentation of your proposal. The limit often is the availability (and goodwill) of your colleagues. Although there may be some theoretical risk of over-practice, it is unlikely to be a serious concern. As with any other task, work at it until you get it right, and then get on with the job.

PREPARING THE ENVIRONMENT

The rule about the environment, the space where you will actually present, is simple: *"Know it, and manipulate it!"* This means that you should inspect the room and arrange it (so far as possible) to suit your purpose. Where particular people sit and the general configuration of seating (as around a table or in a room with freely movable chairs) are first-order concerns. The presence of a lectern, location of light switches, the availability of doors to shut out distracting noise, and the location of power outlets (if in doubt, always bring an extension cord) are all essential information.

If there is a wall-mounted projection screen you intend to use, always pull it down for inspection. More than one unwary novice has discovered an obscene message scrawled there for all to contemplate as the introduction to the first slide! In larger venues, sound systems, projector stands, and lectern lights are never to be taken for granted.

If you are planning to employ one or more assistants to help with demonstrations or the operation of equipment, have them come with you. Where they will sit, how well they can see you, and their familiarity with the environment are matters for your concern.

If you plan to use handouts, having a packet already in place as people enter the room avoids the confusion of later distribution and signals a businesslike atmosphere. If you include a program outline, it can be placed on top with names marked so that advisors or special visitors can have precedence in seating. It always is good to have the most important listeners located where you can keep the closest possible contact with them during your presentation.

The more you can reduce unexpected intrusions and the more you can make the environment comfortable for the audience, the more closely they will attend what you have to say. Take the time to inspect the field of action. If there is not much you can do to adjust it in your favor, at the least let it hold no surprises.

ORAL PRESENTATION

—————————————■—————————————

There are two things most novice speakers do not know (or find difficult to remember). First, virtually everyone is nervous before a public presentation. That is normal and, once you learn how to turn that excitement to your advantage, healthy. A second point is that under almost all imaginable circumstances, everyone in the audience wants you to do well. Even more, most of them are quite prepared to overlook all sorts of minor slips as part of giving you a full and fair hearing. How many times have you sat in the audience and wished the speaker would give a terrible presentation? The answer should afford some comfort for your next effort.

Having something at stake beyond just the challenge of performing well, as in a proposal review or dissertation defense, does add greater pressure to a presentation. In that regard, you will note that we have not said reassuringly, "Don't worry about it." Anyone in that situation will have at least some honest cause for concern. What we do want to point out is that with solid preparation, the possibility of a truly bad presentation is vanishingly small. Formal evaluation of what you have to say is out of our hands—and at the moment you begin, out of yours as well! There is nothing left to do but concentrate on a good clear presentation and let the rest take care of itself.

Take a deep breath, acknowledge the audience (large or small) with a friendly word or gesture of greeting, and then start at a slow, even pace. In the opening sentences, make a special point of trying to match your speaking voice to your normal conversational tone. Many speakers report that the sound of their own voice provides recurrent feedback. If they are able to sound relaxed and confident, they begin gradually to really feel that way. Likewise, if your voice, posture, and movements signal exceptional tension, your audience will be concerned and begin to reflect the tension back. Start easy, breathe, look at people, and just talk to them.

We did not say "smile" as part of our advice because nothing is worse than the frozen rictus of a false smile. Forget your face and concentrate on how your listeners are responding to your words. If you can do that, smiles will come when they are a natural part of the process.

Particularly in the opening minutes, remember to pause when you have made an important point. Do then the kinds of things we all do in conversation: Nod to stress a point, and raise your eyebrows to ask your audience if they understand. Punctuate with a simple gesture, or just wait for a moment as we do when encouraging a listener to contemplate the significance of what we have said.

Later on in your presentation, you will want to consider the need for stimulus variation. Changing the display is one of the key factors in sustaining attention, and the need for it grows as the presentation lengthens. Throughout the presentation, you might change your speaking location, briefly introduce a graphic display, or simply alter your tone and speed of delivery. Any small change can break the dull grip of too much of one thing.

If possible, you should have someone tape record your presentation. It is unlikely to be the last you give, and although being perfect is not a reasonable expectation, getting better is. Be sure, of course, to use long-playing tape to avoid the distraction of having to flip a cassette in mid-course. In addition to making sure you can profit by listening to your own performance, purchase some further insurance by asking several friends to watch for and record the things you will not be able to hear on a tape. Nonverbal signals, for example, are a powerful part of every communication. Knowing about what your body language is saying, good and bad, is part of learning to do effective presentations.

As you close, three things are almost universally appropriate. First, revisit with your audience the essential points that you wish them to retain. Second, provide a graceful transition by reminding the audience about what will happen next, whether that be a break, a period of questions and discussion, return of control to a moderator, or termination of the meeting. Third, and finally, any audience deserves the courtesy of your thanks. While you are struggling to master the difficult craft of presenting research, a patient and forgiving audience will have earned a good deal more. Remember that, when next you are on the other side of the lectern.

MANAGING INTERACTION

Whether you serve as your own moderator or have someone else to preside over a period of questions and discussion, a little advance planning will make it go more smoothly. If you can tape the discussion that follows your presentation, be sure to do so. Valuable points of comment or advice that seem vivid in the excitement of interaction with the audience may be lost to recall. Few people find it possible to take notes and talk at the same time.

If the audience contains both people charged with some official function (such as reviewing your proposal) and others who are visitors or supporters, make a point of setting the ground rules at the outset. It is good to let everyone who has attended have an opportunity to comment or question, but give priority of first opportunity to those who require it. If you are managing the flow of discussion, be sure to spread interaction around. Some people are not skilled in taking turns, and others need encouragement if their comments are to be heard.

In fielding questions, the first rule is *Get it straight!* Be sure you understand what is being asked before attempting to answer. Repeating or rephrasing complex or unclear questions serves the dual purpose of detecting miscommunication and reassuring the questioner that you do understand what he or she wants to know. Repeating every inquiry, of course, is tedious and to be avoided.

When you just do not know the answer, say so. When you just can't understand the question, say so—but also ask if it can be taken up later when there is more time for clarification. If you know something that may be helpful but you suspect it is not exactly what has been requested, ask permission to alter the question as a way of advancing the discussion. If the question is clear enough but you think it is inappropriate to the occasion, acknowledge it politely and suggest that you would be glad to take it up after the meeting is concluded.

If you are pressed for an agreement that, in good conscience, you cannot give, try acknowledging the existence of alternative or competing views. If that does not close the point, ask to defer the matter until there is sufficient time for deeper examination of the argument. Normally, by this time someone will have interceded to redirect the discussion. If help is not forthcoming, there is little to do except to hold your ground, perhaps asking for comment by others in the audience.

Finally, keep an eye on the clock. Just as the presentation proper should end on time, any follow-up discussion should be limited by prior announcement, mutual agreement of those present, or just plain common sense.

THE AFTERMATH

Within several days, make a point of obtaining and processing all the available feedback from your presentation. Listen to the tape, review notes taken by friends, and solicit feedback on both content and delivery. Some people will do this with greater skill than others, and some will feel more comfortable in providing an honest critique. Predictably, there will be conflicting opinions on some points. What one finds helpful, another may not. Rather than attempt to respond by planning some change to accommodate every comment, listen for patterns. Where concerns overlap lie the points at which effort for redesign or further practice will yield improvement.

Finally, encourage people to indicate what they liked and found helpful in your presentation. This is not so that you can revel in their praise but because you may not be aware of what was most effective. If you can learn what worked, strength can be built on strength.

PART
II

---■---

MONEY
FOR RESEARCH

INTRODUCTION

We want to be very clear about the following point. Money, by itself, does not make good research. Good researchers do that. What money can do, however, is allow the design of studies that take advantage of opportunities for producing strong results. Such openings for improving research include larger samples that are more nearly ideal in their characteristics; instrumentation for producing data that are more reliable and precise; needed extensions of time in the field or laboratory; vital participation by technical specialists; travel to acquire training in special skills; a period of freedom from other obligations such as teaching, administration, and student advisement; and budget for expendable items and overhead costs that often accompany a study of even modest dimensions.

Beyond the potential for technical improvements, however, lies another benefit that accrues from finding financial support for your study. In case experience has not yet drawn this to your attention, researchers are people. They have careers to nurture, friends and family to love and support, usually a host of other work-related roles to play, and personal lives to live. There is a powerful tendency, however, for researchers to risk erosion of their status as persons by taking the costs of doing their scholarship entirely out of their own financial (and social) hides. Given the attractions of inquiry, that is a perfectly understandable and, perhaps, even laudatory behavior. Nevertheless, always paying your own way has consequences that extend not just to the quality of research undertaken, but, very often, the quality of life you live as well. Scholarship need not and, indeed does not, require a vow of genteel poverty.

There is money available to support good research by researchers at all levels of career development. Those funds are not evenly distributed across disciplines, do not always come without restrictions, often involve competitive review of proposals, and certainly are not just lying about waiting to be picked up. Nevertheless, the money is there, and it is there in truly astonishing amounts. There are quite literally thousands of foundations and agencies (both public and private) that have the support of research as one of their missions.

Tapping into those sources requires knowledge and skills that are not the same as the requisites for performing an investigation—and in most cases also involves preparation of a research proposal that differs in some important ways from those for theses and dissertations. Sophistication about all of this has acquired the name "grantsmanship." The three chapters in Part II are designed to introduce you to the art of grantsmanship (with its astonishing diversity, local customs, and jargon), the process of preparing a grant proposal for support of a study, and the idea that students (undergraduate, graduate, and postgraduate) can be successful in shaking the money tree.

The chapter titles and text headings should make the organization of Part II self-explanatory. If you are already committed to the idea of seeking research funds, Chapters 8 and 10 should be read in sequence. If you are a student for whom the idea of funding student research is new (or even a bit unimaginable), then Chapter 9 is the place to begin. Wherever you encounter a need for more detailed information than we have provided, please consult the sources we have recommended in each chapter (full citations are in the reference list), and, particularly, those books we have abstracted for your use in Appendix A.

8

$=\!\!\!\Box\!\!\!=$

Money for Research

How to Ask for Help

$\mathbf{G}$rant applications are formal appeals for the award of support, usually in the form of money, for undertakings by individuals or groups, in which the grantor has special interest. In the strict sense, a grant is an award of funds without a fully defined set of terms and conditions for use, whereas a contract is a work order from the grantor in which procedures, costs, and funding period have been established in explicit terms. Thus, the majority of what are commonly called grant proposals are applications for award of a contract—not a grant.

Grants may be sought for projects in which the objective is to provide a needed service, or for research studies in which the objective is to produce knowledge, with any service provided being purely incidental. Specialized guides are available for proposal writers who seek funds for the development of programmatic services. Some of these, such as the texts by Coley and Scheinberg (1990) and Bauer (1995), will be of interest to all novices in the grantsmanship game. Our book is directed specifically to proposals involving research rather than service to a client population.

The grant request contains two components: (a) the application for funding and (b) the proposal that explains in detail what activities the funds—if granted—

will support. Ordinarily, no distinction is made between the application and the proposal, the terms being used nearly interchangeably. Nevertheless, in any application for the support of inquiry, embedded amid budgets, vitae, descriptions of facilities, and plans for dissemination of results, is a research proposal. To that extent, then, the preparation of a grant application requires the same skills as the preparation of any plan for research.

The differences between the research proposal embedded in the grant application and the dissertation or thesis proposals described earlier in this text rest primarily in the need to (a) conform to the grantor's format, which may be specified in considerable detail; (b) present the study in a way that will have maximum appeal to the granting agency; and (c) master skills required to complete other parts of the application that are not directly part of the research plan itself. In all other respects, a sound research proposal is a sound research proposal, whether in a grant application to the National Institutes of Health, a philanthropic foundation, or in a dissertation proposal placed on your advisor's desk.

DECIDING WHERE TO START: CHOOSING THE RIGHT SOURCE

The Track Record: Are You Ready for a Grant?

Most research projects require financial support, either for equipment, for personnel to assist in data collection and management, or for publication and dissemination costs. Because internal sources of support within higher education have declined while research costs have escalated, acquiring external funding for research has become the essential first step for almost all studies. Even after the project is under way, a major function for many investigators is to acquire additional funds needed to complete the project.

Departmental budgets, which formerly had small amounts of money allocated to research projects, now are stretched desperately thin just to ensure that classes are taught. Few departments can supply researchers with even minimal funds. Thus, a major portion of "research activity" is dedicated to funding the project, and this is no different for beginning researchers. In fact, learning to write proposals for research funding has become an important part of the doctoral education experience. Graduate students who have the opportunity to work in well-funded research projects usually share some of the writing responsibilities so that they can learn the process.

The acquisition of funds must be preceded by a written proposal, so preparation of grant applications has become a skill that often is as important as inquiry skills themselves. Each government agency and independent foundation has a specific form to be completed and a unique process through which the proposal must be evaluated. If the proposer of a research project is skilled, diligent, persistent, patient, and possessed of at least a reasonable share of luck, funds can be obtained. The ratio of proposals presently being funded to those being rejected, however, is very low. Fewer than 25% of first-time applicants to the National Institutes of Health are successful, so it is obvious that the task of writing and submitting a proposal cannot be approached in a cavalier manner.

In deciding where to seek support, our first advice is to engage in some serious self-contemplation. Review committees want to feel comfortable in awarding a grant of financial support to an applicant. The committee wants to be assured not only that the proposed study is excellent, but also that the researcher is competent to perform excellent work. The best evidence for competence is a series of publications on the topic to be researched. This has come to be known as a track record in the area of the proposed study. What record of accomplishment will you present to attract and reassure those who review your proposal?

Investigators are more likely to satisfy the review committee that their skills are adequate to perform the study if they include in their research applications reprints of research reports or documentation of pilot studies that verify the reliability of the technique proposed or support the directional hypotheses to be employed. In contrast, when the grant applicant is a complete neophyte, or has not completed a study in the specific area of the proposal, the committee will be forced to depend on less direct evidence of competence and, in the end, mostly on faith and intuition. It is understandable that committees more often avoid investments based mainly on faith and select instead proposals from individuals with a solid track record. Because a strong track record is so important, successful young grant recipients usually are those who have worked through their doctorate in a very active research program and who also have had postdoctoral appointments. In both the doctoral and postdoctoral programs, these new researchers have had ample opportunities to publish with seasoned mentors.

Factors other than track record are weighed by review committees (most notably the quality of the research topic and proposal), and novice researchers or veteran investigators entering new areas do sometimes receive grant support. First-time grant proposals do not automatically encounter a hopeless Catch-22 that demands a display of previous research by the author. The fact remains, however, that previous performance weighs heavily among those factors that determine success.

The track record has been emphasized here not to discourage the beginner but to lend support to a suggestion that the authors of this text have found particularly useful. A good way to build a track record is to begin with limited aspirations and seek limited funding from local sources, particularly from the institution in which the researcher works.

Almost all universities and colleges have faculty and student research funds available. Most major institutions also have federal funds that are provided in block grants to support work in particular disciplines. Such internal sources ordinarily require only a modest proposal document that is not as lengthy or complex as those required by external agencies. A good strategy for eventually obtaining a larger government or foundation grant is to acquire two or three small ($1,000-$5,000) grants, conduct the investigations, submit the results for publication, and subsequently use those reports as the track record supporting a proposal for more extensive funding. This provides you with start-up funds to do the first studies and also indicates to agency reviewers that your work already has been critically and positively reviewed, not only by an editorial board but also by a university funding review committee.

The use of these local grant sources also should emphasize how important it is to have envisioned a systematic research program rather than a single study. Each research project can build on the previous one, providing more and more evidence that your ideas are worthy of major funding. In programmatic research, it is logical sequence, not the accumulated number of studies, that will impress reviewers. Clearly, a fundable proposal could never be supported by a host of experiments aimlessly conducted on a hodgepodge of tenuously related topics.

Agencies and Foundations: Locating the Money Tree

The first step in preparing a successful proposal is knowing where to apply. Finding the funding source that provides the highest probability for successful application often is a time-consuming process. Given the time that will be expended in preparation of the proposal, however, it is a relatively small investment that can return significant dividends.

An effective strategy is to find an individual or service group that maintains a grant library or monitors information sources concerning agencies and foundations. With their assistance, you can identify a preliminary list of grantors with possible interest in your study. Universities often house such a library, and many of their services are computerized to allow highly efficient search procedures. Most research universities also provide postings of grant opportunities that are available for anyone who accesses their Website. For example, the University of California, Berkeley (http://www.chance.berkeley.edu/research/Funding/Funding-byAgency.html), Columbia University (http://cpmcnet.columbia.edu/research/funding.htm), and The University of Texas at Austin (http://www.utexas. edu/research/funding/index.html) list research funding opportunities on their Websites. Most of these university Websites also have a section on regional or local resources. Some universities have specialized lists of resources especially targeted for graduate students, such as those at the University of Massachusetts at Amherst (http://www.umass.edu/research/gsgs) and The University of Texas at Austin (http://www.utexas.edu/ogs/pdn/news/news.html). In addition, all governmental agencies and large foundations have a Website, and much information about availability of grants can be obtained from these. Thus, the absence of information resources at smaller colleges is no longer the obstacle it was before the advent of the World Wide Web.

Many senior professors who have large research programs not only maintain updated information about sources of funding in their particular area but also know and maintain regular communication with key individuals in granting agencies. Such contacts are invaluable for their knowledge about priorities (and changes in priorities) within the funding agency.

It may be beneficial for a novice to collaborate with a senior researcher on one or two studies before attempting a proposal on his or her own. The presence of a well-known researcher's name on a proposal can be very helpful because reviewers have confidence in known quantities and often confer that same confidence on collaborators. Not everyone, however, is in the enviable position of associations with a senior researcher or research staff. Many young scholars must undertake, on their own, the unfamiliar task of locating the money tree.

In this process, the first rule is to throw a wide net and keep an open mind about what might constitute a possible source. Although it sometimes serendipitously happens, do not expect to find an agency with interests exactly matched to your particular research idea. With some creative adaptation, it often is possible to adjust the focus of a study sufficiently to interest a funding agency without distorting the primary intent of the investigation. For instance, a proposal involving the role of motor or play behavior in child development might be of interest to sources as widely disparate as the Center for Research for Mothers and Children in the National Institute of Child Health and Human Development, or an early childhood project within the Office of Educational Research and Improvement, all depending on how the study is presented. For this reason, a flexible point of view is helpful in assembling the initial list of potential funding sources.

There are a variety of computerized retrieval services that can make your search more efficient. For example, the database of the National Technical Information Service (http://www.ntis.gov/index.html) provides information on federal funding sources. The Illinois Research Information Service (IRIS, http://www. library.uiuc.edu/iris) is one of the most comprehensive and widely utilized computer retrieval services. If your institution subscribes to IRIS, you will quickly realize the benefits of a computerized search. IRIS permits those seeking grants to search on a wide variety of keywords (e.g., clinical psychology) and situations (e.g., graduate study or research training programs). In addition, you can create a personal profile of your interests and have periodic notices e-mailed to you to alert you to funding possibilities. Other computerized grant retrieval and notification systems, such as GrantSelect, available through Oryx Press (http://www.oryxpress.com/), provide similar subscription services to individuals. One of the great benefits of most computerized systems is that you can immediately get the grant announcement and other information in an electronic format, saving valuable time that can be used to begin working on a proposal.

If you are pursuing grant support from foundations, *FC Search: The Foundation Center's Database on CD-ROM* will be an invaluable tool. Created by the Foundation Center (http://fdncenter.org/), it includes that center's entire database of foundation and corporate grants. In addition to identifying granting agencies, it provides easy access to other information such as deadline dates and profiles of more than 47,000 foundations and corporations, including the links for Internet access to those foundations and corporations that are on the Web. Your institution's grants and contracts office can inform you as to whether *FC Search* or other systems are available for your use. If you are fortunate enough to live near one of the Foundation Center libraries (in Atlanta, Cleveland, New York City, San Francisco, and Washington, D.C.) you can perform a search there without charge.

In addition to a computer retrieval system, several standard reference works in hard copy may be useful for beginning or extending your search. A comprehensive listing of assistance available from the federal government is contained in the *Catalog of Federal Domestic Assistance* (*CFDA*) (United States General Services Administration, semi-yearly). Published twice a year and available in a searchable format on the Internet (http://www.gsa.gov/fdac/), as well as in CD-ROM format, *CFDA* is an invaluable tool for locating agencies with appropriate interests, as well as general information about support programs within those agencies. Some states publish a catalog that provides similar information for programs of state assistance.

The most useful published tool for identifying nongovernmental sources of support is *The Foundation Directory* (Rich, 1998a). This directory categorizes nearly 9,000 of the largest foundations and includes both application information and the number and kind of grants available from each source. Its companion document *The Foundation Directory: Part 2* (Feczko, 1998) provides similar information on approximately 5,000 mid-size foundations. Also in the private sector, the Foundation Center provides extensive coverage of nongovernmental sources through its publications (*The Foundation Grants Index* [1999] and *National Directory of Corporate Giving* [Hall, 1997]), its fax service for information about U.S. foundations, its regional centers, and the computerized *FC Search* noted above. The center is particularly useful for identifying smaller, local organizations with interest in the support of research.

Many sources in governmental agencies, private foundations, industry, and professional organizations are listed in the *Federal Register* (http://www.access.gpo.gov/su_docs/aces/aces140.html), the *Annual Register of Grant Support* (R. R. Bowker, 1999), the *Directory of Research Grants* (Oryx Press, 1999c), and *The Grants Register* (Austin, 1999). Although the *CFDA*, the *Directory of Research Grants*, and the *Grants Register* provide some overlapping information, each has unique features that justify consulting all three. Directories that list grant opportunities for other areas include the *Directory of Grants in the Humanities* (Oryx Press, 1999b), *Directory of Biomedical and Health Care Grants* (Oryx Press, 1999a), and *Grants, Fellowships, and Prizes of Interest to Historians* (American Historical Association, 1998).

The researcher is likely to use these larger and expensive compendia in the library or at a research center. Once a specific list of potential sources has been developed, however, it often is possible to obtain publications from specific agencies that are free or more moderately priced. Most state and federal agencies publish material that describes their research support programs and application procedures. Examples are the National Institutes of Health's *Guide for Grants and Contracts* (http://www.nih.gov/grants/guide) and the National Science Foundation's *E-Bulletin* (http://www.nsf.gov/home/ebulletin/).

A government Website that may be useful to many is the National Institutes for Health Center for Scientific Review (http://www.drg.nih.gov/), which includes, among other resources, Study Section membership lists (naming those who will review grants in different areas). It is important to know who will be evaluating your proposal. If you have read the papers of those most likely to review your proposal, you will have a clearer understanding of their perspective on the topic.

Another source of information is which funding agencies are supporting research that is published or presented at national or regional conferences. The granting agency or foundation always is listed at the bottom of the first page of a research article. Similarly, at the bottom of abstracts printed in conference programs, the research grant number and funding sources are given. These can tell an observant reader not only what agencies fund research on a particular topic but also specific interest and funding trends for particular sources. In fact, information in abstracts often is the most current information of this type available.

A number of commercial publications and services can meet the need for help in searching out sources for research support. Some of these provide valuable information about approaching foundations, new agency priorities, formulating more competitive proposals, and the legislative processes that precede new governmental programs. Used as a supplement to direct contact with funding agencies, information from such publications as *Grantsmanship Center Magazine* (Grantsmanship Center, http://www.tgci.com/) and *Foundation News and Commentary* (Council on Foundations, Inc., http://www.cof.org/) can help both in correctly targeting proposals and in improving their quality. The familiar series from Peterson's Guides includes an extensive directory of grants available to graduate students (Peterson's, 1998). Information about funding for student research can be found in Chapter 9.

Finally, a potential source of long-term funding is the development of contractual partnerships with business and industry. If you want to pursue this possibility, we recommend reading *Get Funded!* (Schumacher, 1992) before you start.

REVIEWS: THE WEIGHING OF PROPOSALS

Once a completed grant application is received by the funding agency, it will be read and evaluated—a process designated by the generic term "review." In most cases, the application will be processed in company with other proposals that are competing for support during the same funding cycle (such cycles are often yearly but may involve either longer or shorter time spans). In reviewing the submission, the agency or foundation will employ a set of procedural steps to accomplish both the evaluation and, ultimately, the final determination of which submissions will be funded—and at what level of support.

Such review procedures vary enormously and range across a wide spectrum of complexity. At one end of the range are small organizations that may employ a single reader to evaluate and make recommendations. At the other extreme are the large federal agencies and substantial private foundations that utilize teams of both research peers and in-house specialists to complete a multistage review. If you are considering preparation of a grant proposal, it may be useful to acquire some general understanding of what kinds of review procedures you may encounter. The best source for that information, of course, will be the organization to which your application is directed. We can begin that education, however, by offering an example here.

The NIH Review:
Proposing in the Big Leagues

Rather than generate a generic model of a "typical" review procedure, we have elected instead to display the process employed by the National Institutes of Health (NIH). Although few grant applicants will have the opportunity to submit a proposal that receives the kind of elaborate evaluation used by NIH, that model has several advantages as an instructional device.

First, not only is the process real (NIH presently reviews as many as 10,000 applications in each grant cycle), but its characteristics also vividly underscore the common tasks that are shared by all formats for reviewing grant proposals. Complex or simple, short or lengthy, the review must (a) evaluate the practical and theoretical importance of the question in the study, (b) determine the technical adequacy of the proposed study, (c) judge the applicant's ability to execute the research, (d) identify the extent of congruence between the research topic and the organization's mission, and (e) fit those evaluations into a calculus determined by the amount of funding available—to identify which proposal(s) will be supported. Because NIH must apportion limited funds in a careful and equitable manner within a particularly important field of research, its reviews are complex, thorough, rigorous, and not a little daunting to even a veteran investigator.

Those qualities serve to introduce the second advantage in contemplating the NIH review process. Wherever you may apply, you are unlikely to encounter any procedural step that is not represented here, nor will your research proposal ever be dissected with such brutal efficiency. Make no mistake, NIH represents the big leagues for proposal writers.

No diagram can capture all the variations and subtleties of the NIH review system. Further, the process continues to evolve over time as feedback demands new adjustments. Finally, not all proposals follow the precise route displayed in Figure 8.1, though the majority will do so. These are the major steps—and a sample of the jargon that has come to accompany the quest for NIH funding.

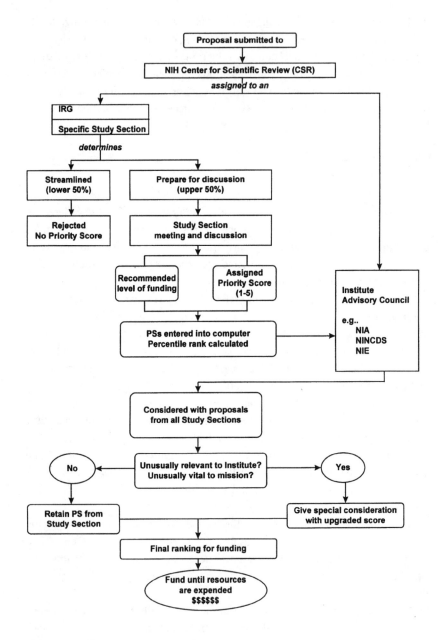

Figure 8.1. Overview of NIH Grant Proposal Review Process

TABLE 8.1 Examples of Websites From Which Electronic Forms May Be
Obtained[a]

Air Force Office of Scientific Research	http://web.fie.com/htdoc/fed/afr/afo/any/menu/any/afrprop.htm
American Cancer Society	http://www.cancer.org/research/grants/rpg_grants.html
Army Research Office	http://www.aro.army.mil/Forms/forms2.htm
Department of Energy	http://www.er.doe.gov/production/grants/forms.html
Department of Health and Human Services	http://forms.psc.dhhs.gov
General Services Administration	http://www.gsa.gov/forms
National Endowment for the Humanities	http://www.neh.gov/html/forms.html
National Institutes of Health	http://www.nih.gov/grants/forms.htm
National Science Foundation	http://www.nsf.gov/home/grants/grants_forms.htm
Small Business Administration	http://www.sba.gov/library/pubs/pubsroom.html

a. Adobe Acrobat Reader will be required to use most of these; however, all these sites provide an easy system for downloading the program from their Web page.

The first step in obtaining funding for a one- to three-year project (known as an RO1) begins when the principal investigator (PI) obtains the Public Health Service Grant Application, PHS 398. This document can be downloaded from the NIH Website (http://www.nih.gov/grants/funding/phs398/phs398.html). It provides guidelines, instruction sheets, and application forms. Also included are samples of completed form pages, a discussion of the peer review process, and suggestions for maximizing your chances to receive a positive review.

Although the PHS 398 packet presently can be obtained in hard copy, NIH, like many large agencies, is rapidly moving to the requirement that all forms be obtained, and all submissions be made, electronically. As evidence, Table 8.1 displays examples of grant sources that already "strongly encourage" such use of computer and Internet technology.

Before an NIH application can be sent on its way, there will be a host of institutional hurdles to navigate. To take one example, acquisition of required signatures alone may require at least a month. Included in a large-scale proposal might be officers in a variety of units and at several different levels: department chairs, program chairs, deans, provost, director of technical facilities (the computer center, for example), a human subjects review committee, business managers, and, in some cases, even the chief executive officer of the institution or state system. Few of these signatures will come without delay, a fact that must be coordinated with the NIH deadline with the greatest care.

Once the proposal is ready for submission, it is transmitted to the NIH Center for Scientific Review (CSR), usually from the institution's office of sponsored projects. At this point, our description of events requires close inspection of Figure 8.1. After receipt of the proposal, CSR Referral Officers will review the contents and assign the document to the most appropriate NIH Institute, such as the National Institute on Aging, and to an Initial Review Group (IRG) which serves that agency, such as "Health Promotion and Disease." In turn, the IRG consists of a cluster of what are called "Study Sections," each with 18 to 20 peer reviewers who specialize in a particular research field such as "Human Development and Aging." Finally, each Study Section is assigned an NIH staff person who serves as the Scientific Review Administrator (SRA) and coordinates the work of that section.

In the first phase of the review, Study Section members, all of whom are active researchers, will evaluate the scientific and technical merit of the proposal. About six weeks prior to the first Study Section meeting, all members receive a package containing the proposals to be considered during the upcoming review cycle. Each member gives each application a preliminary reading. In addition, for each application the SRA assigns two or three members as Principal Reviewers who will develop written reviews of each grant application. Several more members are appointed to serve as the proposal's Discussants at the forthcoming meeting.

One week before that meeting, however, the SRA solicits from each member a list of the RO1 applications judged not to rank in the top half for scientific merit. The proposals so ranked are considered "streamlined." They will not be discussed or assigned a priority score (PS) at the meeting, although a summary review statement will be prepared and returned to the PI. "Streamlining" is not the equivalent of disapproval (though it certainly constitutes rejection of the application in its present form), and many streamlined proposals are resubmitted for review, using feedback from the Study Section, in a subsequent funding cycle.

At the Study Section meeting, members convene around a table to evaluate what, in theory, are the top 50% of the grant applications. The assigned Principal Reviewers and Discussants present their reactions and recommendations. After general discussion, each member assigns a PS to each proposal. The PS is based on the following criteria:

1. *Significance:* Is answering the research question important? Will it advance knowledge? Will it have an impact on the field of study in terms of scientific knowledge and/or practice?

2. *Approach:* Is the methodology sound and appropriate to answer the research question proposed?

3. *Innovation:* Does the proposal describe novel concepts, approaches, or method? Is the study original and creative?

4. *Investigator:* Is the researcher well trained and does he or she have the capability to conduct this study?

5. *Environment:* Is the laboratory, clinic, or field area appropriate to conduct the study? Does it have unique features that would enhance the probability of the success of the study? Does the institution or some other agency support this study?

The Priority Scores may range from 1.0 (highest) to 5.0 (lowest), but because approximately 50% of the proposals have already been "streamlined" out of the process, the reviewers are encouraged to provide scores that range from 1.0 to 3.0. Individual reviewers are free, however, to use the full range of the scale if they feel strongly about a proposal. After the Study Section meeting, the SRA places the PSs into the computer database and each proposal is assigned a percentile rank for scientific merit. It is this rank, along with summary statements from the Primary Reviewers (and the SRA), that are forwarded to begin the second phase of the evaluation.

Now the review process shifts to the right-hand side of Figure 8.1, as the Study Section sends the proposal to the Institute that the CSR earlier had designated as appropriate (indicated by the long descending vertical line at the right of Figure 8.1). In this second phase, the Institute's Advisory Council will consider it along with many proposals forwarded from other Study Sections.

One interesting item of information considered by members of an Advisory Council is each proposal's scientific merit percentile rank, shown in a single list of percentile ranks for all proposals that have been recommended for funding by the Study Section in previous review cycles. This places each proposal in a "historic context" of merit that is much deeper than that offered by its place in the present group of applications. Kelly and Shipp (1991) offer a detailed discussion of how this operates to influence success rates within the review process.

The Advisory Council will lean heavily on the scientific merit percentile ranks that have come from the Study Section, but it also balances funding decisions with other factors, such as the implications of the research topic for the Institute's goals, the similarity of the proposed research to other proposals or to existing funded research programs, and the total level of funding available. In some cases, members of the council will recommend that particular proposals be given special consideration for funding, or they may determine that an application is of questionable relevance to the institute's mission and recommend that it be assigned elsewhere. A reassignment, of course, would require several more weeks to process. That point emphasizes how important it is for the applicant to do everything possible to write the proposal with a specific orientation and to direct it to an Institute that would find it attractive.

At the final step, when consideration is given to funding, the approved applications are listed in order of their percentile ranks, as modified by the Advisory Council, and grants are approved in order as funds permit. Because the proposals are funded on the basis of relative rank and different Institutes have different levels of funding, a percentile rank of 18 may be funded in one Institute but not in another. Thus, a researcher who has submitted a proposal to an Institute with lower levels of funding than others may be disappointed to learn that his or her proposal was not funded, even though it had the same percentile rank as one in another Institute that was funded. Such are the vagaries of life in the world of grantsmanship!

If the proposal is approved and funded, notification is sent to the PI and the sponsoring institution. On occasion, the Study Section will recommend a reduction in budget, or the Advisory Council of the Institute may suggest such an alteration. In these cases, an officer from the Institute will inform the investigator and provide an explanation. Such a recommendation may or may not be negotiable. If the Institute's representative is willing to discuss proposed reductions, the investigator will have to confront inquiries about the necessity of specific budget items. Having a clear rationale for each expenditure is the best method for preventing serious erosion of the budget during such bargaining.

WORKING WITH FOUNDATIONS

Because every foundation has different procedures for working with grant proposals, we cannot provide a single set of specific instructions, as was possible with the NIH example above. We can, however, provide advice about working with foundation staff and offer some suggestions that will improve your chances for a successful application.

The charter of each foundation establishes a mission that is particular to that organization. Some are constrained only to fund programs providing benefit in the community (for example, grants to support development of legal services for the poor) and do not fund research. Other foundations have been created specifically for the purpose of supporting research in particular areas (for example, mental health or education). Still others fund both public programs and research. Foundations in this latter category often are more likely to support studies that deal with problems closely associated with the service aspect of their mission. Even though they are willing to support research projects, their first priority remains the impact of findings on their community and their particular constituents.

Accordingly, when investigating a foundation as a possible source of funding, try first to inform yourself about its mission. If the interests of the foundation appear to have some relationship with your research agenda, the next steps are to obtain a sense of the priorities articulated by its leaders and information about the kinds of studies that have been approved for funding in recent years. If proposals have been funded recently in areas that are related to your research interests, it will be particularly helpful if they can be obtained for review.

The initial contacts with foundation personnel are particularly important. Courtesy to everyone is a rule, whether the executive director, board member, or receptionist, and remembering that their time is valuable is the first way to show respect. If it becomes apparent that the agenda of the foundation does not provide a sufficiently close fit with your present ideas, make a point of thanking staff for their time and withdraw politely. You may wish to return at a future date.

In the highly competitive grant marketplace, trying to force a square proposal into a round foundation is likely to be a poor use of time and effort. If, however, preliminary contacts with staff do suggest that there is some potential for mutual interest, you may wish to extend the discussion with staff before developing and submitting a proposal.

Most foundations welcome the opportunity to have staff discuss possible proposals with prospective applicants. Exploring areas of shared interest and providing some preliminary screening of potential applicants are functions that are in the best interest of the organization. Foundation staff can alert you to deadlines, describe application procedures, indicate areas of investigation for which the foundation currently has particular concern, explain how the review process works, and identify the individuals within the organization who hold final authority for grant decisions.

As with government agencies, some foundations have grant application packets that provide comprehensive information about the required format for all proposals. Others will accept proposals in a variety of formats. Likewise, some foundations make funding decisions only at a specified point (or points) during the year, whereas others make decisions on applications as they are received. It is your responsibility to obtain the existing regulations for the proposal process—and follow them. For example, if the instructions specify that the pages of your proposal be hole-punched, do it (if you really want the money)!

Assuming your proposal reaches the foundation office on time and in the proper form, it will be reviewed. This process may be structured in any of several ways.

1. A single staff member reviews the application and makes a decision based on the technical merits of the proposal, his or her perception of your ability to carry out the research, and how the study relates to the priorities of the foundation. This is the least common form of review, although it still may be encountered in a few organizations.

2. One or more staff members review the application and provide comments on some (or all) of the points noted above. The foundation's board of directors (or a special committee of the board) then uses that information as the basis for making final funding decisions. This process may be as formal as the one described for NIH reviews—complete with rankings—or may be much less formal, with nothing more elaborate than a committee discussion about which proposal will produce the most benefit for the foundation's money.

3. Comments produced by staff review procedures are supplemented by recruiting the critiques of outside specialists with expertise in the area of the proposal. All comments are then forwarded to the next level of the review and decision process.

In the event that a proposal is not funded, it is to your advantage to obtain feedback from the review committee or foundation staff. Not only can you learn how to improve your proposals, but you also may wish to approach the foundation with another application in the future. The more you learn about their review process, and which aspects of the proposal are pivotal in determining acceptance or rejection, the more likely you are to succeed on a subsequent try. In any case, it is important to be businesslike and respectful even in the face of a rejection. As one veteran foundation executive told us, "No one likes whiners." Positive interactions with foundation staff are the basis for future receptivity.

If your proposal is funded, anticipate that the expectation for continued accountability may be higher than that expected from government sources, especially if the foundation is local and the project is nearby. Local foundations expect to receive as much publicity about their investments as possible, because it makes them credible to their board of directors and also helps them raise more money. They may expect several interim reports, and they may expect you to provide oral presentations to their board, television audiences, or participants in community programs sponsored by the foundation.

PARTNERSHIPS WITH BUSINESS:
AN ALTERNATIVE SOURCE OF FUNDING

Funding for research sometimes can be obtained from business or industry, although this is primarily available to university faculty members who hold relatively permanent and high-level appointments. Graduate students, postdoctoral scholars, and untenured junior faculty are rarely considered unless they are included in a team of university researchers. The commercial sector needs research findings from a wide array of academic disciplines. Businesses of all kinds can profit from information that improves their operation in such diverse areas as "planning, finance, facilities, accounting, operations, marketing, sales, customer service, human resource management, training and education, retention of personnel, public and community relations, and so on" (Schumacher, 1992, p. 43). Faculty scholars in almost any discipline may be able to convince corporate executives that their research project merits support if they bring creative ideas and are willing to persevere in the effort to obtain a hearing.

Most large businesses have research and development units assigned primarily to the tasks of applied investigations, although some devote a portion of their resources to basic research. In either case, some of the research work may be subcontracted to sources outside the organization. This, of course, is a primary point of entry for the development of business/university partnerships.

It is not surprising that businesses are unlikely to be interested in funding short-term projects. Given the highly specialized needs of businesses, when research is done for them, it often involves expensive services, equipment, and facilities. Contracting to support such costly activity makes sense only when a partnership between the corporation and the researcher can be sustained over a substantial period of time. Businesses must look to the bottom line of profitability, and that goal is best served when funding can purchase a reliable source of continuing research capability.

Research support from commercial enterprises is a double-edged sword. Not only does it hold potential for support that is substantial in quantity, but additional funding also is much easier to obtain once the relationship is established. The disadvantage, however, is that support must go up or down with company fortunes. When profits go down, management changes, or priorities shift, the company can lose interest, and funds may quickly dry up.

The process of shaking the corporate money tree may be very different from that required for government agencies or foundations. Access here often is achieved through contacts with personnel in the organization—frequently with researchers, technicians, or research managers. Usually it is necessary to have someone inside the organization to advocate for your proposal and assist in moving your ideas for a partnership through the channels of corporate management.

In her informative book *Get Funded!*, which is reviewed in Appendix A, Schumacher (1992, pp. 95-108) suggests a variety of ways you can identify and cultivate company employees who may be interested in sponsoring your proposal for a research partnership. Some of these are paraphrased in the brief list below.

1. Keep in touch with former students and colleagues who have found employment in business or industry.

2. Enlist the help of alumni who may have contacts in the corporate world.

3. Make use of university staff who have corporate relations as a responsibility.

4. Attend on-campus presentations by corporate representatives.

5. Talk to company recruiters when they come to your campus.

6. Make contact with representatives from the business sector who serve on any of your institution's various advisory committees.

7. Make contact with business organizations through your state's economic development agencies.

8. Use cooperative education programs and field placements to locate some of your students in companies with which you may have shared research interests.

9. Search out possible avenues of contact through the School of Business or Management at your institution.

10. Make contact with corporate researchers who publish in your field.

Business and Corporate Foundations

Most business foundations differ sharply from philanthropic foundations. The availability of research funding from such institutions often is not completely insulated from the profitability of the corporate parent and rises and falls accordingly. Frequently, the nature and purpose of the foundation is closely tied to the interests of its business sponsor, although it is common for the mission statement to be written in such general terms that it is difficult to discern the true priorities (and biases) of the organization.

Grants from business foundations often are made preferentially to particular institutions of higher education. This may be on the basis of some historical relationship, such as the undergraduate education of a corporate founder or the existence of familial ties between company and institution managers. For that reason, applications or letters of inquiry sent without the advantage of sponsorship may provoke little interest from the corporate foundation's management. As in the case of direct contacts with business organizations, it is best to locate an inside advocate who can sponsor your proposal for serious attention.

THE REJECTION OF A GRANT PROPOSAL: WHY DOES IT HAPPEN?

Whether you submit a grant application to a governmental agency, a philanthropic foundation, or a business-affiliated organization, it is virtually inevitable that your proposal will be considered in competition with other proposals. Such grant competitions are mediated through review processes that, whatever unique form they may take, ultimately must involve human readers. This fact produces an implacable rule. *What is not noticed is not funded!*

Amid the sometimes formidable stack of proposals, the document that does not catch the eye—and thus the reward of closer attention and consideration—cannot compete on the formal criteria associated with quality of design and congruence with the grantor's priorities. For that reason, in Chapter 10 we will give close attention to the abstract and introduction that must present whatever attractive elements are contained in the research question and proposed methodology.

Beyond the problem of failing to attract attention, the reasons given for rejection may be phrased in diplomatic terms—but they boil down to a surprisingly small set of simple and all too familiar defects. Because in purely statistical terms the probability of rejection for any given proposal is high, beginners in the grant application business have good reason to note the common causes of "submitted, but not funded" with considerable care. As shown in Table 8.2, reasons for rejection fall into four general categories: mechanical, methodological, personnel, and cost-benefit. Having made the point that most rejections are the consequence of proposals that are unsound—often in simple and obvious ways—it is important to note that perfectly sound proposals sometimes are rejected. Research of considerable merit may remain unsupported for no reason

TABLE 8.2 Common Reasons Grant Proposals Are Rejected

Mechanical Reasons

1. Deadline for submission was not met.
2. Guidelines for proposal content, format, and length were not followed exactly.
3. The proposal was not absolutely clear in describing one or several elements of the study.
4. The proposal was not absolutely complete in describing one or several elements of the study.
5. The author(s) took highly partisan positions on issues and thus became vulnerable to the prejudices of the reviewers.
6. The quality of writing was poor—for example, sweeping and grandiose claims, convoluted reasoning, excessive repetition, or unreasonable length.
7. The proposal document contained an unreasonable number of mechanical defects that reflected carelessness and the author's unwillingness to attend to detail. The risk that the same attitude might attend execution of the proposed study was not acceptable to the reviewers.

Methodological Reasons

8. The proposed question, design, and method were completely traditional, with nothing that could strike a reviewer as unusual, intriguing, or clever.
9. The proposed method of study was unsuited to the purpose of the research.

Personnel Reasons

10. As revealed in the review of literature, the author(s) simply did not know the territory.
11. The proposed study appeared to be beyond the capacity of the author(s) in terms of training, experience, and available resources.

Cost-Benefit Reasons

12. The proposed study was not an agency priority for *this* year.
13. The budget was unrealistic in terms of estimated requirements for equipment, supplies, and personnel.
14. The cost of the proposed project appeared to be greater than any possible benefit to be derived from its completion.

---

that can be associated with the quality of the proposal. Because that unfortunate circumstance is a possibility, rejection must not be taken, by itself, as evidence of a fundamental defect.

At any point in time, a proposal simply may not appeal to a reviewer who must make a choice among equally strong contenders. Under such circumstances, subjective factors determine decisions, often leaving no wholly logical explanation for the action. The following section, dealing with resubmission, was prepared with the unfortunate authors of such proposals in mind.

Rejection, Feedback, and Resubmission

A rejection, especially of the first grant proposal submitted for review, should not be unexpected. It is commonplace in academic life—especially for the novice. Just as it takes practice to learn how to perform any complex task truly well, it takes practice to write successful proposals. So long as the applicant has an opportunity to profit from evaluative feedback, each attempt should produce significant improvement.

Most review systems contain some provision for feedback as part of the rejection process. Often in the form of a summary review of the proposal, the feedback statement will list the main criticisms and may even suggest changes. The applicant should consider each point. If resubmission is contemplated, the new draft should address as many criticisms as possible through revisions, clarifications, and strengthened rationales. In addition, when the interval of time between the original submission and the notification of results has allowed collection of new pilot data, or acquisition of additional support from new publications, these should be added.

The easiest critique to respond to is one that raises questions about design or methodology. There the decision is simple: Either provide better substantiation for the choices made or change them. The review, however, may center not on what was proposed, but on the way the proposal was written. In some instances, the absence of any substantial comment about the research question or methodology provides the indirect suggestion of a failure to communicate clearly. In other cases, the reviewers may have understood the proposal perfectly but had reservations about a nontechnical issue such as the ratio of costs to potential benefits. In the former, rewriting for clarity is the needed response. In the latter, the only recourse is either to strengthen the rational for the importance of the study or to find ways to cut the budget.

In terms of devising a response, the more difficult critiques often are those related to the proposed research questions themselves. In such cases, the author must read the reviewers' comments with great care so as to ascertain whether the questions raised are matters of logic and research design, or really are subtle expressions of doubt regarding the value of the research.

Sometimes reviewers signal their disinterest in the proposed study in implicit ways, because they don't want to make the blunt assessment: "I don't think this is worth doing!" In some (unfortunate) cases, this lack of candor leads to a furious hunt for every possible flaw in the proposal (no matter how minor) that can be used to rationalize rejection. That problem in the review process was one of several that led recently to a thorough reexamination of the NIH system. Although that evaluation did not lead to radical changes, it did produce a new question to which every reviewer must respond in his or her critique: How likely is it that the proposed project will make an original and important contribution?

Negative answers to that question offer strong evidence that the problem lies with your research question(s). The only useful responses are either to argue the matter by improving the rationale or to make significant modifications in the question(s) you want to ask. All of this suggests that in making use of reviewers' comments on your proposal, you must read both the lines and between the lines.

Once responses to criticisms have been devised, the rejected proposal may be resubmitted. An accompanying letter should note that the document is a resubmission and request return to the original reviewers. When this can be accomplished, it both makes use of familiarity and avoids a new set of criticisms based on a fresh set of perceptions (and biases). Proposals can be resubmitted several times, provided that feedback encourages revision and there is no suggestion from the grantor that the topic of study is inappropriate.

A telephone or e-mail conversation or meeting with the individual who coordinated the review process often can clear up ambiguities in the feedback provided with rejection. Such assistance is particularly useful when it is not clear whether the primary cause for rejection lay with the research question or with the substance of design and method. Further, a willingness to listen attentively, and politely, can serve to invite suggestions for improvement. In some instances, a staff member at the agency or foundation may even give the applicant an estimate of the probability for success in a resubmission. The applicant should remember, however, that staff members can only provide their personal judgment on such matters. In most cases, final decisions will be made by others.

After the first shock, a rejection should not inhibit the urge to find support for a worthy study. With critical feedback in hand, a stronger proposal can be drafted. Doubtless it is better to have approval and the desired funding. An unsuccessful effort, when properly understood, however, can yet yield something of value—the opportunity to learn how to do it better. That is a grant of assistance that will pay, and pay, and pay.

PLANNING AND PREPARATION: TAKING THE LONG VIEW
---■---

As the competition for sizable grants has grown more rigorous over the years, the amount of detail involved, the advanced planning required, and the complexity of the proposal process itself have dramatically increased. Shaking the money tree is not the straightforward process it was when funds were more plentiful and applicants fewer. Once, one or two weeks was the norm for the time invested in a proposal of modest scope. The same document now may take several months of preparation. Nevertheless, if your goal is to make productive scholarship a part of your career, there is no choice. Particularly if you want to prosper in a university setting, grant writing will be an essential skill for survival.

When the proper steps are taken in a logical sequence, and adequate time is allotted to complete each step, the worst that can be said about proposal writing is that it is exacting and sometimes tiring work. The best one can say is that it is challenging, and even stimulating. This is particularly likely to be the case when investigators in complementary areas of expertise collaborate in the process of developing the research plan. The interaction that occurs among colleagues during formulation of research questions and study design can be educational—and a powerful motivation for sustained effort. When a grant application has been completed, the proposal critiqued by expert reviewers, and the project approved for funding, there is more than just the satisfaction of success. There is the excitement of doing what the money can pay for—a good study.

CHAPTER

9

—◻︎—

Funding Student Research

Very few graduate students apply for grants, awards, or fellowships with which to support their research—whether theses, dissertations, independent study projects, or pilot investigations. This pattern of omission arises from several sources. First, overwhelmed by the difficulties of planning a study and writing the necessary proposal, students find it difficult to imagine they will surmount those hurdles, much less organize an application for funding. Second, faculty advisors often do not encourage students to apply for research grants. Indeed, there sometimes is an unspoken (and, perhaps, unintended) discouragement in professorial attitude that holds student research to be something less than the "real thing" and, thus, not worthy of the effort involved in a search for funding. Finally, given the temporal rhythms of graduate programs, the tasks of planning and writing a grant application many months in advance of a project or thesis often must compete with the more mundane but, nevertheless, essential work of attending classes, preparing for examinations, and meeting assistantship obligations. In that context, the speculative possibility of a grant to support next year's research is disadvantaged by the certainty of what is due on Monday morning.

In the larger universities, of course, where students are part of a research community and often involved directly in funded laboratories or long-term, grant-supported projects, they usually are socialized into a tradition that defines planning for funding as an essential (and routine) part of preparation for a study. Those fortunate interns and research assistants, however, represent a minority of the students proposing and executing research studies. Each year, literally thousands of students do research without funding of any kind, often without any programmatic expectation that they should learn how to search for support, and, even more unhappily, often without strong faculty encouragement to believe they can succeed.

We believe none of the excuses for failing to seek financial support are valid. At the least, all of them are shortsighted and work to the disadvantage of students' education, as well as the quality of their research (and personal lives). We urge you to consider a very different and far more positive perspective on the possibilities for finding money to support your research.

Our reasoning is not complicated. First, if there is any possibility that you will go into a profession, position, or career in which you (or any of your colleagues) will find it advantageous to do research, the process of locating and applying for funds to support your student research will yield invaluable training—whether you get your grant or not! We can assure you that aside from some differences in the sources of funding, the knowledge and skills needed to apply for research support as a student are similar to those employed by postgraduates and career researchers. Grantsmanship is as much an essential skill of modern scholarship as learning to do a literature review or mastering a protocol for data analysis. Graduate departments in which faculty insist that their students not only begin early but also persist in grant seeking throughout their program invariably receive a disproportionately large number of student research grants—year after year. Equally important, such programs are providing training that is essential for success in any career that involves the conduct of research.

A second reason for students to seek research funding is, if anything, even more immediate and compelling. Simply put, money can make a positive difference in virtually any study. With financial help you might (a) take advantage of superior measurement, recording, or processing technology; (b) use a larger sample for data acquisition; (c) follow a time schedule that is more appropriate (whether longer or shorter); and (d) make fewer demands on your family, friends, and personal bank account for support of your investigation. If those advantages are true, and we insist that they often are, then why not make applications for funding part of the same process that produces your proposal?

It is easy to anticipate the *sotto voce* responses to that rhetorical question. Beyond the personal and institutional discouragements noted above, there is the pervasive belief that money for student research is not available, or, at least, is in such scarce supply as not to justify the great investment of time required to make application. That popular wisdom manages to blend a series of false assertions. There *is* money for student research, in some areas it even is plentiful, and there are hundreds of sources for small grants that require no more than a few pages of application information.

We can sum up the matter by revealing the three most important and pervasive prejudices that operate to deny students money for support of their research projects. Granting agencies give money only to those who have: (a) applied for it, (b) completed the application forms exactly as specified in the instructions, and (c) submitted the applications before the indicated deadline. Those who ask, can get. Those who do not ask, do not get. Think about it.

Admittedly, there are other forces at work. For example, it is true that available funds are unevenly distributed across disciplines. It also is true, however, that many awards are made on the basis of factors unrelated to the field of the proposed study (e.g., gender, race, nationality, institution, church affiliation, military status, vocation, organizational membership, geographic location, etc.). It is true that having received a previous grant often is a substantial advantage. It also is true, however, that "trading up" to a higher level of support can be facilitated by very small prior awards ($100-$200) such as those that often are readily available from sources within your own institution. It is true that those who review applications are always more favorably disposed when something in the proposed study fits closely with the primary interest of the granting agency. It also is true, however, that when funding is considered *during* the preparation of the proposal (as opposed to being an afterthought upon completion), small adjustments in purpose, sample, site, method, or justification often can create just such an attractive match without significant sacrifice of the main research objective.

Not all the funding available for support of graduate study can be used for support of a particular research project. Once used exclusively to designate support for tuition, books, and living expenses while pursuing advanced study, the word "fellowship" now includes funding that may, or may not, include research. The words "grant" and "award" now are used so variously that only inspection of funding agency specifications can reveal whether money is available for support of student research. Nevertheless, of the more than 1,400 sources listed in the most recent *Peterson's Grants for Graduate and Postdoctoral Study* (Peterson's, 1998), we estimate that as many as half might be construed to offer some form of financial support for studies proposed by students (we urge you to read our abstract for that invaluable guide in Appendix A).

WHAT EVERY STUDENT RESEARCHER
NEEDS TO KNOW ABOUT MONEY

———————————■———————————

There is a great deal to know about the art and science of applying for research funding. A sound introduction to all of that can be found in Chapters 8 and 10 of this book. What we have done in this short section is to extract the advice that applies with particular cogency to locating and making application for money to support student research.[1] In a few cases, our suggestions arise from genuine differences between the situation of the all-but-dissertation graduate student, postdoctoral scholar, or junior faculty member (what the National Science Foundation now refers to as "New Career Researchers"), and the position of more established applicants. The majority of our recommendations, however, are based on general rules of grantsmanship that the novice simply is unlikely to know—or may find all too easy to forget.

Begin at the beginning. Start right here by skimming Chapters 8 and 10, as well as the abstracts of books in Appendix A that deal with research funding.

Begin at home. If you are enrolled at a college or university, locate the office that deals with research grants. Such units go under a variety of names, but virtually every institution of higher education has one, all deal with supporting faculty in their search for extramural funds, and some will have a separate office or individual to provide assistance for students. Talk to someone on the staff, obtain and read their materials, make use of their training classes, and follow their advice. In addition, virtually every campus has some procedure for making institutional funds available for research by junior faculty and, sometimes, by students as well. Locate that office and find out what is possible. The awards typically are small, but everything helps and even a small success gives you a track record and, thereby, a significant advantage in subsequent applications, both inside and outside the institution.

Do it now. The famous three laws that govern the value of real estate ("location, location, and location") have their analogue in seeking research grants ("timing, timing, and timing"). The typical student novice completes his or her proposal, gains approval from advisors or the graduate school, and turns up at the local equivalent of the Office of Research Affairs with a 50-page document asking, "Where can I get money to do this?" In several respects, that forlorn inquiry already is too late. It is too late to influence the development of the proposal, and thus the best opportunity to make the study attractive to a potential source of funding. More to the immediate need, however, it probably is too late (or far too early) for the cycle of grant deadlines.

The average decision time for student grant applications lies in the range between three and nine months (a long wait often made longer by the time consumed in preparing the application), and 65% of application deadlines for student research funding fall between November and March (85% if you add October and April). Missing the deadline, for many agencies, means a full year delay before a new cycle of application consideration begins.

Learn how to search. The library has hard-copy and electronic database sources for grant searching that you should locate, and with which you should be familiar as soon as you have begun serious work on your proposal. Also, if you do not have it already, you will need to acquire a modest degree of computer literacy. The most powerful retrieval sources are the subscription databases now searchable only through the Internet. None of these involves the skills of rocket science, but all require practice to achieve a reasonable level of search efficiency.

Of the Internet sources, the Illinois Researcher Information Service (IRIS) (http://www.library.uiuc.edu/iris/) and the Community of Science (COS) (http://www.cos.com/) presently are the most comprehensive. All research universities and most of the larger state institutions of higher education maintain membership in either the IRIS or COS networks—and sometimes both. If your home institution is a subscriber, you may wish to take advantage of the IRIS Alert Service. With this, any graduate student can create an individual search profile (congruent with his or her interests and skills) that can be run against the IRIS database of funding opportunities. The resulting matches can then be received via e-mail at intervals specified in a personal profile.

In addition, there are a group of hard-copy volumes, available in most college and university libraries, that still are an essential element in seeking opportunities to fund student research. Very early in the proposal process, you should acquire at least a nodding acquaintance with *The Grants Register* (Austin, 1999), *Foundation Grants to Individuals* (Hall, 1999), *Directory of Research Grants* (Oryx Press, 1999c), and *Peterson's Grants for Graduate and Postdoctoral Study* (Peterson's, 1998), the *Annual Register of Grant Support* (R. R. Bowker, 1999), *The Foundation Directory* (Rich, 1998a), *National Guide to Funding in Higher Education* (Rich, 1998b), and (if appropriate) *Directory of Financial Aid for Women* (Schlachter, 1997).

Finally, there are literally dozens of more specific directories, indexes, and computerized retrieval systems that serve particular kinds of research topics, individual investigators with particular characteristics, and many other categorizations used to determine the client population for funding sources. Your campus research office staff and reference librarians usually can help you identify the listings that will best serve your search needs. As for the most frequently asked question of all, "yes," there are both federal and private sources of financial support for doctoral dissertations.

Be a collector. As soon as the nature of your proposed study has been broadly defined in your mind, begin collecting and reviewing application forms from prospective sources. Because a growing number of granting agencies will not respond to either telephone or mail requests, that restriction will serve to force you into the medium of communication they prefer—electronic mail on the Internet. One of the things you will discover in reviewing application instructions is that for some agencies you also will have to file your application electronically. Whatever the format used for information, instructions, and applications, having all that material at hand is a strong encouragement to consideration of research plans that will have at least some capacity to attract money—while serving your scholarly interests.

Network with students in other fields. There is a strong trend in research funding to favor proposals that employ an interdisciplinary approach to inquiry. This is particularly true of federal agencies and applies in virtually all academic fields. Student projects that take advantage of that disposition not only will have improved chances for an award but also will offer preparation for participation in a collaborative research format that trainees are sure to encounter upon graduation. In some institutions, graduate school regulations even have been adjusted to accommodate theses and dissertations that involve interdisciplinary collaboration.

Whether through informal contacts or by more structured means, discussion with students in other disciplines often reveals that interesting theoretical and practical problems have parallel representation in several fields of inquiry. Some of those represent opportunities for the kind of research that reaches beyond the confines of a single perspective—and that can attract support for students who are ready to "think outside the boxes" of their disciplines.

Apply early and apply often. Unlike the rule on submission of manuscripts to multiple publication outlets, there is absolutely no prohibition against applying to several sources of financial support for the same study. In fact, once you have the main elements of a strong research plan (and the necessary written boilerplate for description), multiple applications should be the rule and not the exception. Further, rejection of one or several requests should not end your search for support. You should learn from each failure, and subsequent applications (and reapplications to the same source) will be more effective as well as easier to complete.

If (surprise!) you receive favorable responses from more than one source, you often need not decline one in favor of another. Most agencies do want to know (and will ask you to report) if your proposal will be funded by another source. "Double-dipping" (the practice of taking research funds from two agencies without informing either) is unethical and could end your career before it starts. Nevertheless, it is not uncommon in the research funding community for agencies to work together in supporting different aspects of the same investigation. For example, one source might be willing to fund a strong pilot study or necessary instrument validation work, while another supported the main investigation. Always (of course) be completely honest about your circumstances in any negotiation, and work for the arrangement that best fits your study.

Get ready to present yourself. In this book (Chapters 2 and 10), we have given much advice about academic resumés (vitae), and once again we urge you to maintain one (or several, to serve different purposes) in up-to-date condition. Keeping your records on a computer disk makes this a simple task. Almost all grant applications require submission of an academic resumé. In addition, many sources of support for student research ask for a "personal description" or "personal profile." This more closely resembles the essay that is part of application for admission to many colleges and universities. Particularly in the case of predissertation doctoral students, granting agencies know they cannot expect a track record of previous funding success or research publications in support of the candidate. Their emphasis, then, must be on selecting student applicants who know why they are in school, why they are engaged in research training, and what really interests them in the world of scholarship. With that in mind, and sufficient time to do multiple drafts and obtain editorial assistance, you can craft a profile that portrays you as a good bet for any agency's investment of grant money. Having those tasks of self-portrayal done in advance simply makes it easier to assemble a prompt and effective response when opportunity knocks.

Attention, undergraduate juniors and seniors! A surprising number of fellowships are designated for award to "entering students" in programs of graduate study (a specification that appears to be increasingly popular among foundations). In fact, some graduate fellowships specify that the applicant must not have accrued any graduate credit hours. Of course, not all these awards include the potential for funding student research, but of those that do so, virtually all will go each year to individuals who identified the opportunity and made application during their junior and senior years of undergraduate study.

Even tuition awards for graduate study may position you to receive priority consideration when later applying (to the same agency) for money to support a program-related investigation. If you think you may be destined for a graduate degree, exploring possibilities for financial support (including research funding) prior to receiving the baccalaureate is just sound career planning.

Not only full-time students need apply. Applications from part-time students and individuals without any current institutional affiliation are welcomed by some granting agencies. In such cases, it often is accomplishments rather than awarded degrees that must carry the day. Demonstrating the capacity to do the work of inquiry is always a central concern, however, and here, as elsewhere, strong and specific recommendations from scholars who themselves are active in the area of your proposed study may be a requirement.

No matter what the result—count your blessings. Searching for money with which to support your study, thinking about your proposal in terms of the perspective taken by funding agencies, and completing the tasks involved in making a sound application are all learning experiences that have lasting value. Among the senior scholars we know, there is not one with a strong record on obtaining research funding who has not also acquired some rejections along the way. It would be surprising if that were not true of student scholars as well. The verdicts "Approved, but not funded" and just plain "Not approved" are hard to digest. We would not try to persuade you otherwise. But going through the process can leave you smarter, more determined, and more likely to succeed on the next try. If rejected, apply, apply, again!

NOTE

———————————————◼—————————————————

1. Many of the suggestions here were formulated by the staff of the Graduate Student Grant Service (GSGS) in the Office of Research Affairs at the University of Massachusetts at Amherst. Since 1979, the GSGS has served as a national clearinghouse for collecting and cataloging information about graduate student and postdoctoral funding opportunities. Their Web page is located at http://www.umass.edu/research/gsgs/.

10

—◻︎—

Preparation of
the Grant Proposal

O nce the funding agency is selected, the first step is to obtain its published guidelines for submitting proposals. These guidelines must be followed meticulously. We will discuss here some of the purposes and the considerations to be dealt with in writing many grant proposals. For each specific proposal, the information in this chapter should be used along with the guidelines that are provided by the funding agency.

ABOUT ABSTRACTS ⌣

The word "abstract" normally designates a brief summary of a larger document. Most published research reports are accompanied by such an abstract. Written in the simple past tense, abstracts of this sort are histories of work already accomplished. In contrast, the abstract of a grant proposal is written in the future tense and summarizes work that will be done. When, as sometimes is the case, the abstract is prepared before the full proposal has been developed, it more properly should be called a *prospectus* or *preproposal*, but such niceties of language are seldom observed.

Abstracts or preproposals are prepared early in the proposal development process to serve several purposes. First, an abstract may focus the thinking of individuals developing the proposal by establishing a clear and explicit goal to which all subscribe. Second, a concise prospectus can be used for internal purposes to obtain preliminary administrative approval or to solicit support and cooperation from other units. Third, many agencies now require submission of a "letter of intent," which, in essence, is a one- or two-page abstract of the proposed study. These letters are screened by a panel of judges who rank them on preestablished criteria. Authors of the best abstracts are invited to submit full proposals for the second phase of consideration. Under such conditions, every-thing rests on the abstract, and no argument is required to convince the proposer that only the best effort will serve. Finally, whatever its function, an abstract prepared prior to development of the full proposal must be revised to maintain perfect congruence with the evolution of that document. Abstracts that do not match the proposal may receive short shrift from reviewers.

Whether or not a letter of intent is required, the abstract that is submitted with the full proposal bears a disproportionate share of responsibility for success or failure. Often limited to a single page, these few paragraphs are what the reviewer will read first. When the bottom of that page has been reached, the reviewer must have a clear impression of the study's objective, method, and justification. If the proposal is to have a fair chance to succeed, however, another impression must have been communicated—that the study contains something of special interest, something that will sustain the reader's attention through the pages that follow. Thus, the abstract must accomplish the dual tasks of providing a concise picture of the study while also highlighting its unique characteristics.

Although different funding agencies require different lengths and types of abstract, in almost all cases there is no space for throwaways. Each word and sentence must convey a precise message to the reader. If a point is not essential to an understanding of the study, it is better left to the main body of the proposal. Because the abstract is a one-way, one-shot communication, absolute clarity is essential. No matter how well a point may be explained in the body of the proposal, if the reader is confused by the language of the abstract, the game may have been lost.

For both of the reasons noted above, economy and clarity, the watchword for writing the abstract is *plain language*. Avoid any special constructs that require definition. Don't coin new words in the abstract. Avoid slogans, clichés, and polemical style. Keep adjectives to a minimum and omit flowery descriptions.

Finally, remember that the sure sign of an amateur is to apply banalities such as creative, bold, or innovative to one's own ideas. Reviewers, unlike graduate advisors, cannot ask what "that phrase" means at the next conference, may not take the time needed to puzzle through a convoluted sentence, and certainly will not bother to figure out what probably is intended by an imprecise description.

Although one can assume that reviewers are both literate and familiar with the research process in broad terms, for the purpose of the abstract it is unwise to assume more. Writing beyond the technical competence of the reviewer can be fatal. The best rule is to imagine that you are explaining your study to an intelligent layperson. By eliminating specialized language and reducing esoteric constructs to their essential components, you can make the abstract intelligible to individuals with a wide range of scientific backgrounds—without appearing to write down to any reader.

The typical format required for a proposal abstract includes the following major elements:

- General Purpose
- Specific Goals
- Research Design
- Methods
- Significance (Contribution and Rationale)

Some agencies may also request that the applicant organization (institution), estimated cost (total funds requested), and beginning and ending dates be included. It is important to read the instructions and include only what is requested, as the space requirements always are limiting in terms of communicating your ideas.

The specific goal section should begin with a statement of what will be accomplished, presented in the format of a research question or testable hypothesis. For example: "The objective of this study is to determine whether the use of foam cushion inserts in athletic shoes will affect the incidence of heel injuries in runners. Frequency and type of injuries over a six-month period will be compared for two groups of 100 subjects of varied age, weight, ability, and sex, one group using shoes with cushion inserts, and the other using uncushioned shoes."

One of the hardest things to do is to reduce objectives and methods to just a few sentences. This difficulty probably contributes to several common errors found in the abstract section of the proposal.

Confusion of objectives with procedures: Taking a survey may be a procedure to be employed in the study, but it is not an objective of the study.

Confusion of objectives with the problem: The conditions that make the study important, in terms of either practical application or contribution to knowledge, are better discussed in the section on significance. In the occasional case in which some appreciation of significance is required before it is possible to understand the objective, the best course of action is to create a short subsection titled "The Problem" as a lead into statement of the objective.

Attempting to specify more than one or two major objectives for the study: Save all sub-objectives for the body of the proposal. Do everything possible to help the reviewer focus on what is essential.

Failure to be explicit: The best insurance is to start with a conventional phrase that forces you to write about your intention. "The objective of this study is to. . . ."

The clarity and precision with which your objectives are presented may control how carefully the reviewer attends to the subsequent section on procedures, but it is axiomatic that *agencies fund procedures, not objectives.* How research is performed determines its quality, and it is here that the competence of the reviewer as a research specialist in the area of your proposal will be brought to bear. If the reviewer finishes the one or two paragraphs of this section with a clear, uncluttered idea of what will be done, a full appreciation of how those actions will accomplish the objectives, and a positive impression of what is intriguing or particularly powerful about your approach, your proposal will receive a full hearing.

The significance of the proposed study should be identified in modest but precise terms. Nothing can serve so quickly to make a reviewer suspicious of the merits of a study as to encounter some Chamber of Commerce enthusiasm in the abstract. In plain language, indicate how achieving your objective would be of value to someone, could improve some service, would fill a gap in an evolving body of knowledge, or would permit the correct formulation of a subsequent question. It also is appropriate, and often effective, to indicate a specific example of how a finding from the study might provide human benefit, even at some point subsequent in time or technical development. It is best, however, not to drown the drama of a simple example in needless embellishment. Finally, when deciding which potential consequence should receive emphasis in supporting the significance of the study, it is useful to examine the existing interests and commitments of the funding agency. When the proposed study takes some of its importance from a potential for contribution to ongoing projects of the grantor, there is a powerful argument for special attention to the application.

As the abstract is developed, revised, and given its final review prior to submission, it will be helpful to remember one of the somber facts that has emerged in this age of endemic grantsmanship. Some heavily burdened review committees are so large that it has become necessary to delegate to a subcommittee the task of giving full proposals a complete reading. The remaining reviewers thus may not see more of a given proposal than the cover sheet, the abstract, the author's vita, and, perhaps, the budget. That prospect should be sufficient to encourage attention to producing the best possible abstract.

COMMUNICATING THE SIGNIFICANCE
OF THE PROPOSED RESEARCH

Most funding agencies require a section in the proposal that has a title such as "Significance of the Proposed Research." Funding agencies are accountable either to the public or to their benefactors for the expenditure of their funds. Try to read your proposal from the *funding agency's perspective*. What will they think is important? What aspect of your proposal will attract their attention and interest? Reviewers seek the applicant's best forecast as to the usefulness and importance of the results of the proposed project. This prediction assists the review committee in determining the cost-benefit ratio of the proposed study. The significance of the investigation might be explained in terms of synthesizing information from several research areas or by showing how the findings might be applied to human services. It could be impressive to point out that the findings might enable development of other types of research that previously had been impossible. The section needn't be long, but it should be carefully reasoned and should address concerns specific to the mission of the funding agency.

STAFFING AND CONSULTANT NEEDS

The staff needed for the research project should be carefully planned and kept as small as possible while maintaining services essential to conducting the study. The staff budget generally is what drives up the cost of a research project more than any other expense. Along with staff salaries, fringe benefits (medical insurance, retirement) and raises for each year of the grant often must be included. The beginner at this game quickly finds that the costs of a project escalate rapidly as more personnel are involved. When a neophyte is attempting a first grant application, the proposal for staffing should be constructed with a frugality tempered only by feasibility.

The staff requirements should be explained in detail, and if a staff member's function dwindles in the second or third year, then that member should be phased out. Reviewers will note a conscientious effort on the part of the applicant to execute the project at a minimal cost. Positions to be funded for the full term of the study with only global explanation of responsibilities and no indication of compelling necessity also will attract attention—all of it negative.

Rumor has it that applicants should pad their budget with some excess and unneeded staff so that the reviewers will have something to cut. This is a foolish notion, because it results in the applicant having items in the budget that are not well justified, which ultimately gives the impression of a casually constructed proposal.

Consultants, too, should be requested sparingly and only when absolutely needed. When they are required, the need should be explicitly stated. If a particular consultant is needed, the applicant should explain exactly why, and a letter of agreement from that consultant should be included in the appendix.

THE TIME FRAME

Many proposals submitted to government agencies are for funding of a three- to five-year project. The application and review process is so time-consuming that the applicant, the institution, and most agencies find the investment of such energy and time best returned if the award is for a substantial period. A time frame, therefore, that states explicitly when specific parts of the project will be completed has several useful functions.

The first and most obvious use of a projected time sequence is that it keeps the investigator and all personnel on schedule throughout a long period. When all members of the research team have a copy of the time frame, and when it is posted in offices, work rooms, and laboratories where every member of the team will have daily exposure to its terms, the effect is to encourage steady application of effort.

A second function of the time frame is to forecast for project personnel, reviewers, and the funding agency the probable contents of each progress report that must be filed (usually annually or biannually over the term of the funding period). Every reader of the time frame can clearly see what events will transpire prior to each progress report and, consequently, will expect a full and punctual accounting. This serves also to discourage investigators from procrastinating and later finding themselves having to accomplish an enormous amount in the month or two that precede a progress report.

A third function that the time frame serves is to document the need for three or five years of funding for the project. If the reviewers can see in the time frame that every month is filled with work to be done, then it is clear that a project of the length proposed is necessary.

Fourth, if the time frame is well described, it will enhance the reviewer's understanding of the entire project and will further document the applicant's organizational skills. A well-conceived time frame, in which each part of the project is estimated in terms of its onset and duration, goes a long way toward convincing the reader that the applicant knows the area, the methodologies to be used, and all other aspects of the project. If it is well written, it also will buffer several possible criticisms—that the project cannot be completed in the amount of time proposed, that it does not require funding for the full period of time requested, or that the investigator does not understand the topic well enough to know how long certain procedures will take.

The time frame should include the schedule for hiring personnel, ordering equipment and supplies, putting equipment and facilities into operation, meeting with personnel from other institutions or agencies, acquiring subjects for the investigation, data accumulation, data analysis, and report write-up. In preparing the time frame, the applicant should try to think through and record every step that will be taken in the project. Then how long each step will take must be estimated. The more people who are involved in a step, the longer it probably will take. The applicant may even find, after working out the time schedule, that the project will take longer than anticipated, and the funding period must be extended. If such extension makes the project too expensive, it may be necessary to consider a more economical design. For all these reasons, the time frame should be carefully worked out before the budget is made final.

The proposal writer also should have a personal time frame that includes the amount of time necessary to get the proposal through all levels of the approval process. This part of the time frame, although not submitted with the final proposal, should aid the writer in understanding the full commitment to the research that will be necessary. In the accompanying illustration of a time frame (Figure 10.1), the first half of Year 1 represents that period of proposal preparation.

Notice first that in the time frame for this research project, 23 weeks (nearly half a year) were required from the initial contact with the funding source (in this case a corporate entity) to receipt of notification that the proposal would be supported. The intervening weeks of intensive effort represented a "risk investment" by the researchers. There was no guarantee of success, but they had made

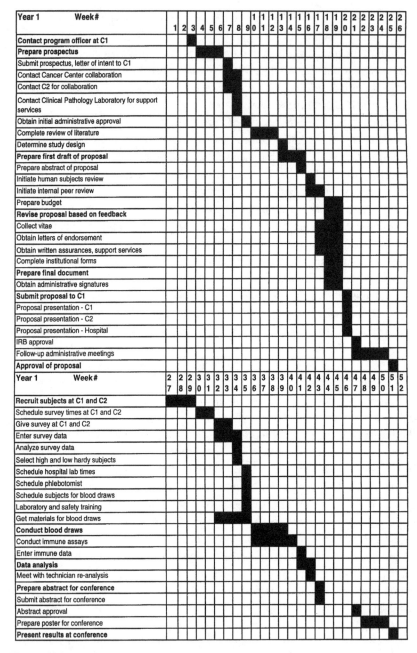

Figure 10.1. Example of Time Frame

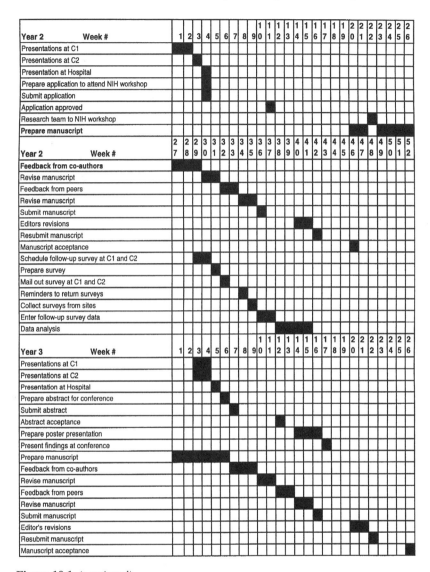

Figure 10.1. *(continued)*

SOURCE: This was developed by Christyn Dolbier, a doctoral candidate in Health Education, The University of Texas at Austin, 1998. C1 = company 1, C2 = company 2.

a judgment that the potential payoff justified the time and effort. It is easy to imagine the feeling of excitement (and relief) when the previous 27 steps of investment, laid out in the time frame plan, led to the 28th!

If you have read the previous chapters in this book, many of the individual steps (note particularly those we have put in bold type) will be familiar. For example, notice the very early creation of a preliminary prospectus for use in recruiting cooperation from one of the participating companies. Also, the fact that it is five weeks from the first draft of the proposal to the last round of revisions and the final document will come as no surprise, given what you now know about the painstaking process by which research proposals are created. Likewise, if you complete this chapter, the provision of three weeks for the creation and collection of academic vitae from participating colleagues will not seem mysteriously excessive.

The steps that follow in the second half of the year include many that are peculiar to the particular study, but some represent generic mileposts in the research process. These will be found in the time frame for any grant proposal. The schedule for recruitment of subjects, acquisition and analysis of data, and preparation of an abstract for the first conference presentation of results represents the heart of all studies.

These steps also involve the activities that absorb a large portion of the allocated funds. In the second and third years, however, you will observe the substantial portion of time (and resources) devoted to dissemination of results—including results from a follow-up study. A journal report was planned as a part of this proposal, for example, and the author budgeted a total of 23 weeks for drafts, reviews, and revisions. This suggests not only the care lavished on the report but also the central importance of dissemination as a part of the research process. That is something well understood by funding agencies of all kinds, a fact that makes careful and explicit plans for dissemination a key part of the time frame presented with any grant proposal.

Although Figure 10.1 displays the time frame for what obviously is a relatively complex study, you should not imagine that such detailed projections are appropriate only to large-scale research projects. The most modest study will contain its own sequences of activity and deadlines for completion of particular tasks. Those steps may be fewer in number, but the notion that they can be adequately captured by a few general (and suitably vague) promises, much less be managed efficiently, without an explicit road map of what must be done—and when—is an amateur's illusion.

Positive responses to grant proposals are facilitated when the research plan is accompanied by a thorough and realistic time frame. Further, as we will assert at the close of this chapter, any study, whether funded under a grant or financed out of the investigator's own pockets, is likely to be significantly strengthened by laying out a flowchart that schedules the salient events—step by step.

SUPPORT SERVICES

Any large project will require an extensive array of support services from the university and any other agency or unit of the community that is involved with the project. Insofar as possible, the need for support services should be anticipated, both by providing money for them in the budget and by ensuring that what must be purchased exists and can be delivered. If a computer graphics person is needed, one should be located to ensure that such a person is available. Specialized computer services may be required from the computer center, or unusual transportation capacity may be needed, such as the need to move video equipment into the community. These types of research support must be located and confirmed as part of preparation for the proposed study.

All space needs such as laboratories, offices, or work areas for technicians should be anticipated. If the research project is going to tax any unit of the university or agency, the people involved should be consulted prior to the final draft of the proposal. Examples include proposed projects in which a large number of telephone calls will be imposed on the departmental switchboard, frequent mass mailings will be planned for the postal pickup, or dozens of students are to wait in lines in a hallway immediately outside classrooms. The applicant should try to anticipate any hardship that the project may create for anyone. This will prevent, insofar as possible, logistic problems that create ill will among support service staff and frustration for the researcher.

When support from other sources is critical to the research project, the researcher should obtain a written agreement from the appropriate officials specifying that the needed service will be available. This letter of agreement may be included in the appendix of the proposal. For example, if a specific school classroom is essential to the project, a letter reserving that facility for the specified period of time should be obtained. It would be an unpleasant surprise, for instance, to begin use of another researcher's environmentally controlled laboratory for a year-long study, then discover that it will not be available for the final two months of the project. Every precaution must be taken to prevent such disastrous accidents.

VITAE: PRESENTING YOURSELF

———————■———————

It would be easy to underestimate the importance of this section in a grant application. For many readers, vitae represent one more instance of the paperwork syndrome that infects higher education. Personal resumés are required, accumulated, and ignored in a host of bureaucratic functions. In consequence, unlike people in the business world, academics often pay relatively little attention to the construction and maintenance of attractive and utilitarian vitae. Like McGee's closet, they simply are allowed to accumulate the residues of scholarly and professional life without much thought to order, economy, or impact.

Two common misapprehensions prevail about the vitae section of a grant proposal: (a) that they are not read by reviewers and (b) that as a *pro forma* section, vitae have little influence on the success of a proposal. Both notions are untrue. Vitae are read. Many reviewers read vitae before they read the body of the proposal. Not only do vitae influence the judgments of reviewers, but they are the one part of the proposal in which the applicant can be aggressive by taking the argument for competence directly to the reviewer's attention.

The resumés of individuals to be associated with the proposed study are the primary vehicles for arguing that the interests, training, and experience of the investigator(s) make support of the study reasonable. The techniques for mounting this offensive are not difficult to imagine.

1. If a format is provided, follow it exactly by revising, reformatting, and reprinting every resumé. If a format is not provided, invent one that will best serve the strategies noted below.
2. Keep vitae reasonably short by being selective about content. Reviewers will be looking for the obvious items, and these should be given prominence:
   a. Publications in the area of the study
   b. Publications in areas related to the study
   c. Receipt of previous grants in the area of the proposal
   d. Receipt of research grants in any area
   e. Involvement in a similar study whether funded or not
   f. Evidence of relevant training completed (e.g., postdoctoral study in the area)
   g. Unpublished papers or conference presentations in the area of the study
   h. Completed pilot studies in the area of the proposal.

Take care to give emphasis to current items. Items more than five years old should not be included unless they continue to be cited in current work or they help to establish a track record that is directly related to the study. Don't burden the reviewer with irrelevant clutter.

3. Use a uniform format that is divided into subsections with prominent headings. The idea is that the format should make it impossible for a hurried reader to miss material that supports the competence of the investigator. Only research publications should be listed, but if there are few, cite relevant research presentations or abstracts to supplement. Be certain, however, that the research publications are listed first, and that abstracts and presentations are categorized as such. It is not wise to list all of these in a mixture, leaving the reviewer to assume that you do not know the difference between an abstract and a publication, or that you are trying to give the impression of a great deal of scholarly productivity by intermingling these three types of activity.

4. Use short sections of highlighted text to provide detail about the exact nature of previous research experiences relevant to conduct of the proposed study. You are not limited just to the citation of dates, project titles, and publications. Tell the reviewers exactly what they need to know in a form that makes the task as easy as possible.

Where a team of investigators is to be involved, it will not always be easy to prepare an effective vitae section. Individualism in personal matters is a common trait among productive scholars, and the vitae is correctly regarded as a personal matter. Nevertheless, this is a place where flexibility and some cooperative effort will improve the chances that all participants will enhance their vitae—by winning a grant to support their scholarship.

DISSEMINATION OF RESULTS

The final step that transforms the personal act of inquiry into research is dissemination of a report into the public domain. Peers must review procedures if results are to be treated as reliable knowledge, and if the knowledge is to be useful, it must reach those who can make application. For those two reasons, many funding sources stipulate that plans for dissemination of results must be included as part of the proposal.

The rules here are reasonably simple.

1. Tell which results will be reported.
2. Indicate which audiences you intend to reach.
3. Specify how you plan to disseminate the final report.

4. Be specific in citing which particular conferences; development projects; local, state, or federal agencies; publications; or colleagues working on related research projects will be informed about the results from the proposed study.

5. Think carefully about how to reach appropriate audiences and go beyond the requisite printed report and ubiquitous paper at a national conference. Consider such strategies as summaries directed to interested scholars in other institutions, use of computer-based retrieval services, and releases through news media.

Typically, costs for dissemination can be built into the budget. Expenditures for everything from travel to conferences, to the printing and mailing of reports, is legitimate. Be sure, however, to base each item on careful estimates of actual costs. For example, obtain cost estimates for copying and collating the reports you expect to produce.

THE BUDGET

Although not a part of the plan for research, the budget is a central element in a grant application. It will be examined in detail by almost all members of a typical review committee, even those who may not be involved in evaluating the adequacy of design and methodology. Most application formats require that the budget be presented in brief form with no more than a page or two of appended explanation. Experience suggests that such explanation should be provided, even if it is not specifically required.

Personnel for whom funds are requested must be essential to the study. The most effective way to demonstrate such need is to specify responsibilities for each position. If project personnel must have special certification or advanced degrees, it is important to tell why a less qualified person could not be used. Enough information should be provided to support the level of commitment required in each position, whether for full-time or fractional employment.

Supplies and equipment must be documented with care. Review committees will appreciate efforts to give exact and realistic estimates of supplies needed, rather than the use of speculative round numbers. For instance, if videotape is to be used, rather than simply requesting $1,125 for the purchase of tapes, the applicant should explain that 15 minutes will be required for 100 subjects on three occasions without possibility of reusing tapes. That will require one tape per four subjects, or 75 tapes at $15 each, or a budget item of $1,125.

If funds for the purchase of large equipment are requested, the budget justification section might explain what attempts have been made to obtain the items by other means and why alternative plans such as rental or sharing will not suffice. Generally, funding agencies are not well disposed to requests for extensive equipment purchases, particularly large and expensive items. The position of many agencies is that the university or college should supply all the basic and less specialized equipment, as well as most large items that represent expensive and permanent investments in research capability. Young researchers may be dismayed to discover that their university takes the opposite position, holding that the investigator should obtain all expensive equipment through extramural funding, but that is the way things often work in a complex society.

Funding agency officers understandably would rather award money to applicants who already have the necessary equipment. In that manner, the agency's funds go directly into research activities rather than into building the capacity to perform research. The only counter to this logic is to make the best possible case for why the applicant's facility is ideally, if not uniquely, positioned for the conduct of the particular study—given the addition of the needed equipment. Another helpful strategy here is to point out any substantial ways the applicant's institution is contributing to the proposed study in terms of equipment, facilities, or personnel assigned to the project. Agency and foundation personnel like to feel that research projects, especially large ones, are a joint university/agency enterprise, and they tend to resent any implication that they constitute a goose that lays golden eggs.

Budget lines for ancillary items such as analysis of data, preparation of manuscript, and communication with consultants may be permitted under the rules for application but should be explained with great care. Consultants, for example, must be justified in detail. In the golden days of research when grants were plentiful, consultants sometimes were included in proposals simply because they were good professional friends who had an interest in the study. Today, a consultant must be demonstrably necessary to completion of the study. Even when such need exists, caution is required in preparing the explanation. If the consultant is needed because the investigator has not mastered a technique that is central to execution of the study, a reviewer may wonder why the grant should be awarded to someone who is deficient in skills commonly used by workers in the area.

Travel costs also require careful explanation. Only travel that is necessary to complete the research and, perhaps, to disseminate the findings should be included in the budget. If travel to specific conferences for the purpose of presenting reports from the study is included, the nature of the audience should be indicated and the relevance of the conference to the study demonstrated. More important, the relevance of the conference attendees to the interests of the funding agency should be specified.

Another major item in a proposed budget will be indirect costs (overhead) that the funding agency will pay directly to the institution. At this time, such costs vary widely and are negotiated by the agency and the university or college. Many large institutions have a standing policy on overhead for all grant contracts. Indirect charges presumably reimburse the university for the cost of building maintenance, processing of paperwork, utilities, and so on—all items that would have to be purchased by the grantor if the study were conducted at a facility owned by the agency. Other budget items dictated by the institution are insurance, retirement, and medical benefits for project personnel.

It is wise to take an early draft of the budget to the university officer in charge of grant negotiations and obtain assistance on all items not directly dictated by the nature of the research process itself. After several projected budgets have been written, the mysteries associated with indirect costs and employee benefits may become understandable to the researcher, but a substantial amount of grief can be avoided on the first effort if competent help is solicited and advice faithfully followed.

As a corollary to budget making, if a significant amount of support is to be provided by the institution in the form of new inputs of equipment, facilities, supplies, or personnel, the researcher must be sure to obtain formal approval from appropriate officers before proceeding too far into development of the proposal. In many institutions, agreement of the chairperson, the dean, and a vice president (at minimum) is required for such expenditures. It is best to have the needed commitments in hand well in advance of the point at which the proposal will be submitted for review.

It may be useful to demonstrate that respected scholars with expertise in the area of the proposed research regard the project as worthy and the investigator(s) as competent. For this purpose, letters containing such endorsements may be included in the proposal (usually in an appendix).

LETTERS OF ENDORSEMENT
AND CONFIRMATION

A second type of letter includes those that confirm the cooperation, support, or participation of organizations or individuals essential to the study. If, for example, schools and teachers or students are to be involved in any way, it is essential to have evidence that the appropriate authorities have reviewed the proposal and are prepared to participate if the grant is awarded. Similar brief notes may be required from the directors of service units such as the computer center, university health services, or laboratory facilities in other departments.

The documentation provided in such cases need not be elaborate or extend beyond what seems essential. The goal is simple. The applicant must provide some assurance that the staff, facilities, support service, and subject populations envisioned in the proposal will, in fact, be available.

USING PLANNING MODELS
AND FLOWCHARTS

Preparation of a grant proposal often involves dealing with a number of individuals in administrative units external to the author's home base. Institutional review and approval, soliciting peer reviews, obtaining letters of support, accumulating budget information, gathering commitments from personnel, assembling vitae, and obtaining multiple signatures all serve to complicate the process. A set of subdeadlines emerges that must be met in serial order. For these reasons, even a relatively straightforward grant proposal may quickly exceed managerial habits that are entirely adequate for the limited scope of theses or dissertations.

In response to the complicated network of steps that are demanded in developing many grant proposals, a number of management models, flowcharts, checklists, and step-by-step guides have been devised to assist the author (see Appendix A). Some of these, such as the PERT (Program Evaluation and Review Technique) system (Gall et al., 1996), lend themselves primarily to larger research or development undertakings.

The best option for the novice who is attempting to stay organized may be to devise a do-it-yourself flowchart, complete with assigned responsibilities and deadlines. Once a problem has been defined and an appropriate funding agency has been identified, the following items can be supplemented as required by local circumstance and displayed with boxes and arrows to form a flowchart of sequenced events with appropriate time frame warnings. This is, in effect, your own personal time frame, one that precedes the one you submit with the grant proposal. Table 10.1 includes the elements that most proposal writers should include when planning their time frame.

The novice will do well to remember the corollary of Murphy's Law that states, "Everything takes longer than you expect." Where one must depend on the voluntary cooperation of busy individuals in other parts of the university, several weeks of cushion are wise when establishing any set of target deadlines. This is particularly true of the typing and collation of the proposal. Even when

TABLE 10.1 Items to Be Included in the Time Frame

Important Dates

    First response to the request for proposals

    Deadline for preproposal or letter of intent

    Deadline for submission to Human Subject Review Committee

    Deadlines for obtaining administrative signatures

        Chairperson

        Dean

        Office of Sponsored Research

        Director of Computer Services

    Deadline for submission to a typist

    Deadline for submission of proposal

    Award announcement date

Major Development Steps

    Obtain guidelines

    Contact program officer at funding agency

    Select primary authors of proposal

    Prepare abstract or preproposal and submit letter of intent

    Contact units for support of collaboration

    Obtain initial administrative approval

    Complete review of literature

    Determine study design

    Prepare first draft of proposal

    Prepare abstract of proposal

    Initiate human subjects review

    Initiate internal peer review

    Prepare budget

    Revise proposal based on feedback

    Collect vitae

    Obtain letters of endorsement

    Obtain written assurances from support sources

    Complete institutional forms

    Type final document

    Obtain administrative signatures

    Duplicate proposal

    Submit proposal

a proposal is produced on a word processor, the typing alone may take several weeks. Invariably, it will take longer than you anticipate. Because a proposal is a large project often involving 50 to 100 typed pages, all of which must have no errors at all, it will take the office staff away from other duties for unacceptable periods of time if typing is left to the last minute. Further, each draft must be checked and double-checked. The end result is a process that makes Murphy's corollary look positively optimistic.

SUMMARY

If you have read this far, we hope you are not immobilized by the thought of undertaking the tasks described. Difficult and demanding as proposal writing can be, the rewards are clear and attractive—a well-planned study and money to make it go. In addition, each time a proposal is written, the process becomes easier. Many of the proposal sections, when written on a word processor, simply can be updated and reused in subsequent documents. For example, each time a proposal is submitted, the basic description of a university research facility simply is updated and reprinted. The same process can occur with a particular methodology used in a line of research. Once the description has been written, it need only be updated and then recycled. Grant gathering, like any other intellectual skill, improves with practice. You may never find yourself regarding the process as enjoyable, but the challenges are always fresh, and the sense of satisfaction in completing a good presentation can be a significant reward. Better still, of course, is obtaining the money!

PART

III

SPECIMEN PROPOSALS

INTRODUCTION

The specimen proposals presented in Part III of this text were selected with several intentions. First, we wished to display proposals that involved both different research paradigms and different designs for data collection and analysis. Second, we thought it desirable to present proposals that dealt with research topics drawn from a variety of disciplinary and professional areas. Third, it was necessary to illustrate proposals for both academic theses and dissertations, and for grant-supported research projects. Fourth, and finally, for the purpose of helping you appreciate the developmental process through which most proposals must pass, we have included exemplars ranging from an early draft to a document in polished and final form. Ultimately, all four proposals presented in Part III did accomplish the purposes of their respective authors—the award of a research grant or approval by a graduate committee and subsequent successful completion of a thesis or dissertation.

We suggest that you examine more than one of these documents. Not only do the proposals involve different research designs, but they also illustrate alternative formats and writing styles. You can obtain valuable ideas about the preparation of your own proposal by observing how the demands for communicating a research plan were met in different contexts for inquiry.

For the first specimen proposal, we selected an experimental study in which the investigator lays out a plan to examine the impact of psychological factors on training programs for strength and flexibility in older women. Second in order is the proposal for a doctoral dissertation involving qualitative research. In that document, the author proposes to examine high school students' perspectives concerning teachers who had a substantial impact on their school careers. The third proposal employs a quasi-experimental design for a study of children's reading comprehension to be conducted in the field setting of elementary school classrooms. The final proposal in Part III is an application for a "competitive renewal research grant." The study plan described there involved the field test of a worksite intervention for the reduction of employee smoking.

Each of the proposals has been edited for the present purpose and is accompanied by our comments. The specimens used here are not presented as models that are perfect in every respect. Instead, we selected proposals that not only served the intentions noted above but also did so in a manner that reflected a consistently high level of general academic competence. As you will see, the proposals also involve both interesting research topics and sometimes challenging problems of study design.

Our accompanying comments are not intended to be critical of the authors. It is easy to play the role of "Monday morning quarterback" when you have ample time and none of the pressures associated with preparing a proposal. The purpose of our commentary is only to draw your attention to crucial elements within each research plan, as well as to underscore the strengths and limitations of presentation in each proposal document.

As you formulate your own critique of the proposals, it will be useful (and a point of fairness) to remember that each of the authors, having now gone through the process of presenting his or her plan for formal approval, and then having actually performed the proposed study, surely could make changes that would improve both the proposal document and the investigation it presents. Hindsight always is 20/20. As you read, give special attention to the points at which clarity or persuasiveness seems to weaken, and then think carefully about what changes in the text might better have served the author. Look also for proposal functions that are executed with precision, economy, and grace—and then go and do likewise!

1

Experimental Study

Strength Training in Older Women: Does Self-Efficacy Mediate Improvements in Physical Function?

Readers are reminded that, as indicated in the Introduction to Part III, this document has been edited for the purposes of both economy of presentation and consistency with the proposal functions presented in Chapter 1. Text that elaborated on particular concepts (once introduced) was abbreviated, and several sections that were essential in the original proposal but are redundant for our present purpose were omitted entirely. What remains here, however, is a faithful reproduction of the basic elements in the author's plan for the proposed study.

AUTHORS' NOTE: This proposal was prepared in 1996 by Shannon Mihalko as part of the dissertation research requirement in the Department of Kinesiology at the University of Illinois at Urbana-Champaign under the direction of Edward McAuley. The dissertation was completed and accepted by the graduate school. Dr. Mihalko currently is an assistant professor at Wake Forest University.

INTRODUCTION

The fastest growing segment of the population in North America consists of those individuals 65 years of age and older (U.S. Bureau of the Census, 1992). This rapid increase among the aging population, often coined "the greying of America," is forecast to continue over the next 60 years (Brown, 1992), resulting in an attendant concern for the health, functional ability, and quality of life in this population (Brown, 1992; Katz, 1983). Although older adults are living longer, whether they are living more functional, active, and independent lives is debatable. This ability to function independently has become an increasingly crucial public health concern (Katz, 1983; Phillips & Haskell, 1995).

> The author has begun by introducing the general social context of the problem to be addressed by the proposed study. The first paragraph was designed to pique readers' interest by discussing changes in our population—changes in which they are (or will soon become) participants. As everyone expects (or, at least, hopes) to grow older, most readers will be interested in the topic and will be drawn along as the author now shifts from gentle introduction to definition of the concepts that form variables within the study. The discussion in the following paragraphs introduces two of those key concepts, agerelated decline in physical function and the role of muscular strength and balance in physical performance by older individuals.

Attempts have been made to identify those factors that are associated with the marked declines in age-related physical function. Physical activity and exercise participation have been consistently identified as important components in improving the quality of life and level of functional independence among aging populations (McAuley & Rudolph, 1995). However, the percentage of aging individuals who participate in physical activity and exercise is extremely low, with epidemiological estimates indicating that less than 40% of those individuals over the age of 65 participate in any leisure time physical activity, whereas over 40% of these adults maintain a sedentary lifestyle (Stephens, Jacobs, & White, 1985).

In addition to declines in physical activity, aging has also been associated with decrements in muscular strength, balance and movement impairments, increased incidence of falls, and reductions in performance of activities of daily living (ADLs) such as eating and drinking, dressing, washing, using the toilet, getting in and out of bed, rising from a chair, and moving about a home (Fiatarone et al., 1990; Goldberg & Hagberg, 1990; Katz, 1983; Tinetti & Speechley, 1989). It has been argued, however, that those physiological deficits often directly associated with aging are not solely due to the process of aging, but are largely a consequence of decreased participation in physical activity (Goldberg & Hagberg, 1990; Mihalko & McAuley, 1996). In fact, substantial physiological gains have been demonstrated in those aging individuals who engage in regular physical activity and exercise (Blair et al., 1989; Fiatarone & Evans, 1993; Goldberg & Hagberg, 1990; McAuley, Courneya, & Lettunich, 1991; McAuley & Rudolph, 1995).

Research examining the influence of regular physical activity and exercise on physiological parameters has demonstrated a wide range of effects on various physical conditions, including the reduction of coronary artery disease and all-cause mortality (Blumenthal et al., 1991), increased levels and performance of ADLs (Gill, Williams, & Tinetti, 1995; Katz, 1983; Phillips & Haskell, 1995), increased muscular strength and endurance (Fiatarone & Evans, 1993; Mihalko & McAuley, 1996), improved balance and movement parameters (Tinetti & Speechley, 1989; MacRae, Feltner, & Reinsch, 1994), and more recently, a decreased risk for falling (Province et al., 1995).

> In the next paragraphs, the construct of "falling" is introduced as a vital concern in the health of elderly persons. Notice how the author first connects the construct to elements in the previous paragraphs, and then extends it by explaining how physical abilities may affect activities of daily living.

Falls and fall-related injuries warrant particularly thorough investigation as they are major contributors to mortality, morbidity, and institutionalization in older adults and therefore pose a significant threat to the aging population (Dunn, Rudberg, Furner, & Cassel, 1992; Rubenstein & Josephson, 1992; Sattin, 1992). A landmark study by Province and colleagues (1995) examined the relationship between exercise levels and the relative risk of falling and fall-related injuries in adults 60 years of age and older. Their meta-analysis of epidemiological evidence was generated using the database from the Frailty and Injuries: Cooperative Studies of Intervention Techniques (Ory et al., 1993). Specifically, the risk factors for falling and fall-related injuries identified as primary outcomes in this meta-analysis included functional status, ADLs, muscular strength, balance, and previous falls. Province et al. (1995) report that assignment to interventions that had exercise as a component was associated with a decrease in the incidence of falls among the elderly.

In previous studies, researchers have compared fallers and nonfallers in an attempt to identify the major risk factors for falling. Throughout that literature, the most consistently identified risk factors that are implicated in falling are lower-extremity strength, levels of balance, and those variables associated with abnormal gait patterns (MacRae et al., 1994; Tinetti, Speechley, & Ginter, 1988). In fact, impairment of gait and balance have been associated with a significant three-fold increased risk of falling, whereas decreases in lower-body strength appear to increase the odds of falling five fold (MacRae et al., 1994).

In aging populations, clear differences have been shown between fallers and nonfallers on parameters that are potential risk factors for falling, as well as on future behavior and lifestyle changes and restrictions. In fact, 26% of those aging individuals who have fallen in the past year report avoiding common daily physical activities (Tinetti et al., 1988). Another study found that fallers report a 41% decrease in physical activity over a one year period as compared to 23% in nonfallers (Vellas, Cayla, Bocquet, dePemille, & Albarede, 1987). Other risk factors for falling consistently identified throughout the literature include: use of an assistive device, such as a walker or cane; impaired vision and a decrease in nocturnal vision; arthritis; self-reported limitations in mobility; and limited levels and/or dependence in ADLs (Langlois et al., 1995).

Activities of daily living are the most common referents of physical disability and functional dependence among the elderly (Guralnik & Simonsick, 1993; Phillips & Haskell, 1995) and are often characterized by primary self-maintaining functions such as bathing, dressing, transferring from bed to chair, climbing stairs, and walking a short distance (Guralnik & Simonsick, 1993; Katz, 1983). This decrease in physical functioning accompanying aging leads to an inability to live independently, often referred to as frailty, and is typically characterized by the need for assistance in carrying out one or more ADLs (Guralnik & Simonsick, 1993). Approximately one-fifth of the U.S. population who are 65 years of age or older require assistance in at least one ADL and may therefore be classified into this category (Guralnik & Simonsick, 1993). Furthermore, 23% of older adults living at home have difficulties with ADLs, and about 10% require help to complete these activities.

The inadequate assessment of functional ability among aging populations suggests the need to make wider use of physical performance tests that are truly relevant to the sample under consideration. In addition, it is necessary to incorporate the assessment of specific tasks and movements that are required to perform these common daily activities (Gill et al., 1995). Typical ADLs, such as climbing stairs, reaching up, and lifting objects, require the involvement of the three components of physical fitness often referred to as "muscular fitness" (American College of Sports Medicine, 1993, p. 48), which includes muscular strength, muscular endurance, and flexibility (Czaja, Weber, & Nair, 1993; Phillips & Haskell, 1995). That is, those aging adults who have undergone declines in muscular fitness are likely to report more difficulty in performing many daily activities, which often require lifting, carrying, pushing, and/or pulling capabilities (Czaja et al., 1993).

> The first sentence of the next paragraph provides a brief summary of the previous discussion (signaled by the opening phrase, "The recent literature suggests . . ."). The closing sentence, however, serves a very different function. It draws the reader's attention to a fact that will become the basis for the proposed study—we do not know whether increased strength reduces falls directly, or through other intermediate agencies (which nicely explains the rhetorical question posed in the title). Using that question as a means of transition, the author promptly turns to a discussion of the relationships involved. Note that the author is in the enviable position of being able to use some of her own preliminary work as part of the supporting literature.

The recent literature suggests that participation in physical activity, specifically resistive strength training programs, is associated with increases in the three components of muscular fitness (Fiatarone et al., 1990, 1994; Frontera et al., 1988). In turn, an increase in muscular strength has been associated with improvements in the levels and performance of ADLs (Fiatarone et al., 1990, 1994; Mihalko & McAuley, 1996) with a potential reduction in the risk for falls and fall-related injuries among aging individuals (Binder et al., 1994; Lipsitz et al., 1994). Whether the association between increased strength and reduced risk for falls and enhanced ADLs is direct or whether it can be explained by other underlying mechanisms is not, however, known.

One logical explanation for the association between greater levels of muscular strength and improvements in ADLs and reductions in the risk for falls and fall-related injuries may simply lie in the resultant changes reported in muscular strength levels from participation in strength training programs. That is, improvements in muscular strength among aging adults via participation in resistive strength programs may directly lead to an increase in ADL levels and performance, as well as to a decrease in falls and relative risk for falls. In fact, preliminary findings (Mihalko & McAuley, 1996) offer limited support for this hypothesis. Here, Mihalko and McAuley (1996) report that strength improvements accounted for 10.3% of the variance in ADL performance following an 8-week high intensity strength training program. Future research to corroborate these findings is necessary, however, since the assessment of ADLs was based on proxy reports rather than on actual performance levels.

In addition to the resultant muscular strength gains consistently reported as a function of participation in resistive strength training programs, it is possible that ADLs and the relative risk for falling may also be influenced by enhanced balance. For example, significant increases in balance parameters were demonstrated by frail older adults participating in an 8-week low to moderate intensity group exercise program (Binder et al., 1994). Moreover, this program led to significant increases in lower extremity strength, gait speed, and self-reported physical function in this cohort of older individuals at risk for recurrent falls. Therefore, increases in balance parameters may indeed augment the influence of physical activity on independent functioning and falls prevalence.

In conjunction with the findings on the effects of physical activity on physical function and the performance levels of ADLs, it has been suggested that a decrease in ADLs is often reported as a result or consequence of falling. More recently, however, reductions in ADLs and decreased performance levels in a variety of ADLs have been investigated and identified as potential risk factors for falling among the elderly (Langlois et al., 1995). Additionally, several investigators (Tinetti & Powell, 1993; Tinetti et al., 1988) have argued that fear of falling may be a significant predictor of falling among aging adults and perhaps, a more considerable problem than falling itself. Fear of falling is typically defined as an enduring concern about falling that results in restriction of daily activities and functioning (Tinetti & Powell, 1993). Specifically, fear of falling, after adjustment for age and gender, has been significantly associated with increased frailty and depressed mood, restriction of mobility and social activity, and decreased satisfaction with life (Arfken, Lach, Birge, & Miller, 1994). The prevalence of falling and the impact of fear of falling on physical activity levels and ADLs among the elderly is overwhelming. In fact, approximately 50% of those older individuals who report fear of falling avoid performing common ADLs and voluntarily reduce their levels of physical activity (Tinetti et al., 1988).

In the paragraph below, the author arrives at the primary destination for all that has preceded—the key concept of self-efficacy, and the suggestion that it may be one of the intermediary mechanisms for functional change. Retrospectively, the step-by-step logic of the presentation now becomes transparent, and the author's thoroughness in that process is impressive. Our only concern is that subsequent to mention in the title, the key concept (self-efficacy) is named for the first time on page 10 (of the original proposal document) and has been preceded by a great deal of dense and heavily documented prose. A reader might be excused if he or she began to wonder "What is all of this leading to?" a number of pages before arriving at the answer.

There are several strategies for circumventing that problem. One would have been to introduce a sketch (perhaps a simple graphic model) of the primary components, in their ordered relationships, at a much earlier point in the introduction, saying "This is the tour we are going to take, here are the primary stops en route, and there is the destination." With that guide in mind, this lengthy "introduction" might not seem at all arduous (or mysterious).

Another strategy simply would have been to reduce the density of the presentation. Although, for example, the many multiple citations probably were familiar and reassuring to advisors who were specialists in the field of gerontology, limiting the documentation to just one or two items for each major point might have served the purpose of the proposal just as well—and allowed other readers to move more easily through the less encumbered text.

Although fear of falling may decrease ADLs and limit physical functioning in older adults, little is known about the determinants of fear of falling or the potential mediating constructs between fear of falling and physical function. As actual behavior is often hard to predict based upon self-report measures of such constructs as fear and fear of falling (Tinetti, Mendes de Leon, Doucette, & Baker, 1994), this fear of a lack of control over one's ability to perform ADLs without falling is often conceptualized and assessed by perceptions of selfefficacy (McAuley, Mihalko, & Rosengren, in press; Tinetti & Powell, 1993; Tinetti et al., 1994). As proposed by Bandura (1977, 1986), self-efficacy is a situation-specific sense of control, concerned with the beliefs or convictions that one has in one's capabilities to successfully engage in a course of action in order to satisfy situational demands. It has been argued (McAuley et al., in press; Tinetti & Powell, 1993) that Bandura's (1986) social cognitive theory offers a potentially useful framework for explaining and understanding the relationships between physical activity, fear of falling, prevalence of falls, and ADL performance levels. Specifically, a social cognitive perspective posits that self-efficacy perceptions may mediate the underlying changes reported in ADLs and falling among active older adults as compared to their less active counterparts.

PURPOSE ⌣

In the statement of the purpose below, after identifying the broad conceptual framework of the study, the author lays out two objectives for the investigation. The first involves comparison of two treatments in terms of consequent changes in the parameters of strength and balance. The second objective, however, is to examine the relationships of those *physical* changes to *behavioral* (performance) changes measured by tests of ADLs and falls, as they may be mediated by *psychological* changes (in perception) measured by tests of selfefficacy and fear of falling. As complicated as that may sound, in operational terms it still boils down to a basic two-treatment group experiment with pre-post measures of six primary variables.

It might also have been helpful at this point if the author had indicated the order in which the variables are presumed to act. For example, does increased strength lead to improved ADL and thus higher perceived self-efficacy? Or might it be that increased strength itself leads to a greater sense of self-efficacy, and thereby to improved ADL performance?

The present study incorporates a social cognitive framework to examine the relationships between the changes in muscular strength and balance resulting from participation in a high-intensity strength training program, and the subsequent changes in efficacy perceptions, ADL performance, fear of falling, and prevalence of falls among an aging cohort. In an attempt to examine the mediational role played by self-efficacy in changes in ADL performance and falling, this study had two primary objectives: (a) to compare strength and balance changes in aging individuals who were assigned to either a high intensity resistive training program or a stretching and flexibility control group and (b) to determine whether unique variation in changes in ADL performance and falls could be attributable to changes in perceptions of control or self-efficacy.

RATIONALE

Although reasons for conducting the study have been woven throughout the introduction, here the author directly addresses the question "Why do this study?" Notice that for the purpose of clarity, the author neatly separates practical and theoretical reasons for conducting the study. The ensuing discussion leads through a series of cumulative steps to the final assertion that although the evidence for each link is as yet inconclusive or incomplete, there is a sufficient chain of evidence to support testable postulates (hypotheses) about the complex relationships involved.

There are both practical and theoretical reasons for conducting this study. From a practical perspective, knowing the benefits of the two exercise programs and how they differ in improving the physical capabilities of the participants will provide information that is valuable to those working with the elderly. If one exercise program is substantially better then physicians and exercise specialists will have a basis from which to make informed decisions.

On a theoretical level, this study will integrate a number of the percepts of efficacy relevant to falling, ADLs, muscular strength capabilities, balance parameters, and physical function and provide information on the factors that decrease fall prevalence and reduce ADL limitations. Moreover, we will better understand whether increases in physical capabilities, such as muscular strength and balance, lead to enhanced perceptions of personal control relative to successful performance of common ADLs without falling. This in turn may provide information on whether self-efficacy influences balance and improves subsequent function, and reduces the fear of falling. Although there is little empirical evidence to date that links physical activity and fear of falling (McAuley et al., in press), improvements in balance (Binder et al., 1994), increases in muscular strength (Fiatarone & Evans, 1993), and a reduction in falls risk (Province et al., 1995) have been consistently related to physical activity and exercise among aging individuals.

Considerable evidence exists to support the hypothesis that successful participation in exercise and physical activity programs can serve to enhance perceptions of mastery or personal control (Ewart, Stewart, Gillilan, & Kelemen, 1986; McAuley et al., 1991; McAuley, Lox, & Duncan, 1993; Rodin, 1986). Specifically, McAuley and colleagues (McAuley et al., 1991; McAuley et al., 1993;

McAuley, Courneya, Rudolph, & Lox, 1994) have demonstrated that participation in exercise programs not only increased levels of self-efficacy, but these perceptions of personal capabilities also led to increased adherence to exercise regimens and subsequent physiological responses to exercise. Thus, a social cognitive perspective (Bandura, 1986) would postulate that fear of falling, falling, and ADL performance are multiply determined by physiological, cognitive, and behavioral influences. It is possible, therefore, that perceptions of self-efficacy may mediate the relationships between physical activity participation and subsequent physiological improvements with changes in ADL performance, fear of falling, and prevalence of falls among aging individuals. The results of this study will substantially contribute to our understanding of these complex relationships.

HYPOTHESES

The complex nature of this study, including both the presence of six major variables (some of which were divided into subvariables) and the need to examine several different types of relationships through complex statistical analyses, required the author to establish a large number of hypotheses. For clarity of presentation and ease of use, these were grouped into six logically derived clusters. For economy, we have included here only representative examples from each cluster, indicating in each case the number of omitted hypotheses.

Notice that each hypothesis is specific to a particular relationship. For example, in Hypothesis 1a the relationship between type of training and pectoral muscle strength will be subject to a statistical test of significance (some form of analysis of variance is implied). When the analysis is complete, the investigator will be able to accept or reject the hypothesis. By returning to our discussion of hypotheses in Chapter 1, you can examine the adequacy of each hypothesis. For example, is the hypothesis unambiguous? Does it express a relationship? Is an appropriate statistical test implied?

You will also notice that some of these hypotheses are directional—positing whether the relationship might reasonably be expected to be positive or negative. The presence of previous research suggesting such directionality encouraged the hypothesis and, in turn, allowed the author (in at least some of the instances) to choose a more powerful statistical test (one allowing greater confidence in its prediction) than the test used with hypotheses that lack specified direction (null hypotheses).

Specifically, it is hypothesized that:

1) Participation in a resistive strength training program will result in greater increases in muscle strength than participation in a stretching and flexibility program, for the:
   a. pectoral muscles
   b. latissimus dorsi muscle
   c. deltoid muscles

We have omitted six additional hypotheses. For hypotheses such as these, it is acceptable to write a separate statement for each measurement to be taken, or to nest a series of such items within a single stem statement. For the sake of economy and simplicity, we prefer the latter (as above).

2a) Participation in a resistive strength training program will result in greater decreases in fear of falling than participation in a stretching and flexibility program.

2b) Participation in a resistive strength training program will result in greater increases in Falls Efficacy Scale scores than participation in a stretching and flexibility program.

We have omitted two additional hypotheses.

3a) Participation in a resistive strength training program will result in greater improvements in self-reported ADLs than participation in a stretching and flexibility program.

4a) Change in muscular strength is negatively related to changes in fear of falling.

4b) Change in balance is negatively related to change in fear of falling.

We have omitted four hypotheses here.

5c) Change in muscular strength is positively related to change in ADL performance.

5d) Change in balance is positively related to change in ADL performance.

6a) Change in muscular strength will predict a unique percentage of the variance in residualized change in fear of falling scores, in addition to that predicted by change in balance and self-efficacy.

We have omitted eight additional hypotheses.

In many proposals, sections would be included at this point to deal with a variety of special needs within the proposal. Among the most common of those are definitions of technical terms that are particular to the investigation or to the author's supporting arguments, and specification (for the reader) of the limitations and delimitations that must be remembered when considering the proposed study. An alternative to segregation of such material into separate sections, and the option used in this proposal, is to weave the information into the text as it becomes relevant. The first time a technical term such as "self-efficacy" was used, for example, it was followed by a brief definition, adjusted to the nature of the immediate context.

The choice between segregating or distributing definitions is partly a matter of personal style and partly a matter of logistics (length of the manuscript, number of unfamiliar terms, complexity of definitions, etc.). If a great number of definitions are required, for example, it is easier to revisit one that appears in a single listing than to locate it embedded somewhere in many pages of text. On the other hand, establishing subsections of the proposal (such as "Limitations" or "Definitions") just for the effect of having them serves no useful purpose. The primary consideration should be to make it as easy as possible for your readers to follow the presentation. In what follows, you can observe exactly how the author has elected to handle these matters.

In the original proposal, the following review of the literature required 42 pages of text. Following the brief introduction, we have selected the first and last subsections of that review for use here. A lengthy middle subsection has been omitted. Because it employed exactly the same review format, for our present purpose the reader will not be deprived by the deletion. A brief summary does provide an overview of the entire review at the close of the section.

LITERATURE REVIEW

This chapter begins with an epidemiological overview of aging in the United States, in order to highlight the importance of examining the aging process from a public health perspective. This section will also discuss the relationship between aging and physical function from an epidemiological perspective, with an emphasis on declines in physical activity and common activities of daily living (ADLs), as well as on the increase in falls risk and prevalence of falls associated with age. This section will be followed by a review of the effects of physical activity and exercise on function in the elderly, highlighting the role played by muscular strength in falls risk reduction and ADL enhancement. Finally, the last section of the chapter will be devoted to reviewing the potential underlying mechanisms proposed to mediate strength effects on these parameters of physical function, with particular emphasis on the role played by self-efficacy perceptions.

At the close of the first paragraph, the reader knows three things about the review of literature in this proposal. First, although citations to prior studies have appeared throughout the sections serving as introduction and definition of primary variables, the concepts involved are sufficiently complex (and numerous) to require further explanation. Much of that discussion will involve the use of research literature to support the design of hypotheses and selection of methods of measurement. Thus, for this proposal it became reasonable to have a separate section designated as "Literature Review." Second, an overview of the chapter indicates that the review will be divided into three subsections—an important step in helping readers to organize their understanding of the author's discussion. Third, and finally, the author has specified the relationships to be treated within each subsection: (a) aging, health, and physical function; (b) physical activity, strength, and physical function; and (c) the mediating role played by self-efficacy between strength and physical function.

This might be an appropriate point for you to revisit our discussion of preparing a literature review (Chapter 4). In particular, we draw your attention to the way the author uses the literature to support an ongoing discussion that is the central element in this section. This contrasts sharply with the ineffective strategy of writing text that consists of long (and boring) sequences of studies only occasionally punctuated by reference to their implications. Note also that extended detail is provided only when appreciating a particular point truly is essential to understanding the proposed study. As we argued in Chapter 4, if the discussion is developed with care, much of it can consist of general statements, with the reader always having the option of recourse to relevant detail in the cited references. As you read, also note how the use of topical subcategories and the insertion of headings and subheads eases the task of following the review. The addition of summaries for each subsection (as well as to the chapter as a whole) makes it difficult to lose track of information despite the complex set of variables involved.

Epidemiological Perspectives

Aging in the United States

According to the United States (U.S.) census (U.S. Bureau of the Census, 1992), individuals over 65 years of age make up the fastest growing portion of the population in North America and have often been referred to as the "fastest growing minority" (Mackintosh, 1978). In fact, the proportion of Americans who are 65 years of age and older is estimated to double from 12% in 1986 to 24% in the year 2020, reaching an approximate number of 52 million (Tinetti et al., 1988; U.S. Bureau of the Census, 1992). Specifically, population estimates have indicated that this segment of the U.S. population had grown to 31.2 million in 1990, as compared to 26 million in 1983. This "greying of America" is projected to continue over the next several decades (Brown, 1992), raising several concerns relative to public health issues and health care economics. The overall impact of this rapid increase in the aged will influence such factors as reductions in independent functioning, the need for long-term care and institutionalization, and ultimately, the prevalence of chronic disease and all-cause mortality and morbidity (Schneider & Guralnik, 1990).

Approximately 85% of those individuals 65 years of age and older have one or more chronic health conditions, with an additional 42% demonstrating limited functional capabilities (Katz, 1983). At present, the proportion of elderly individuals who are functionally impaired and/or dependent is alarmingly high and estimated to grow exponentially in the future (Tinetti et al., 1988). For example, one-quarter million hip fractures that are attributable to osteoporosis and indirectly associated with falls and fall-related injuries are reported each year in the U.S. among those individuals 65 years of age and older (Smith & Tommerup, 1995). As the population ages and becomes more functionally dependent, the impact on society, health care, and the public health system could be overwhelming (Bokovoy & Blair, 1994).

Aging and Physical Activity

As the population of older adults continues to increase, the question posed by many is not how long can we prolong life, but how can we extend the quality of that life? Indeed, although individuals may live longer, they may not necessarily lead more active, happy, and independent lives. In fact, several recent conferences and workshops on health, physical activity, and exercise have emphasized the importance of physical activity and an active lifestyle, recommending the evaluation and promotion of physical activity and exercise among elderly populations (Bouchard, Shephard, & Stephens, 1993; Haskell et al., 1992; King et al., 1992). Additionally, the U.S. Department of Health and Human Services (1990) has identified physical activity and fitness as one of the major objectives for the health of the nation, as well as an integral component of overall health promotion. Specifically, the U.S. Public Health Service (1990) has incorporated the importance of prolonging independent living among this elderly population in their national health objectives for the year 2000, with an emphasis on increasing the rate of participation in regular, appropriate physical activity to 40% in individuals 65 years of age and older.

Although considerable evidence exists to suggest that physical activity and exercise are essential ingredients in successful and healthy aging, the participation rates of North Americans in physical activity and exercise programs are disappointing. Analysis of the 1990 Established Populations for Epidemiologic Studies of the Elderly data base indicates that 26% of the study population were incapable of walking 1/2 mile, 42% were unable to complete heavy household chores, and 19% were not able to climb stairs (National Institute on Aging, 1990). Furthermore, the Healthy People 2000 report indicates that more than two out of every five older adults over 65 years of age lead a basically sedentary lifestyle (Public Health Service, 1990). In fact, disability resulting from this sedentary lifestyle is twice as common in those individuals 75 years of age and older, as compared to those aged 45 to 64 years (U.S. Department of Health and Human Services, 1990).

Unfortunately, many older individuals who attempt to participate in an exercise or physical activity program withdraw prior to the onset of apparent health benefits (Dishman, 1990). This finding is not surprising in light of the well-documented attrition rate in exercise programs, with approximately 50% of those adopting a new exercise regimen dropping out within the first 6 months (Dishman, 1990). With the apparent increase of older populations in which inactivity and decreases in independent functioning are prevalent, the importance of determining the impact of these declines in physical activity on functional status, morbidity, and mortality is abundantly clear.

Aging and Physical Function

Activities of daily living. In addition to the established age-related declines in physical activity, aging has been associated with decreases in various components of functional independence (Gill et al., 1995; Katz, 1983; Simonsick et al., 1993; Tinetti & Speechley, 1989), with a considerable segment of the community-dwelling population over 65 years of age reporting limitations in some aspect of physical functioning. For many older adults, a reduction in levels and performance of ADLs has a greater impact on the preservation of independence in day to day functioning than the chronic diseases from which these reductions had originated (Ensrud et al., 1994). For example, an estimated 10% of nondisabled adults aged 75 and older who are still living in the community become dependent in ADLs each year (Gill et al., 1995) and approximately one-quarter of the aging population has difficulty performing activities that are deemed necessary for self-sufficiency (Dawson, Hendershot, & Fulton, 1987; Young, Masaki, & Curb, 1995).

The ability to live independently in the community is extremely difficult for those older adults who need assistance with or simply cannot perform common ADLs (Czaja et al., 1993). Specifically, 23% of adults aged 65 years and older have difficulty with activities such as bathing and dressing, and about 10% require assistance with these ADLs (Dawson et al., 1987). In addition, 27% need help with more complex activities, such as meal preparation and housework (Guralnik & Simonsick, 1993). Furthermore, there is a high rate of home accidents and falls among this aging population, possibly resulting from the inability to perform these common self-maintaining functions (Czaja et al., 1993; Province et al., 1995; Sattin, 1992). With the present and anticipated aging of the population, the increasing proportion of older adults who are functionally limited or dependent is not expected to diminish in the near future (Manton, Corder, & Stallard, 1993).

Falls Risk and Prevalence. One of the most serious and prevalent sources of medical problems and functional decline among aging individuals in the U.S. is represented by falls and fall-related injuries (Tinetti et al., 1988). Approximately 30% of those individuals 65 years of age and older suffer a fall each year, with about 50% of these elderly persons sustaining more than one fall in this time period (Tinetti et al., 1988; Tinetti & Speechley, 1989). Consequently, serious injuries result from approximately 10% to 15% of these falls (Tinetti et al., 1988). Specifically, 0.2% to 1% of these falls result in hip fractures, 5% in fractures at other sites, 5% in soft-tissue injuries and dislocations, as well as long periods of immobility due to the inability to regain normal gait patterns (Kiel, O'Sullivan, Teno, & Mor, 1991; Sattin, 1992; Tinetti et al., 1988).

Falls and fall-related injuries pose a major threat to aging individuals and are a significant contributor to morbidity, mortality, institutionalization, and immobility (Dunn et al., 1992; Sattin, 1992; Tinetti et al., 1988). Unintentional injury is the 6th leading cause of death among those adults 65 years of age and older.

These unintentional deaths may be largely attributable to falling, especially for those over the age of 85 years (Province et al., 1995; Sattin, 1992). Additionally, these falls have a considerable social, medical, and economic impact.

Several paragraphs have been omitted here that offer details concerning the threats to individuals, as well as the social and public health implications, presented by injurious falls in the elderly.

Summary

This section reviewed the epidemiological literature on aging. People are living longer but that does not necessarily mean they have an optimal quality of life. Many age-related declines occur with aging. Over one-quarter of elderly adults have problems doing simple daily tasks, and accidental death, particularly from falling, is a problem in the aged. Participation in physical activity programs has been recommended for the elderly (U.S. Public Health Service, 1990) and may help reduce the accidental deaths and improve the quality of life.

The middle subsection of the literature review, "Exercise Effects on Function in the Elderly," has been omitted here.

SELF-EFFICACY THEORY

Overview of Self-Efficacy Theory

Self-efficacy theory is a social cognitive approach to behavior that views behavior, physiology, cognitions, and environmental influences as interacting determinants of one another (Bandura, 1977, 1986). Self-efficacy is defined by Bandura (1977) as a belief in one's capabilities to overcome successfully the demands of a situation, in order to achieve a desired outcome. Self-efficacy theory offers a common mechanism by which individuals posit control over their own behaviors and act as self-referent mediators, rather than simply passive acceptors of environmental stimuli and external forces (Bandura, 1977, 1986). Efficacy cognitions are specifically related to the activity or behavior in question, and subsequently, efficacy cognitions are apt to change in response to changing environmental stimuli.

Increases in efficacy perceptions are likely to occur as a function of positive mastery experiences, whereas decreases in efficacy perceptions are likely to result from negative experience and failure. By definition, self-efficacy cognitions are concerned with the convictions or beliefs that an individual possesses about his or her ability to meet the situational demands of a particular course of action successfully (Bandura, 1977, 1986). It is important to emphasize that it is not the skills an individual actually possesses that are important, but rather what judgments the individual forms relative to what can be accomplished with these skills.

Those individuals who have high levels of self-efficacy tend to exert more effort, approach more challenging tasks, and persist longer in the face of obstacles and barriers. For example, an elderly individual who has high levels of self-efficacy for performing ADLs without falling is more likely to engage in ADLs within a variety of environmental situations. On the other hand, when faced with aversive stimuli, those individuals who have low self-efficacy perceptions tend to attribute negative experiences internally, drop out of the activity altogether, and report higher levels of depression and anxiety (Bandura, 1982). In the context of falling, aging individuals who have low levels of efficacy for maintaining balance and believe they are at risk for falling are more likely to avoid these situations altogether.

> Omitted here are several paragraphs that describe self-efficacy theory, its derivation within the social sciences, appropriate forms of measurement, and domains within which it successfully has been applied.

Although self-efficacy theory has been applied to numerous domains, perhaps the domain of most promise is that of health behavior and specifically, that of exercise and physical activity (McAuley, 1992a). Research in the exercise domain has demonstrated that not only is self-efficacy enhanced by the exercise experience, it is also a determinant of physical activity in both diseased (Ewart et al., 1986) and asymptomatic populations (Dzewaltowski, 1989). This has been documented in large-scale community studies (Sallis et al., 1986), and in training studies (McAuley, 1992a; McAuley et al., 1994).

> This last section of the review of literature describes the aspects of the research literature that are most relevant to the present study: the relationships among the dependent and independent variables.

Self-Efficacy Theory, Physical Activity, and Exercise

Exercise behavior has been recognized as a complex, dynamic, and multiply determined phenomenon (Dishman, 1990) with a host of determinants having been identified as having a potential direct or indirect effect on exercise participation and adherence (McAuley, 1993). Self-efficacy theory (Bandura, 1977, 1986) offers a promising and sound theoretical framework from which to examine the interplay between biological, psychological, social, and environmental processes in the specific domains of health, exercise, and physical activity (Dishman, 1990; McAuley, 1992b). A majority of the researchers examining self-efficacy theory within the domains of exercise and physical activity have focused on efficacy as a determinant of exercise behavior (McAuley, 1992b, 1993).

In a large-scale community study, findings indicated that self-efficacy perceptions had influenced the adoption and maintenance of exercise behavior in a general population (Sallis et al., 1986). Further support for this relationship was found in a study of older individuals recovering from acute myocardial infarction (Ewart et al., 1986), who participated in a 10-week exercise rehabilitation program involving either jogging and circuit weight training or jogging and volleyball exercise regimens. The number of minutes above or below the prescribed intensity level that subjects participated in the jogging activities, as well as the strength gains accrued in the weight training program were predicted by levels of self-efficacy. That is, subjects who had higher levels of lifting-efficacy had greater strength gains at program end. Those subjects with greater post-treadmill efficacy also had an increase in their perceived ability to carry out tasks involving arm or leg strength, such as home activities and stair climbing (Ewart, Taylor, Reese, & DeBusk, 1983).

Ewart and colleagues (Ewart et al., 1983, 1986) have demonstrated that those individuals with increased self-efficacy are more likely to participate in a variety of life behaviors than their less efficacious counterparts (McAuley, 1993). With respect to exercise and physical activity, aging individuals who have a greater sense of efficacy in their physical capabilities will adopt a more active lifestyle and perhaps, attempt more ADLs and therefore decrease their levels of functional dependence. In turn, an increase in physical activity and exercise participation may serve as a further means to enhance efficacy perceptions. Indeed, exercise and physical activity have been investigated as a mechanism by which efficacy cognitions concerning one's physical capabilities may be enhanced. In this vein, it appears that efficacy cognitions about one's physical capabilities may be altered and modified by chronic exercise and physical activity (Ewart et al., 1986; Holloway, Beuter, & Duda, 1988).

Most of the research in this area has examined the effects of physical activity on self-efficacy cognitions among middle-aged and older males and females, with the majority of studies involving clinical populations (McAuley, 1993). For example, Kaplan, Atkins, and Reinsch (1984) examined the effect of a walking program on efficacy perceptions for compliance to future exercise programs in subjects with chronic obstructive pulmonary disease (COPD). Not only was efficacy significantly correlated to program compliance among this clinical sample, but efficacy was also found to generalize to other related ADLs. In addition, exercise efficacy was found to be a predictor of five-year survival in another sample of patients with COPD (Kaplan, Ries, Prewitt, & Eakin, 1994). Thus, participation in strength training programs may not only lead to enhanced efficacy for strength training, but also to compliance with future strength training endeavors and increased efficacy for strength-related ADLs.

Here we have deleted several pages presenting additional examples of the pervasive and interactive relationships among exercise, affective responses, and efficacy expectations.

Across these studies, it has been shown that both chronic and acute bouts of physical activity and exercise consistently influence efficacy cognitions in a positive manner (McAuley, 1993, 1994). Through many subsequent studies, evidence has accumulated to support these two related aspects of the exercise/self-efficacy relationship. That is, self-efficacy has consistently been both a reliable predictor of exercise behavior, as well as a positive outcome of the exercise experience. In addition, several studies exist that examine the mediational role played by self-efficacy in affective responses (Bozoian, Rejeski, & McAuley, 1994; McAuley & Courneya, 1992). From this standpoint, physical activity is theorized to influence affective responses indirectly through its positive influence on efficacy perceptions.

Summary

Self-efficacy theory posits that behavior, physiology, cognitions, and environmental influences interact with each other. Self-efficacy theory may help explain the relationships between strength and falling variables in adults. An extrapolation of the findings suggests that self-efficacy plays a mediational role in the relationship between physical activity, falling, and physical function since self-efficacy perceptions have proven to be reliable predictors, outcomes, and mediators of various behaviors, and hold particular promise in the domains of physical activity and exercise. Thus, muscular strength changes that result from participation in a strength training program may both directly and indirectly affect ADLs, falling, and fear of falling, via increased perceptions of efficacy for strength-related activities.

> The transitional section with the heading "Summary of the Proposed Study" serves as a bridge between the preceding review and the following explication of method, measures, procedures, and analyses. Notice how this overview begins with a backward reference to the main points established in the review, then moves through a clear statement of the rationale for the study, and then closes with a paragraph that directs attention forward to what will be accomplished by the study (now to be proposed in detail).

Summary of the Proposed Study

Participation in a high intensity strength training program leads to increases in muscular strength and fitness, as well as improved balance parameters (Binder et al., 1994; Ewart et al., 1986; Phillips & Haskell, 1995). Resistive strength training, once thought to be potentially hazardous for an elderly population, has recently been acknowledged for its role in not only enhancing physiological outcomes, but also in improving ADL performance, reducing the risk for falls and fall-related injuries, and enhancing the quality of life among elderly persons (Brown et al., 1990; Czaja et al., 1993; Ewart et al., 1986; Fiatarone & Evans, 1993: Goldberg & Hagberg, 1990; Phillips & Haskell, 1995). Whether the role played by increased muscular strength in the reduction of falls risk and ADL enhancement is direct or whether it can be explained by other underlying mechanisms has yet to be determined.

Bandura's (1986) social cognitive theory offers a theoretical framework for examining the underlying mechanisms that may explain the effects of resistive strength training on falls prevalence, fear of falling, and ADL performance in aging individuals. Specifically, a social cognitive perspective (Bandura, 1986) would suggest that fear of falling, falls prevalence, and ADL performance are multiply determined by physiological, cognitive, and behavioral influences. Furthermore, it has been argued that self-efficacy perceptions may mediate the relationships between physical activity participation and subsequent physiological improvements with changes in falls prevalence, fear of falling, and perform-ance of ADLs among elderly persons. From a public health standpoint, the integration of the percepts of efficacy relevant to muscular strength, balance, ADLs, falling, and overall physical function may serve not only to decrease falls prevalence and reduce ADL limitations, but may ultimately lead to enhanced physical, economic, and social independence in our aging society.

The present study employs a social cognitive framework to determine the direct and indirect effects of changes in muscular strength and balance resulting from participation in either a high intensity strength training program or a stretching and flexibility program on ADL performance and falling among a sample of older adults, via self-efficacy. As a result, the mediational role played by self-efficacy will be more thoroughly examined and the direct and indirect effects of strength training on ADL performance and falls prevalence will be determined.

METHOD

For most proposals, the brief introductory paragraph is a perfect model of economy and clarity. It provides a simple overview of major steps and then directs the reader to a figure that meshes the individual parts into a diagram of actions in sequential order. In what follows, you will see three other proposal strategies that are worthy of emulation: (a) previous studies by the author, her advisor, and other members of her research group are used as pilot work to support particular decisions; (b) references are cited that provide reliability and validity information for each measure; and (c) complex details, test forms and protocols, and other supplementary materials are placed in appendices.

This study addresses the effect of strength and stretching/flexibility exercise programs on a variety of variables. In addition, the underlying mechanisms that influence increases in ADLs will be investigated. Participants will be recruited and then oriented to the study. Pretests will be conducted on behavioral, physical, and psychological measures. Participants will then be randomly assigned to one of the two exercise programs. At the conclusion of a 12-week exercise program posttests will be administered to all participants. A diagrammatic overview of the design is presented in Figure 1.

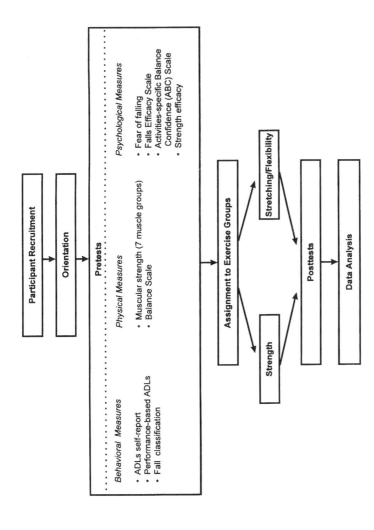

Proposal 1: Figure 1. Figure 1. Overview of the Research Design
NOTE: ADL = Activities of Daily Living.

Participants

Participants for this study will be recruited via local newspaper and radio advertising. In addition, the addresses of retired faculty and staff from a midwest university will be obtained from an established mailing list and these individuals will be sent an invitation to participate in this study. Potential participants will be asked to respond to further announcements which will explain the time commitment and outline the general aspects of the exercise programs. All participants will be required to satisfy the following inclusion criteria: (a) females 60 years of age and above, (b) no history of regular physical activity over the past six months, (c) free of any medical condition that might be further exacerbated by regular physical activity, and (d) an adequate level of functional mental status. In order to screen for declines in the latter criterion, participants will be asked to complete the Pfeiffer Mental Status Questionnaire (Pfeiffer, 1975), which is a short measure and will be administered by interview (see Appendix A). Any of the participants who answer three or more questions incorrectly on this measure will be excluded from this study based on mental status. This cut score of three follows the standard guidelines employed by researchers in the Establishment of Populations for Epidemiologic Studies of the Elderly (National Institute on Aging, 1990).

Prior to participation in the study, participants also will be required to obtain medical clearance from a personal physician. This clearance will ensure that all participants are capable of engaging in the exercise program without aggravating any existing physical condition. Additionally, participants will be asked to document all medications and prescribed drugs that are taken on a regular basis, so factors that might confound the analysis can be identified and, if necessary, be subject to control. Finally, all participants will be required to read and sign the informed consent. The informed consent and the medical clearance form can be found in Appendix B.

Measures

Measures of behavioral (e.g., ADLs and falls), physical (e.g., muscular strength and balance), and psychological (e.g., self-efficacy and fear of falling) function are described in the following sections and can be found in the appendices.

Behavioral Measures

Activities of daily living. Two measurements of activities of daily living will be administered in order to investigate both subjective and objective ADLs. With the current emphasis on performance-based testing (Elam et al., 1991), rather than on proxy assessments (Mihalko & McAuley, 1996), the use of both measures will allow for a comparison between the assessment of ADLs based on performance and self-report (See Appendix C).

> The comparison indicated above certainly would be possible, and it might be of considerable practical interest. As a general rule, however, it is unwise to introduce analytic operations that are not truly part of the study as proposed (which is the case here). If nothing else, such side excursions may distract readers from the main exposition and add little more than a further complication. There is, of course, the alternative of making it a genuinely functional part of the proposal.

The development of the self-report measure of ADLs (Mihalko & McAuley, 1996) was based upon ratings by nursing home administrators on the importance of various ADLs in the daily functioning of their senior residents. This adaptation of Lawton and Brody's (1969) Instrumental Activities of Daily Living Scale was constructed in an attempt to target ADLs relevant to functional ability among sedentary older persons. This measure includes the assessment of daily activities such as getting up and down from a chair or bed, getting in and out of a car, carrying and picking up objects, and reaching up overhead. Participants will be asked to rate 20 ADLs separately on a 5-point Likert-like scale, ranging from 0 to 4, (i.e., 0 = cannot do, 1 = can do with assistance, 2 = can partially do without assistance, 3 = can do independently with some difficulty, and 4 = can do easily). Therefore, scores for this measure of subjective ADLs can range from 0 to 80.

A performance-based assessment of ADLs also will be completed by each subject. Here, all participants will be asked to attempt four ADLs, including reaching up overhead, getting up and down from a chair, stair climbing ability, and walking speed. The first three ADLs will be scored on a 5-point Likert-like scale by objective raters, based upon strict scoring criteria which will mirror the scale of the subjective ADL measure. For example, when attempting to stand and sit from a chair, participants will be given a score of 0 if they need maximal assistance to stand or sit, a score of 1 if they can stand and sit with minimal assistance, a score of 2 if they can stand or sit after several tries, a score of 3 if they can rise to a complete standing position and then sit with the use of the arms of the chair, and a score of 4 if they can stand and sit easily. The last performance-based ADL will assess walking speed by asking participants to walk an 8-foot course with no obstructions (Guralnik et al., 1994). Participants will be instructed to walk at their usual speed with the aid of an assistive device if needed. Two raters will record times for two walking trials and an average of the four times will be used for analysis. For the walking measure, categories will be created in order to allow for a collective performance-based measure of the four ADLs (i.e., 5-point Likert-like scale). That is, participants who can complete the task will be assigned scores of 0 to 4, dependent upon the quintiles of time needed to complete the walking task, with the fastest times being represented by a score of 4 (Guralnik et al., 1994). The four categorical measures will be combined for a total ADL score ranging from 0 to 16. The analysis of walking speed as a variable will utilize average walking times (i.e., actual seconds).

Fall classification. To address the limitations of past fall assessments which have typically employed one-item dichotomous, retrospective measures, falls will be assessed in this study by using computerized dynamic posturography, commonly referred to as the Equitest. The Equitest perturbs the support surface and visual surround in order to examine the contribution of visual, vestibular, and somatosensory components involved in balance control. Any time the subject steps forward or begins to fall, the computer stops the particular task and records the occurrence as a fall. Therefore, falls will be calculated by summing the number of times that the subject "falls" over the course of the test. Participants will be supported by a loose harness, thereby preventing the occurrence of an actual fall.

> When participants are to be exposed to a complex situation or activity such as that presented by use of the apparatus described above, it usually is wise to plan some form of acclimatization procedure. This would be the appropriate point to briefly sketch how that would be accomplished.

Physical Activity History. A short inventory assessing participants' exercise history will be employed to determine overall physical activity background (see

Appendix D). Specifically, participants will indicate: (a) the number of days per week they typically engage in physical activity; (b) the number of minutes per session of physical activity; (c) the intensity level of each session, ranging from 1 "easy" to 4 "hard"; and (d) the mode of activity in which they typically engage.

Physical Measures

Muscular Strength. Levels of muscular strength will be assessed for the following muscle groups: pectorals, latissimus dorsi, deltoids, biceps, triceps, hamstrings, and quadriceps. The strength level of each muscle group will be determined by the individual's one repetition maximum (1 RM) or the greatest amount of resistance that the individual can move one time throughout a full range of motion about the working joint. For example, participants will attempt an exercise for each muscle group at a relatively light resistance, contracting with enough force to overcome the resistance, thereby causing the resistance to move throughout the full range of motion. The resistance will be progressively increased for each subsequent attempt until the subject is no longer capable of completing the exercise. The resistance level for the last completed attempt will be recorded as the subject's maximal strength score for that exercise and muscle group. In addition, the five muscle groups of the upper body, as well as the two for the lower body separately will be combined in order to have a composite measure of both upper and lower body muscular strength. Finally, the upper and lower body strength scores will be combined in order to calculate a composite measure of total muscle power or strength.

Balance. Level of balance ability has been shown to predict future falling risk and to be associated with enhanced ADL performance (Binder et al., 1994). Furthermore, exercise programs have been related to increased levels of balance among the elderly (MacRae et al., 1994; Nichols et al., 1995). Therefore, the Balance Scale (Berg, Wood-Dauphinee, Williams, & Maki, 1992) will be employed to assess participants' balance to determine whether the exercise program had a positive influence on balance levels and whether changes in balance are associated with improved ADL performance and reduced falls. The Balance Scale is a 14-item scale and will be scored by trained objective raters on a 0-4 metric with scores ranging from 0 to 56 (see Appendix E). In contrast to the limited one-item assessment of balance typically employed, this measure asks participants to execute 14 movements that are essential to daily living in the elderly, including turning, standing, moving and reaching, transferring, and standing on one foot. The Balance Scale possesses adequate psychometric properties (Berg et al., 1992) and McAuley et al. (in press) have reported an acceptable level of internal consistency ($\alpha = .90$).

Psychological Measures

Fear of falling. Although fear of falling has been suggested as one potential cognitive mediator of the relationship between physical activity, ADLs, and falling among the elderly (Arfken et al., 1994; Tinetti et al., 1988), little is known about the determinants of fear of falling or the mediating constructs between fear of falling and physical function. In order to more clearly understand the construct of fear of falling, a single item 1-5 Likert-like scale will be employed and participants will be asked to indicate the degree to which they are afraid of falling (McAuley et al., in press). Using this format provides data regarding the fear of falling in a continuous form, as opposed to the more typical dichotomous assessment of the construct (see Appendix F).

Self-Efficacy. Research examining physical activity, ADLs, and falling requires a multi-dimensional approach. Therefore, a number of measures will be employed to assess self-efficacy cognitions relative to falling, balance, and strength capabilities in order to tap different aspects of physical function (see Appendix G). For all self-efficacy assessments, participants will indicate their degree of confidence on a 100-point percentage scale comprised of 10-point increments, with 100% indicating complete confidence and 0% indicating no confidence at all. Total strength of self-efficacy for each measure will be calculated by summing the confidence ratings and dividing by the total number of items in each scale, resulting in a maximum total efficacy score of 100. The assessment of self-efficacy in this manner is in accord with the recommendations proposed by Bandura (1986).

In order to assess one's perceived self-confidence for avoiding falls while performing common ADLs, the Falls Efficacy Scale (FES; Tinetti et al., 1990) will be employed. The FES is a 10-item scale which assesses participants' beliefs in their capabilities to carry out basic ADLs without falling. Tinetti and her colleagues (1990, 1994) have shown falls efficacy to be an important correlate of ADLs and physical function in a community sample of older persons and the FES to be a reliable and valid measure across a variety of samples. Adequate internal consistency ($\alpha > .90$) for the FES has been consistently reported in the literature (McAuley et al., in press; Tinetti et al., 1990, 1994).

The second measure of self-efficacy will be the Activities-specific Balance Confidence (ABC) Scale (Powell & Myers, 1995). In the rationale for the development and utilization of the ABC scale, Powell and Myers (1995) have argued that the FES consists of fairly global activities and may not be sensitive enough to assess balance confidence among highly functioning older adults. By employing both the FES and the ABC scale in the present study, a comparison can be made to determine which is the most sensitive measure for aging populations. The newly developed 16-item ABC scale assesses one's confidence in performing various ADLs without compromising one's balance and has initially promising psychometric properties, with adequate internal, convergent, and construct validity (Powell & Myers, 1995). In addition, the ABC scale taps a broader continuum of activity difficulty than the FES, including such items as picking up an object from the floor, standing on a chair to reach, and walking on icy sidewalks.

Again, we must caution readers that the introduction of "potentially interesting" comparisons that are not, in a direct sense, a part of the primary design of the study puts both economy and clarity at risk. Given the presentation here, it seems reasonable to believe that it might be fruitful to compare the sensitivity of the FES and ABC Scale when used with the participants in this study—but that matter certainly can be pursued without including it in the proposal.

The last measure of efficacy was developed for the study and was geared toward the assessment of efficacy beliefs for successfully completing strength-related activities. This measure of efficacy will be employed to tap efficacy cognitions which are specifically related to the activity in question, i.e., strength training. The strength efficacy measure is comprised of 10 items, which assesses one's confidence in lifting objects which increased in weight by small increments. For example, the first item will ask participants how confident they are in their ability to lift an object weighing 3 pounds for 10 times without stopping. Adequate internal consistency ($\alpha > .91$) was found for the strength efficacy measure in a similar sample.

Procedures ✓

Orientation

An initial meeting will be held to inform potential participants about the randomly assigned exercise program, detailing time commitment, possible risks, and providing a description of the exercise protocol. Interested participants will then attend an orientation session conducted by the primary investigator one month prior to the exercise intervention. At this time, all interested participants will complete the informed consent, medical and physical histories, and the Pfeiffer Mental Status Questionnaire by interview. Immediately prior to the beginning of the intervention and before the balance and Equitest assessments are completed, participants will attend a second meeting at which the medical clearance will be collected and the remaining measures and physiological tests will be completed. Participants then will embark on a 12-week strength training or stretching and flexibility exercise program.

> Group administration of paper and pencil tests (and, particularly, psychometric instruments) always holds the potential for introducing unintended data artifacts. Both the context and the process must be planned with great care and executed with meticulous observation of protocol. Who will be present? How will instructions be delivered? How will responses be recorded? Will participants be allowed to ask questions? In what order will the measures be administered? Detail about all of this might be relegated to an appendix, but we would prefer to be reassured that the author has thought it through.

High Intensity Strength Training Program

The protocol for the strength training program will follow the guidelines developed by Fiatarone and her colleagues (1990, 1993) which entails working with 80% of the one repetition maximum (1 RM). Participants will begin the program at 60% of their 1 RM, which will be assessed at the second orientation session immediately prior to the exercise intervention. The resistance progressively will be increased to 80% of the 1 RM, as participants become accustomed to the training regimen.

A trained exercise specialist will demonstrate proper form and technique for each exercise as follows: incline bench press, front or side-lateral raises, one-arm bent-over row, biceps curl, triceps kickback, leg extension, and leg press. Specifically, each subject will be instructed to complete one set of up to 12 slowly conducted repetitions for each exercise. Once a subject can complete 12 repetitions at their pre-determined resistance level, the weight will be increased by one increment for the next exercise session. For example, if a subject can complete 12 repetitions at 5 lbs. for the side-lateral raises with proper form, the weight will be increased to 8 lbs for that exercise at the next exercise session. Exercise sessions will be held three times per week on alternate days, lasting approximately 30 minutes, and progressively increased from 60% to 80% of the 1 RM. In order to ensure that participants are indeed working at 80% of their current 1 RM, an assessment of maximal strength will be taken during the 6th week of training. Finally, exercise frequency for all participants will be recorded with a log of completed exercises for each session.

Stretching and Flexibility Control Program

The stretching and flexibility exercise group will serve as an attentional control group against which the effects of the strength training program can be compared. This group will meet on the same basis as the strength training group, be supervised by an exercise specialist, and therefore receive the same amount of attention and feedback. The focus of the stretching and flexibility program will be on general stretching and flexibility exercises for the whole body. For example, participants will be led by the exercise specialist in progressive exercises that involve constant, controlled, and steady stretches for all large muscle groups. Each stretch will be held for approximately 20-30 seconds and repeated 5-10 times. Furthermore, each session will start and finish with 5 minutes of warm-up and cool-down exercises. Finally, exercise frequency will be recorded by the exercise leader in an attendance log for all participants.

Post-Testing

Immediately following the 12-week exercise interventions, participants will complete all psychological, behavioral, and physiological testing. In addition, participants will be given guidelines for continuing their exercise programs upon cessation of the organized training intervention. For example, the use of resistive equipment and objects that can be found in the home for strength training exercises will be discussed.

Data Analysis

Repeated Measures Multivariate Analyses of Variance (MANOVA) will be employed to assess between-group and within-subject changes over time in the variables of interest as a function of the exercise interventions. Univariate and simple effects analyses will be used to follow-up any significant multivariate effects indicating between group differences. If any pre-treatment differences in the variables of interest exist between groups, the pre-treatment value will be used as a covariate in subsequent analyses. Multiple regression and correlational analyses will be employed to investigate the hypothesized relationships among the dependent variables of interest. Specifically, the analyses that will be employed to test each hypothesis are detailed below.

The reader is reminded that only selected examples within the six clusters of hypotheses and subhypotheses have been presented in this abbreviated version of the original proposal. Notice how the three forms of analysis (variance, correlation, multiple regression) are organized around hypotheses to which they are applied. This simple arrangement allows for both economy and clarity.

Hypothesis 1, 2, 3: A series of mixed model repeated measures MANOVAs with treatment groups as the between-subjects factor and time as the within-subjects repeated measures factor will be conducted to examine changes in (a) muscular strength and balance, (b) self-efficacy and fear of falling, and (c) ADL performance and falls prevalence, as a function of the exercise interventions.

Hypothesis 4, 5: Correlational analyses will be conducted to investigate the relationships between changes in muscular strength and balance with changes in self-efficacy and fear of falling (hypotheses 4a-d), and ADLs and falling (hypotheses 5a-d).

Hypothesis 6: Hierarchical multiple regression analyses will be employed to determine whether self-efficacy mediates the relationship between muscular strength and balance changes and changes in ADL performance, fear of falling, and reported falls. First, residualized change scores for the psychological variables will be calculated by regressing the post-program scores onto the pre-program scores. Although simple pre-post change scores are acceptable for those physiological variables that possess high reliability, such strategies are less advisable for assessing change over time in psychological variables (Cohen & Cohen, 1985).

The original proposal included a list of references as well as the appendices noted below.

Appendix A. Pfeiffer Mental Status Questionnaire
Appendix B. Informed Consent and Medical Clearance Forms
Appendix C. Self-report Forms Activities of Daily Living, and the Record Form for Performance-based Test of Activities of Daily Living
Appendix D. Physical Activity History Form
Appendix E. Balance Scale
Appendix F. Fear of Falling Scale
Appendix G. Falls Efficacy Scale, Activities-specific Balance Confidence (ABC) Scale, and Strength Efficacy Scale

2

─═□═─

Qualitative Study

NOTE TO THE READER

The proposal that follows involves use of the qualitative paradigm for research. If you are unfamiliar with this kind of inquiry, a prior reading of Chapter 5 will help you to understand the particular problems that were confronted by the author, both in planning the study and in preparing the proposal document. Also, if you are familiar only with experimental and quasi-experimental designs, Chapter 5 will explain what may seem to be unorthodox or, at least, unexpected ways of handling some elements in the proposal.

As you read, it will become increasingly clear that the author's assumptions about the nature of such matters as reliability, objectivity, validity, replicability, and generalizability differ from those made by investigators using traditional models of quantitative science. Although those differences sometimes are more apparent than real, they do exist, and they are vital to an understanding of qualitative research.

The special and uniquely valuable powers of the qualitative paradigm reside precisely in how it is different from other forms of inquiry. Changing the starting assumptions allows research questions of a very

AUTHORS' NOTE: The original of this proposal was prepared by Belinda J. Tucker under the direction of Professor Linda C. Wing, in partial fulfillment of the requirements for the Ed.D. in the Graduate School of Education at Harvard University. The ensuing doctoral dissertation was completed and accepted by the Graduate School in 1997. Now Dr. Belinda J. Minor, the author, lives in California where she is a school administrator and part-time lecturer in administration and teacher development.

different order. In the following proposal, for example, the author lays out a plan for asking a group of senior high school students what they think (and feel) about the role played in their school careers and lives by particular teachers. The research questions served by that process demand much more than just a reconstruction of events, or the simple collection and tabulation of opinions. The author is proposing to ask the participants to reflect upon and discuss the perceived influence of teachers on their motivation, academic achievement, persistence in school, and aspirations. Questions of that kind, and the data collected to serve them, are quite unlike what one expects to encounter in a quantitative study.

To the extent, then, that qualitative researchers start with different assumptions about some aspects of inquiry, their proposals likewise will display some distinctively different characteristics. At bottom, however, there must be rules of thought and procedure that ensure that qualitative designs represent research that is systematic, transparent, rigorous, and faithful to the demands of its own paradigmatic assumptions. Proposals for qualitative research must allow a clear distinction between what is science, on one hand, and what is no more than careful reportage, thoughtful observation, or connoisseurship, on the other. To have different rules for inquiry is not the same as having no rules for inquiry. For that reason, some investment in prior study will make your reading of the following proposal both much easier and far more profitable.

Finally, we want you to take particular note of the fact that the following document was selected for use here because it represents a relatively early stage in proposal development. Authored by a well-prepared and highly motivated doctoral candidate, and guided by the efforts of a competent and helpful graduate advisor (and thesis committee), the draft seen here was subsequently revised into a final form that received prompt approval. For our readers, however, the particular advantage in this document lies in the opportunity to look over the shoulders of the author and her advisors during the process of tweaking the proposed study toward a finished level of polish. As they did, you can work at the task of considering additions and alterations that would further strengthen this strong initial effort.

Teachers Who Make a Difference: Voices of Mexican American Students

Title for Retrieval. Granted, this is no more than the tentative title used for the proposal, but this is the place to start crafting one that will best serve its primary function—retrieval of the study by potential readers. The present title clearly identifies the two groups that will be of central interest in the study: (a) Mexican American students and (b) teachers. Furthermore, although less explicit, the wording would lead most readers to assume that the study will involve quoted material of some kind from students, as well as an effort to describe the influence of their teachers. Brief, nonpedantic, and nicely phrased to seem intriguing, the title may well serve to attract interest—but can do so only for those who read it!

It is important to remember that in most instances titles are read only when they are retrieved from some type of index, whether from a data-based computer retrieval system or the pages of a hard-copy volume. When indexing is based on keywords assigned by the author (or a review specialist), an artistic title such as the one used here can serve perfectly well. When, however, the assignment of the study to index categories is done on the basis of the words actually appearing in the title, what was aesthetically attractive may become functionally inadequate.

In an index based on title words alone, persons searching for qualitative studies of student life in secondary schools, investigations of student achievement in high schools, research employing pheno-menological interviewing with adolescents, or even studies that iden-tify variables related to teachers' influence on students will be unlikely to retrieve this study. Research method, social context, school level, and primary variables may be inferred by the present title, but they are not actually specified.

By all means, write graceful titles. Be sure, however, to use the key words that might be important in placing your study into index categories where it can be noticed and retrieved by people who will find it valuable. Our suggestions in Chapter 6 concerning the design of titles should help you to achieve that goal.

A standard title page was omitted here.

ABSTRACT

This qualitative study will describe and analyze the perspectives of Mexican American high school seniors regarding the influence of their teachers on their learning, school careers, and lives. The theoretical framework undergirding this study is "effective teacher" research. The research design will involve "in-depth phenomenological interviews" (Seidman, 1991), focus groups, and observations involving a primary sample composed of twelve Mexican American seniors. In addition, a second sample of six will be interviewed in a separate focus group as a "member check" (Guba, 1981). The research will have implications for educators who want to make a positive difference in Latino students' learning, achievement, and persistence to high school graduation.

Theoretical Framework. In terms of the definition we have used throughout this book, a body of research is not, in itself, a "theoretical framework." The author apparently is using the term in its more general sense to indicate the source of theoretical constructs and empirically based assertions that formed the background for designing the study and developing the proposal. It is our strong preference, however, to reserve use of the term *theoretical framework* to designate a particular (and formal) theory, or network of related theories, used as the singular vantage point for defining a research problem and interpreting the results of an ensuing study. In that sense, then, a theoretical framework is a coherent set of postulates about the nature and functioning of some aspect of the world.

In light of demographic changes in the United States—distinguished by a large, young, and quickly growing Latino[1] population—coupled with a sizable and historically persistent achievement gap between Latino and Anglo students, the education of Latino students is a critical challenge facing our nation. The life challenges confronting most high school dropouts, including higher unemployment and lower wages, as well as the costs to society are well-documented (Catterall, 1985; Fine, 1991; U.S. Department of Education, 1993).

Since the publication of *A Nation at Risk* by the National Commission on Excellence in Education in 1983, national leaders have exhorted schools to eliminate the achievement gap, and to educate **ALL** children to high standards. However, many teachers today question their ability to meet this goal because they locate the source of students' academic and motivational problems in their families, peers, SES, culture, or personality and believe that, in relation to those external factors, their influence is of little consequence. (Clark, 1990; Grant & Secada, 1990; Harris, 1991; Hidalgo, 1991; Ladson-Billings, 1994; Paine, 1989). Tragically, teachers' self-perceived lack of "efficacy"[2] may actually contribute to the low achievement of students (Ross, 1945).

Research is needed to help educators appreciate and understand their influence on Latino students' achievement. Despite the numerous factors that are, or seem to be, beyond their control, teachers must understand how they can use that influence in ways that make a positive difference in their students' lives.

This study will contribute to meeting this need by responding to the following research questions: **What do Mexican American[3] high school seniors report as the salient qualities and behaviors of teachers who have made a difference in their lives? How do the students characterize the influence of these teachers on their motivation, learning, academic achievement, persistence in schools, and aspirations?[4] In what other ways do pivotal teachers influence students' lives?**

Abstract. Not all graduate schools require an abstract in the prescribed format for dissertation proposals (abstracts invariably are required in grant proposals). Because preparing an abstract for the proposal provides practice on a vital skill (see our discussion of abstracts in Chapter 10), we are much in favor of the requirement and suggest that you develop one whether or not it must be included in the formal document.

It would be inappropriate to attempt a critique of the proposed study as presented in the abstract. Technical details can be judged only in the context of their explanation. It is possible, however, to consider the adequacy of the abstract as a mechanism for accomplishing its primary purposes: (a) concise communication of the study's purpose, method, and justification; and (b) suggestion that the findings will contain something of special interest.

In this abstract, the writing is crisp, graceful, and a model of efficiency. The first paragraph touches on purpose, method, and justification without use of jargon or technical terms likely to be unfamiliar to reviewers. Use of footnotes and citations in an abstract would not be our preference, but they do serve a clear purpose in this instance.

Three of the five paragraphs are employed to develop further the argument for the importance of the study (and they do so very effectively). That, however, leaves only the opening and closing paragraphs to deal with a formal statement of the research questions— and methodology. Necessarily, a great deal must be left out. Two of the missing bits of information are among those that most reviewers will be looking for: (a) method for selection of participants and (b) means of data analysis. Although we can anticipate that those will be specified in detail in the subsequent body of the proposal, most readers will expect some brief indication in the abstract. Even if there is a word or page limit on the length of the abstract, that small expansion should not be difficult to achieve. The opening sentences of the third paragraph, for example, might be sacrificed without serious loss as a way of providing space to identify the type of participant selection and data analysis being proposed.

Headings. Note that the use of an underscored, centered heading is not allowed in either APA or Chicago style. Unless otherwise specified by the graduate school (as may have been the case here) or funding agency, it is best to employ one of the heading styles commonly used in the discipline or professional field of the study. The correct number and type of headings in the APA format, for example, can easily be established by consulting the "Level of Headings" section of the *Publication Manual of the American Psychological Association* (1994). Headings for subsequent sections of this proposal have been revised to conform to APA guidelines.

TABLE OF CONTENTS

Table of Contents. A glance through the table of contents will remind you that when they are carefully done, as is the case here, tables of contents serve not only as a way of locating particular topics within the proposal document but also as an excellent outline of how the author has developed the presentation. The 14 appendices indicate that the author has tried to keep the main text as compact and tightly focused as possible, relegating supportive materials, complex technical definitions, forms, and protocol specifications to attachments that can be consulted as needed. Because virtually all readers will want to read the material on sample selection, however, we think it inappropriate to force them to flip back and forth between appendices (F and G) and the main text. Appendices are for non-essentials only.

INTRODUCTION

Background

This qualitative study will describe and analyze the perspectives of Mexican American high school seniors regarding the influence of their public school teachers on their learning, school careers, and lives. The theoretical framework undergirding this study is "effective teacher" research. The research design will involve "in-depth phenomenological interviews" (Seidman, 1991), focus groups, and observations involving a primary sample composed of twelve Mexican American seniors. In addition, a second sample of six will be interviewed in a separate focus group as a "member check" (Guba, 1981). The research will have implications for educators who want to make a positive difference in Latino students' learning, achievement, and persistence to high school graduation.

The Problem

In light of demographic changes in the United States—distinguished by a large, young, and quickly growing Latino population—coupled with a sizable and historically persistent achievement gap between Latino and Anglo students, the education of Latino students is a critical challenge facing our nation. Latino school enrollment has doubled over the past twenty years. Historically, Latino students have attained lower standardized test scores[5] and have suffered lower high school completion rates and substantially higher dropout rates than Anglo and African Americans (supporting data are presented in Appendix A). The life challenges confronting most high school dropouts, including higher unemployment and lower wages, as well as the costs to society are well documented (Catterall, 1985; Fine, 1991; U.S. Department of Education, 1993).

Since the publication of *A Nation at Risk* by the National Commission on Excellence in Education in 1983, national leaders have exhorted schools to eliminate the achievement gap, and to educate ALL children to high standards. However, many teachers today question their ability to meet this goal because they locate the source of students' academic and motivational problems in their families, peers, SES, culture, or personality and believe that, in relation to those external factors, their influence is of little consequence (Clark, 1990; Grant & Secada, 1990; Harris, 1991; Hidalgo, 1991; Ladson-Billings, 1994; Paine, 1989). Tragically, teachers' lack of self-perceived "efficacy" may actually contribute to the low achievement of students (Ross, 1994).

Research is needed to help educators appreciate and understand their influence on Latino students' achievement and to understand how they can use that influence in ways to make a positive difference in students' lives, despite the numerous factors that are, or seem to be, beyond their control (see Appendix B).

This study will contribute to meeting this need by responding to the following research questions: What do Mexican American high school seniors report as the salient qualities and behaviors of teachers who have made a difference in their lives? How do the students characterize the influence of these teachers on their motivation, learning, academic achievement, persistence in school, and aspirations? In what other ways do pivotal teachers influence students' lives?

Introduction. At first glance, this introductory section appears to be a repeat of the abstract, a tactic that, in itself, is perfectly acceptable so long as both texts perform the functions needed at each location. Closer reading, however, will reveal that there is additional detail here, along with changes in wording and references that lead the reader to supplementary material in the appendices—all signals that we now are in the main body of the proposal.

Research Questions. Because research questions are such a central element in a proposal, we would prefer that they always be listed individually, in numbered serial order, rather than be embedded in the text of a paragraph. That helps the reader treat them as separate entities, each with its own demands on methodology.

Sample. Although the main exposition is yet to come, this introduction will cause most readers to post caution flags at three points: (a) How will the sample groups be selected? (b) Will 12 participants be sufficient in number to serve the relatively ambitious goals presumed by the research questions? and (c) How can six *different* participants be used as a "member check" when use of that term generally is taken to mean a confirmation of data by the original sources?

Assumptions. Finally, there is an opportunity at this point to test your own ability to think through a problem in study design. In formulating the research questions above, the author has made a very important (though tacit) assumption about her participants, and about their experience of schooling in particular. We do not refer here to the usual assumptions about method (participants will volunteer, will not deliberately mislead the interviewer, etc.), but to how the students understand what happened to them in school. As with Poe's famous *Purloined Letter*, what the author has assumed is so obvious (and taken for granted) that it easily becomes invisible. Examine the research questions carefully and watch for further clues as you read—and leave our "Postscript" following the proposal until you have finished a complete reading of the document.

LITERATURE REVIEW

Since the turn of the century, educational researchers have conducted many investigations in an attempt to find ways to define and measure attributes of "effective" education. Nevertheless, no consensus has emerged concerning either criteria for or quantification of that elusive construct.

Three lines of inquiry have dominated such studies: "effective schools" and "effective educational practices" research (Appendix C), and investigations of "effective teachers" (Appendix D). As explained below, the study proposed here will contribute to the latter.

Cruickshank (1990), in his comprehensive review of the effective teacher research from the 1890s through the 1980s, notes two historically distinct periods of research that differ theoretically and methodologically. Research on "effective teachers" conducted prior to 1960 used subjectively derived items and vague terms created by *administrators* to describe teacher attributes and behaviors that they *presumed* to be effective. That line of study proved to be of little value.

Subsequent to the publication of the so-called *Coleman Report*[6] researchers turned their attention to identifying specific teacher behaviors present or operative when pupils were succeeding (Cruickshank, 1990). Conducted in the 1970s and 1980s, these quantitative studies used a host of new instruments to record classroom behaviors, which were then analyzed systematically. The goal of this methodology was "to determine *how and to what extent teachers perform a group of precise actions and the extent to which performing these actions is related to other desirable attendant classroom events and/or pupil learning*" (Cruickshank, 1990: 68, emphasis in original).

Cruickshank's table of 85 "promising teacher effectiveness variables" (Appendix D), culled from his review of ten other reviews of roughly 2350 studies, shows few areas of agreement about which variables are most closely associated with effective teaching. Only eight of the 85 variables associated with effective teachers appear in at least four of the reviews. These are: clarity, attending/monitoring behavior, use of more pupil participation, equitableness of pupil participation, structure, time-on-task persistence and efficiency, use of feedback, and criticism (the latter is negatively related to effectiveness).

One of the main limitations of the quantitative methods used in the above studies is that, because they are based primarily on *observations*, they cannot explain why certain teacher qualities or behaviors appear to be associated with student outcomes. *The connections* between what students perceive teachers to be doing and the students' motivation and achievement remain invisible to the observer and must be speculated by him or her.

Researchers who study "effective teachers" do not disaggregate data to examine what kind of teachers and teaching are effective for students from different ethnic or cultural backgrounds. Instead, when they differentiate among student groups, they use terms such as "low SES," "disadvantaged," or "at-risk," to refer to poor students of all ethnic backgrounds. The extent to which these or other variables are salient for effective teachers of Latino students remains unclear. The proposed study will focus on "effective teachers" for one somewhat heterogeneous (Matute-Bianchi, 1991; Suarez-Orozco & Suarez-Orozco, 1995) cultural group: Mexican Americans.

One large, quantitative study not mentioned in Cruickshank's review (possibly because it involved teacher *ineffectiveness*) was conducted by the U.S. Commission on Civil Rights (1973), and focused specifically on the behaviors of teachers with Mexican American students. The investigators used the Flanders Interaction Analysis (Amidon & Flanders, 1963) to code observations of 494 classrooms in 430 southwestern schools. They found that teachers were "failing to involve Mexican American children as active participants in the classroom to the same extent as Anglo children." The study reported:

Combining all types of approving or accepting teacher behavior, the teachers responded positively to Anglos about 40 percent more than they did to Chicano students. Teachers also directed questions to Anglo students 21 percent more often than they directed them to Mexicans (U.S. Commission on Civil Rights, 1973: 43).

Clearly, several of the behaviors of "effective teachers" were withheld from Mexican American students. Low Mexican American achievement was associated with teachers' inequitable treatment of the students, but the researchers inferred the causal connection between teacher behavior and student outcomes. In the proposed study, I will seek to explore the substantive connections between teachers' pedagogy (broadly defined to include all teacher behaviors including curricular choices) and students' motivation, learning, achievement, and aspirations by soliciting the perspectives of the students themselves.[7]

My study will join others that focus on "effective teachers" of students from culturally diverse backgrounds. These contain two new types of research: 1) *cross-cultural quantitative studies* of the numerous factors (including teachers) associated with student motivation and achievement (e.g. Gibson & Ogbu, 1991; Stevenson & Stigler, 1992; Suarez-Orozco & Suarez-Orozco, 1995)[8], and 2) *qualitative studies* in which methods from anthropology, sociology, and psychology are used to investigate the relationship between teacher attributes and culturally diverse students' achievement.

Literature. In this section, the author has elected to shift from the brief introductory sketch of the study directly to a discussion of related literature. Some readers might find that transition somewhat abrupt. At the least, they might reasonably feel that a more complete overview of the study would be helpful in understanding how prior research clarifies and supports formulation of the questions and design of the research methodology. We think that most readers, however, will be reassured when it becomes clear that the primary concern here is with explicating the research questions and the choice of a design from within the qualitative paradigm.

The author's primary purpose in these pages is to explain the nature and importance of the research questions. That is, as was true in much of the abstract, the points developed in this section deal with describing the educational problems faced by Mexican American students, testifying to the importance of dealing effectively with those problems, explaining what research can and cannot tell us about that process, and asserting how the proposed study will contribute.

Organizing for Explicitness. We can suggest only that appreciating how the research literature supports these arguments might be made easier if the steps of logic were made more explicit. A simple strategy commonly employed in research writing would be to organize this same content around each research question in sequence. If preferred, common-language points of logical development (like those laid out in the previous paragraph) could be used to achieve the same end. Either strategy would serve to focus the reader's attention on one point at a time, yielding both greater clarity and a more powerful cumulative effect.

Our preference for such explicit organization notwithstanding, given the generally high level of exposition here we doubt that any reader will miss the primary points being made. The author is using a body of educational research to explain both a set of social problems and how results from the proposed study might be employed in resolving those problems. In what follows, she continues the argument that her investigation might do so in a unique and potentially powerful manner.

This body of qualitative research, while still in its infancy, describes some effective teacher behaviors—including listening to students, caring, and showing respect for students' cultures—that were not noted in prior research. Indeed, they are entirely absent from the list of 85 "teacher effectiveness variables" enumerated by Cruickshank. The four main foci of the qualitative research included:

Lists of citations have been omitted in the four categories below.

1) Studies of dropouts. These studies reveal, primarily through interviews with dropouts, how dropouts attribute much of their loss of motivation and lack of achievement to ineffective teaching practices. The students commonly identify these practices as: lack of caring, and prejudice against students of color.

2) Studies of minority teachers' memories of influential teachers. These studies find qualities such as: caring that students learn, connection of material to "real life," not moving on in the curriculum until the students have mastered a lesson, pushing students to think, and getting to know students and their families, to be attributes of effective teachers for students of color.

3) Studies involving interviews and direct observation of teachers whom parents, administrators, or colleagues deem "effective." These studies find that, among other attributes, effective teachers of students of color use "cultur-ally relevant" pedagogy.[9]

4) Studies involving ethnographies and/or interviews with students, individually or in focus groups. These studies, like the studies of dropouts, point to the importance of teacher "caring" and "respect" demonstrated through instructional practices that elicit and value all students' learning.

My study will fit into this fourth category, as it attempts to understand Mexican American students' experiences with and perceptions of the influence of teachers on their motivation, achievement, persistence in school, and personal lives.

> *Human Attribution.* We draw your attention to the phrasing in the sentence immediately above. A literal interpretation would lead the reader to believe that the study, an inanimate entity, is going to do something that only an animate entity (a human, in this case) can achieve—that is, to understand something. We confess that this has become a commonplace of construction in writing about research, and it is likely to remain so. Nevertheless, we prefer to write as though it were the investigator, or the reader of the research report, who is described as performing human functions—understanding, exploring, theorizing, and the like. Thus, we would much prefer: "My study will fit into this fourth category, and through it I hope to better understand Mexican American students' experiences. . . ." As you can see, this is not a matter of correct or incorrect grammar (which might be resolved by application of the appropriate rule), but rather a problem in the logic of word usage. We think you will serve your readers better by attributing things attempted to the researcher and not the research.

The only study that has been directed exclusively at Latino students' perspec-tives on the influence of teachers on their learning was conducted by Gladys Cappella Noya for her Harvard Graduate School of Education doctoral thesis, completed in 1995. Noya's sample includes eleven adolescents, Puerto Ricans and Dominicans, whom she engaged in "collective discussions, writing, and individual conversations." She found the following themes to be salient:

> . . . participants' perceptions that teachers play a determinant role in the demar-cation of the depth to which students are willing to bring themselves into the

classroom; students' needs to express their doubts, questions and disagreements; and young people's appreciation for relationships among students and teachers which acknowledge human dimensions beyond their respective teacher/student status, and which transcend hierarchical boundaries (vii).

Noya found the students in her sample described effective teachers as teachers who demonstrate caring and respect for students. Participants indicated that teachers demonstrate respect by listening to student comments in class without cutting them off or humiliating them with criticism. Students particularly value teachers who can create a class climate in which everyone feels free to ask questions and think aloud. These teachers convey a sense that the students are intelligent people, capable of doing challenging work and contributing to the construction of knowledge in the classroom. They enable students to bring their whole selves into classrooms and reciprocate respect.

Further review of Noya's findings has been omitted here.

Although my research questions are similar to Noya's, and there will be some similarities in our methodology, the proposed study will differ both methodologically and theoretically from Noya's in some important ways. First, Noya's methodology employs what could be considered "extreme" sampling (Patton, 1990: 169). Her sample includes only students who have been rejected from traditional American public schools and students who attend a relatively affluent school on the island of Puerto Rico. My methodology will use "intensity sampling." "Using the logic of intensity sampling, one seeks excellent or rich examples of the phenomenon of interest, but not unusual cases" (Patton, 1990: 171). My sample will be drawn from students who attend a typical, urban public high school.

Second, Noya's analysis does not consider how students perceive teachers' responses to their ethnicity or social class. I intend to look for the relevance of these qualities for Mexican American students.

Third, and finally, since Latinos are not a unitary population, and Mexican Americans may have different experiences and perspectives from Puerto Ricans, due to differences in region, history, and culture (Suarez-Orozco, 1995), when contrasted with Noya's findings it is likely that there will be differences in my participants' perceptions of teachers.

Prior Research. Here the author has introduced a key reference—one
with which her advisors are likely to be familiar. Not only does she
make skillful use of the results to support her proposal, but she also
carefully shows how her own work will make a distinctive contribution
that moves beyond the prior investigation.

METHOD

The purpose of this research is to describe and analyze the perspectives of
Mexican American adolescents regarding the influence of their teachers. The
central questions are: **What do Mexican American high school seniors report
as the salient qualities and behaviors of teachers who have made a difference
in their lives? How do the students characterize the influence of these
teachers on their motivation, learning, academic achievement, persistence
in school, and aspirations? In what other ways do pivotal teachers influence
students' lives?**

These phenomenological[10] questions will be investigated through a qualitative research design that will consist initially of interviews, focus groups, and
observations of eighteen students. Lincoln and Guba (1985: 225) caution that "the
design of a naturalistic study . . . *cannot* be given in advance; it must emerge,
develop, unfold . . ." (emphasis in original). Thus, where it seems reasonable to
modify the design, I will do so and will "report fully on what was done, why it
was done, and what the implications are for the findings" (Patton, 1990: 62).

A qualitative approach seems to be the most reasonable approach for answering these research questions, since qualitative research is especially appropriate
for studies where little empirical research exists (Patton, 1990).

Site

The site for this study will be a typical urban California public high school
with a predominantly Latino student body. I have chosen a predominantly Latino
school because more than two thirds of the Latino students in the United
States are educated in racially isolated schools (Appendix A-1). The site is in
California because California has the largest Mexican American school population. I have selected a typical, rather than an "exemplary" school because I want
to learn how individual teachers can make a difference to Latino students in
average schools, under typical circumstances. I chose a high school as the site

for the research because I am interested in interviewing seniors who are on the brink of "making it" through the system. Their insights concerning the influence of teachers on their motivation, learning, and achievement may have implications for supporting other students in ways that will lead to the same end result.

One site is sufficient for this study because a number of schools "feed" into the high school and the district has a voluntary school choice program. Thus, I can select students who previously have been exposed to a wide range of teachers and pedagogy while conducting my study at this site.

Repetition. Is it really necessary to repeat the research questions here? Probably not, but we think it a good idea, if only because some reviewers turn directly to the methods section.

Flexibility. Is the second paragraph note about necessary flexibility appropriate? Indeed it is in a qualitative study, though with a novice researcher the license to make such adjustments should be used with great caution. The apt quotation from Patton notwithstanding, in most dissertation proposals it is customary to make it explicit that changes will be made with the advice and consent of the primary advisor, or, for major changes, all members of the thesis committee.

Why Qualitative? The claim for appropriateness of the qualitative paradigm in the third paragraph might better be made by noting that only a qualitative study would be appropriate for answering the questions posed. The argument that qualitative studies are best where little is known can too easily lead to the assumption that they are valuable only for "exploratory research." That view weakens the position of qualitative designs as viable alternatives for any question that they fit—irrespective of the status of existing knowledge.

Defining Terms. Based on our experience with many thesis committees, we can predict that if a distinction is made such as "typical" rather than "exemplary," someone will ask for a definition of what the author considers to be "typical." It might be better to deal with that here, rather than in an extemporaneous exchange with advisors.

Variability. Finally, we think that the author intends to assert that one school is enough because the substantial variety of teaching present in feeder schools will produce a participant sample within which a wide range of educational experiences are represented (that is an important condition for the study). Although the argument seems plausible enough, we would prefer that it be made even more explicit. It is important to avoid any implication that diversity of students somehow makes this "typical" school site more representative of urban high schools (a caution the author does make in a subsequent section of the proposal). Qualitative studies of this type do not have strong claims to external validity (transferability of results) as a consequence of sampling (although they may address the matter of generalizability through other means).

Appendix. As illustration for our earlier criticism of placing the explanation of sample selection in the appendices, you must now turn periodically to F and G while reading the following (and do so if you are to understand our comments on that section).

Sample

The primary sample will be twelve Mexican American high school seniors— the intensive focus of the study; a second sample will be six additional students who will participate in a focus group serving as a "member check" (Guba, 1981) at the end of the study. I will purposefully select participants from a pool of volunteers in order to include a range of diverse characteristics including: males and females, students from various academic programs, students of varying grade point average, and first and second generation Mexican Americans (see Appendix F). The primary sample of twelve students will each be interviewed three times. From these twelve, two will be selected for observation and six for participation in ongoing focus group interviews (see Appendix G).

I will interview twelve students in order to select a cross-section of students who have been exposed to diverse school and life experiences. While this is not a study specifically about gender, track, grades, or generation, prior research indicates that students' experiences and perceptions vary systematically along those dimensions (Gilligan, 1982; Oakes, 1995; Suarez-Orozco, 1995). Thus, those factors will serve as "sensitizing concepts" (Patton, 1991: 391) in my data analysis. By including a cross-section of students along these dimensions, I hope to discover perceptions of effective teaching that are either widely shared or that differ categorically (Patton, 1991: 172). By selecting six other students for focus groups, using these same criteria, I can test my findings from the interviews and seek further information.

Since Fine (1991) suggests that many students of color "make it" despite rather than because of teachers and the system, this sample of "achievers" will be asked to locate the influence of their teachers in particular. Acknowledging that other people and institutions impact their lives, I will be cautious and not presuppose a causal relationship between teacher influence and student success in school.

How Many? Unlike the situation in many quantitative studies, there is no reliable mechanism for definitively answering the question "How many participants are needed?" In the end, establishing that number will be a matter of judgment. There are, nevertheless, some simple rules of thumb (discussed below) that apply to conditions like those in the proposed study.

Complicating Conditions. As the author skillfully argues, one of the desired conditions is representation of particular characteristics in the sample group. Her citation of prior research to sustain that point is exactly correct. From a reading of Appendix F, however, we also know that maintaining a degree of balance among those characteristics is an additional requisite (for example, a final sample with only one out of twelve student participants to represent the "second generation" condition clearly would be unacceptable). This is further complicated by the fact that the author obviously wants to maintain an even gender balance (or close to it) as a priority consideration.

A Rule of Thumb. The applicable generalization here is that as the number of desired characteristics increases, and as you add provisions about maintaining a minimum balance of characteristics in the total sample, the number of participants also must be increased. Finding participants with exactly the right characteristics simply is too difficult (with a small, all-volunteer initial pool to draw from, it may be impossible). Given the specifications as proposed, we think it is highly unlikely that the desired sample can be obtained. Either the total number of participants must be increased (at least twofold would be our rough guess), or the number of characteristics decreased (or, ideally, both might be adjusted).

Building the Sample. Although it preempts the later discussion of selection procedures, it may be helpful here to insert our advice about how the desired sample (size and nature) might be obtained. We would urge the author to proceed with a pilot recruitment at the study site. Using only the three original criteria for preliminary selection (senior class status, Mexican American, volunteer), the initial group of recruits thus generated can then be inspected for representation and balance of other characteristics. Given a pool of sufficient size, it may be possible to make necessary adjustments by purposeful selection of candidates for the final (now much larger) participant sample. If that does not produce a sample with the desired characteristics, the option of a further "targeted" recruitment effort may be available. Beyond those strategies lie the less desirable alternatives of simply working with whatever the call for volunteers has provided or of moving on to a different site for another try.

Access and Sample Selection

I have negotiated access to the district and school where I plan to conduct the study between January and March, 1996. In January, I will solicit participants by posting announcements and by staffing a sign-up table where students can meet me, ask questions, and fill out questionnaires. I will perform the contact work myself because, "building the interviewing relationship begins the moment the potential participant hears of the study" (Seidman, 1991: 37). I will select the participants from the pool of students who complete the demographic information questionnaire (copy in Appendix H) and whose parents co-sign the "informed consent" agreement (Kimmel, 1988: 67-76).

Because Latino students are not dispersed equally among the different academic tracks, and because the sample size is so small, the sample will not be "representative" of the school population, nor is it intended to be (Patton, 1990: 185). Using the logic of qualitative inquiry, I am more interested in understanding, in depth, the experiences and perspectives of diverse individuals than being able to generalize those experiences to a larger population. To be considered for participation, students must be seniors of Mexican origin who have attended schools in the U.S. for at least five years (so that they have experience with teachers in at least two U.S. schools).

> *Groundwork.* It is clear that the author has done her homework, completing preliminary negotiations for access to the site and drafting informed consent forms and other study documents. All of that is powerfully reassuring to advisors. Again, readers are cautioned against any assumption that the sample is intended to represent the population at the school site, or the student populations in urban schools more broadly. Planning to handle the recruitment tasks herself (on site) is particularly important, for reasons that she makes clear.
>
> *Appendix I.* It is essential that Appendix I, "Interview Guide," be read in conjunction with the following. Again, the decision to relegate an item to the appendix has worked to the disadvantage of the reader.

Interviews

I will use in-depth, phenomenological interviewing with twelve Mexican American seniors as my primary method of data collection. Consistent with Seidman's (1991) model, each participant will be interviewed three times. Interviewing is important because, as Seidman (1991: 4) asserts, "If the researcher's goal . . . is to understand the meaning people involved in education make of their experience, then interviewing people provides a necessary, if not always completely sufficient, avenue of inquiry."

In order to provide context for understanding the participant's perspective, the first interview in Seidman's model (1991: 11) focuses on the person's life history. Using an "interview guide approach" (Patton, 1991: 288) consisting of open-ended questions (see Appendix I), I will focus on the participant's school life history, particularly on experiences with and perceptions of past teachers. The second interview focuses on the "concrete details of the participant's present experience in the topic area of the study . . . upon which their opinions may be built" (Seidman, 1991: 12). In this interview, I will ask students to describe their lives and the impact of current teachers. "In the third interview, participants are asked to reflect on the meaning of their experience" (Seidman, 1991: 12). In this interview, I will ask students to make connections between pivotal K-12 teachers and the students' motivation, achievement, persistence in school, and aspirations. I will also ask students to reflect on how teachers can support students in ways that will help them achieve at high levels in school and beyond.

Whenever possible, I will conduct interviews at least one day, but not more than one week, apart with each participant, in order to give them a chance to reflect on their experience and to build rapport over time. I will tape record each interview. A bilingual transcriber will assist me in transcribing half of the interviews. I will transcribe the other half and will listen to all the tapes as I proofread and annotate the transcripts. Immediately following each interview, I will record field notes (Patton, 1991: 239).

Seidman's Protocol. Although phenomenological interviewing in the format provided by Seidman is a complex process that requires considerable interpersonal skill, careful attention to detail, and a thorough understanding of purpose (as well as a period of guided practice), the brief description given here is entirely adequate. The Seidman book provides a definitive source, and most advisors are likely to be familiar with the methodology involved. Where that is not the case, prior conversations and provision of reference materials can serve as preparation.

Transcribing. Even though the author is bilingual (a point made clear in a later section of the proposal, along with her intention to give each participant the choice of language for their interviews), the use of a bilingual transcriber for a portion of that difficult task is a significant addition. Providing for an external check on her own technical skill reflects the author's concern for maintaining a high standard of accuracy in the data—again a signal her advisors will interpret as indicative of sound preparation and readiness for the long task ahead.

Cuing Participants. As some of you may already have concluded from a reading of Appendix I, however, there may be some reason for concern about the author's plans for collecting data from interviews. An interviewer's choice of words can signal the interviewee as to what sort of responses are anticipated. Given the probability that in the context of a friendly, nonthreatening setting, most participants already will have some inclination to say things that please the investigator, such signals can serve as a powerful source of data contamination. That being the case, advisors will be looking for clear assurance that the author intends (initially, at least) to avoid giving her participants any indication that teachers should be identified as influential figures in their lives.

Whether teachers are called "memorable," "influential," "pivotal," "effective," or simply "good," those descriptors constitute a clear signal about what is expected when students talk about teachers. Even a seemingly neutral word like "memorable" can give more direction than intended. Stimulating participants to reflect upon and talk about the behaviors of teachers whom they perceive as having fallen into any of those positive categories will be an appropriate (even necessary) part of the proposed study. *It will be so, however, only after students have, of their own unprompted volition, indicated that teachers were among the people "who made a difference" for them.* In other words, it is essential to first establish the "whether" of things, before moving on to the "how"!

It is easy to understand how the author, committed to the vital significance of the research questions, steeped in the supportive literature, and eager to move ahead to conducting the study, might have overlooked the possibility of cuing her participants. Happily, the correction is easily made—and there is clear evidence in the proposal that she knows precisely how to do it. To paraphrase points already made in her presentation: Don't rush, lead with comfortable, nonprescriptive questions that invite students to share their stories, listen intently and show interest in the participants' perceptions, be prepared to use follow-up probe questions when needed to clarify or extend a response, and move the conversation only gradually (perhaps in the later interviews) toward the explicit questions that address such matters as teacher effectiveness. The reader should note that a modest pilot trial of the interview guide might have sensitized the author to this matter before presentation of this preliminary draft for review.

Observations

I plan to observe at least two of the participants from when they rise in the morning until they prepare to retire in the evening. By spending a day with the students I expect to get a sense of how the students negotiate their home, school, and work cultures, which may prove helpful in contextualizing the information and ideas that they share about the relative influence of teachers in their lives.[11]

During the observations, I will take field notes (see Appendix J)[12] and will type them soon after, adding reflections. I will use the data from the observations to inform my follow-up questions in the interviews and to generate tentative hypotheses.[13]

Rationale. We are not convinced that the proposed observations will contribute significantly to the data collected from other sources. Furthermore, given what is provided here (and elsewhere in the proposal) concerning observations, we are not sure the author herself has fully come to grips with the how and why of this part of the research plan. With an already demanding schedule of data collection, and the arduous tasks of transcription and analysis beyond that, unless more persuasive arguments can be advanced, we are inclined to advise dropping this component of the proposed study.

Focus Groups

"Groups are not just a convenient way to accumulate the individual knowledge of their members. They give rise synergistically to insights and solutions that would not come about without them" (Brown et al., 1989: 40). Both Hidalgo (1991) and Noya (1995) conducted focus groups with Latino adolescents and found the sessions fruitful. In this study, I will facilitate two groups. One will consist of six of the twelve primary interviewees. We will meet as a group three times for fifty minutes to discuss the attributes of influential teachers. The six participants in the member check group will meet once for ninety minutes, near the end of the study, to critique the developing analysis.

Citing Sources. The rationale for obtaining focus group data makes good sense in the context of this study (although for some readers a much more thorough definition of the term might have been required to make that apparent). That conclusion is furthered by documentation of the fact that the technique has previously proved to be a helpful supplement to interviews. Because the formation and facilitation of focus groups requires considerable knowledge, skill, and planning, we would normally expect to see both citations to standard works on the methodology (see Chapter 5 for our suggestions in that regard) and indication of successful pilot work by the author.

Trustworthiness

I have made several choices to increase "trustworthiness" (Lincoln & Guba, 1985) and to minimize common threats to validity. First, I have selected a school where neither students nor teachers know me to minimize threats to validity arising from personal bias towards participants or individuals named by them. Second, because I am bilingual, I will interview students in the language they prefer. The bilingual transcriber will assist me in checking the accuracy of both direct quotes and translations. Third, the final focus group will provide a member check on the analysis. Fourth, I will discuss the possible influence that my own life experiences—for example, as a former teacher and administrator who worked for ten years in southern California with many Mexican American students—may have on my perceptions and thinking. Finally, by conducting multiple interviews over time, as well as by using multiple data collection strategies, I will minimize the chances that the findings will be based on idiosyncratic data.

Getting It Right. It is impossible to define here the complex of criteria and procedures that qualitative researchers assign to the word "trustworthiness." Advisors will know what is intended, however, and a full discussion is not required in the proposal. At bottom, trustworthiness has to do with the quality (goodness) of qualitative research. Thus, in practical terms, it has to do with establishing and meeting criteria that will lead readers of the study report to conclude that the investigator "got it right!" Put another way, the term denotes a revision of traditional criteria such as reliability, internal and external validity, and objectivity, to make them more appropriate to the assumptions made in the qualitative paradigm.

What the author presents here are procedures that will serve the ends of trustworthiness, though we would have preferred that the several components of that construct be made explicit (the usual list of criteria includes credibility, transferability, dependability, and confirmability), and then proposed strategies for meeting each be discussed in turn.

Coming Clean. We were particularly pleased to note that the author plans to write a thorough explication of the nature and potential influence of her own life experiences as they might be expected to shape the research process. Of course, that discussion will be necessary for an informed appreciation of the study's conclusions.

Confirming Data. We continue to be concerned about the proposed use of a secondary sample of students who were not interviewed, for the purpose of conducting a "member check." The word "member" here ordinarily designates a full participant who has been selected to read through transcripts to ensure accuracy of what has been recorded, or to review products of data analysis such as thematic statements or individual profiles. The purpose is to detect any substantial discrepancies between the perceptions of the participants (whether as individuals, or as members of a group) and the investigator's reconstructions and representations. If that is the intention, then it is the participants in the primary sample who will have to do the checking.

Ethical Concerns

Due to the nature of the research questions, the confidentiality provided through carefully maintained participant anonymity, and my status as a graduate student with no connections to the teachers or school administration, there is minimal threat to the well-being of the students in the study as a result of their participation.

My stance of "empathetic neutrality"[14] should minimize the threat of "interviewing as exploitation"—a process that turns others into subjects so that their words can be appropriated for the benefit of the researcher" (Seidman 1991: 7) that presents ethical problems in some studies.

Protecting Participants. The author's careful reassurances notwithstanding, hard experiences have taught us that there *always* is the lurking possibility of harm to participants in a naturalistic field study. Anonymity never can be guaranteed, if only because it is not entirely under the researcher's control. In a typical school, everyone will know who the participants were and exactly what was asked in the interviews and discussed in the focus groups. Furthermore, if member checking is done, whatever is checked has the potential to become public and, correctly or incorrectly, will be assigned to every participant.

We think the author's arguments about meeting her ethical responsibilities are reasonable. Certainly, she has given us good reason to
believe that she has given serious consideration to the problem and
will protect her student collaborators in every possible way. We want
to warn our readers, however, that ethical concerns are never simple.
Careful forethought in planning and watchful diligence in execution
are responsibilities that come with the decision to do qualitative
research.

Limitations

As with all exploratory research, the findings of this study will be tentative.
It is important to note: 1) the sample size and procedures for participant
selection, while appropriate for a qualitative study, will not support generalization to a larger population of Mexican Americans, and 2) the relationship
between students' perceptions of effective teachers and empirical measures of
"teacher effectiveness" has yet to be defined. The exploration of that relationship
is beyond the scope of this study.

Data Analysis

Because this is an exploratory study, I will begin coding data from interview
transcripts, field notes, and focus group transcripts using coding categories
(Patton, 1991: 402) suggested by the literature (Appendix K), but I will actively
seek patterns of data suggesting new categories as well. Using data organized
and displayed in that fashion, I will return first to an analysis of interviews from
individual participants, as separate cases, and only then consider the wider
matter of cross-case analysis. Such a sequence of analytic steps would conform
broadly to the suggestions of Glaser and Strauss (1967), who have argued that
an understanding of individual cases (before they are aggregated in any way) is
the best guarantor for theoretical assertions that are grounded in specific contexts
and real-world patterns.

Next, because "a phenomenologist assumes a commonality in those human
experiences and must use rigorously the method of bracketing to search for those
commonalties" (Eichelberger, 1989: 6), I will read across interviews, noting
similarities and differences. I will then use pattern coding (Miles & Huberman,
1994) to identify common themes. While I will examine the entire sequence of
responses about teachers by each participant, I will also distinguish between

those categories generated by the students themselves and those discussed in response to probes. For example, if the students mention nothing about the relevance of the instructional materials to their lives, I might inquire about the connection, but will indicate that I needed to probe to elicit that information.

Finally, I will prepare the data analysis by briefly describing each of the twelve participants, and, by using quotes from their interviews, will illustrate common themes as well as atypical responses. Transcripts from the focus groups will be utilized primarily as a check for confirmation of the salience of themes across the sample, although I will include in my thesis excerpts of dialogue that illustrate important points of consensus or disagreement. The observations will be used both to describe two of the participants more fully and to fill in descriptions of the school.

Keeping Honest Books. Again, the procedures indicated here (coding, category development and sorting of data, identification of patterns, construction of thematic statements, and writing grounded descriptions of participants) are all appropriate to the research task. We can add several suggestions that might strengthen the plan for analysis.

First, it would be wise to consider use of one of the software programs for computer-based analysis. This study will generate such an enormous volume of data that hard-copy manipulation will be difficult. Second, it will be important to maintain a record of the exact source for each category. Not only are advisors often curious about such origins, but the final report will require writing about category development long after immediate memory has dimmed. Third, if at all possible, do some pilot trials of the proposed analysis using interview data obtained from a source outside the study site (an appendix showing that this has been accomplished successfully always is reassuring to advisors). Finally, make it an absolute and inviolate rule not to ignore or discard data that run contrary to initial expectations, or that appear not to fit comfortably into emerging categories for analysis.

CONCLUSION

This country cannot afford, ethically or economically, to fail to educate another generation of Mexican American students. While many factors outside the control of teachers may contribute to underachievement of Latinos in the United

States, evidence abounds to confirm that teachers can make a difference, although many teachers question their ability to do so. In the proposed study I will explore Mexican American high school seniors' perspectives on what constitutes effective teaching and their perspectives on the influence that teachers have on their learning, school careers, and lives. It is my hope that teachers who are actively seeking ways to support the achievement of their Mexican American students will find, in reading this thesis, useful ideas that will support them in their important work. It is equally my hope that teachers who have doubted their ability to make a difference in their Mexican American students' achievement, may reconsider their thinking and pedagogy upon contemplating this research.

The Bad News and the Good News. We were delighted to find the author still enthusiastic and convinced of the potential utility in her proposed study. Sad to report, hardly anyone reads theses and dissertations—except other graduate students! The encouraging flip side of that rule, however, is that publications based on theses and dissertations can be aimed at any audience the researcher desires to reach—other scholars, professors, policy makers, and practitioners at any level of education—including, of course, the teachers specified above. All that is required is preparation of a sound manuscript based on the dissertation (or some part thereof) and selection of an outlet that reaches the intended readers. Good proposals lead to good studies, and when appropriately translated and disseminated, the findings from good studies can make a positive difference in any professional field.

A POSTSCRIPT TO THIS PROPOSAL

The Rest of the Story. This proposal, already well along in its development, was reviewed by a committee of thesis advisors, the author was given feedback and suggestions for improvements, the revisions were executed, and with the full support of the advisory committee the study was approved by the Graduate School. In that process, some, though not all, of the points in our critique above found their way into the final proposal. Notably, the observation component suggested in the first draft was dropped (as was the "member check" procedure), the sample size was expanded (to 34 participants), the specifications for representation and balance of characteristics were maintained in somewhat less demanding form, and discussion of teacher influence was placed at the end of the interview sequence.

As for our earlier note about the author's assumptions concerning the role played by teachers in the cosmology of influences that shape student school experience, by this point most readers will have detected that her unspoken but pervasive expectation was that some (if not most) of her participants would nominate (and describe) particular teachers as pivotal individuals in their school careers. From the outset, we found ourselves asking, "What if none (or very few) of her participants nominate teachers as influential in making it through to graduation?" At the least, that outcome would limit a search for the attributes of effective teachers—although it might well open the door to other important insights into students' perceptions of what and who were helpful in their school careers.

Given her own life experiences, the personal values that are evident in the proposal, and the nature of her continuing professional development, the expectation that teachers might be salient was perfectly reasonable. Indeed, in the case of several of her participants, the assumption was verified by direct and persuasive testimony. Virtually every one of the study participants indicated that they had encountered one or more teachers whom they considered to have been excellent. Furthermore, they unanimously affirmed the proposition that the quality of teaching makes an important difference in school.

Nevertheless, the main direction of findings ran contrary to some of the assumptions apparent in the first draft of the author's proposal. *The majority of students perceived their education and lives to have been shaped more profoundly by their interactions with parents, friends, and peers than with teachers.* That her study was sensitive to just such a possibility, and that she was ready to make that unexpected and (thereby) particularly valuable finding the center of an articulate and powerful report, *were the consequence of thorough preparation, strong advisement, and development of a sound research plan through successive revisions of her proposal.* The lesson to be taken here is that effort expended on construction of a carefully considered proposal for qualitative research may well be as important as conduct of the study itself.

REFERENCES

The reference list has been omitted here.

APPENDICES

Except "F," "G," and "I" below, all appendixes have been omitted here.

APPENDIX F: SAMPLE SELECTION

I intend to select a cross-section of students for participation in both samples, the primary sample of 12 and the "member check" group. Ideally, the sample will assume a form approximately like this:

Composition of Primary Sample

All must be seniors of Mexican decent who have attended US schools for at least five years.

1 male in honors classes

1 female in honors classes

1 male in "regular" classes who is getting good grades (A's & B's)

1 male in "regular" classes who is getting average grades (C's & F's)

1 female in "regular" classes who is getting good grades (A's & B's)

1 female in "regular" classes who is getting average grades (C's & F's)

1 male in "basic" or special education classes

1 female in "basic" or special education classes

1 male first-generation Mexican American

1 female first-generation Mexican American

1 male second-generation Mexican American

1 female second-generation Mexican American

Total = 12

Composition of Secondary Sample

All must be seniors of Mexican decent who have attended US schools for at least five years.

1 male first-generation Mexican American

1 female first-generation Mexican American

1 male second-generation Mexican American

1 female second-generation Mexican American

1 male or female honors student

1 male or female student in "basic" or special education classes

Total = 6

APPENDIX G: SAMPLE AND METHODOLOGY

Participant Number	*Activity*
1	3 in-depth, individual interviews + one day observation
2	3 in-depth, individual interviews + one day observation
3	3 in-depth, individual interviews + 3 focus group interviews
4	3 in-depth, individual interviews + 3 focus group interviews
5	3 in-depth, individual interviews + 3 focus group interviews
6	3 in-depth, individual interviews + 3 focus group interviews
7	3 in-depth, individual interviews + 3 focus group interviews
8	3 in-depth, individual interviews + 3 focus group interviews
	Note: participants 3-8 will all be in the same focus group that will meet three times.
9	3 in-depth, individual interviews
10	3 in-depth, individual interviews
11	3 in-depth, individual interviews
12	3 in-depth, individual interviews
13	"member check" focus group interview
14	"member check" focus group interview
15	"member check" focus group interview
16	"member check" focus group interview
17	"member check" focus group interview
18	"member check" focus group interview
	Note: participants 13-18 will all be in the same focus group that will meet once for ninety minutes.

APPENDIX I: INTERVIEW GUIDE

Interview #1: Personal Educational History

I'm interested in hearing about your experiences in school, particularly with memorable teachers, starting back as far as you can remember.

(I will listen for and possibly probe: when the participants began school, where they attended, what level groups they were assigned to, memorable experiences, the kinds of grades they got, their attendance patterns, any changes in their experiences or feelings towards school or teachers over time, and descriptions of memorable teachers—especially good ones—and their influence; and anything else that the students share about their school history.)

Interview #2: Concrete Details of Present Experience

A) Last time, you told me about your past experiences in school, especially with teachers, and I have found them very powerful. Today, I'm wondering if you could tell me about your life now—both inside and outside school.

B) What do you see as the influence of the teachers you now have on your motivation, learning, achievement, and plans for the future?

(In addition to listening to the students' responses to these questions, I may ask them to describe the best teacher whom they have at present.)

Interview #3: Reflections on the Meaning of Experience

A) Now that you've told me a lot about your school experiences, I'm wondering if you could help me see what some of the long-term and short-term influences that you think specific teachers have had on your life.

(Here I may follow up on stories from the previous interviews)

B) What advice would you give to a teacher who really wants to make sure that all of the students in his/her class are both motivated to learn and able to succeed in school?

(Here I will listen for students' connections between "effective" and "ineffective" teachers and their own motivation, achievement, persistence in school, and aspirations. If they have not already done so, I will ask them to describe to me the qualities and attributes of an effective teacher, either based on someone they know, or based on how they imagine one could be.)

NOTES

1. In this proposal, the terms "Latino" and "Hispanic" refer interchangeably to people, or their descendants, who hail from diverse Spanish-speaking regions such as Mexico, Cuba, Puerto Rico, the Dominican Republic, and parts of Central and South America (Suarez-Orozco & Suarez-Orozco, 1995).

2. Teacher efficacy measures the extent to which teachers believe their efforts will have a positive effect on student achievement.

3. I will focus the study on Mexican Americans, rather than on all Latinos, as Mexican Americans constitute more than half of the Latino population. I have chosen to use the term Mexican American, rather than Chicano, Mexicano, or any other terms because many people prefer it (Nieto, 1992).

4. These terms ("motivation," etc.) will be defined by the students.

5. The validity of these tests for Latino students is questionable (Valencia, 1991).

6. U.S. Department of Health, Education, and Welfare (1966).

7. The relationship between students' perceptions of effective teachers and empirical measures of teacher effectiveness is unknown and is beyond the scope of this study.

8. These investigations focus primarily on "macrosystem factor," (LeCompte & Dworkin, 1991: 57) such as family variables and school structure (see Appendix B), rather than teacher effectiveness *per se*, thus they will not be discussed further here.

9. Definitions of "culturally relevant pedagogy" differ, but often include involving students' families and connecting subject matter with students' lives and experience in meaningful ways (see Appendix E-1).

10. Phenomenological inquiry focuses on the question: "What is the structure and essence of experience of this phenomenon for these people?" (Patton, 1990: 69).

11. My experience visiting homes of Mexican Americans while working for Migrant Education leads me to believe I will not have difficulty finding participants who are willing to bring me into their homes.

12. I will assign pseudonyms to the school and to teachers mentioned by participants.

13. The focus of this study is on *students' perceptions*; therefore, I will not observe teachers.

14. Empathetic neutrality: "Empathy . . . is a [caring] stance towards the people one encounters, while neutrality is a stance toward the findings" (Patton, 1990: 58).

3

—◻—

Quasi-Experimental Design

Teaching Children to Question What They Read:
An Attempt to Improve Reading Comprehension
Through Training in a Cognitive Learning Strategy

This is a particularly interesting proposal as it involves a quasi-experimental treatment in a topic area, the acquisition of reading skills, that is not often studied in such fashion. The strength of the introduction is that it immediately convinces the reader of the seriousness of the topic—the need to be able to read in our society.

INTRODUCTION

One of the main tasks assigned to schools is that of training students to be linguistically competent. In an industrialized society and national political

AUTHORS' NOTE: This proposal was prepared by John David MacDonald as part of the dissertation research requirement in the Department of Educational Psychology at The University of Texas at Austin. The dissertation was supervised by Beeman N. Phillips and Claire E. Weinstein. The completed dissertation received the Outstanding Dissertation Award from the Southwest Educational Research Association. Dr. MacDonald currently is a school psychologist with the North Kitsap School District, Poulsbo, Washington, and is an adjunct faculty member at Western Washington University, Bellingham.

culture such as the United States, this requires competence in the written as well as the spoken word. It is, for example, very difficult to administer secret ballots except in writing. In the workplace, instructions to workers, including safety precautions, are in printed form. Reading is a means to gain control over one's life, whether one is reading about an upcoming election or one is choosing where to shop for food economically.

While reading may be a necessity for everyday living, evidence is ample that many people never acquire the skills necessary for reading. Several years ago, Gibson and Levin (1975) suggested that as many as 25% of all school children are more than one year below grade level in reading. In some inner-city schools in New York City, the proportion may be as high as 85% (Fuentes, 1980).

Here the author reveals the purpose of the study. As you will note, later in the proposal a problem and question also are stated.

The purpose of the proposed study, therefore, is to assess the effectiveness of a proposed reading intervention technique, a technique that appears conceptually to be consistent with the recent developments in cognitive learning. Not learning to read has, of course, more than social and economic costs. It has personal costs as well. Never to know the intricacies of John Le Carré's plots, or Joseph Conrad's evocative descriptions, or even the self-awareness that comes from reading about one's own condition, is to be isolated from the national culture, and to some degree, to be a person without a past or a present. Calling the over-60 age group the single largest cohort of functional illiterates, the White House Conference on the Aging (Kasom, 1981) suggested that this population is more at risk for mental health problems due to the isolation, poverty, and boredom that result from being illiterate. But personal satisfaction and participation in national culture are not the only costs of illiteracy.

In the paragraph below, the author makes the critical point that reading is the underpinning for success in all school subjects. This provides a strong rationale for a study in which the major purpose was to identify an effective method with which to improve reading skills. So that the reader will not miss this important rationale, the author both coins and italicizes an important word, *keystone*, to describe the construct.

Reading may serve as a "keystone" for other curricular skills, that is, certain skills may be prerequisite to curricular skills in science, social studies, literature, and so on. While some authors complain, perhaps correctly, that the reason for "scientific illiteracy" is the emphasis on basic skills or reading instruction for its own sake, it is difficult to imagine a student obtaining a scientific education while not reading. Because of this *keystone quality*, a lack of reading skills may result in low achievement and premature school dropouts. Curtis, Doss, Mac-Donald, and Davis (Note 1) found that the best predictor of late dropouts was below-average scholastic grade-point average, and many of the dropouts who were interviewed reported chronic reading problems and that they withdrew because they believed these problems were insurmountable.

> Here the author shows that the need for reducing school dropout rates by improving reading performance is relevant to the city in which the study is to be conducted. Thus, the problem of developing reading skills is not an abstraction. It is specific to the locale, and new information will have potential for immediate consequences, a point that will not be lost on the university committee or the public officials who must approve the execution of the study in the school system.

Withdrawal from school can have dire economic consequences: In this city, 48% of non–high school graduate males aged 16-21 were unemployed, but only 18.4% of the same age high school graduates were unemployed (Bureau of the Census, 1973). It is not inconceivable that illiteracy is related to unemployment.

> The section below is an excellent example of demonstrating the need for the study. It directly answers the query we posed in Chapter 1, "Why bother with the question?" Sometimes the answer to this is woven into the rationale, as shown below. An alternative, which is sometimes required by committees or funding agencies, is to separate the "need for the study" section from the section on rationale. If this were the case, the earlier discussion of the personal costs of not knowing how to read, the potential for mental health risk, and the likelihood of employers shunning nonreaders could be shortened and combined into an effective section on "need for the study."

Employers seem reluctant to hire illiterate workers because they view them as more likely to injure themselves and their fellow workers, and because they view them as more likely to cost the company large sums of money for misreading instructions (Lauterborn, 1981). Of 800 companies Lauterborn surveyed, 35% thought it necessary to supplement their employees' education with basic English and business writing. The increasing sophistication of modern weaponry and support equipment along with the failure of the armed services to attract more highly educated recruits has led the Army to invest $37,000,000 over a four-year period in the research and development of instructional systems in basic skills, English as a second language, life-coping skills, and cognitive learning strategies (Begland, 1981). Thus good reading skills are of more than personal benefit for the reader; they are related to the economic and defense interests of the nation.

While the reading skills of the nation's school children may be viewed by many as distressing, there are some encouraging indications that reading performance is improving and that poor reading is less of a problem. The National Assessment of Educational Progress (Burton & Jones, 1982; National Assessment of Educational Progress, 1976a, 1976b) has reported improving performance on both literal and inferential comprehension items for 9-year-olds, and improvements have surfaced in literal comprehension among 13- and 17-year-olds. Differences in reading scores between whites and blacks have declined from a 17 point difference in inferential comprehension in 1970 to a less than 10 point difference in 1980 (Burton & Jones, 1982).

Below is a section that does not speak directly to the question at hand. The volume of specific detail breaks the flow of the introduction. The reader will be struck by the observation that the style of writing is not parallel with the rest of the introduction. It seems clear that the introduction would not suffer if this section were located elsewhere.

In the 1972 assessment, the National Assessment of Educational Progress (NAEP) sponsored a special survey of students' attitudes toward reading and literature. These results are encouraging, if one accepts the validity of student responses to adult interviewers. Of the 13-year-olds interviewed, 43% strongly agreed that it is important to study literature, while an additional 34% somewhat agreed with the statement. In the inner-city schools, 58% strongly agreed with the statement. The majority of 17-year-olds (90%) believed literature should be taught in every school. A majority of the 9-year-olds (84%) and 13-year-olds (78%) reported they read for their own pleasure at least once a week, with 54% of the 9-year-olds and 44% of the 13-year-olds reporting they read for pleasure every day. When asked if they had read a particular type of literature on their own (e.g., short story, novel, poetry, etc.) 98% of the 13-year-olds replied they had read at least one of the types, and 86% gave verifiable titles when asked. For an adult sample, 89% replied they had read at least one genre, while 76% gave verifiable titles (NAEP, 1973).

In general terms, the outlook is hopeful. However, there remain substantial numbers of children and adults for whom reading is troublesome. Unless they receive effective interventions, their economic prospects are grim, they are disenfranchised from the political process, and much of the world's cultural heritage bypasses them. For the 78% of the 1973 13-year-olds who reported reading at least once a week, 6% of them reported never having read for pleasure. In the 1980-81 school year, some 5% to 6% of the students in the city Independent School District's average daily enrollment had reading problems so severe they required classification for special education services under the category of Learning Disabilities (Bass, Note 2). Knowing what to do for these students to help them improve their reading is troublesome for teachers, learning disability specialists and school principals. Yet these individuals are legally mandated with providing an appropriate education for these students, that is, charged with improving these students' reading (McClain, 1981). Despite a large number of research studies of reading instruction, little is presently known about the relative effectiveness of different methods of teaching reading (Maxwell, 1972; Pflaum, Walberg, Karegiones, & Rasher, 1980). Most children arrive in kindergarten not knowing how to read, and most leave high school as fairly competent readers; thus although we know little about effective reading instruction, most children do learn how to read while in school. It is likely that few students who do not attend school will attain the same reading competence as they would if they attended 12 years of school, although this interpretation of descriptive studies of school nonattendance suffers from selection factors.

Here the author begins establishing a background for the particular approach to be used in this study, that is, the identification and measurement of behaviors specific to reading competence.

It seems likely that acquisition of reading competence is directly related to teacher and student behaviors, although at this stage in reading research it is difficult to state precisely what these behaviors are. The attempt to define them to validate their effectiveness as mediators in the acquisition of reading competence should contribute to "cracking the problem of what happens to reading achievement after the second or third grade" (Glaser, 1979, p. 8). Identification of these behaviors may then contribute to a system of intervention practices with regard to reading problems.

The following discussion provides a historical framework through which to understand the significance of the study here proposed. New techniques to determine teacher and student behaviors relevant to reading acquisition make possible acquisition of heretofore inaccessible information.

The field of reading diagnosis and intervention has been plagued by systems of nonexperimentally-validated constructs regarding the processes involved in reading, resulting in assessment instruments with unacceptably low levels of reliability. In turn, the use of poor assessment instruments has contributed to ineffective intervention procedures (Arter & Jenkins, 1979; Hammil & Larsen, 1974a, 1974b; Hammill, Goodman, & Wiederholt, 1974; Larsen & Hammill, 1975; Minskoff, 1975). However, three developments have improved the likelihood of identifying those teacher and student behaviors involved in the acquisition of competent reading. The first development is the identification of a series of learner behaviors that are directed at constructing meaning from text (Bransford, Barclay, & Franks, 1972; Perfetti & Lesgold, 1977; Rumelhart, 1975), behaviors that are directed at understanding and recall (DiSibio, 1982; Weinstein, 1978; Weinstein, 1982; Weinstein & Underwood, 1983; Wittrock, 1979; Wittrock, Note 3), and the discovery that these behaviors can be learned and can be brought within the cognitive control of the learner (Rothkopf, 1970; Weinstein, Cubberly, Wicker, Underwood, Roney, & Duty, 1981).

The second development is in the application of task analysis to the acquisition of curricular knowledge (Chi & Glaser, 1980; Gage & Briggs, 1974; Glaser, 1976; Resnick, Wang, & Kaplan, 1973). It is now possible to model complex hypothesized reading and knowledge acquisition strategies through the use of task analysis. The third development involves methodologies for determining causal relations (Blalock, 1971; Duncan, 1975; Wolfe, 1980; Wright, 1971) and methodologies for evaluating aptitude treatment interactions (Cronbach & Snow, 1977), which have been called, along with the developments in cognitive learning (Wittrock, Note 3), "the most significant developments of the past 5 to 10 years, developments that may have significant if not greater influence on educational research during the 1980s" (Kerlinger, 1982, p. 120). The study of causal relations is now being applied to the experimental validation of task-analytic models of curricular skill acquisition (Bergan, 1980; Hill & McGaw, 1981). These developments are of great importance for the assessment of learning problems and for the design and implementation of interventions for learning problems.

> At this point, the author included an extensive review of the literature. A variety of topics were covered including reading comprehension, individual differences, methodology, and analysis. Because we have suggested a shorter, concise review focusing specifically on decisions for the proposed study (see Chapter 4), we have chosen not to include the review of the literature here.

STATEMENT OF THE PROBLEM

A small number of children do not attain functional reading skills and suffer economically, socially, and politically. The consequences for these children necessitate that effective reading remediation strategies be developed and implemented. Remediation strategies need to be derived from theories of what it is that good readers do that enables them to be competent readers. Although such theories are in their infancy, they are now specific enough in their implications that specific intervention strategies may be developed and evaluated.

> The author now has identified a problematic area (some students do not attain functional reading skills), but only later on does he actually state the question for the study. The paragraph below is intended both to introduce and support the treatment to be examined. For the reader, it would have been helpful to undertake the two communication tasks separately, and in sequential paragraphs.

One such strategy that has been recommended to reading teachers is having students generate their own questions about the content of the reading material and then having students seek the answers to these questions. This recommendation has appeared in teacher preparation texts (Durkin, 1978), in journals directed to reading teachers (Alexander & Fuller, 1973; Dillworth, 1980; Eeds, 1980; Hopkins, 1979; Olmio, 1975; Seifert, 1980), in journals directed to learning disabilities specialists (Wong, 1979), and in publications directed at psychologists (*Comprehension is the Key*, 1981). Without exception, these authòrs have presented the technique in a favorable, noncritical light, but little data have been presented in these articles to support this position.

> Here the case is made that, although the technique of having children generate their own questions about reading material facilitates reading skills, children must be trained to generate these questions. Here, the proposed study is seen to be firmly grounded in the current understanding of how children learn to read. By identifying the limitations of previous research, the author positions himself to argue for the design features of the proposed study.

Experimental evaluations of this technique have recently appeared (e.g., Andre & Anderson, 1979; Dreher & Gambrell, Note 5; Frase & Schwartz, 1975; Weiner, 1978), which suggest that at least one qualification be made to the recommendations for the use of this technique. This qualification is that children may need to be trained in how to generate questions that are targeted on important ideas in order for the technique to be effective.

Unfortunately, previous studies of the efficacy of training students how to use this technique have serious flaws. While the finding that students who generate good questions benefit more from the use of this technique than do students who generate poor questions is a well-established one, these authors (with the exception of those of one study) have failed to demonstrate that improvements in question-asking lead to improvements in reading comprehension and reading recall when using the technique (Andre & Anderson, 1979; Dreher & Gambrell, Note 5; Frase & Schwartz, 1975). This failure appears to have been the result of too brief or inappropriate instructional activities.

> The statements below argue the need for an intervention of longer duration with a wider range of student abilities. Again, this establishes the grounds for selecting a particular research format.

The author of the one study in which significant improvements in reading recall following training were shown used a more extensive training program than did other investigations (Weiner, 1978). Weiner's subjects had above-average reading skills, however, as did the subjects in the other training studies. Thus although the recommendation to use this technique has been directed at teachers of below-average readers, the efficacy of training these students to use this technique has never been tested.

Differential treatment response by reading level groups will be an important variable in the proposed study. The following discussion introduces this concept so that the reader will later understand why an analysis by skill level is proposed.

This technique appears promising, based on the theoretical rationale underpinning its design. Empirical trials of the use of the technique, however, indicate that its implementation is problematic. Recently, some progress has been made in preparing average and good readers for its use, but the critical question is how poor readers might be best prepared to benefit from the technique. If the technique cannot be made accessible to poor readers, then teachers attempting to use it may have a detrimental effect on their students' reading skills, if only because time spent learning and implementing the technique may be time spent off-task. Understanding how to make the technique accessible to poor readers is thus of critical importance before further recommendations for the technique can be made.

Below is the actual statement of the question. It expresses two questions succinctly. It could have been stated much earlier. Also, from a research perspective, it would have been more explicit to substitute a nonvalue-laden phrase for the word "better," such as "higher order" or another appropriate term.

Specific hypotheses appear on the following pages, but this study will be directed at answering the following questions: Can students with adequate vocabulary skills for the material they will be reading be trained to generate good questions, and if so, will the improvement in question-asking result in improved reading comprehension and reading recall when students are told to use the technique?

Hypotheses

In this study the following hypotheses will be tested:

1. A group of junior-high-school students who are below average in reading and who receive training in generating good questions will ask better questions than will a group of similar students receiving a control training program (when posttest question quality is controlled for pretest question quality).

2. A group of junior-high-school students who are below average in reading and who receive training in generating good questions will perform better on a task of reading recall than will a group of similar students receiving a control training program (when posttest free recall quality is controlled for pretest free recall quality).

3. The amount of improvement (pre to post) in free recall will be directly related to the amount of improvement (pre to post) in question quality.

METHOD

An overview of the research design would have been helpful at the start of this section. This is a complex study in which many measurements will be utilized. A flowchart or brief outline (see our suggestions in Chapter 1) would assist the reader in understanding how each type of measurement contributes to the overall purpose of the study.

The first paragraph in this section provides information about the subjects. Inasmuch as the author has suggested earlier that failure to control for grade and reading ability has been an important confounding factor in previous research involving the proposed treatment, it is especially important to provide details about these factors.

Subjects

Students in reading classes in a rural, central Texas school district will serve as subjects in this study. About half will be students in seventh-grade required reading classes who demonstrate a wide range of reading ability. The other subjects will be students in eighth-grade remedial reading classes; these students represent about the lower third of the district's eighth-graders in terms of reading comprehension scores on the Science Research Associates (SRA) Achievement Series (Thorpe, Lefever, & Naslund, 1973). Subjects will range in age from 12 years to 15 years.

This next section gives details about the specific tests to be used in the study. Six tests will be used: four that were previously available and two that were designed for this study. The author provides details on the purpose and reliability of each test. Note that reliability for the first test has been reported elsewhere. Accordingly, the author provides just the reliability coefficient and a citation. Interested readers can obtain the reference, and the proposal is not cluttered with unnecessary detail. The description of why this subtest was selected is excellent. Readers may wonder, however, why the subtest was administered exactly six months prior to treatment and not at some other time. The timing of test applications is a particularly important factor and should be justified with care.

Instrumentation

SRA Achievement Series (Thorpe, Lefever, & Naslund, 1973). This test yields both reading comprehension and reading vocabulary subtest scores. Confounding of these subtests occurs, however, because the vocabulary subtest uses the same materials as the comprehension subtest (Fry, 1965; Guthrie, 1972). Therefore, only the comprehension subtest (SRA-C) will be used in this research, while another test will be used to assess pretest vocabulary skills. The SRA-C subtest requires students to answer questions concerning main ideas, supporting details, and inferences from a series of reading passages. It has been reported to have an alternate-form stability coefficient of $r = .83$ (Guthrie, 1972) after a one-year test-retest interval. The SRA-C subtest will be administered to the subjects six months prior to the training program.

Three other tests were presented in a similar fashion: (a) Test of Reading Comprehension-General Vocabulary (TORCGV), (b) Test Reading Comprehension-Paragraph (TORCPR), and (c) Test of Reading Comprehension-Syntactic Similarities (TORCSS). The fifth test, Question Quality Rating, was created by the author. Because no reference is available for this test, greater detail is provided. The author alerts the reader to why the content was chosen and particular procedures devised for administering the test. Note, however, that the actual test is included in an appendix.

Question Quality Rating. This test was created for use in this research, and it will be used as both a pretest and a posttest measure. The reading passages and instructions to subjects are contained in Appendix A. Two reading passages (A and B) were selected from sixth-grade social studies texts that had not been in previous use in the district. Passage A, 984 words long, is a discussion of the economies of the British North American colonies (Jones, Young, & Boutwell, 1971, pp. 38-43). Passage B, 695 words long, is a narrative about the struggles to control Mexico from colonial times until the twentieth century (Chapin, McHugh, & Gross, 1971, pp. 62-66). These passages were chosen because students were likely to be somewhat familiar with the content (although much of the content would be new), because the style and readability of the passages are similar to text materials students are and will be required to learn from in their school program, and because the passages are complete and long enough to be sensitive to the use of efficient reading strategies while being short enough to allow testing during a single class period.

Subjects will read either Passage A or Passage B on the pretest, and the other passage on the posttest; subjects will be randomly assigned to passages. They will be instructed to write down, while reading, "the best questions about the story that [they could] think of . . .[,] questions that [they] could ask someone else [in order to] find out if they had read the story too." Fifteen minutes will be given to complete this task, and they cannot get help from each other. They can request help from the experimenter if they do not understand a specific word; the experimenter will then define the word for all subjects.

The questions that the subjects will generate will be rated on a 1 to 5 equal appearing interval scale with "1" representing a poor question and "5" representing an excellent question. Raters will receive training and practice materials before rating and will be told to base the rating of question quality on the degree to which the question targets important information in the passage and on the degree to which answering the question requires the reader to organize the content of the text. If these two qualities are present to a high degree, raters also are to consider the amount of elaboration required by the question, and the degree to which answering the question taps the higher levels of Bloom's taxonomy, for example, understanding, application, analysis, synthesis, and evaluation. If raters do not understand the question, it will be rated "1," or poor.

In the paragraph above, the author provides detail on how the raters will score this test. Below he provides a careful description of the raters. In this study, the raters serve as a form of instrumentation, and because a good proposal requires that all instrumentation be described fully, the paragraph is needed.

The ten raters are either graduate students in educational psychology ($N = 5$) at the university or advanced undergraduate education students who have completed a course in Tests and Measurements and have been recommended by their instructor as being skilled at evaluating test items. All raters have had courses in Tests and Measurements, five have had courses in Psychometric Theory, and one has taught Tests and Measurements courses. Seven raters were experienced teachers at either the elementary or secondary level with a median of 4.0 years of experience. The questions generated by students and the instructions and training materials given to raters are contained in Appendix B.

> In the paragraph below, the author presents the reliability for each of the passages in the test. Because individual questions were rated, but means were used in the analysis, the author provides reliability estimates for both.

To determine reliability of the test, pre- and posttest questions for the same passages were combined and question order was randomized. Five raters (similar to those used in the study) rated all questions for Passage A and five rated all questions for Passage B. The mean of the five ratings for a question was used as the estimate of the quality of that question. Interrater agreement by the Spearman-Brown formula (Winer, 1971, pp. 283-287) was estimated to be $r = .84$ for Passage A questions and $r = .73$ for Passage B. Subjects generated between 0 and 9 questions. The quality estimates for all the questions a subject asked were combined and the mean of these was taken to be the estimate of that student's question-asking skills. Reliability of this estimate by the Spearman-Brown formula was estimated to be $r = .96$ for Passage A and $r = .92$ for Passage B.

Throughout the rest of this proposal, the estimates of student questioning skills are referred to by the mnemonics PREQUES and POSQUES, for pretest and posttest question ratings, respectively.

> A second test, Free Recall Quality Rating, also was created for this study. The author presented it in much the same way as the test above, and that material has been omitted here. A final item of data will be collected by interviewing students, and that step is presented here. Note that the experimenter will debrief the subjects as a part of the final process of data collection.

Other measures. In addition to the previous measures, the *number of questions* asked on both the pretest (PRENUM) and on the posttest (POSNUM) will be included in the analyses. After the posttest, subjects in the experimental training group will be asked if they have *used the strategy* they had learned about, and will be told to write down their answers on experimenter-supplied paper without writing their names. The experimenter will then explain to the subjects that he or she did not know whether this strategy would work, but in order to find out if it did, their help was needed, because they were the only ones to know if they had really tried to use the strategy.

> The procedure for collecting pretest and posttest data is presented in the next section. The level of heading (not separate from the paragraph) should be changed so that it is the same as "Subjects" and "Instrumentation." Note that the author plans for the contingency that some students may not return the parent permission slip. Because it is unlikely that all students will get permission or remember to bring back the letter, it is wise to address this in the proposal.

Procedure. During the second week of the fall semester, the subjects' regular reading instructor will explain to them the nature of the research project and distribute parent permission forms to be reviewed and signed if desired by the subjects' parents. This form is contained in Appendix C. If any students are not permitted by their parents to participate, these students will work on individual assignments during assessment sessions and participate in the control group training because the control training is part of the regular instructional program.

> The paragraph below performs the function of an overview paragraph. Notice how a simple diagram, as suggested in Chapter 1, would help in grasping the overall pattern of the study.

Subjects next will be administered the Test of Reading Comprehension–General Vocabulary (TORCGV) subtest, the Pretest Question-Asking task (PREQUES) and the Pretest Free Recall task (PRECALL). SRA Reading test scores are available for subjects who had been present the previous spring. Following pretesting, subjects will be randomly assigned to control and experimental groups.

> The author provides a concise depiction of the treatment group. Details of the specific instructional objectives for the treatment are presented in Table 1. The figure is logical and easy to read. Presenting this information separately from the text gives the reader the option of reading it for greater detail.

Experimental Group. What occurs during the experimental group training is critical to testing the main hypotheses of this study. The training the students will receive involves four components: (a) instruction and practice in problem solving (as a prerequisite to presenting reading comprehension as a problem-solving task), (b) instruction and practice in question asking, (c) instruction and practice in recognizing text structure, and (d) practice in asking questions while reading. In Table 1 more details are contained about specific instructional objectives of these four components. The instructional manual for this experimental training is contained in Appendix D.

The experimental training will be conducted by the experimenter, and all experimental sessions will take place in the subjects' regular classroom. The experimental training will last nine sessions for a total of 7.5 hours of allotted instructional time. All students must attend seven or more sessions to be included in the final data analysis.

The last sentence above establishes the minimum participation standard required for each subject. Those who do field research, particularly in school settings, are aware of the fact that it is *very* unlikely that all subjects will be present for the entire treatment. As we indicated in Chapter 4, it is better to anticipate and resolve such problems before collecting data than to be faced with difficult decisions after the data have been collected and disagreements between student and committee become potentially disastrous.

Below, the author provides concise information on the control group and posttests. Note that students were debriefed after the posttest and that each student then received the alternative treatment, even though further data were not collected for the study. The reversing of treatments ensures that all the subjects have the chance to experience the primary intervention. If in fact the treatment provides significant benefits, the control group has equal access to them, *after* all data essential to the study have been collected.

Control group. The control group will receive instruction and practice in using a dictionary, a thesaurus, and the library. The instruction will be done by the regular reading teacher and will take place either in the library or in an alcove adjacent to the regular classroom. Precautions will be taken to ensure that the control group cannot hear teaching that occurs with the experimental group.

PROPOSAL 3: TABLE 1   Specific Instructional Objectives for the Four
Components

Problem Solving	Questioning Skills	Text Structure	Applications
1.1 Students will be able to identify a situation as problematic and the reason why it is a problem.	2.1 Given a word or phrase from text, students will be able to identify attributes of that word or phrase.	3.1 Students will be able to identify similarities between reading to learn information and problem-solving.	4.1 When given a text, the topic, and the first paragraph, students will be able to generate explicit statements of information they want to obtain from the text.
1.2 Students will be able to list the six steps for solving problems.	2.2 Given a word or phrase from text, students will be able to state implied attributes of that word or phrase (e.g., "postpone" implies an event, a person controlling its occurrence, a previous time for the event and a new time).	3.2 Given a short passage of discourse, students will be able to identify the probable intent of the author.	4.2 When given a text, students will generate questions about the text and will search for answers in the passage.
1.3 Given either an example of a school (intellectual) problem or a general social problem, students will be able to identify the steps they will follow in seeking a solution.	2.3 Given a word or phrase from text, students will be able to state what information is missing about implied attributes.	3.3 Given a passage of discourse, students will be able to identify the main ideas and their supporting details, and will be able to outline the passage without omitting, adding, or distorting main ideas.	
	2.4 Students will list several types of strategies aimed at obtaining information and will be able to identify several types of questions and the type of information they elicit.	3.4 When given a passage of text and a set of questions about the passage, students will be able to identify where the answers to the questions about the passage are likely to be found and will successfully find answers to these questions.	

PROPOSAL 3: TABLE 1 *Continued*

Problem Solving	Questioning Skills	Text Structure	Applications
	2.5 Students will demonstrate improved skills in asking constraint-seeking questions by reducing the number of questions necessary to win the "twenty questions" game.		
	2.6 Students will demonstrate improved skills in domain-seeking questions by reducing the number of questions necessary before a correct subordinate class is identified in the "twenty questions" game.		
	2.7 Given a problem to solve, students will be able to rank a series of informative facts as to their value in solving the problem.		
	2.8 Given a problem to solve, students will be able to make a statement about a possible solution and will be able to test the truth value of the statement by obtaining and interpreting appropriate information.		

Posttesting. One day after the last training session and three weeks after pretesting, the subjects will be administered the TORCPR, the TORCSS, the Posttest Questioning task (POSQUES), and the Posttest Free Recall task (POS-CALL). After posttesting, all subjects in the experimental group will be asked if they had used the strategy, about advantages and disadvantages of the technique, and about whether or not they would use the technique again. The nature of the research will again be explained to the subjects and any questions they have about the study will be answered to the best of the experimenter's ability at that time. The following week, treatment conditions will be reversed, with the control group receiving the experimental training, and vice versa.

In the final section of the body of the proposal, the focus is on data analysis. The author reports all the techniques to be used for each part of the analysis. More detail would help many readers. It would be particularly helpful if the author had discussed the analysis in the light of each hypothesis stated earlier. Including sample tables for the analyses to be performed is a good idea for all studies, particularly when there are as many variables as in this study. An illustration of the path analytic model to be tested, such as the one presented in Chapter 1, should be included here so the model to be tested is apparent.

Data analysis. Reliability estimates for PREQUES, POSQUES, PRECALL, and POSCALL were calculated using a hand calculator with programmable statistics functions. These estimates were double checked by the experimenter. All other analyses will be performed using the Statistical Package for the Social Sciences (SPSS) statistics package (Nie, Hull, Jenkins, Steinbrenner, & Bent, 1975), edition 8.3, on the CDC 6000/Cyber 700 computers at the university. Data-checking activities will include running subprogram FREQUENCIES to check on variance distributions and plotting distributions on probability paper. Subprograms FREQUENCIES and CROSSTABS will be used to generate the characteristics of treatment groups. Subprograms REGRESSION and PLOT will be used to run preliminary path analyses and to check that regression assumptions have been met, and subprogram REGRESSION will be used to run the final, restricted model path analysis. Subprogram PLOT will be used to generate figures that illustrate significant aptitude-treatment interactions.

4

=▭=

Funded Grant

A Competition Strategy for Worksite Smoking Cessation

This is a proposal for a "competitive renewal grant." The investigator is seeking funding to continue a project that already has been supported. Such applications are called "competitive" because the proposal must be evaluated with all other proposals submitted within a given time frame, including both renewals and those that are new. If the study is of particular interest to the funding agency and is technically sound, a competitive renewal application will have the advantage of a "halo effect"; that is, the reviewers will recognize that the investigation already has been deemed meritorious enough to have received funding from the grantor.

AUTHORS' NOTE: The original of this proposal was prepared by Nell H. Gottlieb, Ph.D., while a faculty member at The University of Texas at Austin. Dr. Gottlieb is a Professor in the Department of Kinesiology and Health Education and in the Department of Sociology at UT-Austin. This grant was part of a comprehensive research agenda that focuses on the reduction of behaviors that are linked to cancer and was funded by the American Heart Association-Texas Affiliate.

The competitive renewal, however, faces the additional challenge of providing a rationale for continuation—in some cases, despite the fact that the goal of the original study has been achieved. The proposal presented here met that challenge and was funded for continued work. One of the particular strengths of this proposal is that it is unusually concise, yet it manages to communicate the details of the proposed study very effectively. This is well illustrated by the abstract below, which conveys a surprisingly complete account of the study in the small space permitted.

SUMMARY OF PROPOSED RESEARCH

This research uses a quasi-experimental design to assess the effectiveness of competition/high social facilitation on the recruitment of employees of a large state human resources organization to participate in a self-help smoking cessation program and on the treatment outcomes of the self-help program. Two pairs of regions will be assigned at random to the experimental condition, an inter-program area competition to increase the percentage of smokers and nonsmoking supporters participating in the cessation program or to the control condition, which employs only the usual marketing of program availability. The program will be offered in conjunction with the Great American Smokeout and with Valentine's Day. Besides testing the effect of social facilitation on program recruitment and smoking cessation using a controlled intervention, we will specify a general model of the process of smoking cessation, which includes cognitive, behavioral, social influence, and social structural variables. Smoking behavior will be measured using a self-report and the physiological markers of saliva thiocyanate and, for quitters only, cotinine. This research will contribute to the knowledge base of social psychological factors related to smoking cessation and will be immediately applicable to the design of more effective worksite-based smoking cessation programs.

The author provides a brief overview of the notion of health interventions in the workplace. This serves as the kind of "gentle introduction" discussed in Chapter 1 of this guide—a preface that will be particularly helpful for reviewers who did not read the proposal for the original study.

AIMS OF THE RESEARCH PROGRAM

The worksite offers unique opportunities for cardiovascular disease risk reduction programs. Organization-wide, on-site interventions are convenient and sanctioned for employee participation and provide increased social support for individual behavior change. Self-help behavior change programs, which do not require employer-subsidized time off the job, offer the potential for cost-effective worksite health promotion.

Here the author provides a concise description of the intervention. This is given at an early point in the proposal so that the reader can use it as a general frame for considering the details that follow.

We propose to field test two conditions of social facilitation, measuring the impact on the recruitment to and outcome of a self-help worksite smoking cessation intervention, which uses previously evaluated materials. In the high social facilitation condition, a region-wide competition among Texas Department of Human Services (TDHS) program areas to involve the most smokers and smoker-supporters (nonsmokers who assist smokers to quit) will be used to generate enthusiasm and strong social reinforcement for program recruitment, adherence and outcome. In the standard social facilitation condition, smokers will be recruited, using the same intensity of marketing but without the competition aspect, to participate in the self-help program. The research will test the impact of the two social facilitation conditions on the proportion of smokers employed at the worksite who volunteer for the program (program penetration) and the proportions of quitters/program participants and quitters/smoking employees at program completion and 6 months following the program. Four regions of TDHS (two competition and two noncompetition) will participate. Two will hold the recruitment drive during the Great American Smokeout (GASO) and two during a Valentine's Day "Save a Sweetheart" program.

By the end of this paragraph, the reader will know both the nature and length of the intervention, as well as the benefits to be gained—both theoretical and applied.

We will also determine the relationship of cognitive factors (intention to quit, beliefs about the consequences of smoking, and self-efficacy to cope with urges to smoke), social support (the smoking behaviors of co-workers, family, and friends and their attitudes towards the smoker's quitting), smoking history (frequency and duration of smoking, number and duration of quitting attempts), and demographic variables to smoking behavior over the 6-month follow-up period. Smoking behavior will be measured by self-report for respondents to the health promotion survey and, for program participants, levels of saliva thiocyanate (SCH) and, to confirm quitting, cotinine. The findings will demonstrate the effect of social facilitation on smoking behavior change and will increase our knowledge about the cognitive, behavioral, and social factors underlying the process of quitting smoking. In addition, application of the research will lead to more effective worksite smoking cessation programs.

PREVIOUS WORK

In this section, the author describes recently completed research in two areas that are directly related to the proposed study. This demonstrates the long-term interest of the investigator and, by accentuating the fact that her work in the area already has been approved and funded, she lays claim to both success and competence. The proposed study is characterized as a replication of successful work already undertaken in a different environment. This serves to underscore continuity of interest and the programmatic nature of the author's research agenda.

Our research has two primary foci: (a) evaluation of the effects of a competition among program areas on recruitment into categories of a smoking cessation program and (b) analysis of the relationship between individual differences in cognitive structure, smoking history, and demographic variables and the likelihood of quitting smoking.

Our 1986-87 American Heart Association (AHA)-funded research compared the effects of a competition between two worksites in each of three regions of a large state human services agency on employee participation in the Great American Smokeout (GASO) in three categories: number of nonsmoking supporters, number participating in a 20-day, self-help smoking cessation program, and number of smokers quitting for the GASO day only. The incentive was a cold turkey buffet for the total worksite on the day following the GASO for the worksite with the highest proportion of supporters and smokers joining the self-help program. Quitting for the day did not count in the competition. Significant differences ($p < .001$) between competition and noncompetition worksites were found for the proportion participating in each of the categories (69% versus 12% of nonsmokers were adopters; 24% versus 4% of smokers joined the self-help program; and 46% vs. 28% of smokers quit for the GASO day only). However, the total participation in the worksites was variable (ranging from 16% to 97% in the cooperation and 0% to 69% in the noncompetition worksites) and in half of the sites more smokers quit for the day than joined the cessation program. The results of the competition are promising, although the involvement is lower than that reported by Klesges and colleagues for banks (1). The low social facilitation condition is comparable to the participation we found for the Great American Smokeout in an implementation of "Heart at Work" conducted at an insurance company (2). We propose to replicate this research (a) using competition among program areas, which seems to be a more natural line of competition in this agency than individual worksites, and (b) organizing the program around a Valentine's Day "Save a Sweetheart" theme in addition to GASO, which involves quitting during the holiday season. We also propose a more in-depth qualitative evaluation to examine the process of implementing the programs in the competition and noncompetition sites.

> The next paragraph develops the theoretical base for the study. In the process, however, the author underscores several benefits to be achieved by funding the study. These include attractive outcomes at a number of different levels (levels likely to correspond to the differing interests of members of the review committee) such as improved design of cessation programs, improved worker health, and improved understanding of personality and behavioral characteristics of people who quit or persist in smoking.

The second focus of this research is individual differences in smoking cessation. The applicant's major research interest has been the social epidemiology of lifestyle health behaviors, with special emphasis on smoking. She has used local and national data to develop and specify a multi-level theoretical model of smoking, which includes cognitive, behavioral, and social structural variables (3,4). Using this model, she has shown gender differences in smoking to be related to gender-specific modeling effects of peer and parental smoking, group membership, and marriage. In addition, education, not attending church, life events, and belief in susceptibility to heart disease were directly associated with the likelihood of smoking for both men and women (3-9). Differences were also found by ethnicity in a national probability sample. Hispanic males and females were less likely to be current smokers than their Black and Anglo peers, while Anglo males and females had the highest proportion of quitters (10). In a probability sample of Texas residents, Gottlieb, Lloyd and Bernstein (11) found men more likely to smoke than women (34% vs. 27%) and recommended worksite-based programs as an especially effective way to reach adults younger than 65. Our current AHA-funded research involves testing the relative influence of social learning theory variables (including self-efficacy), behavioral variables, social facilitation, and demographic variables on smoking status immediately after and at six months following a self-help smoking cessation program. The 1986 GASO competition did not yield sufficient subjects in the self-help program to test these hypothesized relationships. Continued funding would allow recruitment of enough subjects for this aspect of the research.

> Below, the author points out the specific ways in which this proposal is superior to previous studies: how it corrects errors in research design, and how its theoretical framework will allow the results of the study to be more than purely descriptive. The author makes clear not only that she is aware of the problems that attended previous research on the topic but that she knows how to circumvent them as well.

Our AHA-funded research addresses several problems often found in smoking studies. Much of the research suffered from inadequate sample sizes to detect differences in quit rate, the use of self-report of smoking status as the sole dependent variable, and the use of cross-sectional surveys, which does not allow causal inferences to be made regarding the relationships of the independent variables and smoking behavior. At a level more fundamental than these methodological problems is the lack of an adequate theoretical model of smoking behavior to guide research. Such a model must move beyond the psychological level of explanation, to include social and cultural influences. In our current and proposed research, the two social facilitation groups are large enough to detect expected differences in quit rates, smoking self-report is confirmed using biochemical measures, and participants are followed through their participation in the self-help program and six months thereafter. Based on our theoretical approach, we include variables at the cognitive, behavioral, and social structural level in our analysis and manipulate social facilitation, using an organizational level intervention, in our controlled experiment.

Other investigators have examined the effect of competitions as an incentive to change health behavior. Brownell and colleagues have reported effective weight loss using competitions between organizations and divisions or teams within organizations (12). The cost/benefit ratio of this program was reported to be substantially better than other worksite-based weight reduction programs. Klesges and colleagues used a competition strategy to recruit smoking employees in three banks to participate in a self-help smoking cessation program (1). Almost all (88%) smokers in the organizations participated and the quit rate at 6 months following the treatment was 18%. The opposite result, however, was found in a competition among naturally occurring divisions of a nursing staff (13). No nurses volunteered for the self-help smoking cessation project. This was attributed to a boycott of the program by influential nurses. It appears that competition has great potential for increasing motivation and reinforcement for entering smoking cessation programs, adhering to them, and quitting smoking. However, the conditions must be carefully directed. The importance of worksite culture is receiving increasing attention (14). Sorensen, Pechacek and Pallonen have recently reported different norms for co-worker discouragement of quitting attempts, perceived prevalence of smoking, and interest in quitting across worksites (15). We will examine these variables. We will also follow the advice of organizational theorists who have pointed out the necessity of examining organizational change from a process as well as a variance approach (16). While most of our proposed work on program outcome falls within a variance framework, we will carefully document the process of implementation using key informant interviews, observation, and other qualitative techniques.

In the next paragraphs, the author provides a rationale for selecting the intervention to be used in the study. Documenting the appropriateness of self-help programs, and combining this with a discussion of results from a recent pilot study, adds strength to the proposal.

The American Lung Association (ALA) self-help program we use has been evaluated and found to have a nonsmoking prevalence rate at 12 months of 18%

and a continuous nonsmoking rate of 5% (17). These rates are comparable to those found for other self-help manuals (18). Windsor et al. obtained a quit rate of 6% and a quit/reduction rate of 20% using the ALA manual and a 10 minute health education skills counseling session in a study of pregnant women using a health department clinic (19). Preliminary results from a study of the effects of social support on quit rates using the ALA self-help manual show 20% quit rates with high social support and 6% with low social support (20).

Self-help programs for smoking cessation have several advantages over therapist-directed interventions. They can be made available to a large number of people, and those who quit using self-help can attribute quitting success to themselves rather than a therapist (21). Although these programs are not as effective as more intensive interventions, they may be more cost-effective than clinics and reach the large segment of the smoking population who wish to stop smoking without professional assistance (22).

> The next paragraph is one of the few that might be deleted. It introduces a sharp change in the focus of the section, without contributing additional information that will help reviewers make a judgment about the present proposal.

Individual differences in cognitive structure, social reinforcement of smoking, social status, and smoking history have been shown by a number of investigators to be predictive of smoking, both independent of treatment type and, in some cases, in interaction with treatment type. DiClemente has studied the influence of self-efficacy expectation, a key variable from social learning theory, on the maintenance of smoking cessation (23). Ratings of one's ability to cope with various situations that provide cues to smoke, and the degree of temptation each situation presented, were predictive of recidivism following a cessation program. Horwitz, Hindi-Alexander and Wagner found that recidivists, in comparison to abstainers, had lower scores on internal locus of control, did not actively cope with others smoking, and had less support from spouse, other family, and friends. In that study, continuing smokers held the strongest beliefs that smoking causes heart disease and emphysema (24). Intention to stop smoking and normative beliefs about the expectations of significant others regarding one's smoking were found to predict smoking status in college women by Fishbein and colleagues (25).

CONTEMPLATED METHOD
OF APPROACH TO THE PROBLEM

Research Questions

> The author now provides a clear introduction to the two major research problems. She then goes on to establish directional hypotheses based on previous research findings. This is a good example of the strategy discussed in Chapter 1 of this guide of using powerful directional hypotheses and listing them in a sequential order that parallels the logic of the research problem.

Our research questions fall in two categories, the findings regarding our controlled intervention and the specification of a general model for the process of smoking cessation. First, we will ascertain whether the competition/high social facilitation condition is more effective in the control of smoking at the worksite than the control/low social facilitation condition. We will test the following research hypotheses:

1. A higher proportion of smokers will volunteer for the smoking cessation program under the high social facilitation condition than the low social facilitation condition.

2. Of those smokers who volunteer for the program, a higher proportion will quit smoking at the end of the program in the high social facilitation group than in the low social facilitation group.

3. Of those smokers who volunteer for the program, a higher proportion will be abstinent six months following the program in the high social facilitation group than in the low social facilitation group.

4. The change from pre- to post-program saliva thiocyanate level will be greater for the high social facilitation group than for the low social facilitation group at the end of the program and at the six-month follow-up.

We will then specify models for the prediction of the process of smoking cessation and maintenance of cessation. The models will include the following independent variables: cognitive variables from social learning theory (self-efficacy, intentions, motivations for smoking), behavioral variables (smoking history, level of self-help program adherence), social facilitation (modeling of smoking by others, normative beliefs regarding others' expectations, assignment to competitive or control condition), and socio-demographic variables (ethnicity, age, pay level, education, gender). Their relative influence on (a) the probability of quitting after the 20-day self-help program, (b) the probability of abstinence at the 6-month follow up, and (c) the change in thiocyanate level at the 6-month follow up will be specified.

Here, a new idea with an extended purpose is introduced. If it is a truly important part of the study, it would have been better to have included it at an earlier point in the proposal. Given the late introduction and the small amount of detail provided, the idea runs the risk of being regarded as "filler," or as a last minute inspiration that has not been thoroughly thought through by the author.

Besides these variance-oriented research questions, we will conduct case studies of the process of implementation in each region. We will be particularly interested in documenting the sequence of events, explanations of decisions made during implementation, and program area leaders' and employees' perception of the recruitment and cessation processes.

Subjects

Potential subjects are 4781 Department of Human Services (DHS) employees from four regions: Houston, San Antonio, Beaumont and Austin. The numbers of employees by program area within regions are shown in Table 1. The two smallest programs will be collapsed to make approximately equal groups.

In an earlier section, the author proposed to analyze results by age, gender, salary level, and education. Thus, in addition to the information provided in Table 1, it would be appropriate to present a breakdown of the subject population by those factors (a footnote directing reviewers to an appendix containing that information would keep the main body of the proposal uncluttered while sustaining the image of thorough attention to detail).

The employees are predominantly female, and ethnic breakdowns vary by region. In 1983, a needs assessment of the central office and Travis County region of the Department of Human Services, which was designed by the applicant, indicated that 22.4% smoked, that 36% of the smokers had tried to

PROPOSAL 4: TABLE 1 Description of Employees by Program Areas Within Regions

| | PROGRAM AREA | | | | | |
REGION	*Administration*	*Protective Services*	*Aged and Disability*	*Income Assistance*	*Family Self-Support*	*TOTAL*
San Antonio	125	247	171	504	75	1122
Houston	180	594	220	998	95	2087
Austin	93	256	212	353	61	975
Beaumont	59	144	118	272	44	637

quit in the last 2 years, and that 70% of the smokers would be likely or very likely to use a stop smoking program at work. Most (81%) of the respondents agreed/strongly agreed that "Cigarette smoke is in the air I breathe at work."

Study Design

This paragraph shows how data from previous work could supplement the data and interpretations from the proposed study. Again, this reminds reviewers that approval would provide funds for a sustained effort in an important area of health behavior.

The study employs a quasi-experimental control group design (26). Because our intervention is an organizational one, random assignment of individuals to treatment conditions is not possible. We have already conducted three replications of high/low social facilitation conditions using worksite-based competitions. For the renewal of this grant, we will assign two social facilitation conditions (based on competition among program areas within a region) to two geographically defined regions of the Texas Department of Human Services in two replications. The first replication will be in conjunction with the Great American Smokeout and the second with Valentine's Day. Although the groups are nonequivalent, we know that employees of TDHS are similar, and we will have additional comparisons on smoking characteristics and other relevant variables from the initial health promotion survey. Our research design will control adequately for such threats to internal validity as history, maturation, and testing.

The author provides here an exemplary demonstration of thoughtful planning for sample size. As indicated in Chapter 4 of this guide, the power analysis yields concise and credible support for the proposed decision concerning sample size. This also has the double advantage of adding credence to the funding requests that will come later in the proposal. The closing sentence of the paragraph, however, is unfortunate in that it alludes to a recruitment process (not mentioned elsewhere in the proposal) that already is under way. Reviewers might well regard such action as premature. At the least, the reference will leave them puzzled.

The experimental regions employ 1612 persons, of whom 403 (25%) are expected to be smokers; 3209 are in the control worksites, of whom 802 are expected to be smokers. A smoker is defined as a person who had smoked at least one cigarette in the 7 days previous to the orientation assessment. From the work of Klesges (1), the 1983 TDHS needs assessment, and our 1986 self-help program recruitment figures (24% in competitive sites and 54% in noncompetitive sites), we estimate a 30% recruitment rate using competition and a 10% rate in the standard condition, yielding 121 and 80, respectively, in the smoking programs in the two conditions. A power analysis, using estimates from Klesges (1) and Lowe (20) for recruitment rates under low and high social facilitation, indicates that, with $alpha = .05$, power $= .80$, a 20% difference in program recruitment ($p^1 = .30$; $p^2 = .10$) can be detected using 71 subjects per group. Similarly, using treatment outcomes under low and high social support conditions from the literature (17,19,20), groups with 58 subjects are needed to detect a 20% difference in cessation rate ($alpha = .05$; power $= .80$; $p^1 = .05$; $p^2 = .25$) (27). We currently have 47 subjects in the high social facilitation and 9 in the low social facilitation cessation conditions.

An organization-wide health promotion survey to determine the number and characteristics of smokers will be administered to employees in each region in September, 1987. For three weeks prior to GASO or Valentine's Day, an intensive recruitment campaign for smokers to enlist in the minimal intervention cessation program will be conducted in each region. Sessions to introduce the self-help materials, along with recruitment and program awareness activities, will be held during this period. Contest awards will be made on either the day of the Great American Smokeout, an important time for antismoking awareness for the population at large, or Valentine's Day. Program participants will be pretested at their orientation session and will receive posttests at the end of the 20-day program and 6 months later.

Description Of Interventions

The section that follows provides a detailed description of the intervention. Because the incentive value of rewards is one of the driving forces behind the competitive aspect of the intervention, it would have been helpful to give reviewers an explicit example of how they would be determined—a point on which the opening paragraph is not entirely clear.

In the high social facilitation condition, social support to quit will be engendered through a competition among the four program areas to enroll the most smokers in the intervention and to enlist the most smoker supporters. The contest will be highly publicized, and progress will be visually presented in a region-wide newsletter distributed to all employees and in a lobby display at the regional headquarters. Besides this recognition of winning, participants from the program area that enrolls the highest proportion of smokers and smoker-supporters will have a chance to win a $100, $50, or $25 savings bond in a drawing on GASO or Valentine's Day.

In the standard (low social facilitation) condition, recruitment to the program will be through messages directed to smokers. The amount of publicity (number of memos, numbers and size of posters, etc.) will be the same in both groups. Also, visible signs of program participation ("I Quit" buttons, no smoking desk and wall signs, etc.) will be available for employees in both treatment conditions.

The marketing interventions will be coordinated by the research assistants, who will work closely with the DHS Regional Wellness Coordinators and designated DHS employees in each region. Smokers and smoker supporters will return program registration forms to the designated DHS employees. Smokers will be assigned to a group orientation at their convenience, and smoker supporters will receive a packet of materials to assist them in encouraging smokers to quit.

The self-help intervention to be received by all smoking cessation program participants will be *Freedom from Smoking in 20 Days*, a 64-page cessation manual (28). Subjects who report quitting at the completion of this program will receive *A Lifetime of Freedom from Smoking*, a 28-page maintenance manual (29). These materials, which use a cognitive/behavioral approach with emphasis on self-management, have been evaluated (17,19,20). We will add an orientation session to this self-help treatment following the protocol developed and tested by Windsor and colleagues (19,30). In 1986, we produced and used a videotape introduction to the program. The tape included TDHS employees who served as coping and mastery models for smoking cessation, describing why and how they quit and remained abstinent. A clinical psychologist provided an overview of the self-help manual, discussed ambivalence about quitting, and attempted to raise viewers' self-efficacy about quitting. The orientation is aimed at enhancing commitment to cessation, social support, and skills in behavioral self-monitoring and deep-breathing used in smoking cessation. All subjects will be told that the biochemical tests at the orientation and 6-month follow-up will measure exposure to cigarette smoke.

Commitment to adherence and cessation will be enhanced by having participants pay $5.00 to join the program, which will be refunded if they turn in their self monitoring sheets and have quit smoking by the end of the program. Funds not returned will be pooled and divided among the smokers who have quit. This will be done within each program area in the noncompetition regions. In the competition regions, the funds will be pooled across program areas and divided among the quitters in the program area with the highest proportion of quitters.

Collection Of Data

Data will be collected four times. A 25% sample in each region will be requested to complete the initial health promotion survey. The self-help program participants will be asked for information at the orientation session, at the completion of the program, and at the 6-month follow-up. The smoking supporters will be queried concerning their activities 1 month after they volunteer.

> Here the author creates an effective summary by listing all the variables in a single table. By grouping them within the sequential steps of the study, she provides the reader with a sense of the wider time frame for the investigation. In addition, examples of survey and measurement instruments are referenced to an appendix—where they are available for interested reviewers without intruding on the main presentation. It would have been helpful to note that the follow-up system also appears in an appendix.

The specific variables to be measured at each of the four time periods are outlined in Table 2. Description of measurement of the dependent and independent variables and copies of the 1986 questionnaires are included in the Appendix. The longest instrument (75 items) will be completed during the group

PROPOSAL 4: TABLE 2 Overview of Data Collection: Variables by Testing Times

Initial Health Promotion Survey/All Employees (18 items)	*Self-help Program Participant Pretest (75 items)*	*Self-Help Program Participant Immediate Posttest (38 items)*	*Self-Help Program Participant 6-Month and 1-Year Follow-up (33 items)*
Age	Age	Smoking Status	Smoking Status
Sex	Sex	Self-efficacy for Coping with Urges	Self-efficacy for Coping with Urges
Pay Group	Pay Group	Program Component Usefulness	Saliva Thiocyanate
Education	Education	Co-worker Support	Saliva Cotinine (quitters only)
Family History of CHD	Family History of CHD		
Smoking History	Smoking History		
Intention to Quit	Intention to Quit		
	Perceived Consequences of Smoking		
	Smoking Topology		
	Smoking Models		
	Normative Beliefs about Smoking		
	Motivation to Quit		
	Self-efficacy for Quitting		
	Saliva Thiocyanate		

orientation session. For the initial employee survey, we will use two follow-ups, with a post card system to ensure anonymity, for the initial survey. Program participants will be followed-up by mail and telephone to ensure completeness of the data for each case.

Data Analysis

Tests of proportion using Chi-Square (27) will be used to test differences in the proportion of smokers who volunteer under the two conditions, the proportion of volunteer smokers who quit (using self-report confirmed by SCN level) at program completion, and the proportion of smokers who are abstinent at 6 months following completion of the program. Regional differences in quit levels within treatments will also be tested. Participants will be compared to smokers at the worksite using the health promotion survey and pre-test data to see whether they differ in demographic, smoking history, or heart disease risk characteristics.

Analysis of covariance, using baseline SCN as covariate, will be used to examine the main effects of treatment group and region upon the dependent variable of SCN level at the 6-month follow-up. Significant regional differences may be a function of the ethnic or other demographic differences of employees within region, organizational variation in the way the marketing conditions were implemented or some other factor, such as smoking policies, unique to a region. A better understanding of such differences may be gained through the regression models of influences on reduction, quitting, and abstinence from smoking.

At the next stage of our analysis, we will examine the influences of individual difference variables that would be expected to influence changes in smoking behavior under both social facilitation conditions. Logistic regression, a multivariate technique for binary dependent variables analogous to least-squares regression, will be used for smoking status dependent variables. Logistic regression models will be used to study the selective effects of social support, health locus of control, self-efficacy expectations for quitting or coping with urges to smoke, smoking history, ethnicity, education, occupation, and level of program participation on the logarithmic-odds of quitting and abstention from smoking at 6 months. A similar analysis using SCN at the 6-month follow-up as the dependent variable and the psychosocial, behavioral, and social structural variables as independent variables will be carried out using multiple regression. Hierarchical models will be used to isolate the relative explanatory power of program adherence, smoking history, psychosocial correlates of smoking, and demographic variables consistent with our multilevel theoretical orientation.

EXPERIMENTAL PROBLEMS

This is a section of the proposal that is specified in the application format used by the funding agency. In the process of responding to the demand for comment on the experimental problems, the applicant takes the opportunity to point out the close and ongoing relationship she has with both the managements at the test sites where the study will be conducted and the administrators of state and regional health agencies to be involved.

No experimental problems are expected in the course of this research. The proposed research is an extension of the TDHS smoking cessation programs begun in 1986 under AHA funding. The self-help smoking cessation intervention is widely used and has been evaluated. Likewise, the testing procedures have been used in many studies. The adequacy of the competition to generate high social facilitation is dependent on the cooperation and active support of management at each of the worksite offices. The investigator worked closely with the TDHS regional wellness coordinators and with the state wellness coordinator and personnel director (see letters of support). The research project is embedded within the regions' wellness programs, which have the full support of DHS management.

SIGNIFICANCE OF THE RESEARCH

In the following section, the author relates potential findings to several areas of benefit: the participants, the worksites, the theoretical basis for the field of public health, and, of considerable interest to reviewers from the American Heart Association, the implementation of state legislation through agencies charged with responsibility for public health.

The 1987 Surgeon General's Report "The Health Consequences of Involuntary Smoking" calls for smoke-free worksites (31). This report will add impetus to the movement to establish worksite smoking policies and to reduce ambient tobacco smoke in the worksite. When such policies are established, it is important to offer smoking employees opportunities to quit smoking. Self-help smoking cessation programs offer great promise in the worksite setting because of their flexibility. Recruitment to programs and maintenance of cessation following a program are key concerns. Our research utilizes a worksite setting to field test the impact of high social facilitation generated through a competition to increase the penetration and effectiveness of an already evaluated self-help smoking cessation program.

In addition, we will specify a multilevel model of smoking behavior, including the relative influence of self-efficacy, health locus of control, social support for smoking and quitting, smoking history, and demographic variables upon quitting, independent of the social facilitation condition. Programs may then be designed to augment levels of those variables shown to be important and individual treatment approaches based on these factors can be planned.

Our research findings are immediately useful for the implementation of the Texas State Employee Health Fitness Act. The Governor's Commission on Physical Fitness (GCPF), which is responsible for overseeing the development of health programs in state agencies, needs field-tested, turn-key risk reduction programs for the worksite. Based on our findings, the GCPF can recommend a smoking cessation program to the state agencies and provide guidelines and training for its implementation.

ETHICAL ASPECTS OF
THE PROPOSED RESEARCH

The risks to the participants in this project are minimal and are far outweighed by the benefits of stopping smoking. Successful quitters may feel some discomfort during withdrawal from cigarettes and nonsuccessful quitters may feel some sense of failure and low self-esteem. These outcomes are common, but are not serious. They are experienced by all smokers who attempt to quit. The competition approach to recruitment may exert some social pressure on smokers to participate and thus carries some risk of coercion. The possibility of perceived coercion from the competition is real, although the competition emphasizes improvement of health and the importance of local support, and the stakes are low. These risks will be minimized by providing techniques for dealing with withdrawal symptoms and specific behavioral strategies for "What to do if you fall off the wagon." The potential for coercion in the competition will be reduced by using a positive supportive approach in the marketing, as has been done with the Great American Smokeout. Nonsmoking supporters will be given specific instructions for being supportive to smokers attempting to quit. The health promotion hotline questionnaire is completely confidential, with no identifying number. Program participants' records are linked by a code (available only to the principal investigator) that will be destroyed following completion of data collection. Informed consent will be obtained from all project participants (see letters).

The budget for the proposed study is presented below. Notice both the level of detail provided and how the following justification section is used to rationalize individual items. Inclusion of experience from previous studies lends powerful support to these arguments.

OUTLINE OF PROPOSED BUDGET

ITEM

Personnel (itemize)	
Graduate Research Assistant II (B.S.; 9 mo; 50%)	$6,470
Graduate Research Assistant II (B.S.; 9 mo; 50%)	6,470
Social Security and other benefits	3,105
Subtotal	16,045
Equipment (itemize)	
30MB half-height hard disk and cable	560
Desktop publishing software and PC mouse	675
2 Tape recorders, microphones, and transcription equipment	350
Subtotal	1,585
Supplies (itemize major purchases)	
Thiocyanate and cotinine analysis	3,100
Videotapes, computer tapes, diskettes	100
Postage (posttest questionnaires, correspondence)	400
Photocopying	100
Stationery supplies, paper for questionnaires and forms, posters and displays	350
Long distance telephone	150
Competition prizes and incentive for survey returns	450
Subtotal	4,650
Other expenses, including travel and printing	
Travel of PI and Research Assistants to sites	1,620
Travel of PI to professional meetings	700
Publication costs	400
Subtotal	2,720
Overhead (10%)	2,500
TOTAL	$27,500

JUSTIFICATION OF BUDGET

Graduate Research Assistant (GRA) II: The two half-time (50%) Graduate Research Assistants II will assist the principal investigator in the administration of this project and will be responsible for the collection of qualitative and quantitative data in Houston and San Antonio in the fall and Austin and Beaumont in the spring. They will be responsible for the management of data collection, the organization of the recruitment campaigns, and will conduct focus groups, interviews, and observations at the regions. They also will conduct the behavioral skills sessions for the project participants. They will not receive university credit for this work. My experience in conducting the research program last year in these regions (one of which was Austin) with one GRA II has led to a request for two such positions. It is essential that one person maintain full attention on one region for the program to be implemented successfully. The expanded qualitative research makes this even more essential.

Equipment: The hard disk will be used for back up on the computer system funded in 1986, which has one half-height hard disk drive. The desktop publishing software and mouse will be used to prepare professional quality newsletters for publicity at the sites. The tape recorders are for use by the GRAs in the conduct of interviews and focus groups for the qualitative research.

GRA II and PI travel to sites: The organization and implementation of the program and conduct of the qualitative research will require extensive time on site. The budget item covers 6 trips to Beaumont (@ $50) and 11 trips to Houston (@ $120). This essential item was underbudgeted in the 1986 grant.

Note: Self-help smoking cessation materials are being donated by the American Lung Association of Texas. Data entry will be provided at no charge by the Texas Department of Human Services.

At this point, the proposal included the list of references and four appendices: (a) letters of support, (b) questionnaires, (c) consent forms, and (d) information concerning measurement of the primary variables. We have reprinted here only selected portions of the last two appendices. The letter to employees and the attached postcard are reproduced below because they represent a unique means of obtaining consent—one particularly appropriate to the conditions of the proposed study.

PROPOSAL 4: APPENDIX 1
CONSENT FORM FOR QUESTIONNAIRE

You have been selected in a random sample of employees from two regions of the Department of Human Services. You are invited to complete this questionnaire regarding your lifestyle health habits for a worksite health promotion research project funded by the American Heart Association and being conducted by the University of Texas at Austin. The questionnaire is completely anonymous. It will take approximately 10 minutes to complete. An interoffice postcard is attached to the questionnaire. Your signing and returning it will remove your name from the mailing list. If you agree to fill in the questionnaire, return it separately through interoffice mail. When we receive your postcard, we will eliminate your name from the follow-up list so you will not be contacted again regarding your completing the questionnaire.

Thank you for your assistance. It is very important that you respond so that we will have a complete picture of employee health behavior at your worksite before we begin the research program. Your decision whether or not to complete the questionnaire will not prejudice your future relations with the University of Texas at Austin or the Department of Human Services. Please call me at 512-555-1234 if you have any questions about the questionnaire or the research project.

Sincerely,

Nell H. Gottlieb, Ph.D.
Assistant Professor
Principal Investigator

The content of the attached postcard is indicated below.

- --

Please return this postcard through interoffice mail.

I have read the information at the beginning of the survey.

___ I have agreed to fill in the health promotion questionnaire for The University of Texas at Austin and have returned the questionnaire separately through interoffice mail.

___ I do not wish to complete the questionnaire.

Please remove my name from the follow-up list.

_____   _____
Signature   Date

(Please print first initial and last name if your handwriting is difficult to read)

- --

PROPOSAL 4: APPENDIX 2
MEASUREMENT OF DEPENDENT
AND INDEPENDENT VARIABLES

The original appendix contained detailed descriptions of how each variable would be measured, complete with references to information on reliability and validity. That material is reproduced here in abbreviated form.

Self-reported smoking will be measured using the Health Insurance Study Smoking Battery (32,33). These items include whether or not the respondent uses specific tobacco products and the frequency and duration of current or former cigarette smoking. In addition, the number of attempts to quit smoking, the types of approaches used, and the longest duration of abstinence will be obtained. Intention to quit smoking in 3 months will be measured on a 4-point Likert scale from "very unlikely" to "very likely." For the follow-ups, whether or not the respondent has been continuously abstinent since the program will be asked. At the orientation and follow-ups, respondents will be asked the number of hours per day they are exposed to second-hand cigarette smoke. This will be used to evaluate borderline thiocyanate measures for validation of cessation.

Saliva thiocyanate (SCN) and *cotinine* will be used as physiological indicators for smoking (34,35). Thiocyanate is a metabolite of the hydrogen cyanide in smoke, which has a half-life of 14 days. Although estimates vary, specificity (93%) and sensitivity (98%) using a cutoff point of 85 M/L to distinguish smokers from nonsmokers have been reported. Limitations include dietary interference from passive smoking, marijuana smoking, consumption of beer and certain other foods, and the inability to distinguish light smokers from nonsmokers. Cotinine, a metabolite of nicotine, is unique to tobacco, has a half life of 30 hours, and is able to distinguish light smokers from nonsmokers. Costing four times as much as SCN, it is too expensive to use for all subjects. However, it will be used to confirm quitting. Saliva samples will be taken at the orientation session and at 6-month follow-up. The biochemical assays will be carried out by the Division of Epidemiology, University of Minnesota, which does this as a nonprofit service.

Self-efficacy to cope with specific urges to smoke is measured using the 31 item Smoking Situations scale of DiClemente and Prochaska (23,32). Respondents are asked to rate on a 5-point Likert scale, "How tempted would you be to smoke in this situation?" and, "How confident are you that you would not smoke in this situation?" for such situations as "when alone and feeling depressed" and "when I am feeling accepted by someone." The *alpha* reliability scores for the temptation scale (.97) and confidence scale (.98) are very high. Inter-item correlations for the self-efficacy scale ranged from .44-.93 (mean = .69).

Annotated Bibliography of Supplementary References

Information that might be helpful in preparing a research proposal can be found in publications of several different types. For example, valuable direction can be obtained from some textbooks that focus primarily on other topics. Among such references are books that deal with the conduct of research. Some of them do contain sections or chapters on the proposal, but because the central concern of the text is with the technical specification of design and method, the treatment of the proposal generally is brief and superficial. Standard references of this type, such as Gall, Borg, and Gall (1996), are available in most college libraries, and we have not included examples in this appendix. If desired, colleagues, advisers, and research professors can help the novice locate a general research method text that will best serve his or her particular proposal.

Another, and very different, category of potentially helpful books are those designed to assist in obtaining a grant—for support of research or (more commonly) a development project. In many of these, the focus is on how to locate funding sources, how to match proposed projects with agency agenda, and how the proposal evaluation process works. We have included several such guides in the annotations below, but again, because the primary focus often is not on the development of a research proposal, readers will do well to examine library or bookstore copies before purchase.

A small additional category of publications consists of documents prepared by professional and scholarly organizations as guides in the area of research ethics, as manuals for document preparation and format, or as general advice for those embarking on careers in research. An appropriate selection of these should be on the desk of everyone who does research, and the novice will find that the standard references among them, such as the *Publication Manual of the American Psychological Association* (American Psychological Association, 1994), quickly become dog-eared with use. We have not attempted to include annotations of such documents for each disciplinary specialization, but some of the most helpful generic examples are abstracted here.

Finally, a growing number of texts are now available that, like this one, are directed specifically to the needs of people faced with the task of preparing a research proposal—whether for academic or grant solicitation purposes. Some of these presume investigation in certain areas (education, medicine, or social services, for example), but others are directed to a more general audience. Most are oriented toward empirical/quantitative studies, but some, like Marshall and Rossman's *Designing Qualitative Research* (1999) or Maxwell's *Qualitative Research Design: An Interactive Approach* (1996), serve investigators who intend to employ other paradigms. The political and social circumstances that are unique to graduate study are made central in some of these texts, whereas the logic of formulating design and method (or the mechanics of writing the formal document) are given greater attention in others. Accordingly, we have tried to include a wide selection of the proposal books now on the market. The best choice for many novices would be to combine several of those that serve your particular needs—for use in combination with the present text (of course).

American Psychological Association. (1982). *Ethical principles in the conduct of research with human participants.* Washington, DC: Author.

This classic monograph lays out 11 ethical principles that should guide the conduct of research involving human participants. These are powerful statements that are not easily forgotten. The accompanying text provides a discussion of the ethical issues that were considered in developing the principles. The fact that the passage of nearly two decades has not necessitated any revision in this document suggests that the framers got it exactly right on the first try. If your proposed study will require human participants, this is an essential reference.

American Psychological Association. (1994). *Publication manual of the American Psychological Association* (4th ed.). Washington, DC: Author.

This paperbound manual contains a comprehensive set of guidelines for the particular format commonly called "APA," as well as substantial sections that deal with other aspects of the process of scholarly writing. The manual is the standard reference for those students and professors in the social and behavioral sciences for whom APA is either a choice or a requirement of publication. The major topics covered are (a) content and organization of the manuscript, (b) expression of ideas (style, grammar, and reduction of bias), (c) APA editorial style, (d) manuscript preparation and sample paper, and (e) manuscript acceptance and production (submission, review, and proofreading). The guidelines for reduction of bias (gender, race, disability, and sexual orientation) in language will be particularly valuable for proposal writers. The section devoted to handling of materials from on-line information sources and other electronic media reflects standards as of the date of publication. Given the rapidity of changes in this area, authors should seek more recent guidelines. The APA format and citation style are now accepted or required by a large number of universities and journals. If you are going to be using APA in the future, the proposal represents the perfect vehicle for mastering the details of that format.

Becker, H. S. (1986). *Writing for social scientists.* Chicago: University of Chicago Press.

This is not another style and form manual. The book is a collection of nine elegantly simple essays dealing with the problems of writing about research (a 10th chapter on confronting the psychological risks of writing is contributed by sociologist Pamela Richards). Becker attends to the day-to-day work demands of producing a document—whether a research proposal, dissertation, or journal report. These include the familiars of procrastination, writing successive drafts, editing your own work, getting help, using (or not using) a word processor, and how to write clear and attractive prose within the confines of academic conventions.

It takes a special kind of confidence to write a book about good writing, particularly if that book also has to give helpful advice to people who do not know how to do it. The author does it with such grace and gentle encouragement that many readers will be reminded of another slim volume—Strunk and White's (1979) *The Elements of Style.* Becker indeed is an established scholar with a formidable reputation for his writing style; he succeeds here by remembering exactly why writing is not easy for most people. If you do not have confidence in your prose voice or the established work habits required to accomplish a piece of extended writing, this is the book for you.

Campbell, D. T., & Stanley, J. C. (1963). *Experimental and quasi-experimental designs for research.* Chicago: Rand McNally.

Although this is ordinarily thought of as a classic treatise on research design (certainly it is one of the most lucid treatments of design ever produced for a broad readership), the authors of this elegant monograph also have much to say about fundamental standards for systematic inquiry. Building on the format provided by a theoretical model of validity in research, the authors examine 16 different quantitative designs for research. In doing so, they address a host of vital issues that are relevant to preparing a proposal. This is essential reading for those proposing quantitative studies. At the same time, it is a valuable reference point for those who plan work that is guided by the assumptions of the qualitative paradigm. Acquiring good data is fundamental to all inquiry, but a firm grasp on how an alternative perspective demands different ways of defining and achieving that desideratum must begin with a clear answer to the question, "Different from what?" For nearly four decades, Campbell and Stanley have offered a solid start toward that kind of clarity.

Coley, S. M., & Scheinberg, C. A. (1990). *Proposal writing* (Sage Human Services Guide, Vol. 63). Newbury Park, CA: Sage.

This lively little paperback is directed specifically at the task of preparing grant proposals (applications to agencies and foundations for funding of any activity—including research). Thus, it is an ideal companion for Chapters 8 and 10 in the present text. The format is a straightforward and highly pragmatic walk through the process of proposal development from conceptualization to follow-up activities after the proposal is submitted. The authors even attend to such sophisticated topics as management of multisource funding, strategies for obtaining continuation funding, and activities that enhance possibilities for future grants.

Clear and concrete guidelines and examples are provided at every step, including a particularly useful appendix containing a specimen grant proposal accompanied by full critique and evaluation as they would be prepared by an agency reviewer. The single limitation of this otherwise excellent resource is that by attending to proposals for a wide range of human service activities, it does not focus exclusively on the particular case of funding for research—and thereby requires a degree of "translation" by the reader. Notwithstanding this minor problem, if soliciting funds for research is the purpose of your proposal, this guide represents an excellent investment.

Committee on Science, Engineering, and Public Policy, National Academy of Science, National Academy of Engineering, and Institute of Medicine. (1995). *On being a scientist: Responsible conduct in research* (2nd ed.). Washington, DC: National Academy Press.

This 27-page booklet was a project of the National Academy of Science, National Academy of Engineering, and the Institute of Medicine's joint Committee on Science, Engineering, and Public Policy. It provides an overview of ethical principles as they apply to the process of research. As a statement reflecting the positions of the sponsoring organizations, this is essential reading for those beginning research careers, as well as a source of continuing guidance for experienced investigators. A wide variety of topics is covered, including the social foundations of science, conflicts of interest, human error, negligence and misconduct in science, allocating credit and authorship practices, and responding to violations of ethical standards. Easy to read, with helpful sidebars to supplement the main text, this booklet is well worth the modest price ($5.00 at the time of this writing) and the investment of reading time.

Creswell, J. W. (1998). *Qualitative inquiry and research design: Choosing among five traditions.* Thousand Oaks, CA: Sage.

In this substantial book (403 pages), the author undertakes an ambitious and unusual task. He has set out to illustrate in detail how the choice of a particular "type" of qualitative inquiry (also called a qualitative research "tradition") will shape the design—and, thus, the subsequent proposal for a study. That is not a purely theoretical matter, because just as is true within other research paradigms, all those who propose to do a qualitative study must answer the question "What type of qualitative study?" The considerable array of alternatives that, at least in theory, are available to the novice can be overwhelming. Creswell has selected five (biography, phenomenology, grounded theory, ethnography, and case study) and proceeds to explain how each component of the study design (definition of the study problem, collection of data, analysis, and preparation of the report) is shaped by the selection of one of the qualitative genres. Previously published study reports representing each of the five types are reprinted in appendices, as is a glossary of terminology unique to each type of research.

The section most closely related to our own text (Chapter 2, "Designing a Qualitative Study") offers only a general overview of the proposal process; nevertheless, if you are puzzling about which kind of qualitative research best fits your problem or question, capabilities, resources, and personal dispositions, then this text should help you to make an informed decision. That the detail contained in your proposal will be powerfully shaped by that choice is convincingly demonstrated in this book.

Fink, A. (1998). *Conducting research literature reviews: From paper to the Internet.* Thousand Oaks, CA: Sage.

This book is designed for those who wish either to assess current knowledge in a particular area of research or to produce a literature review themselves. The former, of course, is relevant to your preparation for writing the proposal. As we have indicated here in Chapter 4, however, the latter is not the appropriate model for most proposals. The attention given to electronic search procedures, as well as to strategies for screening what is found, is both up to date and relevant to any area of inquiry. Although some sections in this comprehensive text go beyond what most readers will require at the proposal stage of development, we think the book can serve both as an excellent resource for organizing the effort to identify and digest related literature and as a strong stimulus to get started.

Fitzpatrick, J., Secrist, J., & Wright, D. J. (1998). *Secrets for a successful dissertation.* Thousand Oaks, CA: Sage.

Written by three women who have only recently completed doctoral degrees in educational leadership, this book reflects the graduate student's point of view on the process of meeting the dissertation requirement. Accordingly, it contains a degree of irreverence about both institutional protocol and the unwritten norms sustained by faculty. Some readers even may feel that the vantage point taken in this book approaches outright cynicism. In counterbalance, however, our judgment is that the authors have offered an honest and highly realistic road map of the perils to be encountered, as well as the means to overcome them. The book's primary strength is as a support for graduate student intellectual self-esteem, sense of control, and feelings of authenticity—all of which can be eroded by the stress of completing a dissertation.

It is inevitable that the book attends primarily to matters of emotional support, program politics, sustaining motivation, and efficient use of time and resources, rather than the detail of planning, conducting, and writing about an investigation. The opening chapter, "Writing the Doctoral Proposal," is couched almost exclusively in general terms. Some of these we regard as highly laudable, such as an appeal to invest time and effort in preparing the best possible document so that it can later serve as the opening chapters of the dissertation. Nevertheless, this text was not intended to serve as a guide for doing the work of writing a proposal—or of conducting a study. It is intended to improve the probability that those tasks will be completed with the least personal trauma and the greatest possible satisfaction (and profit) for the student investigator. Purchased for those purposes, this book may well serve your needs.

Geever, J. C., & McNeil, P. (1997). *The Foundation Center's guide to proposal writing* (Rev. ed.). New York: The Foundation Center.

If you are going to apply to a foundation for research funding, this book should be the first stop after reading Part II in our own text. Written by two authors with wide experience in the worlds of corporate and nonprofit foundation funding, this is a definitive resource if you are considering preparation of an application for research support from either of those sources. Although the procedures and standards described were designed primarily for those proposing to undertake program initiatives, in most cases they will be the same as those used in reviewing requests for research funding.

Interviews with 21 foundation executives responsible for evaluating proposals and making funding decisions (in a wide variety of foundation settings) were used in the development of the text. Information from those discussions is used throughout the book where it highlights the fact that foundations often employ very different approaches in their handing of applications.

The book is organized around the sequential steps in proposal development. Of particular interest is the concentration on creating a "master proposal" that can be used as the basis for applications to a variety of funding sources. So far as we are aware, the chapter on "contacting and cultivating potential funders" is unique in the literature (and is a source of practical advice on that delicate topic). Specimen letters and a complete proposal are provided in an appendix.

Glatthorn, A. A. (1998). *Writing the winning dissertation.* Thousand Oaks, CA: Corwin Press.

Although not indicated in the title, this "step-by-step" guide was prepared explicitly for graduate students in the field of education. Despite that focus (all the illustrative material involves school settings), first-time proposal authors will find a great deal of practical advice that is relevant to the generic problems of formulating research plans in any professional field.

Ten chapters are devoted to activities that occur prior to actual execution of the study. In two of them, the author urges first the development of a preproposal (a "prospectus"), and then its subsequent use in conferences with advisers (advice that we heartily second). Additional chapters take the reader through developing, writing, and formally presenting the proposal.

As the author himself observes, this book was not prepared as an exercise in sophisticated scholarship. It is a handbook intended to give technical assistance to people who have never performed the tasks they now face—identifying a research topic, designing a study, and preparing the written proposal. Although purists may wince at the suggestion that novices have to learn how to "sound academic" when they write about their study, some acquaintance with the prose styles found in published research reports will suggest that the observation contains more than a grain of truth. In any case, Glatthorn is far more concerned with helping the novice achieve clarity than he is with giving advice about creating the right image.

As an experienced dissertation adviser, the author has accumulated a substantial fund of suggestions that, though they often deal with routine matters, are at the heart of getting the work done. Such homey things as keeping duplicate records, maintaining a planning chart, and settling the first person versus third person question early in the writing process are better attended to than neglected. This modest paperback will allow anyone to profit from what hard experience has taught others about preparing research proposals.

Janesick, V. J. (1998). *"Stretching" exercises for qualitative researchers.* Thousand Oaks, CA: Sage.

The author's primary purpose in this slim paperback was to present a series of training exercises for individuals preparing to do a qualitative study. Although the primary focus is on helping investigators develop their skill as observers and interviewers, because the exercises presented are learning activities for beginners in qualitative research, the resulting text is what might well be called "a prelude to the proposal" (our characterization, not Janesick's). That use of the text is supported by the extensive set of appendices containing such materials as lists of topics and questions that are appropriate for qualitative research, examples of consent forms for participants, an outline of suggested components in a qualitative prospectus, and sample doctoral dissertation proposals for several different types of qualitative inquiry. Although a book such as this ideally would be used in connection with a course or seminar that provided the guidance of an experienced investigator (and the opportunity for group processing of training experiences), it could easily serve individual students at the early stage of thinking through a qualitative proposal.

Locke, L. F., Silverman, S. J., & Spirduso, W. W. (1998). *Reading and understanding research.* Thousand Oaks, CA: Sage.

Our motives in suggesting this text actually are not entirely self-serving. For the beginner, reading and making sense out of research reports will occupy a major part of the time and effort expended in preparing to write a proposal. Knowing how to do that work from the outset can make the whole process far more efficient—and rewarding. Further, having at least rudimentary skills in estimating the quality of research represented in a report (and, thus, the degree of confidence warranted for its findings) will serve the novice well, both when conversing with advisers and when preparing the related literature portions of the proposal. Those three functions—reading, understanding, and making critical assessments—are the central topics of our "other" book.

Written in a style similar to the text you now have in hand, *Reading and Understanding Research* is designed as a guide for the novice investigator, whether used as a textbook in a formal course or as a do-it-yourself handbook for independent study. The text contains step-by-step study and practice procedures as well as a variety of recording forms and checklists designed to support beginners during their first encounters with actual reports. The book is intended for use with a variety of paradigmatic formats (both quantitative and qualitative) as they are employed in the social sciences and fields of applied study.

Among the sections that will be of particular interest to proposal writers are those devoted to (a) an overview of the types of research encountered in reports, (b) a discussion of the sources of credibility in published studies, (c) identification of reasons to suspend trust in the findings of an investigation, (d) a list of basic questions to ask when reading research with a critical eye, and (e) directions for "explaining" reports as a means of improving your understanding of what they contain. Appendices include a beginner's guide to reading statistics (in reports), as well as summary explanations of actual examples of both research reports and research reviews.

Madsen, D. (1992). *Successful dissertations and theses* (2nd ed.). San Francisco: Jossey-Bass.

This text is explicitly devoted to the needs of graduate students preparing to write proposals, dissertations, and theses. With logical organization, non-technical prose, and skillful use of examples drawn from actual proposals, it fully deserves its reputation as a sound and utilitarian handbook.

Unlike many dissertation guides, this one focuses on the proposal rather than on performing the research or writing up the results. Addressed to an audience working within the broad rubric of educational research, it is more eclectic than many such texts (it includes, for example, proposals for both experimental and historical studies). The book does not, however, give specific attention to qualitative models for research—a substantial limitation. The three chapters covering use of reference sources, library retrieval, and the transition from notes to document collectively represent a fine introduction to that phase of proposal preparation. Altogether, this is a thoughtfully prepared guide for the first-time investigator.

Marshall, C., & Rossman, G. B. (1999). *Designing qualitative research* (3rd ed.). Thousand Oaks, CA: Sage.

This remains one of the few books devoted exclusively to the topic of formulating plans for qualitative research (also see Maxwell, below). The authors treat the proposal document as a framework for organizing the many activities that go into thinking through and presenting a research design. Although this is not a how-to-write-it guidebook for preparing the proposal, neither is it a standard how-to-do-it research methods text for beginners. The book is intended to provide clear, practical guidance for anyone at the starting point of a qualitative study, whether novice or experienced investigator. The target throughout is thorough and systematic consideration of the major problems in designing a study—from identifying and defining the problem to defending the proposed method of investigation.

Discussion of the design process is cast as the development of an argument that will convince funding agency reviewers or dissertation committee members of the importance and feasibility of a qualitative study—and of the author's competence to bring it to a successful completion. Each step is illustrated with brief (one to three pages) vignettes that underscore the nature of problems encountered and the solutions available. The twin themes of maintaining design flexibility and marshaling supportive evidence are used throughout to weld the individual parts of the process into an integrated whole.

The text is sensitive to the many alternative approaches to qualitative study, including feminist research, critical ethnography, and qualitative evaluation formats. Graduate students will find the chapter devoted to defending the value and logic of qualitative research particularly helpful. The authors understand that some of their readers will have to argue their case before reviewers who either are unfamiliar with the paradigm or are uneasy about the adequacy of qualitative methods. Their commentary on this problem avoids defensive posturing by staying firmly positive and pragmatic. Also of particular value for first-time authors of qualitative proposals will be the unique chapter on estimating and managing time and resources—a topic almost invariably ignored or underestimated by the beginner.

It is impossible for us to imagine a qualitative thesis or dissertation proposal that would not profit from a close reading of this volume, as early in the process as possible. Teamed with our own text, this book offers a solid foundation for preparing a successful proposal.

Maxwell, J.A. (1996). *Qualitative research design: An interactive approach* (Sage Applied Social Research Methods Series, Vol. 41). Thousand Oaks, CA: Sage.

Although this small paperback has only one full chapter devoted to writing the proposal for a qualitative study, in a real sense the entire book is about preparing to write that proposal. The author simply regards the research "design" as the logic of a study and the research "proposal" document as a vehicle for communicating that logic to a particular audience.

As a result of the author's "interactive approach," the reader is engaged in a series of provocative questions and lively writing exercises that are precisely those required to create a research plan: (a) Why are you doing this study? (b) What do you think is going on? (c) What do you want to understand? (d) What will you actually do? and (e) How might you be wrong? The last question in that sequence deals with the problem of reassuring proposal readers about the validity of the study. Because that is one of the most commonly asked questions in the presentation/defense of a qualitative proposal, such attention gives particular strength to the text. A full proposal for a qualitative study is contained in an appendix—complete with the author's commentary on each section.

This is not a compendium of methods for data collection and analysis, nor is it a thorough explication of the philosophical and theoretical underpinnings of the qualitative paradigm. Instead, it is an overview of what qualitative researchers must actually do in thinking through the study they wish to propose.

Meloy, J. M. (1994). *Writing the qualitative dissertation.* Hillsdale, NJ: Lawrence Erlbaum.

This is a highly unusual book in that it was produced by a collaboration between the listed author (Meloy) and 20 individuals who have prepared proposals for qualitative studies and, in some but not all cases, successfully completed subsequent dissertations. In a sense, the text is a research report—albeit one presented in an informal and easy to read format. The author sets out to capture what a group of successful and unsuccessful doctoral candidates now believe they learned about conceptualizing, writing, executing, and defending their proposals and dissertations. The author posed a set of initial questions and then engaged her participants in a lengthy dialogue (by telephone, mail, and direct interview).

The text rises above the level of merely "telling war stories" as a consequence of the author's skill in weaving together contrasting (and sometimes surprisingly congruent) versions of how, what, and from whom graduate students learn while dissertating. A full chapter is devoted to preparation of the proposal document and the proposal "defense." The section dealing with students' perceptions of the crucial role of "ambiguity" in preparing the qualitative proposal offers an unusual insight that will be valuable to many readers. This is not a how-to manual, nor is it another attempt to give advice on how to survive graduate school. The book simply offers an opportunity to hear the authentic voices of people who tried to write proposals and dissertations—and learned a great deal in the process. For that reason, it is early in the process of preparing your proposal that this text will be most useful.

National Academy of Science, National Academy of Engineering, and Institute of Medicine. (1997). *Advisor, teacher, role model, friend: On being a mentor to students in science and engineering.* Washington, DC: National Academy Press.

The title of this 84-page booklet suggests that it is applicable only to those in the natural sciences, medicine, and engineering, and is directed only to advisers. Our experience indicates a very different conclusion. We commend this thoughtful treatise to graduate students in any area of scholarship. If you want to know the characteristics of a healthy and fruitful adviser-student relationship, the model established here is both comprehensive and flexible enough to meet a variety of circumstances. Throughout the text, highlighted insertions offer examples of mentoring along with commentary on the actions taken by a fictional mentor. Because most proposals presume a partnership between faculty adviser and student, this booklet offers an ideal place to begin.

Panel on Scientific Responsibility and the Conduct of Research. (1992). *Responsible science: Ensuring the integrity of the research process* (Vol. 1). Washington, DC: National Academy Press.

Published as a cooperative effort by the National Academy of Sciences, the National Academy of Engineering, and the Institute of Medicine, this volume contains a comprehensive and critical examination of the factors that influence integrity in research. With details about how the panel developed its recommendations, an executive summary provides 12 standards intended to guide researchers working in a wide variety of contexts. Included are discussions of misconduct in research, handling allegations of misconduct, and guidelines for encouraging responsible behavior by investigators. The book will be of particular interest to those whose first proposal is intended to mark the start of a career in research. A definitive explanation of exactly what constitutes ethical behavior and highly pragmatic advice about the consequences attending various decisions in research make this a prudent investment for the bookshelf of any aspiring scholar.

Penslar, R. L. (Ed.). (1995). *Research ethics: Cases and materials.* Bloomington: Indiana University Press.

This book fills a gap that has long existed in the literature on the ethical problems that arise in planning, conducting, and reporting research. The editor's intention in this text, which is designed as a casebook, was to present materials that would lead research workers to think more deeply about the ethical problems presented by the human circumstances accompanying formal inquiry. The book includes chapters on both ethical theory and the teaching of research ethics. Case materials are grouped into (a) natural sciences, (b) behavioral sciences, and (c) humanities. Case examples are followed by questions designed to stimulate individual reflection or group discussion. Touching on such issues as scientific misconduct, authorship, animal and human subjects, deception, faculty-student relationships, intellectual property rights, and other areas of ethical concern, the text both extends and reinforces our own discussion in Chapter 2. The proposal is the appropriate point at which to begin your consideration of ethics, and *all* studies require such consideration.

Peterson's (1998). *Peterson's grants for graduate and postdoctoral study* (5th ed.). Princeton, NJ: Author.

This 566-page volume may mark the end of an era. The advertisement of opportunities for funding graduate student and faculty research is rapidly moving from hard copy (posters, flyers, and compendia like this one) to the Internet. Even applications for grants, awards, and fellowships offered by the 1,400 sources profiled here must, in many instances, be obtained and submitted (in part or in whole) electronically. Although fully current at the end of 1998, the source profiles contained in this guide gradually will become dated, and thus less reliable and complete. At this time, no final decision has been made concerning publication of a new (6th) edition (up-to-date information on financial aid will continue to be available at http://www.peterson's.com/). What is certain, however, is that in the future, proposal authors will increasingly seek research support through subscription databases on the Internet such as the Illinois Researcher Information Service (IRIS) and the Community of Science (COS). Both of those comprehensive sources are introduced in Chapters 8 and 9.

The brief introduction to the grant-seeking process offered in this paper-bound volume, however, is by far the most succinct, thorough, and helpful available from any source, and is likely to remain so for many years to come. If you are a graduate student or new faculty member, find a copy of this guide in your library or bookstore and read the 20 pages of advice about how (and when) to shake the money tree. Moreover, read them *before* you complete preparation of your proposal. What you learn may be worth a great deal—to your scholarship, your career, and your pocketbook.

Pyrczak, F., & Bruce, R.R. (1992). *Writing empirical research reports: A basic guide for students of the social and behavioral sciences.* Los Angeles: Pyrczak Publishing.

At first glance, this 8 × 11-inch book appears to be just another how-to-do-it cookbook. First impressions, however, are not always accurate. In fact, this text offers a fund of very sound and often quite sophisticated advice for anyone who writes about research. Even though the authors concentrate on the particular task of writing the final report (as distinct from the proposal), much of the material is generic. Each chapter, for example, is devoted to a section of the typical report (e.g., title, hypotheses, introduction, method) and provides a simple set of principles to guide writing that particular part. In turn, the principles are illustrated both by examples and "improved versions" that emphasize effective expression. The appendices contain a checklist of all the principles (itself probably worth the modest price of this paperbound book), a list of suggested support materials, and a useful article explaining what reviewers look for in research manuscripts.

Reis, J. B., & Leukefeld, C. G. (1998). *The research funding guidebook: Getting it, managing it, and renewing it.* Thousand Oaks, CA: Sage.

This books starts with a provocative question: What should you do if your proposal for a research grant has been rejected? That premise is not as farfetched as it might seem: Many research grant applications are funded only after initial rejection, revision, and resubmission. The authors believe (as do we) that in securing funding, the quality of the application as a written document (including the study proposal contained therein) is fully as important as the purely technical features of the research plan.

Readers undertaking their first application for a research grant will find the sections on "Application Preparation" and (quite possibly) "Resubmitting a Not-Funded Application" to be particularly helpful. Although the authors have used the National Institutes of Health model for submission and review, those procedures are sufficiently generic to provide general application to a wide variety of funding sources. Along with the many tables and checklists, the most immediately practical component of the book may be the effort to help proposal authors to understand their application from the reviewer's perspective. It is a hard but unavoidable fact that the advice concerning how to read reviewers' comments on your proposal (and manage your reactions to them) may also have relevance to your work.

Rossman, G. B., & Rallis, S. F. (1998). *Learning in the field: An introduction to qualitative research.* Thousand Oaks, CA: Sage.

Given the overlap of authorship, you might expect to find that the task of preparing a proposal is described here in the same broad terms as were used in Marshall and Rossman's book on designing qualitative studies (see above). Although the lengthy chapter devoted to the planning and proposing process indeed does summarize some of the material from that other text, we believe there still are good reasons to consult *Learning in the Field* as part of your preparation for writing a proposal.

The first rationale for that recommendation is that the tight focus and economy of presentation used here make some complex ideas initially more accessible than they are in texts offering more extensive treatments. For example, the tactic of using the research literature to build the proposal's conceptual framework is discussed here in terms that are particularly lucid (and memorable) because they are so pointed and brief. Second, the proposal process is framed in terms of learning about inquiry, with particular emphasis on learning from experience (our own persistent appeals for the use of pilot studies are reflected in that) and learning from a continuous exchange with colleagues and advisers (again, advice that is congruent with our own). Third, we think that many readers will find the authors' strategy of describing how three fictional graduate students gradually developed very different proposals is an effective teaching device. Through imaginary conversations, the reader is made aware of how experience gradually leads people with differing interests and research goals toward different types of inquiry—and proposal content. Because all proposals must argue for the logic of links between researcher, research goal, and research method, this text can assist beginning investigators to gradually forge those connections on the anvil of their own experiences.

Schumacher, D. (1992). *Get funded!* Newbury Park, CA: Sage.

This small book is advertised as a "practical guide for scholars seeking research support from business." It begins with an explanation of the corporate environment, gives suggestions on how the researcher can discover needs and interests within that culture, outlines strategies for convincing corporate managers that a proposed study might contribute to their objectives, and ends with a practical discussion of ways of organizing such privately sponsored research once it has been funded. Throughout, the emphasis is on thinking in terms of a partnership with business—with the necessary reciprocity that entails.

Declining governmental support for research in some areas dictates that many investigators will have to widen their search for funding. As the author suggests, building partnerships with business may well be the wave of the future. Those who wish to test the corporate waters should find this text an excellent place to begin.

Tashakkori, A., & Teddlie, C. (1998). *Mixed methodology* (Sage Applied Social Research Methods Series, Vol. 46). Thousand Oaks, CA: Sage.

This is a most unusual book. It presents an important new statement about what is possible in designing and conducting good research in the social sciences and applied professional fields. In addition, it differs from many research texts by being sufficiently nontechnical for novice investigators to understand exactly what the authors are espousing. Finally, it is unique: There presently are no truly comparable books in the marketplace. All of that constitutes a remarkable accomplishment for a small paperback!

For 50 years, scholars in the social and behavioral sciences have been conversing about (and often hotly disputing) the true nature, relative merits, appropriate uses, and compatibility (or, more often, incompatibility) of qualitative and quantitative research. Meanwhile, back in the daily business of doing research, where finding ways to answer questions served as the ultimate arbiter of what was possible, life went on. Investigators completed studies, journals published reports, dissertation committees approved proposals, agencies granted funding, and (most important) people made successful use of findings—in each case involving a growing number of investigations that utilized some form of mixed methodology.

Once again, practice had confounded ideologically driven theory, not by resolving all the problems and points of conflict but simply by getting on with the work. The authors explain how that came about and then present their own version of pragmatism as a paradigmatic alternative. In the process, they provide what we believe is one of the best and certainly the most digestible account of recent disputes between proponents of quantitative and qualitative approaches to inquiry (what many observers have characterized as the "paradigm wars").

Many of you will be tempted (probably for good reasons) to mix either methods from the qualitative and quantitative traditions, or the paradigmatic models themselves (a distinction explained by the authors). In Chapter 5, we present both our support and our reservations concerning such choices when made by a novice. Whatever your stage of development, however, if mixed methodology is to be considered, then this book—with its brisk prose style, transparent reasoning, and carefully selected exemplars of design, analysis, and interpretation—should be your first stop.

APPENDIX

B

Standards for the Use of Human Subjects and Specimen Forms for Informed Consent

M ost colleges and universities have an Institutional Review Board (IRB) responsible for overseeing and approving research involving human subjects. At some larger universities, departments may have human subject review committees that first act on the proposed research and then report to the IRB. Whether the study proposal is associated with a graduate degree or with a grant application, investigators should obtain the guidelines for human subject review at their institution, and do so early in the preparation process.

An almost universal step in conducting research with human subjects is obtaining the informed consent of each participant. Subjects must have the opportunity to be informed about the study (particularly what they will be required to do, and the risks and benefits of their participation), ask any questions they might have, make a decision as to whether they wish to participate, and sign a letter of informed consent. Chapter 2 contains a detailed discussion of informed consent accompanied by a listing of the primary requirements in that process.

Figure B.1 presents a consent form checklist that will be useful when preparing consent letters. It contains all information that might be included on

ITEMS	YES	NO	COMMENTS
1. Does the title of the study appear at the top?			
2. Is the general purpose of the study stated—what the researcher expects to learn?			
3. If for student research, is how the study relates to the student's program of study specifically stated (project, thesis, dissertation)?			
4. Is a statement included indicating to the participant his or her right to choose to participate?			
5. Is a statement included indicating why and how the person was selected as a possible participant? Are the population and sample clearly identified?			
6. Is the procedure to be followed in implementing the project explained (time, frequency, nature of information, questions asked)?			
7. Is a statement included that addresses possible discomforts and inconveniences that the participant might expect?			
8. Are any participant risks that are involved in the project described? If pregnancy presents a risk, have specific precautions been taken?			
9. Are benefits, if any, to the participant identified?			
10. If the project requires that any standard treatment is withheld, is this clearly designated? If alternative treatments are available, are they described?			
11. Is participant confidentiality explained? Is the use of any tapes and other materials (e.g., audio- or videotapes, photos, use of data for other purposes) explained and the disposition of materials clear?			
12. Are compensation and costs included in the project, and are they specifically identified for the participant?			
13. Is the location where the participant can contact the investigator to have questions answered indicated? If a student is the investigator, is the supervising professor also identified and a phone number given?			
14. Is it specifically stated that the participant can withdraw at any time from the project? Are procedures indicated for orderly withdrawal from a complex study? Are procedures described for terminating a subject's participation?			
15. Does it state that the participant is entitled to a written copy of the consent form?			
16. Does a statement exist explaining that the participant's signature indicates a willingness to participate?			
17. Are there places for the participant's signature, the investigator's signature, the parent's signature (if required), and dates?			
18. Is provision for child assent (generally for children 7-18 years old) made?			

Figure B.1. Consent Form Checklist

SOURCE: This checklist was adapted (with permission) from Office of Sponsored Projects, The University of Texas at Austin (1987), *Policies and procedures governing research with human subjects.* Austin: Author.

a consent form. All items are not appropriate for every consent form—for example, if subjects are not receiving compensation, that item does not need to be included.

The three informed consent letters presented in this appendix are edited examples from successfully completed research projects. The individual documents reflect the specific demands for informed consent in each research context. The first example is from a laboratory study. The second and third examples are from a field study conducted in a school setting where both teacher and parental consent were required. By changing the details, these letters can be adapted for use in other research settings.

SAMPLE A: LABORATORY STUDY

letterhead of the institution/agency

The Effects of Age, Modality and Complexity of Response, and Practice on Reaction Time

You are invited to participate in a study in which the response speed of young and older adults is examined. You are being asked to participate in the study because you fall into one of the age classifications and responded to a request to participate. If you choose to participate in the study it will be necessary for you to be tested on three occasions. You will be asked to do the following tasks: (1) react as rapidly as possible to a light stimulus by saying the consonants "ss" and "zz" into a microphone, and (2) react as rapidly as possible to a light stimulus by pressing one or two fingers against microswitches. All trials on each occasion should take less than one hour.

Data compiled from your performance will be kept in strict confidence at all times. Only the investigator and supervising professor will have access to the information. Following the collection of data your individual identity will be removed from all records. In this manner, information regarding your participation will be kept confidential.

Possible risk factors from your participation are no greater than normal daily activity. However, you cannot expect to be compensated for any discomforts or injury as a result of your participation in the experiment described here.

The investigator in this study is L. L. Student and the research is being completed to fulfill the thesis requirement for a master's degree. The supervising professor is Dr. X. Bert Supervisor. If you have any questions that we have not answered in person you may contact either of us at 555-1234.

Your signature below indicates that you have decided to participate in this study and that you have read and understood the information in this consent form. Your decision to participate in this study will not prejudice your present or future association with this university. If you decide to participate, you are free to withdraw consent and discontinue participation at any time without prejudice. If you desire a copy of this consent form, one will be provided for you.

Thank you.

Participant's signature _____ Date _____
Investigator's signature _____ Date _____
Witness's signature _____ Date _____

SAMPLE B: FIELD STUDY

letterhead of the institution/agency

A Comprehensive Investigation of the Correlates of Instructional Effectiveness

I would like to request your cooperation in the conduct of a study of instruction in classes you are teaching this year. You were selected to participate in this study because you teach third grade students in a school in the Innovative School District. We hope to learn more about how teacher and student behaviors are important for learning. This information will contribute to research in education, and may be beneficial to future teachers.

If you should decide to participate, you will be asked to teach a two week unit of instruction for approximately 30 minutes per day wearing a miniature microphone. The class will be videotaped for future coding of teacher and student behaviors. Students will be pretested and posttested. Your students will be asked to maintain their normal seating patterns throughout the course of instruction. Should you decide to participate, one thirty minute orientation session will be required prior to beginning the study. Except for normal preparation time, no other time outside of class will be required. Possible risk factors from your participation are no greater than your normal school activity.

Any information obtained in connection with this study that can be identified with you will remain confidential and will be disclosed only with your permission. Only averages and other descriptive statistics will be reported in any publication. In addition, only three trained coders associated with the university will view the tapes and none will be able to identify you by name. Your decision as to whether or not to participate will not prejudice your relations with the Department of Education or the University. If you decide to participate, you are completely free to withdraw consent and discontinue participation at any time.

If you have any additional questions, please contact me (A. Professor) at 555-1234. Thank you.

You may keep a copy of this form.

I have decided to participate in a study of learning, to wear a miniature microphone while teaching the unit of instruction, and to allow my class to be pretested, posttested, and videotaped. My signature indicates that I have read the information above and have decided to participate. I realize that I may withdraw without prejudice at any time after signing this form should I decide to do so.

_____   _____

Teacher's Signature   Date

_____   _____

Investigator's Signature   Date

SAMPLE C: PARENTAL INFORMED CONSENT

letterhead of the institution/agency

Date

Dear Parent:

I am presently involved in the preparation of future teachers at State University. I am interested in the aspects of schooling that relate to how students learn to read. This information is valuable in preparing teachers and can contribute to our knowledge of how to help students improve their reading skills.

I would like permission for your child to participate in a study that will be conducted as a part of his or her regularly scheduled class. The study is titled "A Comprehensive Investigation of the Correlates of Instructional Effectiveness." Your child was chosen to participate in this study because he or she is in a class in which the teacher has agreed to participate. The only changes from the normal class will be an initial test of student reading ability and that each class, for a two week period, will be videotaped. Possible risk factors from your child's participation are no greater than his or her normal school activity.

Your son or daughter will be identified on the videotape, but at no time will his or her scores on the tests or their videotapes be available to anyone but researchers involved in this study. Students will not be identified by name at any time in any reports of this research. If you decide to allow your child to participate, you or your child are completely free to withdraw consent and discontinue your child's participation at any time.

As the results of this study are completed, I will provide the principal of your school with a summary, which will be available to you upon request. If you have any questions, please contact me at 555-1234.

Please sign and return this form as soon as possible. Thank you very much.

Sincerely,

A. Professor
Assistant Professor

Please check here if you would like a copy of this form for your records _____

I have decided to allow my child to participate in a study of learning that will be conducted in his or her regularly scheduled class. My signature indicates that I have read the information above and have given permission for my child to participate. My child's signature indicates that he or she understands that a study will be conducted in class and agrees to participate. I realize that I may withdraw my child (or my child may withdraw) without prejudice at any time after signing this form should either of us decide to do so.

Child's Name _____

Parent's signature _____ Date_____

Child's signature_____ Date_____

References

Adler, T. (1991, December). Outright fraud rare, but not poor science. *The APA Monitor, 22*(12), 11.

Altheide, D. L., & Johnson, J. M. (1994). Criteria for assessing interpretive validity in qualitative research. In N. K. Denzin & Y. S. Lincoln (Eds.), *Handbook of qualitative research* (pp. 485-499). Thousand Oaks, CA: Sage.

American Educational Research Association. (1992). Ethical standards of the American Educational Research Association. *Educational Researcher, 21*(7), 23-26.

American Historical Association. (1998). *Grants, fellowships, and prizes of interest to historians* (1998-99 ed.) Washington, DC: Author.

American Psychological Association. (1982). *Ethical principles in the conduct of research with human participants.* Washington, DC: Author.

American Psychological Association. (1990). Ethical principles of psychologists. *American Psychologist, 45,* 390-395.

American Psychological Association. (1994). *Publication manual of the American Psychological Association* (4th ed.). Washington, DC: Author.

Austin, R. (Ed.). (1999). *The grants register* (17th ed.). New York: St. Martin's.

Bailey, C. A. (1996). *Field research* (Pine Forge Press Series in Research Methods and Statistics). Thousand Oaks, CA: Pine Forge Press.

Bauer, D. G. (1995). *The "how to" grants manual: Successful grantseeking techniques for obtaining public and private grants* (3rd ed.). Phoenix, AZ: Oryx.

Becker, H.S. (1986). *Writing for social scientists.* Chicago: University of Chicago Press.

Bell, R. (1992). *Impure science: Fraud, compromise, and political influence in scientific research.* New York: Wiley.

Bogdan, R., & Biklin, S. (1992). *Qualitative research for education: An introduction to theory and method* (2nd ed.). Boston: Allyn & Bacon.

Brownowski, J. (1965). *Science and human values.* New York: Harper & Row.

Burgess, R. G. (1989). *The ethics of educational research.* London: Falmer.

Campbell, D. T., & Stanley, J. C. (1963). *Experimental and quasi-experimental designs for research*. Chicago: Rand McNally.

Carr, W., & Kemmis, S. (1986). *Becoming critical: Education, knowledge and action research*. London: Falmer.

Carspecken, P. F. (1996). *Critical ethnography in educational research: A theoretical and practical guide* (Routledge Critical Social Thought Series). New York: Routledge.

Coffey, A., & Atkinson, P. (1996). *Making sense of qualitative data: Complementary research strategies*. Thousand Oaks, CA: Sage.

Coley, S. M., & Scheinberg, C. A. (1990). *Proposal writing* (Sage Human Services Guide, Vol. 63). Newbury Park, CA: Sage.

Committee on Science, Engineering, and Public Policy, National Academy of Science, National Academy of Engineering, and Institute of Medicine. (1995). *On being a scientist: Responsible conduct in research* (2nd ed.). Washington, DC: National Academy Press.

Creswell, J. W. (1994). *Research design: Qualitative and quantitative approaches*. Thousand Oaks, CA: Sage.

Creswell, J. W. (1998). *Qualitative inquiry and research design: Choosing among five traditions*. Thousand Oaks, CA: Sage.

Datta, L. (1994). Paradigm wars: A basis for peaceful coexistence and beyond. In C. S. Reichardt & S. F. Rallis (Eds.), *The qualitative-quantitative debate: New perspectives* (pp. 53-70). San Francisco: Jossey-Bass.

Delamont, S. (1992). *Fieldwork in educational settings*. London: Falmer.

Delamont, S., & Atkinson, P. (1995). Purity and paradigms: Semi-scholarship and ethnographic research methods. In S. Delamont & P. Atkinson, *Fighting familiarity: Essays on education and ethnography* (pp. 193-206). Cresskill, NJ: Hampton.

Denscombe, M. (1998). *The good research guide for small scale research projects*. Buckingham, UK: Open University Press.

Denzin, N. K., & Lincoln, Y. S. (Eds.). (1994). *Handbook of qualitative research*. Thousand Oaks, CA: Sage.

Eisenhart, M. A., & Howe, K. R. (1992). Validity in educational research. In M. D. LeCompte, W. L. Millroy, & J. Preissle (Eds.), *The handbook of qualitative research in education* (pp. 643-680). San Diego: Academic Press.

Eisner, E. W. (1981). On the differences between scientific and artistic approaches to qualitative research. *Educational Researcher, 59*(4), 5-9.

Eisner, E. W., & Peshkin, A. (Eds.). (1990). *Qualitative inquiry in education: The continuing debate*. New York: Teachers College Press.

Emerson, R. M., Fretz, R. I., & Shaw, L. L. (1995). *Writing ethnographic field notes*. Chicago: University of Chicago Press.

Fanger, D. (1985, May). The dissertation, from conception to delivery. *On Teaching and Learning: The Journal of the Harvard-Danforth Center, 1*, pp. 26-33.

Feczko, M. M. (1998). *The foundation directory: Part 2*. New York: The Foundation Center.

Fetterman, D. M. (1998). *Ethnography: Step by step* (2nd ed.) (Sage Applied Social Research Methods Series, Vol. 17). Thousand Oaks, CA: Sage.

Fielding, N. G., & Lee, R. M. (1998). *Computer analysis and qualitative research*. Thousand Oaks, CA: Sage.

Fink, A. (1998). *Conducting research literature reviews: From paper to the Internet*. Thousand Oaks, CA: Sage.

Fitzpatrick, J., Secrist, J., & Wright, D. J. (1998). *Secrets for a successful dissertation.* Thousand Oaks, CA: Sage.

The Foundation Center. (1999). *The foundation grants index* (27th ed.). New York: Author.

Gahan, C., & Hannibal, M. (1998). *Doing qualitative research using QSR NUD*IST.* Thousand Oaks, CA: Sage.

Gall, M. D., Borg, W. R., & Gall, J. P. (1996). *Educational research: An introduction* (6th ed.). White Plains, NY: Longman.

Geever, J. C., & McNeil, P. (1997). *The Foundation Center's guide to proposal writing* (Rev. ed.). New York: The Foundation Center.

Gitlin, A. (Ed.). (1994). *Power and method: Political activism and educational research.* New York: Routledge.

Glatthorn, A. A. (1998). *Writing the winning dissertation.* Thousand Oaks, CA: Corwin.

Glesne, C., & Peshkin, A. (1992). *Becoming qualitative researchers: An introduction.* White Plains, NY: Longman.

Golden-Biddle, K., & Locke, K. D. (1997). *Composing qualitative research.* Thousand Oaks, CA: Sage.

Greenbaum, T. L. (1997). *The handbook for focus group research* (2nd ed.). Thousand Oaks, CA: Sage.

Guba, E. G., & Lincoln, Y. S. (1989). *Fourth generation evaluation.* Newbury Park, CA: Sage.

Guba, E. G., & Lincoln, Y. S. (1994). Competing paradigms in qualitative research. In N. K. Denzin & Y. S. Lincoln (Eds.), *Handbook of qualitative research* (pp. 105-117). Thousand Oaks, CA: Sage.

Guston, D. H. (1993). Mentoring and the research training experience. In Panel on Scientific Responsibility and the Conduct of Research, Committee on Science, Engineering, and Public Policy, National Academy of Sciences, National Academy of Engineering, and Institute of Medicine (Eds.), *Responsible science: Ensuring the integrity of the research process* (Vol. 2, pp. 50-65). Washington, DC: National Academy Press.

Hall, L. V. (Ed.). (1997). *National directory of corporate giving* (5th ed.). New York: The Foundation Center.

Hall, L. V. (Ed.). (1999). *Foundation grants to individuals* (10th ed.). New York: The Foundation Center.

Howe, K. R. (1988). Against the quantitative-qualitative incompatibility thesis: Or, dogmas die hard. *Educational Researcher, 17*(8), 10-18.

Jacob, E. (1987). Qualitative research traditions: A review. *Review of Educational Research, 57,* 1-50.

Jacob, E. (1988). Clarifying qualitative research: A focus on traditions. *Educational Researcher, 17*(1), 22-24.

Jacob, E. (1989). Qualitative research: A defense of traditions. *Review of Educational Research, 59,* 229-235.

Janesick, V. J. (1998). *"Stretching" exercises for qualitative researchers.* Thousand Oaks, CA: Sage.

Johnson, R. B. (1997). Examining the validity structure of qualitative research. *Education, 118,* 282-292.

Jorgensen, D. L. (1989). *Participant observation* (Sage Applied Social Research Methods Series, Vol. 15). Newbury Park, CA: Sage.

Kelly, D. E., & Shipp, A. (1991). Odds of being funded by NIH. *The Psychologist, 1,* 28-29.

Kimmel, A. J. (1988). *Ethics and values in applied social research* (Sage Applied Social Research Methods Series, Vol. 12). Newbury Park, CA: Sage.

Kraemer, H. C., & Thiemann, S. (1987). *How many subjects? Statistical power analysis in research.* Newbury Park, CA: Sage.

Kroll, W. (1993). Ethical issues in human research. *Quest, 45,* 32-44.

Kuhn, T. S. (1970). *The structure of scientific revolutions* (2nd ed.). Chicago: University of Chicago Press.

Kvale, S. (1994). Ten standard objections to qualitative research interviews. *Journal of Phenomenological Psychology, 25,* 147-173.

Kvale, S. (1995). The social construction of validity. *Qualitative Inquiry, 1,* 19-40.

Lancy, D. F. (1993). *Qualitative research in education: An introduction to the major traditions.* White Plains, NY: Longman.

Lather, P. (1991). *Getting smart: Feminist research and pedagogy with/in the postmodern* (Routledge Critical Social Thought Series). New York: Routledge.

LeCompte, M. D., Milroy, W. L., & Preissle, J. (Eds.). (1992). *The handbook of qualitative research in education.* San Diego: Academic Press.

Lincoln, Y. S. (1995). Emerging criteria for quality in qualitative and interpretive research. *Qualitative Inquiry, 1,* 275-289.

Lincoln, E. S., & Guba, E. G. (1985). *Naturalistic inquiry.* Beverly Hills, CA: Sage

Locke, L. F., Silverman, S. J., & Spirduso, W. W. (1998). *Reading and understanding research.* Thousand Oaks, CA: Sage.

Lofland, J., & Lofland, L. H. (1995). *Analyzing social settings: A guide to qualitative observation and analysis* (3rd ed.). Belmont, CA: Wadsworth.

Macrina, F. L. (1995). *Scientific integrity: An introductory text with cases.* Washington, DC: ASM Press.

Madsen, D. (1992). *Successful dissertations and theses* (2nd ed.). San Francisco: Jossey-Bass.

Maguire, P. (1987). *Doing participatory research: A feminist approach.* Amherst: Center for International Education, University of Massachusetts.

Marshall, C., & Rossman, G. B. (1999). *Designing qualitative research* (3rd ed.). Thousand Oaks, CA: Sage.

Maxwell, J. A. (1992). Understanding and validity in qualitative research. *Harvard Educational Review, 62,* 279-300.

Maxwell, J. A. (1996). *Qualitative research design: An interactive approach* (Sage Applied Social Research Methods Series, Vol. 41). Thousand Oaks, CA: Sage.

Meloy, J. M. (1994). *Writing the qualitative dissertation.* Hillsdale, NJ: Lawrence Erlbaum.

Merriam, S. B. (1998). *Qualitative research and case study applications in education.* San Francisco: Jossey-Bass.

Miceli, M. P., & Near, J. P. (1992). *Blowing the whistle.* New York: Lexington Books.

Miles, M. B., & Huberman, A. M. (1994). *Qualitative data analysis* (2nd ed.). Thousand Oaks, CA: Sage.

Miller, S. M., Nelson, M. W., & Moore, M. T. (1998). Caught in the paradigm gap: Qualitative researchers' lived experience and the politics of epistemology. *American Educational Research Journal, 33,* 377-416.

Morgan, D. L., & Krueger, R. A. (1997). *The focus group kit.* Thousand Oaks, CA: Sage.

Morse, J. M. (Ed.). (1997). *Completing a qualitative project.* Thousand Oaks, CA: Sage.

National Academy of Science, National Academy of Engineering, and Institute of Medicine. (1997). *Advisor, teacher, role model, friend: On being a mentor to students in science and engineering.* Washington, DC: National Academy Press.

Office of Sponsored Projects, The University of Texas at Austin. (1987). *Policies and procedures governing research with human subjects.* Austin: Author.

Oryx Press. (1999a). *Directory of biomedical and health care grants: 1999* (13th ed.). Phoenix, AZ: Author.

Oryx Press. (1999b). *Directory of grants in the humanities: 1999/2000* (13th ed.). Phoenix, AZ: Author.

Oryx Press. (1999c). *Directory of research grants* (annual). Phoenix, AZ: Author.

Panel on Scientific Responsibility and the Conduct of Research. (1992). *Responsible science: Ensuring the integrity of the research process* (Vol. 1). Washington, DC: National Academy Press.

Patton, M. Q. (1990). *Qualitative evaluation and research methods* (2nd ed.). Newbury Park, CA: Sage.

Penslar, R. L. (Ed.). (1995). *Research ethics: Cases and materials.* Bloomington: Indiana University Press.

Peterson's. (1998). *Peterson's grants for graduate and postdoctoral study* (5th ed.). Princeton, NJ: Author.

Przeworski, A., & Salomon, F. (1995). *The art of writing proposals.* New York: Social Science Research Council. (Available at http://www.ssrc.org/artprop.htm/)

Pyrczak, F., & Bruce, R. R. (1992). *Writing empirical research reports: A basic guide for students of the social and behavioral sciences.* Los Angles: Pyrczak Publishing.

Reece, R. D., & Siegel, H. A. (1986). *Studying people: A primer in the ethics of social research.* Macon, GA: Mercer University Press.

Reis, J. B., & Leukefeld, C. G. (1998). *The research funding guidebook: Getting it, managing it, and renewing it.* Thousand Oaks, CA: Sage.

Ribbens, J., & Edwards, R. (Eds.). (1997). *Feminist dilemmas in qualitative research.* Thousand Oaks, CA: Sage.

Rich, E. H. (Ed.). (1998a). *The foundation directory* (20th ed.). New York: The Foundation Center.

Rich, E. H. (Ed.). (1998b). *National guide to funding in higher education* (5th ed.). New York: The Foundation Center.

Riessman, C. K. (Ed.). (1994). *Qualitative studies in social work research.* Newbury Park, CA: Sage.

Roberts, G. C. (1993). Ethics in professional advising and academic counseling of graduate students. *Quest, 45,* 78-87.

Rossman, G. B., & Rallis, S. F. (1998). *Learning in the field: An introduction to qualitative research.* Thousand Oaks, CA: Sage.

R. R. Bowker. (1999). *Annual register of grant support* (32nd ed.). New Providence, NJ: Author.

Rubin, H. J., & Rubin, I. S. (1995). *Qualitative interviewing: The art of hearing.* Thousand Oaks, CA: Sage.

Safrit, M. J. (1993). Oh what a tangled web we weave. *Quest, 45,* 52-61.

Schlachter, G. A. (Ed.). (1997). *Directory of financial aid for women: 1997-1999.* El Dorado Hills, CA: Reference Service Press.

Schmidt, F. L. (1996). Statistical significance testing and cumulative knowledge in psychology: Implications for training of researchers. *Psychological Methods, 1,* 115-129.

Schumacher, D. (1992). *Get funded!* Newbury Park, CA: Sage.

Schwandt, T. A. (1997). *Qualitative inquiry: A dictionary of terms.* Thousand Oaks, CA: Sage.

Seidman, I. (1998). *Interviewing as qualitative research* (2nd ed.). New York: Teachers College Press.

Sieber, J. E. (1992). *Planning ethically responsible research.* Newbury Park, CA: Sage.

Stake, R. E. (1995). *The art of case study research.* Thousand Oaks, CA: Sage.

Strauss, A., & Corbin, J. (Eds.). (1997). *Grounded theory in practice.* Thousand Oaks, CA: Sage.

Strauss, A., & Corbin, J. (1998). *Basics of qualitative research* (2nd ed.). Thousand Oaks, CA: Sage.

Strunk, W., & White, E. B. (1979). *The elements of style* (3rd ed.). Needham Heights, MA: Allyn & Bacon.

Swazey, J. P., Anderson, M. S., & Lewis, K. S. (1993). Ethical problems in academic research. *American Scientist, 81,* 542-553.

Tashakkori, A., & Teddlie, C. (1998). *Mixed methodology* (Sage Applied Social Research Methods Series, Vol. 46). Thousand Oaks, CA: Sage.

Taubes, G. (1995). Plagiarism suit wins: Experts hope it won't set a trend. *Science, 268,* 1125.

Tesch, R. (1990). *Qualitative research: Analysis types and software tools.* New York: Falmer.

Thomas, J. (1992). *Doing critical ethnography.* Newbury Park, CA: Sage.

Thompson, B. (1996). AERA editorial policies regarding statistical significance testing: Three suggested reforms. *Educational Researcher, 25*(2), 26-30.

Thompson, B. (1997). Rejoinder: Editorial policies regarding statistical significance tests: Further comments. *Educational Researcher, 26*(5), 29-32.

Thornton, S. J. (1987). Artistic and qualitative scientific approaches: Influence on aims, conduct, and outcome. *Education and Urban Society, 20,* 25-34.

United States General Services Administration. (Semiannual). *Catalog of federal domestic assistance.* Washington, DC: Author.

Van Maanen, J. (1988). *Tales of the field: On writing ethnography.* Chicago: University of Chicago Press.

Weitzman, E. A., & Miles, M. B. (1995). *Computer programs for qualitative data analysis.* Thousand Oaks, CA: Sage.

Willoughby, T. L., & Bixby, A. R. (1991). Cross-validation of the Quarterly Profile Examination. *Educational and Psychological Measurement, 51,* 691-697.

Wolcott, H. F. (1990). *Writing up qualitative research* (Sage Qualitative Research Methods Series, Vol. 20). Newbury Park, CA: Sage.

Yin, R. K. (1993). *Applications of case study research* (Sage Applied Social Research Methods Series, Vol. 34). Newbury Park, CA: Sage.

Yin, R. K. (1994). *Case study research: Design and methods* (2nd ed.) (Sage Applied Social Research Methods Series, Vol. 5). Thousand Oaks, CA: Sage.

Index

About the Authors

LAWRENCE F. LOCKE is Professor Emeritus of Education and Physical Education at the University of Massachusetts at Amherst. A native of Connecticut, he received his bachelor's and master's degrees from Springfield College and a Ph.D. from Stanford University. He has written extensively on the production and utilization of research on teaching and teacher education. He has authored a number of books related to research utilization and research methods. As a teacher, graduate adviser, and consultant, he has supervised many student research projects. Much of his present work focuses on the use of the qualitative research paradigm in the study of teachers, teaching, and teacher development. He makes his home in Sunderland, MA, but with his wife, Lorraine Goyette, he spends much of each year writing, running, and exploring the Beartooth Mountains at Sky Ranch in Reedpoint, MT. At both locations, he can be contacted at larrylo@delphi.com.

WANEEN WYRICK SPIRDUSO is the Mauzy Regents Professor in the Department of Kinesiology and Health Education at The University of Texas at Austin. She is a native of Austin and holds bachelor's and doctoral degrees from The University of Texas and a master's degree from the University of North Carolina at Greensboro. Her research focuses on the effects of aging and the mechanisms of motor control. She has been a prolific contributor to the research literature and has authored textbooks related to research methods and aging. She has taught research methods and directed student research for more than three decades and has received numerous research grants from the federal government and foundations. She is an avid golfer and lives with her husband, Craig Spirduso, in Austin, TX. Her Website is http://www.edb.utexas.edu/coe/depts/kin/faculty/spirduso/index.html

STEPHEN J. SILVERMAN is Professor of Education and Physical Education Program Coordinator at Teachers College, Columbia University. He is a native of Philadelphia and holds a bachelor's degree from Temple University, a master's degree from Washington State University, and a doctoral degree from the University of Massachusetts at Amherst. His research focuses on teaching and learning in physical education and on the methods for conducting research in field settings. Hc has authored numerous research articles and chapters, and he is coauthor of a number of books. He is an experienced research consultant, has directed graduate students, and has, for many years, taught classes in research methods, statistics, and measurement. He enjoys running and following politics and lives with his wife, Patricia Moran, on the Upper West Side of Manhattan. His Website is http://www.tc.columbia.edu/academic/health/html/professors_3.htm